S0-DUU-639

STUDIES ON VOLTAIRE
AND THE
EIGHTEENTH CENTURY

177

General Editor

HAYDN MASON

School of European Studies
University of East Anglia
Norwich, England

PQ
2105
A2
S8
v.177

AHMAD GUNNY

VOLTAIRE
AND
ENGLISH
LITERATURE

*a study of English literary influences
on Voltaire*

THE VOLTAIRE FOUNDATION
AT THE
TAYLOR INSTITUTION, OXFORD
1979

© *1979 The Estate of Theodore Besterman*

ISSN 0435-2866
ISBN 0 7294 0119 7

*Printed in England by Cheney & Sons Ltd
Banbury, Oxfordshire*

To my wife and parents

Contents

Preface

THE idea of this book stems from the doctoral dissertation I submitted to London University in 1970. It later became clear that parts of the work could form the basis for a fuller investigation of the subject of Voltaire's indebtedness to English literature. Previous writers have stressed the importance of English 'thought' to Voltaire or have studied English reactions to him. My aim is different: it is, primarily, to assess the impact of English 'literary' influences on Voltaire. At times, however, I discuss thought, as the nature of the subject renders such a discussion unavoidable.

It is with pleasure that I express my gratitude to the following: professor W. H. Barber, Birkbeck College, for his unfailing and invaluable help as the supervisor of my thesis and for his encouragement at all times; professor P. W. Edwards, King Alfred professor of English literature, Liverpool, who elucidated points of English literary history for my benefit; dr R. Shackleton, Bodley's librarian, Oxford; professor A. M. Rousseau, Université de Provence and professor Vivienne Mylne, Kent, for their helpful suggestions.

I also wish to thank the editors of *Studies on Voltaire and the eighteenth century* and the *Revue de littérature comparée* for permission to use material from my articles published by them. I am particularly indebted to the general editor, professor H. T. Mason, for accepting to publish my work in *Studies on Voltaire*.

A.G.

Abbreviations

The titles of periodicals are abbreviated in accordance with the list given in the *MLA International bibliography*.

Bénac   Voltaire, *Romans et contes*, ed. H. Bénac (1960).

Best. D   *Correspondence and related documents*, ed. Theodore Besterman (1968-77), in the *Complete works of Voltaire*, vols 85-135.

Carcassonne Voltaire, *Le Temple du goût*, ed. E. Carcassonne (1938).

M.   Voltaire, *Œuvres complètes*, ed. L. Moland (1877-83).

Notebooks *Notebooks*, ed. Theodore Besterman (1968), in the *Complete works of Voltaire*, vols 81-82.

Taylor   *La Henriade*, ed. O. R. Taylor (1970), in the *Complete works of Voltaire*, vol. 2.

Vercruysse *La Pucelle*, ed. J. Vercruysse (1970), in the *Complete works of Voltaire*, vol. 7.

Watson *John Dryden, Of dramatic poesy and other critical essays*, ed. G. Watson (1962).

White   *Voltaire's Essay on epic poetry*, ed. Florence D. White (1915).

Williams *Commentaires sur Corneille*, ed. David Williams (1974-75), in the *Complete works of Voltaire*, vols 53-55.

Introduction

In the latter part of the seventeenth and in the eighteenth century, most French writers willingly acknowledged the supremacy of the English in the field of ideas. When it came to literature, they became more reticent. They would concede that the English had genius sometimes, but taste never unless Englishmen followed the example of Addison and wrote in the French manner. Rapin claimed that the English surpassed the French in sublimity of thought and boldness of expression, but were inferior to them in matters of taste and form.[1] Even those who were most well-disposed to English literature attacked English taste. Prévost,[2] for instance, declared that the best English works often lacked a certain perfection in taste which was always present in French books. The well-intentioned abbé Yart made this plea on behalf of English writers in the Preface to his *Idée de la poésie anglaise* (1749): 'que la bisarerie de quelques unes de leurs métaphores, que la confusion et le désordre, qui règnent quelquefois dans leurs livres, & enfin que l'inégalité de leur style nous rebutent point. Creusons dans ces mines profondes; séparons l'or de la terre qui le couvre, enrichissons nos terres de ces plantes étrangères.' It was this sense of superiority in matters of taste which led Rivarol to claim in *De l'universalité de la langue française* (1784) that France had provided her neighbours with a theatre, dress, taste, manners, a language and a new style of living.

To the popular antithesis 'esprit-coeur' which one frequently comes across in eighteenth-century French literature and which Voltaire often derided as a cliché, one might perhaps add another relating specifically to England: that of thought and literature. French writers of the eighteenth century upheld the myth of a dichotomy between English thought and literature which had been growing, and more often than not it was English thought that they preferred. England was then regarded as the country which could teach the rest of the world how

[1] *Réflexions sur la poétique d'Aristote* (Paris 1674), p.111.
[2] *Le Pour et contre* (Paris 1733-40), iv. 283.

to think. Voltaire himself wrote to his friend Thieriot about freedom of thought in England and added: 'Si je suivois mon inclination ce seroit là que je me fixerois dans l'idée seulement d'apprendre à penser' (Best.D299, 12 August 1726). Yet in a letter prefixed to his tragedy of *Mérope*, addressed to Scipio Maffei and published in 1744, he joined in the general condemnation of English taste. He complained that England had produced great thinkers, but was deficient in the liberal arts and gave the following warning: 'si les Anglais ne s'appliquent sérieusement à suivre les préceptes de leurs excellents citoyens Addison et Pope, ils n'approcheront pas des autres peuples en fait de goût et de littérature' (M.iv.184). Incidentally, Aaron Hill who adapted *Mérope* in 1753 severely criticized Voltaire for this letter in the preface to his play where he denounced French literary and political ambitions.

It was not just Voltaire and the French who attacked English literature from an aesthetic point of view and at the same time extolled the virtues of other literatures, especially French. Well-known English figures such as Pope, Addison and Bolingbroke – who, admittedly, were thoroughly familiar with French writings – helped to strengthen the prejudice against English literature. One could almost detect an inferiority complex in them. Addison felt that the taste of most English poets as well as readers was extremely Gothic and further clarified his meaning by explaining that the Goths in poetry 'like those in Architecture, not being able to come up to the beautiful Simplicity of the old Greeks and Romans, have endeavoured to supply its Place with all the Extravagancies of an irregular Fancy'.[3]

As has been pointed out,[4] Pope himself shared the Elizabethan fear that the English language had a limited future. In the *Essay on criticism*, he gave expression to this fear when he lamented:

> Our Sons their Fathers' *failing Language* see,
> And such as *Chaucer* is, shall *Dryden* be.[5]

Pope acknowledged the supremacy of French literature in general in the *Imitations of Horace: EP.II.i* (Butt, p.644):

> We conquer'd France, but felt our captive's charms;
> Her Arts victorious triumph'd o'er our Arms:
> Britain to soft refinements less a foe,
> Wit grew polite, and Numbers learn'd to flow.

[3] *The Spectator*, ed. D. F. Bond (Oxford 1965), i. 268.
[4] G. Tillotson, *On the poetry of Pope* (Oxford 1950), p.100.
[5] in *The Poems of Alexander Pope*, ed. J. Butt (London 1968), p.159.

In a letter addressed to Pope in 1723/24, the cultured Bolingbroke wondered why English poetry was so little in demand among foreigners, considering that England had produced as much genius as any country. He thought the main reason was that 'we have not one Original great Work of that kind wrote near enough to perfection to pique the Curiosity of other Nations as the Epick Poetry of the Italians, and the Dramatick Poetry of the French pique ours.'[6]

A more pernicious influence than Bolingbroke's must have been that of the fourth earl of Chesterfield, destined to become Montesquieu's friend. Chesterfield, with whom Voltaire had a long friendship, told his son that he could not possibly read through his countryman Milton, though he acknowledged that Milton had some sublime passages and some prodigious flashes of light. Then he added in his letter dated 4th October 1752:

But . . . that light is often followed by *darkness visible* . . . Besides, not having the honour to be acquainted with any of the parties of his Poem, except the Man and the Woman, the characters and speeches of a dozen or two of angels, and of as many Devils, are as much above my reach as my entertainment.

(see *The Letters of lord Chesterfield*, ed. B. Dobrée (London 1932), v. 1952-53). Chesterfield wanted this information to be kept a secret, lest he should be 'abused by every tasteless Pedant, and every solid Divine in England'. It is not unlikely that he may have provided Voltaire with some material for the section 'D'un passage d'Homère' of the article 'Anciens et Modernes' of the *Questions sur l'encyclopédie*. Despite his intention, his letter did 'run into a dissertation' on epic poets.

When one has taken into consideration the reservations of eighteenth-century French writers on English taste, and the feeling of inferiority shown by English francophiles of the same period, one can appreciate why an English literary influence on Voltaire is minimised by earlier scholars. In the face of the combined attack by Frenchmen and Englishmen, in an atmosphere so hostile to English taste, how can one talk of any English literary influence at all on Voltaire? What is less understandable is that an eighteenth-century attitude should have persisted even in later times, although concessions have been made in certain areas such as tragedy. In this connection, T. W. Russell stresses

---

[6] *Correspondence of Alexander Pope*, ed. G. Sherburn (Oxford 1956), ii. 220.

the importance of Dryden in his book entitled *Voltaire, Dryden and heroic tragedy* (1946). Such an emphasis has its dangers: apart from being at Shakespeare's expense, it tends to exaggerate the influence of Dryden the dramatist on Voltaire. Russell almost completely ignores Dryden's satirical impact on him.

If what Pope says in the *Imitations of Horace* represents the whole truth about the situation, then it is unlikely that Voltaire was subjected to any English literary influence. Many a modern English-speaking francophile thinks that the outward form and style of English literature naturally made no impact on Voltaire. Ballantyne, for example, argued that English literature had nothing to teach Voltaire which he did not know already.[7] He implied that Voltaire's knowledge of English literature did not extend much beyond the time of Pope's death, that is, 1744. This is far from being the case and Ballantyne's conclusions therefore rest on insecure foundations. As late as 1777 Voltaire was reviewing Sterne's *Tristram Shandy* in the *Journal de politique et de littérature*. Even in respect of earlier authors mistakes have been made. In an interesting paper entitled 'Milton's fame on the Continent', read to the British Academy, J. G. Robertson argued that Milton's actual influence on French literature remained small and unimportant, since his genius had, after all, no very firm hold on the French mind in the eighteenth century.[8] This erroneous view was supported by F. C. Green in *Minuet* (1935) and more recently by I. O. Wade in *The Intellectual development of Voltaire* (1969).

Moreover, one cannot restrict the impact of English literature on Voltaire to Dryden, Pope and Swift. Whoever has lived in the company of Voltaire knows that he did not discriminate between greater and lesser writers when it was a question of engaging in controversy. Had it not been for Voltaire's quarrel with him, no one would have heard of La Beaumelle today. Similarly when it came to tapping a possible source for a polemical writing, Voltaire never hesitated to use a 'minor' writer like Matthew Prior. Any survey of English literary influences on Voltaire ought to take into account writers as varied as Shakespeare, Addison, Fenton, Milton, Rochester, Butler, Sterne, Richardson and Fielding.

It seems that on the whole French-speaking scholars of the twentieth century such as Dédéyan have done some justice to English literature.

[7] A. Ballantyne, *Voltaire's visit to England 1726-1729* (London 1893), p.332.
[8] *Proceedings of the British Academy* (1908), iii. 328.

His *Voltaire et la pensée anglaise* (1956) is a brief introduction to the subject of English literary influences on Voltaire, while André Michel Rousseau's book on *L'Angleterre et Voltaire* (1976) is primarily a study of English reactions to Voltaire. Jean Gillet's book *Le Paradis perdu dans la littérature française de Voltaire à Chateaubriand* (1975) studies the significance of *Paradise lost* for Voltaire: however, it sometimes overemphasises the political element in Voltaire's attitude to *Paradise lost*, an element which the author thinks is totally absent in Voltaire's reactions to Shakespeare (p.67).

What follows is therefore an attempt at a fuller investigation of the whole question of Voltaire's indebtedness to English literature. It is not suggested that all the authors Voltaire mentioned in his works made an impact on him. Even when he has the highest praise for an author, it does not follow that the latter's influence can be traced in Voltaire's writings. On the other hand, someone he does not mention or whom he denigrates may well be more significant. The appropriate background to Voltaire's reactions to English men of letters is Voltaire's own thoughts on the various genres in which he writes. Such a background is often enriched by factors of a non-literary nature which have to be taken into account.

Perhaps one should point out here that Voltaire could not have benefited fully from his contact with English men of letters and their works before 1721 as he probably started learning English just after that.[9] In the 'Advertisement' to the *Essay on epick poetry* he wrote:

It has the Appearance of too great a Presumption in a Traveller, who hath been but eighteen months in England, to attempt to write in a Language, which he cannot pronounce at all, and which he hardly understands in Conversation.[10]

However, his poor oral performance in English in 1727 is no evidence of his incompetence in the written language: after all, a reliable method of developing one's proficiency in a foreign language even now requires one to spend as much time as possible in the foreign country. In the text of the *Essay*, Voltaire said he hoped that the reader would look with some indulgence on its diction and 'pardon the Failings of

[9] Voltaire could of course read English literature in translation. For a more detailed treatment of Voltaire's knowledge of English, see A.-M. Rousseau, *L'Angleterre et Voltaire*, Studies on Voltaire 145-147 (1976) i. 39-51.

[10] *Voltaire's Essay on epic poetry*, ed. Florence D. White (Albany 1915), p.75.

one who has learn'd English but this year' (p.88). His progress in English seems to have been too rapid for this statement to be literally true. Even if the possibility of some assistance from Young whom he had met in 1727 is not excluded, Voltaire must have started learning English a few years before and acquired a fair grasp of it by 1723. Otherwise there would have been no point in his asking for an English *Mariamne* in that year.

A classification into genres may appear arbitrary, yet it is convenient. Although an English literary influence is very obvious at times, Voltaire does not necessarily use the English material in the same genre in French. While in theory he is generally opposed to the mixing of the genres, does he not help break down barriers as often as he can in his works? An investigation by genres still has its advantage. It clarifies one's view of this complex subject, without restricting one to a particular type of writing.

For the sake of convenience again, this study attempts to stress the 'literary' aspect of English influence on Voltaire, and generally omits the 'thought' aspect, except in the case of Prior. This is not because 'thought' is considered less important. Indeed it is often impossible to draw a line of demarcation between English 'thought' and 'literature'. Moreover, in Voltaire's time and even much later, English literature suffered from certain misconceptions. Has not the time come to explode the myth created by some of a dichotomy between 'goût' and 'génie' in English literature from Shakespeare to Sterne?

English tragedy and Voltaire

i. *Voltaire's conception of tragedy*

VOLTAIRE'S tragedy has in the past roused considerable interest both in France and abroad. The views he held on this *grand* genre attracted as much attention as the plays themselves. What he says on tragedy in his prefaces, *dissertations*, *discours* and *épîtres* can be regarded as his own attempt to renew Aristotle's *Poetics* which made a great impact on the seventeenth century.[1] However, since he was not essentially a theorist like d'Aubignac, but communicated his thoughts in accordance with the needs of the moment, we have to follow him through a variety of writings. When the exercise is completed, we might have the impression that nothing very new emerges. On the other hand, if we have this body of critical opinion constantly before us as a framework of reference it should be easier to establish whether his views of English tragedy were based on purely literary principles or whether other factors were involved.

The young and successful author of the tragedy of *Œdipe* had no hesitation in giving a critical commentary on his own version and those of Sophocles and Corneille in 1719 in the *Lettres sur Œdipe*. His main grievance against Sophocles is that the latter does not observe *vraisemblance*[2] since his Oedipus knows absolutely nothing of his predecessor Laïus (M.ii.19). He acknowledges the simplicity of the Greek theatre, but this very simplicity which is synonymous with aridity does not provide scope for a modern play in five acts. Corneille

---

[1] in his letter prefacing *Mérope*, Voltaire described the *Poetics* as immortal (M.iv.180).

[2] in the *Remarques sur les trois discours* following the *Commentaires sur Corneille* (1764) Voltaire observes that the marvellous is meant for opera, whereas tragedy is 'le pays de l'histoire, ou du moins tout ce qui ressemble à l'histoire par la vraisemblance des faits et par la verité des mœurs'. One can invent in tragedy provided the story is 'vraisemblable', moving and tragic, the style is pure and the poetry beautiful. See Williams, iii. 1029, 1046.

therefore had to make good this deficiency by falling back on his inventive powers (M.ii.29). In the Thésée-Dircé episode which he invented in his play, he sinned against decorum by allowing Dircé to hurl abuse at her mother and was also guilty of *invraisemblance*. Lack of verisimilitude is understandable when one is hampered by the bizarre events of certain tragic subjects. In such cases, one must aim at being interesting rather than precise, 'car le spectateur pardonne tout, hors la longueur; et lorsqu'il est une fois ému, il examine rarement s'il a raison de l'être' (M.ii.38). The appeal to the emotions is obviously based on classical sources.

The idea of pandering to the taste of the public is reinforced in the preface to *Mariamne* in 1725 (M.ii.162-64) where Voltaire says that one of the fundamental rules is to depict heroes as they were or rather as the public imagines them: it is easier to influence people by using the ideas they have than by giving them new ones. So the disagreeable characters must be softened, for it is necessary to think of one's public even more than one's hero and to follow history, though not blindly, if one's aim is to move.

To combat the trend against poetry which culminated in the prose tragedy of La Motte's *Œdipe* in 1726, Voltaire felt obliged to add a preface to the 1730 edition of his own *Œdipe*. His argument is that rhyme may not by itself constitute the merit of a poet or give pleasure to the reader. Certain metres are indeed difficult. Whoever limits himself to overcoming a difficulty merely for the sake of overcoming it is mad, but he who extracts from these very obstacles beauties that please everyone is a very wise, almost unique man (M.ii.57). Voltaire also defends the unities against the attack of La Motte (M.ii.48-49). The French, says Voltaire, were among the first of the modern nations to revive these 'wise' rules of the drama.[3] Today even English authors claim that the duration of the action of their plays is equal to that of the performance. All nations begin to consider as barbarous the times when the rule of the unities was unknown to geniuses such as Lope de Vega and Shakespeare. The fact that Addison and Maffei, like Corneille and Racine, observed the rules is in itself sufficient to prevent anyone from violating them.

---

[3] with regard to unity of action, Voltaire believes that a tragedy cannot have subordinate plots and diverse interests. A single action without any episode such as that of *Athalie* is perfection in art (*Remarques sur les trois discours*, Williams, iii.1050). Voltaire modifies his views on unity of place. He now considers this unity to be almost impractical

The *Discours sur la tragédie* (1731), which forms the dedication of *Brutus* to Bolingbroke, stresses the differences between the English and the French theatres. One of the essential differences is that where the English are free to write in blank verse the French are slaves to rhyme. But rhyme is essential to French poetry. Moreover, so many great writers – Corneille, Racine and Boileau – have accustomed their ears to this harmony that the French could not put up with any other device (M.ii.313). These very exacting demands of rhyme and versification account for the excellent works to be found in the French language. Neither lord Stair (see below) nor Francis Atterbury, bishop of Rochester, whom Voltaire mentions in the *Discours* and with whom he says he quarrelled on the subject of rhyme succeeded in influencing his attitude in this matter.

It is clearly implied in the *Discours* that any language that avoids rhyme and versification cannot produce excellent tragedies. This explains why Voltaire spoke highly in favour of English dramatists who wrote in the French tradition and was less well-disposed towards others who used prose and blank verse in tragedy. English tragedy lacks 'cette pureté, cette conduite régulière, ces bienséances de l'action et du style,[4] cette élégance, et toutes ces finesses de l'art qui ont établi la réputation du théâtre français depuis le grand Corneille' (M.ii.314). Yet the most irregular English plays have a great merit, that of action, whereas French tragedies are conversations rather than the presentation of an event. Voltaire does not approve of the 'delicatesse excessive' of the French who refuse to show new spectacles and who are used to turning into ridicule anything that is not usual.

Swinging to the other extreme will not do either: there are too many revolting spectacles in the Greek theatre and the Greeks have failed to distinguish between horror and terror,[5] between what is revolting and unbelievable and what is tragic and awe-inspiring.[6] If

because of the poor construction of French theatres and he concludes 'L'unité de lieu est tout le spectacle que l'œil peut embrasser sans peine' (p.1053).

[4] cf. *Lettres philosophiques*, letter xviii.

[5] this does not prevent Voltaire from advocating in the verse *Discours* prefaced to *Eriphyle* (1732) that terror should reappear in French tragedy (M.ii.458). This was, however, a defence of his own play where, under the influence of *Hamlet*, a ghost is introduced.

[6] the Greeks, however, had simplicity – an essential requirement of tragedy. In the first 'Epître dédicatoire' to *Zaïre* (1733), Voltaire claims that simplicity was one of the strong points of the Ancients. He seems to deplore its absence in English tragedy, for his advice was 'Anglais, que cette nouveauté / S'introduise dans vos usages. / Sur votre

the English and the Greeks have sometimes gone beyond the limit of decorum, the French have not attained real tragedy through fear that they might pass beyond these limits. There are situations which however disgusting and horrible they may appear to the French could produce aesthetic pleasure if they were well-handled and above all toned down by the charm of fine poetry. The laws of decorum are rather arbitrary, unlike those of the unities which are fundamental. Voltaire seems to suggest that there is no harm in showing one dead body on the stage, as happens in Addison's *Cato*.

In these critical writings, much attention is devoted to love, *galanterie*, *tendresse* and their role in tragedy. In the section entitled 'De l'amour' of the *Discours sur la tragédie*, Voltaire states that introducing love in all tragedies shows a rather effeminate taste; banishing it completely is very unreasonable (M.ii.323). The theatre, be it tragic or comic, depicts human passion. So love must not be rejected unless it is badly handled or treated without art. Voltaire acknowledges that love in French tragedy is often *galanterie*. To be worthy of the tragic stage, love must be fundamental to the play and not arbitrarily imposed so as to fill a gap. This is a defect found in both English and French plays which are too long. Love must be a truly tragic passion, and treated like a weakness: it must be assailed by remorse and lead to misfortune and crime if it is to appear dangerous. Or let virtue triumph over it, and show that it is not invincible. Otherwise it is only worthy of the eclogue or comedy.[7]

If love is a blemish in tragedy, the second dedicatory epistle to *Zaïre* (1736) makes it clear that it is a blemish where the French have achieved more than all nations ancient and modern put together. Love appears on the French stage with 'des bienséances, une délicatesse, une vérité' not found elsewhere (M.ii.551). Voltaire accounts for this by the fact that there is more social intercourse among the French than among any other nation and French sophistication is due to the presence of women in society. The English were until the time of Charles ii deprived of this advantage mainly because of their austerity, their political quarrels and religious wars which made them 'farouches'. It is therefore hardly surprising that their treatment of love is not that

théâtre infecté / D'horreurs, de gibets, de carnages, / Mettez donc plus de vérité, / Avec de plus nobles images' (M.ii.539).
[7] here Voltaire seems to be attacking Corneille who was responsible, in his view, for that mixture of the sublime and *galanterie* which infected the French theatre.

of the 'honnêtes gens'. Voltaire's final recommendation to Fawkener is that the English should submit to the rules of the French theatre, as the French should embrace English philosophy for 'l'art de plaire semble l'art des Français, et l'art de penser paraît le vôtre' (M.ii.554).

In the letter to Maffei Voltaire claimed that the Italian author was the first in the eighteenth century to have written a play without *galanterie*[8] and worthy of the Athenians at their best. He takes the opportunity of referring to an English version of *Mérope* in 1731 and of chastising the English for having depicted the love passion in the worst possible manner (M.iv.184). The English disfigured a play where maternal love is the mainspring of the action. Even if the English *Merope*, in which love appears ridiculous, proved a failure, the very fact that it was performed proved that the English theatre was not yet 'épuré'. Voltaire is referring to the *Merope* of George Jeffreys, which was performed at the Lincoln's Inn Fields Theatre in February 1730-31. He is well-informed: despite some attempt at novelties, the play was a failure.[9] Jeffreys, on the other hand, in an edition of *Merope* published in *Miscellanies in verse and prose* in 1754, boasted that he had reformed his Italian model (Maffei) in a few instances and that Voltaire did him the honour to adopt every one of them. He even accused Voltaire of 'petty larceny'.

Voltaire adds that the same cause that deprives the English of the genius for painting and music accounts for their failure in tragedy (M.iv.184). He objects to the custom of English dramatists of ending a tragedy with a poetic image. Where the French insist that the heroes alone should speak, the English let the author intervene. The French public represented by Voltaire will not allow princes and ministers to use poetic imagery in a grave crisis (M.iv.188).

The *Dissertation sur la tragédie ancienne et moderne* (1748) which precedes *Sémiramis* reveals new aspects of Voltaire's conception of tragedy. He shows increasing interest in scenic effects when he asks where one can find an equivalent of the spectacle of the Greek theatre.[10] He thinks that Italian opera perhaps provides the answer. But he does not intend that external scenery should be a substitute for tragic action and emotion; it must be an essential element of the play (M.iv.500):

[8] Corneille and Rotrou are specifically condemned for their 'intrigues galantes' (M.iv.182).

[9] see Allardyce Nicoll, *A History of English drama 1660-1900* (Cambridge 1955), ii. 95.

[10] the Greeks could, however, learn from the moderns in France the art of skilful presentation and the liaison of scenes.

quand je parle d'une action théâtrale, je parle d'un appareil, d'une céré-monie, d'une assemblée, d'un événement nécessaire à la pièce, et non pas de ces vains spectacls plus puérils que pompeux, de ces ressources du décorateur qui suppléent à la stérilité du poète, et qui amusent les yeux quand on ne sait pas parler à l'oreille et à l'âme.[11]

Here he is proposing that tragedy should appeal to the eye, the ear and the mind at the same time. Voltaire's notion of display and pomp excludes the introduction of a horse on stage. He says that when he was in London he saw an English play dealing with a coronation in which there was a horse. Commentators often fail to take this reference into account when they discuss his knowledge of the English theatre. What Voltaire has in mind is a lavish production of *Henry VIII* at Drury Lane in honour of the coronation of George II in 1727. It included a grand coronation scene.[12] He is against any fireworks display as well: four lines of good poetry are better than this.

Voltaire militated in favour of a widening of geographical frontiers in tragedy so that the customs of other times and far-away places could be depicted. In *Zaïre* (1731), he had set the scene in Palestine and the timing of the action was that of the Crusades; in *Alzire* (1736) we are transported to Peru, in *Zulime* (1740) the action is set in North Africa while *L'Orphelin de la Chine* (1755) takes us to China. In the dedicatory epistle to the last play, Voltaire defines his attitude to tragedy and manners: 'Les aventures les plus intéressantes ne sont rien quand elles ne peignent pas les moeurs' (M.v.299). However, there must be something new in these sketches to stimulate interest. In the preface to *Les Scythes* (1768), he claims that his play shows this 'nouveauté' in that it depicts manners that had never been seen before on the tragic stage. He goes on to explain what he had been doing in plays like *Tancrède*, *Zaïre*, *Alzire* and *L'Orphelin de la Chine* in order to satisfy the public taste for novelty: 'un amateur du théâtre a été forcé de mettre sur la scène l'ancienne chevalerie, le contraste des mahométans et des chrétiens, celui des Américains et des Espagnols, celui des Chinois et des Tartares' (M.vi.267). He approves the mixing of charac-ters from high and low classes of society. Ordinary people can become

[11] what Voltaire wanted for tragedy was picturesque tableaux. In a letter to Damila-ville, he wrote: 'J'ai toujours songé autant que je l'ai pu à rendre les scènes tragiques pittoresques. Elles le sont dans Mahomet, dans Mérope, dans l'Orphelin de la Chine, surtout dans Tancrède. Mais ici toute la pièce est un tableau continuel' (Best.D10397, c. 30 March 1762).

[12] see *King Henry VIII*, ed. R. A. Foakes (London 1957), p.lxiii.

the subject of tragedy, provided the bombastic element is excluded.

Following Rapin[13] and André Dacier, Voltaire believed in the moral basis of tragedy and he showed this moral preoccupation from the early 1730s.[14] Thus in the *Discours* prefaced to *Eriphyle*, he remarked (M.ii.458):

> Ah! qu'à jamais la scène, ou sublime ou plaisante,
> Soit des vertus du monde une école charmante!

The *Dissertation sur la tragédie ancienne et moderne* distinguished between tragedy and moral treatises. Good tragedy is the school of virtue[15] and the only difference between a 'purified' theatre and moral treatises is that the didacticism found in tragedy is all in the action, it is interesting and it appears with the beauties of an art which was once invented to teach mankind and bless heaven and which, for this reason, was called the language of the gods (M.iv.505). In the dedication to the *Orphelin de la Chine*, Voltaire states that the depiction of customs is nothing more than frivolous amusement unless it inspires virtue (M.v.299). In 1767 in the *Discours historique et critique* which precedes *Les Guèbres*, he defines the aim of the play even more positively: it is to inspire respect for laws, universal charity, humanity and tolerance. Voltaire is convinced that the moral teaching of his play is so pure and touching that it can contribute to public happiness.

Like part of the *Discours sur la tragédie* the *Appel à toutes les nations* (1761) draws attention to some of the weaknesses of French tragedy. Voltaire agrees with Saint-Evremond that French plays do not make a stong enough impression, that pity, emotion and horror tend to be replaced by *tendresse*, shock and astonishment. An element of warmth has always been missing and Voltaire attributes the lassitude and weakness of French tragedy to the way French theatres are constructed, to the shabbiness of the spectacle and to the declamatory style of the actors (M.xxiv.219):

[13] in the *Dissertation sur les principales tragédies anciennes et modernes* which precedes *Oreste* (1750), Voltaire quotes Rapin to prove that tragedy 'est une leçon publique, plus instructive, sans comparaison, que la philosophie' (M.v.169).

[14] Voltaire does not mean that the hero himself should moralise: he should reason as little as possible. As passions form the basis of tragedy, he should feel and act. See *Remarques sur les trois discours* where Voltaire condemns long conversations, maxims and the 'lieux communs' of politics in Corneille (Williams, iii.1029-30).

[15] this, of course, did not rule out the essentially Voltairean technique of self-contradiction. Did not Voltaire also write in the *Discours sur l'homme*: 'Malheur à l'auteur qui veut toujours instruire' (M.ix.419)?

Cette forme, qui excluait toute action théâtrale, excluait aussi ces grandes expressions des passions, ces tableaux frappants des infortunes humaines, ces traits terribles et perçants qui arrachent le cœur; on le touchait, et il fallait le déchirer.[16]

Even when he is writing about satire and satirists, Voltaire cannot resist the temptation to make invidious comparisons with tragedy. This is what happens in the *Parallèle d'Horace, de Boileau, et de Pope* (1761). Fortunately, the digression enables Voltaire to emphasize some of the duties a tragic author must perform (M.xxiv. 226-27):

créer un sujet; inventer un nœud et un dénoûment; donner à chaque personnage son caractère, le soutenir, le rendre intéressant, et augmenter cet intérêt de scène en scène . . . faire dire à chacun ce qu'il doit dire, avec noblesse et sans enflure, avec simplicité, sans bassesse; faire de beaux vers qui ne sentent point le poète, et tels que le personnage aurait dû en faire s'il parlait en vers.

The playwright must do more. For without terror and pity there is no tragedy. Terror and pity are not enough by themselves, the poetry must be excellent, otherwise one remains a mediocre writer.

The section entitled 'De la bonne tragédie française' from the article 'Art dramatique' in the *Questions sur l'encyclopédie* (1770) stresses further the difficulties of French tragedy which nevertheless manages to assemble in one place heroes of antiquity, makes them speak in French verse and say only what they had to say. Moreover French tragedy uses a reasonable number of stage exits and entrances; it is written in a magic style which is neither bombastic nor familiar, and remains always decent and interesting. It is hardly surprising that there should be no more than twenty good French tragedies. Should tragedies which appeal to the heart not be preferred to those which appeal only to the mind? (M.xviii.405). A few scenes which are 'bien raisonnées, fortement pensées, majestueusement écrites' can arouse admiration. But this feeling is transient and leaves the soul unmoved. However beautiful these scenes may be – perhaps the ancients themselves never experienced such beauty – something more is required:

---

[16] Voltaire could be much harsher towards French tragedy. For instance, he stated in a letter to Desfontaines that 'notre goût, ou plutôt notre habitude de ne mettre sur le théâtre, que de longues conversations d'amour, ne plaît pas chez les autres nations. Notre théâtre est vide d'action et de grands intérêts, pour l'ordinaire. Ce qui fait qu'il manque d'action, c'est que le théâtre est offusqué par nos petits maîtres; et ce qui fait que les grands intérêts en sont bannis, c'est que notre nation ne les connaît point' (Best.D940, 14 November 1735).

one must take control over the heart by degrees, rouse it, tear it apart and join to this charm the rules of poetry and those of the theatre which are countless (M.xvii. 406).

Voltaire's *Remarques sur les trois discours* in 1764 are quite useful in clarifying his thoughts on tragedy. It is defined as 'un tableau des grands événements de ce monde'. The more virtue is 'infortunée', the truer the picture. Voltaire admits that he does not understand 'this medecine' which the purgation of the passions is. He cannot understand how pity and fear purge, although he knows that terror and pity move a spectator for two hours and that without these elements, everything languishes in the theatre (Williams, iii. 1030-31). It is the actor who must create pity and fear if he is to be interesting: whether the spectator is purged or not is an idle question (p.1040).

It is obvious that many of Voltaire's critical comments restate principles or ideals formulated at the beginning of his career. For example, he constantly affirms that the theatre should present love that is truly tragic, that tragedy is much more than a long conversation[17] and that despite the annoying requirements of rhyme it is a noble genre. He believes that beautiful poetry can be linked to spectacle and display to achieve the artistic. At the time of *Brutus* he is very interested in scenic effects, dress and setting. He says he introduced with a feeling of apprehension on the French stage Roman senators proceeding to the council chamber in their red togas. Another innovation on that occasion was the stage direction relating to costume, for his aim was to 'frapper l'âme et les yeux à la fois'. Although he made a few innovations such as these, increased the number of characters, widened the geographical boundaries and consciously used his plays as an instrument of anticlerical and political propaganda,[18] he was, as far as the theatre was concerned, a conservative at heart. However liberal he may have been in his attitude to epic poetry in the *Essay on epick poetry* where he acknowledged that there is no absolute in taste and where he was 'very far from thinking that one Nation

----

[17] A. Bellessort provides a useful summary of Voltaire's conception of tragedy when he defines it as the most moving of sermons, the exaltation of virtue, the terrifying spectacle of the dangerous nature of the passions, an appeal to humanity in a language which is unlike that of ordinary people and where pomp must be sublime in some way. Tragedy must take place before a gathering 'des plus belles personnes et des plus grands personnages' (*Essai sur Voltaire* (Paris 1925), p.82).

[18] see R. S. Ridgway, *La Propagande philosophique dans les tragédies de Voltaire*, Studies on Voltaire (1961), xv.

ought to judge of its Productions by the Standard of another' (p.135), when he comes to the drama, he regards the rules as eternally fixed.[19] In the latter part of his career, his criteria for assessing any tragedy are increasingly those of French classicism, and in particular those of Racine. 'Sans Racine point de salut', Voltaire wrote to Condorcet (Best.D20453, 6 December 1776). To a certain extent does he not recall Vaugelas and his successors who were pursuing the same objective, albeit in a different field, that of 'fixing' the French language once for all?

The merit of the comparative approach often followed by Voltaire in these critical essays is that it enables him to pinpoint the strengths and weaknesses of both English and French tragic dramatists. If such an approach is interesting from a theoretical standpoint, it should be even more rewarding in any survey of Voltaire's reactions to English dramatists and individual plays. French weaknesses might explain his interest in English tragedy just as French achievement in tragedy might account for the harshness of his comments on English playwrights.

ii. *Voltaire's reactions to Shakespeare*

When in his 'Prologue' to *Zara*, Aaron Hill's adaptation of *Zaïre*, Colley Cibber wrote:

> From English plays Zara's French author fir'd,
> Confess'd his muse, beyond himself inspir'd;
> From rack'd Othello's rage he rais'd his style,
> And snatch'd the brand that lights this tragic pile

he was probably overstating the case for Voltaire's indebtedness to English tragedy, Shakespearian tragedy in particular. What the Frenchman had actually said in his first dedicatory epistle to *Zaïre* was that the English theatre was responsible for the daring he had shown in using the names of French kings and of ancient families of the kingdom. He felt that this was a novelty and that it could provide a type of tragedy unknown as yet to the French, but necessary to them (M.ii.542). Presumably Voltaire was thinking of Shakespeare's history plays.

---

[19] *Voltaire on Shakespeare*, ed. Th. Besterman, Studies on Voltaire (1967), liv. 41.

In a way, Cibber is fairly representative of the defenders of English literature and less extreme perhaps than Baretti, the author of a *Discours sur Shakespeare et sur monsieur de Voltaire* (1777). The Italian was so eager to please an English public and was so hostile to Voltaire that he made some violently anti-French statements. Remarks such as 'les Pièces à la Française rassasient, parce qu'elles ne sont point susceptibles d'une variété aussi grande que celles faites à l'Anglaise' (p.62) and his prophecy that Corneille's works would be banished from the stage and relegated to libraries (p.63) are matched by the equally chauvinistic, jingoistic views of English tragedy held by Frenchmen, including Voltaire. It is this state of affairs that bedevils any attempt at a fair assessment of Voltaire's reactions to Shakespeare. Yet this assessment can only take place if prejudices are put away on both sides.

Although what Voltaire says on Shakespeare in the *Discours prononcé à l'Académie française* (1746) and in the *Dissertation sur la tragédie ancienne et moderne* (1748) is not without significance, commentators have so far found it convenient to situate his remarks into two major and distinct phases, one starting from the period 1726-35 and another from the 1760s to the end of his life in 1778. Such a division appears justified at first sight since the reactions of the earlier period appear rather favourable despite Voltaire's reservations, while those of the later period are clearly hostile. However, on closer analysis, it may be seen that the difference is not so much in the substance as in the form and tone. Granted that there is a difference, how are we to account for it?

If Voltaire's strictures against Shakespeare are viewed against a static background in which the rigid canons of French taste apply and are to be explained by opposing attitudes to tragedy prevailing in France and England, had the rules governing tragedy not better be invoked in the first period when non-literary factors hardly come into play? It may well be that most, if not all, of Voltaire's adverse criticisms arise from a misuse of words and from a matter of vocabulary. Shakespeare himself, if he had not lived long before Voltaire, might have asked 'What's in a name?' All the criticisms on irregularity, mixture of genres and so on perhaps stem from the fact that Shakespeare's plays were called *tragedies*.[20] In this connection, the author of the

[20] Samuel Johnson's remark that Shakespeare's plays are not in the rigorous and critical sense either tragedies or comedies, but compositions of a distinct kind is most relevant here. See the preface to *The Plays of William Shakespeare* (1765), p.10. The

important 'Dissertation sur la poésie anglaise' published in the *Journal littéraire* at the Hague[21] and partly reprinted in the *Mercure de France* in June 1727 and January 1728 observed as far back as 1717 that Shakespeare's plays were not tragedies (ix.202). To the French the use of the word tragedy to describe Shakespeare's plays automatically meant that they belonged to a well-defined, traditional genre with universally accepted rules, as if no tragedy had been written in France before the rules were proclaimed or reasserted in the seventeenth century! They would have been happier if Shakespeare's plays had been called *drame*, a new genre which was to be tried in France and which denoted something quite different and independent of Aristotle, Horace and modern theorists of tragedy.[22]

Shakespeare's impact on Voltaire may be seen in 1726 during the latter's visit to England. In a letter to Thieriot written in English after his sister's death, Voltaire is full of melancholy and his state of mind is very conducive to introspection in the manner of Hamlet. He continues in these terms (Best.D303, 26 October 1726):

Life is but a dream full of starts of folly, and of fancied, and true miseries. Death awakes us from this painful dream, and gives us, either a better existence or no existence at all.

Voltaire is visibly moved by Hamlet's monologue 'To be or not to be' which he was to translate. A few years later in the 'Cambridge notebook',[23] Voltaire talked of puerilities in *Hamlet*, a defect it shared with the *Hippolytus* of Euripides (*Notebooks*, i. 106). Although Shakespeare and the Greek dramatists wrote few good plays, Voltaire's point is that they wrote noble scenes and were rightly esteemed (i.108). He was so impressed by *Hamlet* that he thought of imitating it in *Eriphyle* in 1732. But his tragedy failed because of its incredible situations. After all the corrections he made to his melodrama, he confessed to his friend Cideville that he had begun another play (*Zaïre*) in order to forget *Eriphyle* (Best.D493, 29 May 1732).

opinions of eighteenth-century English critics on Shakespeare are conveniently assembled in *Eighteenth-century essays on Shakespeare*, ed. D. Nichol Smith, second edition (Oxford 1963). I quote from this edition.

[21] the author could have been Van Effen or Saint-Hyacinthe, the latter more probably. See R. Naves, *Le Goût de Voltaire* (Paris 1938), p.123.

[22] see Paul Van Tieghem, 'La découverte de Shakespeare sur le continent' in *Le Préromantisme* (Paris 1947), iii. 98-99.

[23] this notebook was written at different times and over a period of several years from 1727, possibly 1726 (*Notebooks*, i. 19).

Zaïre's indebtedness to *Othello* has always been hotly debated.[24] Both plays certainly have in common the theme of jealousy, although Orosmane's jealousy is not developed in the same way as Othello's. Besides, Orosmane is not the hero of Voltaire's play as Othello is in Shakespeare's. If an imitation is to be sought, it is perhaps in the language used at the end of *Zaïre*. At the sight of Othello's body falling on a bed, Lodovico exclaims: 'The object poisons sight. Let it be hid.' In *Zaïre*, the dying Orosmane says to Nérestan: 'Remporte en ta patrie cet objet que ma rage a privé de la vie' (v. x). The word 'object' in *Othello* therefore appears to be literally transposed to *Zaïre*. On the other hand, it is quite possible that when Voltaire uses 'objet' he means 'cherished woman' or he is trying to observe the conventions of French classical tragedy which would not allow 'cadavre'.

In the *Discours sur la tragédie* (M.ii.316-18), Voltaire tells Bolingbroke how pleased he was to have seen a performance of *Julius Caesar* in London. He does not approve of the barbarous irregularities found in it, but he is surprised that there are so few of them in a work written in a century of ignorance by a man who did not know Latin and who was only guided by his genius. Amidst its gross mistakes, he was thrilled by the sight of Brutus holding a bloodstained sword and addressing the crowd. He found that Mark Antony's speech had more pathos than Brutus's which he had just translated. He tries to give a balanced commentary, taking into account French taste which would not allow a chorus of commoners to come on stage and Caesar's blood-stained corpse to be exposed to public view. What happens in Shakespeare's play has to be set against what happens in the numerous Greek plays which Voltaire lists and which are no less revolting in their horror. The blemishes of the Greek and English stages are due to the fact that art was in its infancy at the time of Aeschylus and Shakespeare. Despite these, one finds true pathos and strange beauties in their plays. If the French were to condemn English tragedies on the basis of translations and hearsay evidence, they would be like blind men. What Voltaire advocates in the *Discours* is that tradition which governs the world should change the taste of nations and turn aversion into

[24] see, for instance, H. Lion, *Les Tragédies et les théories dramatiques de Voltaire* (Paris 1895), p.73; T. R. Lounsbury, *Shakespeare and Voltaire* (London 1902), pp.78-79, 119; G. M. Haines, *Shakespeare in France* (London 1925), p.15 and H. C. Lancaster, *French tragedy in the time of Louis XV and Voltaire* (Baltimore 1950), pp. 142-43.

pleasure. His tone here is in keeping with that of the *Essay on epick poetry*, which shows him at his most liberal. Had he not proclaimed there that such a thing as a national taste exists, but that each nation should pay a little more attention to the taste and manners of its neighbours so that a general good taste might eventually emerge? (pp.86, 135).

Voltaire's liberalism did not last long. In his chapter on Homer in the *Essai sur la poésie épique*, written shortly after the *Discours*, he says Shakespeare will enable him to prove his point about the paradox to be found in Homer, a writer who, in his view, was a mixture of gross mistakes and great beauties. Yet he ends up with putting the emphasis on Shakespeare's weaknesses: his plays are monsters in tragedy, some last many years, the hero is baptised in the first act and dies of old age in the last act; witches, peasants, drunkards, clowns and grave diggers appear; the latter sing carousing tunes and play with dead skulls (M.viii. 317-18). Voltaire says that the English, like himself, saw the gross defects of their favourite author, although they had a better understanding of his beauties.

Since in the *Letters concerning the English nation* (published in London in 1733),[25] the first version, in English, of the *Lettres philosophiques*, Voltaire is dealing specifically with tragedy, in letter xviii, he writes at greater length on Shakespeare and tries to be fair to him in his own way. He says (pp.166-67):

Shakespear boasted strong, fruitful Genius: He was natural and sublime, but had not so much as a single Spark of good Taste, or knew one Rule of the Drama . . . the great Merit of this Dramatic Poet has been the Ruin of the *English* Stage.[26]

Voltaire takes up the point made in the *Notebooks* about the existence of noble scenes in Shakespeare's plays, here styled 'monstrous Farces, to which the Name of Tragedy is given'. They are 'such beautiful, such

[25] quotations in English are from this edition. For later editions, quotations are from *Lettres philosophiques*, ed. G. Lanson, revised by André-M. Rousseau (Paris 1964).

[26] in conversation with Martin Sherlock in 1776, Voltaire is reported to have said that Shakespeare spoiled the taste of the nation, that he had been its taste for two hundred years. He implied that Shakespeare had permanently fixed the taste of the English. See Martin Sherlock, *Letters from an English traveller* (London 1780), quoted in *Voltaire on Shakespeare* (p.173). Yet in his Academy discourse of the same year, Voltaire thought it was fortunate that Shakespeare had not obliterated all other taste except his, since some modern French tragedies were well received by the English, that judicious and enlightened nation! (*Voltaire on Shakespeare*, p.205).

dreadful Scenes that they have always been exhibited with great Success'. Shakespeare's mistakes, his 'whimsical, gigantic Images', hallowed by time, became almost sublime. As was to be the case with the imitators of the English sentimental novel later, Voltaire disliked Shakespeare's imitators in particular as they had none of his touches and descriptive skill. These imitators were so bad that they created the impression that Shakespeare was inimitable. As for Shakespeare's plays themselves, Voltaire objected to the grave diggers' scene in *Hamlet*, the jokes of the cobblers in *Julius Caesar* and the strangling of Desdemona on stage in *Othello* (pp.168-69).

Voltaire claims that Shakespeare's critics notice only his errors[27] and that no one has translated any of 'those strong, those forcible Passages which atone for all his Faults' (p.169). Still relatively liberal and well-disposed towards Shakespeare, he explains this situation by saying that it is easy to write a prose commentary on Shakespeare, but difficult to translate his beautiful poetry. In order to defend Shakespeare and other great writers, he attacks the critics because they compile whole volumes instead of displaying the beauties of great geniuses. One should note Voltaire's consistency here. In his attitude to the writer and the critic, his stand is the same as in his contemporary essay in criticism, the *Temple du goût*, where he shows the contempt of the man of letters for those who are devoid of creative genius. The commentators are ridiculed when they compile big volumes about a word they do not understand and show complete indifference to good taste.[28] Since in the *Temple*, he is applying the criteria of beauty and good taste to criticise French authors and he is applying the same criteria in the *Lettres philosophiques* to judge Shakespeare, Voltaire cannot be accused of double standards. Whether he lacks perception or not in his appreciation of Shakespeare, whether he seems vain or not, Voltaire's stand appears to be in accordance with the logic of the writer who had identified himself as 'La Critique' with a harmonious trinity where the god of taste, the public and 'La Critique' are a manifestation of one and the same force (Carcassonne, p.126).

One may detect in Voltaire's early reactions to Shakespeare some English influence. Dryden, Mulgrave and Addison all stressed the importance of having a balanced view, of describing faults as well as

---

[27] the irony is obvious; for much of the later phase of his interest in Shakespeare, Voltaire was an inveterate sinner in this respect.

[28] *Le Temple du goût*, ed. Elie Carcassonne (Paris 1938), p.66.

beauties in a writer. In the *Spectator* (no.262), Addison refused to harm the reputation of anyone: his aim was to show the beauties and merits of contemporaries rather than their defects. In *On the genius and writings of Shakespear* (1712), Dennis thought that Shakespeare's beauties were entirely his own and due to the force of his nature, whereas his faults were due to his education and to the age that he lived in. He pointed out Shakespeare's ignorance of the rules and blamed it for the introduction of 'things into his Tragedies, which are against the Dignity of that noble Poem, as the Rabble in *Julius Caesar*' (*Eighteenth-century essays on Shakespeare*, pp.23-25). One finds in Shakespeare, as Pope suggests in the preface to his edition of Shakespeare's works, 'the most numerous as well as the most conspicuous instances, both of Beauties and Faults of all sorts' (p.44). However, did not Pope add that to judge Shakespeare by Aristotle's rules was like trying a man by the laws of one country who acted under those of another (p.47)?[29] It is therefore no longer satisfactory to see in Voltaire merely the reflection of views held by Englishmen whom he knew or whose works he had read.

In the *Letters concerning the English nation*, Voltaire's sound view is that the rules, however important they may be, must not be observed at the expense of beauty. To support his thesis, he says that some new plays have been written after Addison's time, which were very regular, but at the same time very flat and insipid. He goes to the extent of suggesting that one might think that the English had been created to produce irregular beauties only: that is why the 'shining Monsters of *Shakespear* give infinite more Delight than the judicious Images of the Moderns' (pp.179-80).

It was convenient for Voltaire to take refuge behind Shakespeare and other English writers for his own polemical purposes. He deliberately distorted some lines in his translation of the 'To be or not to be' soliloquy in *Hamlet*. For instance, Hamlet's

> Whether 'tis nobler in the mind to suffer
> The Slings and Arrows of outrageous Fortune,
> Or take arms against a sea of troubles (p.171)

becomes (p.173):

---

[29] Nicholas Rowe had earlier said that it would be hard to judge Shakespeare by a law he knew nothing of. See 'Some account of the life of mr. William Shakespeare' (1709) in *Eighteenth-century essays on Shakespeare*, p.15.

Dieux cruels, s'il en est éclairez mon courage...

Prévost who had seen the *Lettres philosophiques* in manuscript before September 1733 made some interesting remarks on letter xviii. He thought that Voltaire was particularly well-qualified to judge the work of others and that the defects Voltaire saw in Shakespeare were acknowledged by the English themselves. In general he praised Voltaire's translation, but he condemned the above line when he said: 'Voilà un blasphème que l'Auteur prête gratuitement à Hamlet. Il n'y a rien d'approchant dans l'Anglois, & rien n'est si contraire au caractère de la Pièce' (*Pour et contre*, i. 278-80). It is likely that Voltaire took note of the remarks made by the anglophile critic for he subsequently altered the line. In 1761 in the *Appel à toutes les nations*, it read: 'Dieux justes, s'il en est, éclairez mon courage', while in the article 'Art dramatique' of the *Questions sur l'encyclopédie* (1770) it became: 'Ciel, qui voyez mon trouble, éclairez mon courage.' Voltaire's version made in accordance with the spirit and not the letter of the original, as he suggests, also includes the following lines:

Eh! qui pourroit sans Toi supporter cette vie,
De nos Prêtres menteurs bénir l'hypocrisie.

This thought is nowhere to be found in the original: it is a complete fabrication on the part of Voltaire.

Moreover, Voltaire's boast that no one had translated Shakespeare before[30] and that this justifies his own free translation does not stand. In fact someone had done. Hamlet's speech to the ghost of his father in act I, scene iv, beginning 'Angels and Ministers of grace' was translated and published anonymously in Amsterdam some twenty years before in the French version of *The Spectator*, *Le Spectateur ou Socrate moderne* (1714). It was unfortunate that the anonymous author first attributed *Hamlet* to Otway and *Macbeth* to Dryden. The mistake was corrected in the 1716 edition of the periodical.[31] Although the French

---

[30] in the preface to the 1736 edition of *La Mort de César*, Voltaire again claimed that he was the first to have vulgarised English literature in France (M.iii.309), while his letter to Horace Walpole contains the categorical statement that he was the first to have introduced Shakespeare to the French (Best.D15140, 15 July 1768). This letter is also interesting because it contains Voltaire's objection to the introduction of an official fool in Shakespeare's plays. He thinks that this fashion, which was unknown to Sophocles and was good only for backward times, is abominable.

[31] see Simon Jeune, '*Hamlet* d'Otway, *Macbeth* de Dryden, ou Shakespeare en France en 1714', *RLC* (Paris 1962), xxxvi. 500-504.

translation of *The Spectator* was a major vehicle for the diffusion of interest in English literature in France in the early eighteenth century, this mistake must have prevented Shakespeare and the *Hamlet* translation from reaching a wider public. Voltaire therefore retains his importance as a vulgariser of English literature or more accurately Shakespeare as seen through his distorted eyes. Is it not the same situation that obtains with regard to the vulgarization of certain aspects of English thought? The publication of his *Discours sur la différente figure des astres* in 1732 should have made Maupertuis the pioneer in the introduction of Newtonian physics in France, but it was through Voltaire that the public at large knew of Newton.

In his three-act tragedy, *La Mort de César* (1735) where he has Shakespeare's *Julius Caesar* constantly in mind, Voltaire invented a new character, a senator called Dolabella. He reached a compromise between showing the murder of Caesar on the stage as happens in Shakespeare and giving an account of the death of a character as usually happens in French tragedy. He ensured that the shouts of the conspirators who are behind the stage and performing the murder are heard by Dolabella who is before the audience. Algarotti pointed out in a letter written in Italian to Franchini-Taviani that Voltaire imitated Shakespeare and that the last two scenes were the best models of eloquence in the theatre (Best.D927, 12 October 1735). The imitation is particularly close in the last scene (III.viii), where Mark Antony delivers his funeral oration over Caesar's dead body. The essential parts of act III, scene ii of *Julius Caesar* are faithfully rendered.

The introduction of a corpse on stage was a striking innovation. Voltaire was putting into practice what he had advocated in his critical remarks on *Cato* (see below). He may also have been inspired by a five-act play, *The Tragedy of Julius Caesar* (1722), adapted from Shakespeare by John Sheffield, duke of Buckingham. It had been written earlier since Dennis referred to it in 1710/11. Buckingham divided Shakespeare's play into two: *The Tragedy of Julius Caesar* and *The Tragedy of Marcus Brutus*. To achieve unity of action in his *Julius Caesar* he used only the first three acts from Shakespeare. The time of the action 'begins the Day before *Caesar's* Death, and ends within an Hour after it'. Voltaire's play followed a similar pattern since his aim in reducing it to three acts was to maintain unity of action. He was certainly aware of Buckingham's version which he mentioned in the preface to the 1736 edition of *La Mort de César* (M.iii.310).

The *Tragedy of Marcus Brutus*, also published in 1722, contained two choruses written by Pope who supervised another edition of the two plays in 1723. *Marcus Brutus* included the character of Dolabella, Antony's friend and probably gave Voltaire the idea for his creation in *La Mort de César*, although he did not mention Buckingham's second play.

Voltaire thought that his last scene was a rather faithful translation of *Julius Caesar*. In a letter to the abbé Asselin[32] he claimed that his play gave a true notion of English taste,[33] adding that a prose translation would not disseminate knowledge of the poetic genius of a nation: one had to imitate their taste and their manner in verse (Best. D937, 4 November 1735). To Desfontaines, who he thought had been unfair to him in his review of the play, he wrote that the last scene and some pieces translated word for word from Shakespeare provided great scope for his scholarship and taste. Moreover, France was not the only country where tragedies were being written (Best.D940, 14 November 1735). Voltaire's acknowledgment of his debt to Shakespeare did not prevent him in the preface to *La Mort de César* from minimising the fact that Shakespeare was a great genius and insisting that he lived 'dans un siècle grossier' and that one finds in his plays 'la grossièreté de ce temps beaucoup plus que le génie de l'auteur' (M.iii.309). This is a point he takes up in the *Essai sur les mœurs* where he credits Shakespeare's genius with having shone through barbarism, as Lope de Vega did in Spain. But, he added, what a pity that there was more barbarism than genius in Shakespeare's works.

The *Discours prononcé à l'Académie française* (1746) did not give Voltaire much scope to talk of Shakespeare. He, however, conceded that the barbarian Shakespeare 'mit dans l'anglais cette force et cette énergie qu'on n'a jamais pu augmenter depuis sans l'outrer, et par conséquent sans l'affaiblir' (M.xxiii.210). The *Dissertation sur la tragédie ancienne et moderne* enabled him to write a longer analysis of *Hamlet*. He says he is far from justifying everything in the tragedy, a gross and barbarous play which would not be tolerated by the vilest rabble in France and Italy. One would have thought that it was the

---

[32] the previous day he had written to Cideville on the defects and merits of Shakespeare who was a 'grand fou, d'ailleurs et ressemblant plus souvent à Gilles qu'à Corneille. Mais il a des morceaux admirables' (Best.D934).

[33] in the preface to his play, Voltaire said that instead of translating 'l'ouvrage monstrueux de Shakespeare' he wrote 'dans le goût anglais, ce *Jules César*' (M.iii. 309).

product of the imagination of a 'drunken brute'. Despite gross irregular features which make the English theatre so absurd and barbarous, one finds sublime touches worthy of the greatest geniuses. In Shakespeare, nature assembled the grotesque and the sublime.

What Voltaire is emphasizing here even more clearly than in the *Lettres philosophiques* is the dichotomy between *goût* and *génie*. He is so impressed by the ghost of Hamlet's father that he thinks it is the most striking dramatic event in the play. When he says that it produces a powerful effect on the English, he certainly includes himself. For he tried to introduce a ghost in *Ériphyle* and in *Sémiramis*, but without much success. He cannot however be put in the same category as French dramatists of the early eighteenth century like Gilles de Caux and Crébillon. They misunderstood the nature of Racinian tragedy and failed to appreciate that its greatness lay in the subtlety of its psychological analysis. Voltaire was not really taken in by the external element. He was fully aware of the difference between art and artifice. Had he not stated in the *Discours sur la tragédie*: 'Plus on veut frapper les yeux par un appareil éclatant, plus on s'impose la nécessité de dire de grandes choses; autrement on ne serait qu'un décorateur, et non un poète tragique' (M.ii. 320)? The message is driven home with as much clarity in the preface to *Les Scythes* (1768). He wrote (M.vi. 269-70):

L'appareil, l'action, le pittoresque, font un grand effet sans doute; mais ne mettons jamais le bizarre et le gigantesque à la place de la nature, et le forcé à la place du simple; que le décorateur ne l'emporte point sur l'auteur; car alors, au lieu de tragédies on aurait la rareté, la curiosité.

The *Dissertation sur la tragédie ancienne et moderne* does not argue that any ghost will do. In corroboration of this view, Voltaire refers to the ghost of Darius in Aeschylus's play, *The Persians*, and he points out how weak it is. To Voltaire, the ghost in *Hamlet* represents justice and divine retribution (M.iv.502). One has also to remember that the ghost was far from being the only thing that impressed him in the play: he was always alive, for instance, to the beauty of Hamlet's 'To be or not to be' soliloquy which he could not help reproducing in his own translation in the *Appel à toutes les nations* and in the article 'Art dramatique' of the *Questions sur l'encyclopédie*.

Perhaps one might suggest that after the late 1740s, Voltaire ceases to judge Shakespeare solely in accordance with aesthetic criteria. Patriotic sentiment becomes inextricably merged with purely literary considerations. In fact, Voltaire's patriotic feelings against England may be traced back to the battle of Fontenoy. On the occasion of the great victory the French army under Maurice de Saxe won at Fontenoy in the presence of Louis xv, Voltaire wrote to the marquis d'Argenson, the foreign minister, to say what a fitting subject this victory was for an historian. He added that for three hundred years the kings of France had achieved nothing as glorious and that he was overcome with joy (Best.D3117, 13 May 1745). He said that he too had waged war and that he had more trouble in celebrating victory than the king in winning it (Best.D3121, 20 May 1745). He even sent him a great number of copies of his *Poème de Fontenoy* for distribution 'à tous ceux qui auraient été honnis en pays étranger si nous avions été battus' (Best.D3127, 29 May 1745).

However, despite the dream of hegemony over Europe by d'Argenson and despite the military success of Maurice de Saxe, France achieved virtually nothing in the war of Austrian Succession which ended with the signing of the treaty of Aix-la-Chapelle in 1748.[34] Her colonial struggle with Britain overseas continued after that treaty and in 1754 it intensified in Canada and India. In June 1755 a French convoy was attacked by admiral Boscawen off Newfoundland: two French ships were captured, while the rest escaped. Although Britain and France were not officially at war, the British navy was ordered to seize all French ships wherever they might be. As a result of a policy that was closer to piracy than to privateering, more than three hundred French merchant ships were captured in a few weeks in the latter part of the year. In January 1756, the two colonial powers were openly at war: the Seven Years War had started.

The above events may have had a bearing on Voltaire's reactions to Shakespeare. A true picture of his position regarding the English playwright at the time can be had from a letter the young Claude Pierre Patu wrote to David Garrick on the 1st November 1755 (Best.D6562). Patu, a young man of letters who knew English well and who had visited Voltaire at Les Délices in 1755 and 1756, told Garrick how he had taken Voltaire to task for his hostile attacks on Shakespeare and added:

Quant au naturel, à la chaleur, aux idées admirables répandues dans les pièces de Shakespeare, il est tombé d'accord, et convient en riant que si vous

[34] see A. Cobban, *A History of modern France* (Harmondsworth 1966), i. 72-74.

nous preniez moins de vaisseaux et ne *piratiez* pas ainsi sur l'océan, il aurait plus ménagé le créateur de votre théâtre!

Since Voltaire was not indifferent to the conflict opposing England and France, his reported comment, uttered as a joke, should not be treated lightly. Neither was it a passing reference. The colonial argument is repeatedly invoked by Voltaire in support of his attack against Shakespeare.

It seems that from 1745 to 1776 Voltaire was not simply reacting against the popularity of English literature and English taste in France, that of Shakespeare in particular. It is clear from his letter to mme Du Deffand, that he was annoyed with the English, not only because they had written that their Shakespeare was vastly superior to Corneille, but also because they had taken Pondicherry from him! (Best.D9452, 9 December 1760).[35] He told Duclos that it was good to humble the pride of the English who thought they lorded it over the theatre as they did over the seas and who did not hesitate to put Shakespeare above Corneille (Best.D10279, 20 January 1762). These letters were supported by an unpublished writing entitled *Mémoire important*. Composed in 1764, it remained in the archives of Voltaire's friend, J. B. Suard, until it was edited for the first time in 1955.[36] It has since been published by Th. Besterman as a letter addressed to the d'Argentals (Best.D11645, c. Jan. 1764). Voltaire wrote:

Cecy est une affaire d'Etat sérieuse. Tant que les Anglais se sont contentés de prendre nos vaisseaux et de s'emparer du Canada et de Pondichéri, j'ai gardé un noble silence. Mais à présent qu'ils poussent la barbarie jusqu'à trouver Racine et Corneille ridicules, je dois prendre les armes. Voicy une petite Lettre écrite aux auteurs de la gazette Littéraire. L'auteur y venge, autant qu'il le peut, la nation et le bon goût, sans dire aucune injure à mr Home qui les outrage . . . Ces petites guerres d'ailleurs sont agréables, elles tiennent le public éveillé, et peuvent contribuer au succez d'un journal.

On the other hand, the same Voltaire was capable of reacting in an extraordinary manner in the same period. Such was his idea of patriotism that he celebrated Wolfe's capture of Quebec with great gusto at Tourney. The celebrations included the performance of a tragedy and a

---

[35] see his letter to the d'Argentals: 'Le zèle de la patrie m'a saisi. J'ay été indigné d'une brochure anglaise dans laquelle on préfère hautement Shakespear à Corneille' (Best. D9474, 16 December 1760).

[36] see L. A. Boiteux, 'Voltaire et le ménage Suard', *Studies on Voltaire* (1955), i. 25.

fireworks display. The stage was decked with emblems of liberty bearing the inscription: Libertati quieti / Musis Sacrum / Sp[ite] of the F[rench]. The *Public advertiser* of 27 November 1759 described the play as *Le Patriot insulaire*, but no such play by Voltaire exists. The reference was really to *Tancrède* which celebrates the freedom of Sicily from the Moors and was performed three times in Voltaire's theatre at Tourney at the end of October 1759.[37]

At the height of his anti-Shakespeare campaign, which culminated in his *Lettre à l'Académie française* in 1776,[38] Voltaire claimed in a letter to d'Argental that he was going to die leaving France 'barbare', but that if his letter were published perhaps one day the nation would be grateful to him for his sacrifice to its cause (Best.D20232, 30 July 1776). In a letter to d'Alembert, Voltaire compared himself to a certain mr Roux of Marseille who went to war against the English in 1756 in his private capacity (Best.D20248, 10 August 1776). To La Harpe he said that d'Alembert and others were serving a patriotic and worthy cause in defending in the Academy, Sophocles, Corneille, Euripides and Racine against Shakespeare and Le Tourneur[39] (Best.D20258, 15 August 1776). For his part, d'Alembert seems to have urged Voltaire on.[40] His vocabulary and general tone were like Voltaire's and he polarised the issue as if the survival of Racine depended entirely on the destruction of Shakespeare. He wrote (Best.D20266, 20 August 1776):

Je regarde ce jour comme un jour de bataille, où il faut tâcher de n'être pas vaincus comme à Crecy & à Poitiers . . . Il faut que Shakespear ou Racine demeurent sur la place; il faut faire voir à ces tristes & insolens Anglois, que nos gens de lettres savent mieux se battre contre eux que nos soldats & nos généraux . . . Je crierai dimanche en allant à la charge, Vive st Denis Voltaire, & meure George Shakespear!

[37] see R. E. Pike, 'Voltaire: *le Patriot insulaire*', *MLN* (1942), lvii. 354-55 and Best.D8573 (6 November 1759).

[38] some of Voltaire's complaints, as they appear in his letter to d'Argental, were that in his *Shakespeare traduit de l'anglois* (Paris 1776-82), P. Le Tourneur had put Shakespeare forward as the model of true tragedy and had sacrificed all the French without exception to his idol. Corneille and Racine were not even mentioned (Best.D20270, 19 July 1776).

[39] whom he called a deserter in his letter to d'Argental (Best.D20286, 8 September 1776). In the *Lettre à l'Académie française*, he accuses him of wishing to humiliate his country.

[40] Voltaire won d'Alembert's approval for his attack on Shakespeare as he had won mme Du Deffand's in his attack on Milton in *Candide* in 1759 (Best.D8559, 28 October 1759).

After the discourse was read at the Académie française, d'Alembert told Voltaire that some Frenchmen were displeased: not content with being beaten on land and at sea, they wished to be defeated in the theatre as well. He confessed that his own pride was involved, 'car j'avais fort à cœur de ne pas voir rater ce canon, lorsque je m'étois chargé d'y mettre le feu' (Best.D20272, 27 August 1776). Memories of the colonial wars between France and England, particularly those involving Canada and India, were revived in that denigration of Shakespeare. Voltaire was to tell Jean de Vaines that he did not know whether after his declaration of war[41] with England he could now make peace with her. For he had no Canada to give her, no East India Company to sacrifice to her! (Best.D20279, 4 September 1776). In fairness to Voltaire, it must be said that other writers found it convenient to exploit the political climate. Arthur Murphy, for instance, took shelter behind injured national pride in attacking Voltaire in his famous *Letter from the author of the orphan of China* (see below). French translations of the letter appeared in the *Journal étranger* (1760) and the *Variétés littéraires* (1768).

All this does not mean that literary criteria were no longer valid with Voltaire as from the 1740s. Rather when they were applied, Voltaire made it harder for Shakespeare to pass the test. In the *Essai sur les mœurs*,[42] he asks why no Shakespearean play had crossed the seas while entire scenes from Guarini's *Pastor fido* are known by heart in Sweden and Russia. His explanation is that if Shakespearean tragedy were really good, it would have been sought after by other nations. A nation that satisfies only its own taste could never claim that it had good taste (M.xii.246-47). The *Appel à toutes les nations* states that every European reader knew Corneille or Racine, but very few knew Shakespeare (M.xxiv.112). The correspondence insists on universality as a criterion. In a letter to Keate, Voltaire says he is not impressed by the genius of a tragic writer if none of his plays can be performed anywhere else in the world.[43] No one more than he sees the purple

[41] Voltaire claimed in his letter to mme de Choiseul written some years before that he was at war with the English (Best.D15141, 15 July 1768). He considered Walpole's letter to him (Best.D15161, 27 July 1768), which he had not yet received, to be the latter's declaration of war.

[42] this section entitled 'Usages des xve et xvie siècles et de l'état des beaux-arts' had already appeared in fragmentary form in the *Mercure de France* (1745-46) See Williams, i.281.

[43] he makes the same the same point in 1776 in the *Lettre à l'Académie française.*

passages to be found here and there in Shakespeare, but he will concur with Pope that it is not 'un nez et un menton qui fait un beau visage et qu'il faut un assemblage régulier' (Best.D8858, 16 April 1760). The only concession he makes to Shakespeare when he writes to Saurin is that apart from London, Canada is the only other place where Shakespeare's plays give pleasure. Considering that Canada was a rather barren and desolate country in the eighteenth century, this is virtually no concession (Best.D13025, 4 December 1765).

With the passage of time, the rules, especially those of the unities, assume increasing importance in Voltaire's assessment of Shakespeare. One might be tempted to say that he was acting in accordance with dramatic principles he firmly believed in. However, it will be seen that here too external factors influence his judgement. When he feels provoked,[44] he is no longer prepared to turn a blind eye to the violation of the rules for the sake of genius. Had not the anonymous writer of the article 'Parallèle entre Shakespeare et Corneille' which was published in the *Journal encyclopédique* of 15 October 1760 concluded that Shakespeare had too much genius to submit to the rules? One would look in vain, he thought, in Corneille's writings for this 'fonds inépuisable d'une imagination également pathétique et sublime, fantastique et pittoresque, sombre et gaie, et cette prodigieuse variété de caractères, tous si bien marqués, tous si bien contrastés, qu'il n'y a pas un seul de leurs discours qui puisse être transporté de l'un à l'autre; talent qui est particulier à Shakespeare, et dans lequel il surpasse tous les autres poètes. Il est, pour ainsi dire, le miroir de la nature' (cf. Paul Van Tieghem, p.252).

To Voltaire this 'Parallèle' meant that the reassertion of the rules had become a necessity.[45] That is why in his letter to mme Du Deffand,

---

But by that time J. F. Ducis's version of *Hamlet* (1769) and his *Romeo et Juliette* (1772) had already been performed. Voltaire, however, did not consider these remote adaptations as being truly Shakespeare, cf. *Voltaire on Shakespeare*, p.206, n.

[44] Arthur Murphy, author of *The Orphan of China* (1759) complained that Voltaire seemed determined in many of his late writings to live in a state of hostility with the British nation and mentioned the 'vein of prejudice, which had discoloured almost all your *fugitive pieces*' (Best.D8278, 30 April 1759). Murphy kept using Voltaire's own expressions of contempt in this letter: he hoped that his own tragedy would not appear to him a *monstrous farce* and begged Voltaire not to make it the criterion by which he would decide on the taste of the English nation. The actor playwright had in 1756 defended Shakespeare against Voltaire's criticism in *The Gray's-Inn journal*. See H. H. Dunbar, *The Dramatic career of Arthur Murphy* (New York 1946), p.7.

[45] lord Kames's *Elements of criticism* (1764) provoked equally strong reactions in

he draws attention to the way in which *Richard III* violates the rules of the unities (Best.D9452, 9 December 1760). In the *Appel à toutes les nations*, after a lengthy account of the plot of *Hamlet*, Voltaire states that tastes vary considerably between nations. Here, however, he is not moved by the same spirit that prevailed at the time of the *Essay on epick poetry*. The diversity in taste is simply mentioned in order to show how the English violated all the rules and consequently could not have high standards. His point is that when one is thinking of the barbarous English it is useless to talk of the rules of Aristotle, of the three unities, of decorum, to show how necessary it is that the stage is never left empty and how important it is to weave a plot with art, to unfold it in a natural way, to express oneself in noble and simple terms, to make princes speak with the decency they always have or wish to have and never to stray from the rules of language. One can delight a nation – the English, that is – without taking so much trouble. It is because Shakespeare deviated from these rules that he is considered superior to Corneille. Voltaire explains his success in England by the fact that he pandered to the taste of the rabble, which unfortunately influenced that of the court as well.

Another reason for his dislike of the marvels of the 'divine' Shakespeare, as he ironically put it, is mentioned for the first time in the *Appel*. It is that Shakespeare obtained all the plots of his tragedies from novels: he simply put in dialogue form the novel of Claudius, Gertrude and Hamlet which was entirely written by Saxo Grammaticus. Voltaire took up this point in the *Lettre à l'Académie française*, where he says that the tragedy of *Othello* came from the novel of Cinthio. He was certainly right with regard to the source of *Othello*. The influence of Dryden is visible here, for in the preface to *An Evening's love* (1671), he wrote: 'Most of Shakespeare's plays, I mean the stories of them, are to be found in the *Hecatommithi* or *Hundred Novels* of Cinthio' (Watson, i.154). If he could criticise Corneille on the grounds that his plays borrowed too much from romance, it was logical for Voltaire to use the same criterion against Shakespeare. We know how at first[46]

Voltaire. Because Kames had attacked Corneille and Racine, Voltaire retaliated by attacking the vocabulary of *Othello* and the tone of Hamlet's soliloquy 'Frailty thy name is woman' which he took pains to translate. His conclusion was that the English had nothing better to offer: in any case, they did not care for decency, nobility, soundness of ideas, the beauty and harmony of poetry (M.xxv.159-63). Voltaire's review of the *Elements of criticism* was published in the *Gazette littéraire* of the 4th April 1764.

[46] see below, p.236.

he despised the novel as a genre. There was a change in his attitude to the novel subsequently, but he never accepted that romance could be freely used in tragedy.

Despite all his reservations on Shakespeare, Voltaire could not help betray some admiration for him in parts of his later works. Even in the *Appel à toutes les nations*, he takes considerable pains to reproduce from memory his translation of Hamlet's soliloquy 'To be or not to be' and to add a more literal version. He pays homage to the genius of the English language, its naturalness, its energy, its daring which those unaccustomed to foreign turns of speech will think is grandiloquent nonsense. One will discover truth, depth and 'je ne sais quoi qui attache, et qui remue beaucoup plus que ne ferait l'élégance' buried under this veil. He thinks everyone in England knows this monologue by heart because he himself has been so impressed: it is a raw diamond with stains. However, if it were polished, it would lose its weight. The conventions of the French theatre such as the use of rhyme and eloquence and the presence of a highly cultured audience made Corneille's task more difficult. This explains why in his letter to Keate Voltaire almost envied Shakespeare's liberty to do as he pleased on stage (Best.D10322, 10 February 1762). To Saurin he confessed (Best.D11727, 28 February 1764):

Gilles Shakespear avec toute sa barbarie et son ridicule, a ... des traits si naïfs et si vrais, et un fracas d'action si imposant, que tous les raisonnemants de Pierre Corneille sont à la glace en comparaison du Tragique de ce Gilles. On court encor à ses pièces, et on s'y plait en les trouvant absurdes.

It was an advantage to do without rhyme. While commenting on act III, scene iv of Corneille's *Horace*, Voltaire says that Corneille had failed to observe the first rule of 'always hurrying on to the crisis'.[47] But, he adds, who has always observed this rule? He acknowledges that Shakespeare is of all tragic writers the one who has fewer scenes of pure conversation; there is almost always something new in every scene. Even if it is at the expense of the rules of decorum and verisimilitude, even if Shakespeare mixes the grotesque and the sublime, he still moves (Williams, ii. 268).

Perhaps some of the most balanced judgements[48] of Voltaire on

---

[47] Horace, *Ars poetica*, i. 148.
[48] notwithstanding his desire to make the Académie laugh at Shakespeare's expense. He suggested that if d'Alembert wanted to laugh, he should be present at the Académie

Shakespeare are those he inserted after his translation of the first three acts of *Julius Caesar*, which appeared as part of his commentary on Corneille in 1764.[49] The prose text of *Julius Caesar* is literally translated; the verse part is not an exact translation, although the sense and tone of the original have been preserved.[50] As consistency is rarely automatic with Voltaire, it is worth noting that despite his campaign against Shakespeare and his patriotic sentiment, he maintained the balanced position he had taken about *Julius Caesar* in the *Discours sur la tragédie* more than thirty years earlier. Here, however, his analysis has more substance. He is surprised that a nation known for its genius and for its success in the arts and sciences can enjoy so many monstrous irregularities, such as the sight of Caesar who now talks like a hero, now like a braggart in farce; cobblers and senators who speak as if they were in the market place. To show that he is not prejudiced against Shakespeare, Voltaire mentions the common traits that the Englishman shares with Calderón: ignorance, an inflated style, a mixture of the grotesque and the sublime.

Why do two nations which are so different show such similarities in taste? Voltaire's explanation is that the poor taste in which these strange, wild plays are written does not prevent them from being genuinely interesting. When he saw the performance of *Julius Caesar*, his interest and emotions were roused right from the start. Every conspirator made him feel curious and however ridiculous and uneven many of the scenes were, he was moved by the play as it was so natural. This natural tone is often low, vulgar and barbarous. The characters are not really Roman, but country people of previous centuries who conspire in a tavern. Caesar hardly resembles the Caesar of history – a sound judgment from Voltaire. Shakespeare goes to extremes in being ridiculous, without being weak. Yet Voltaire confesses that he would rather have this monstrous spectacle than the 'longues confidences d'un froid amour, ou des raisonnements de politique encore plus froids'.

There is also an attempt to account for Shakespeare's success by the spectacular element in *Julius Caesar*. Even the aristocracy liked

when *Héraclius* of Calderon and *Julius Caesar* translated in blank verse word for word were read (Best.D10515, 17 June 1762).

[49] see *Voltaire on Shakespeare*, pp. 93-154.

[50] d'Alembert had misgivings about Voltaire's translation. He impressed upon him the importance of retaining the spirit of the original so that the English might not accuse him of betraying his ignorance of English idiom or disfiguring their idol (Best.D10697, 8 September 1762).

scenic effects. In defence of Shakespeare is the argument that one must have a cultured mind and a developed taste, like the sixteenth-century Italians and the seventeenth-century French, 'pour ne vouloir rien que de raisonnable, rien que de sagement écrit, & pour exiger qu'une pièce de théâtre soit digne de la cour des Médicis, ou de celle de Louis xiv'. It was Shakespeare's misfortune that his genius should have blossomed at a time when taste had not yet been formed. Voltaire could not be fairer to Shakespeare.

In the article 'Art dramatique' of the *Questions sur l'encyclopédie*, Voltaire gives other examples of what he calls the sublime in *Julius Caesar*, but the greater part of this article is against Shakespeare simply because he feels provoked by Samuel Johnson's remarks in his edition of Shakespeare and by lord Kames's failure to appreciate lines from *Iphigénie*. In Johnson's view, Voltaire is one of those critics who base their judgements upon narrower principles: this explains why Voltaire censures Shakespeare's kings as not completely royal. Voltaire perhaps thinks decency is violated when the Danish usurper is represented as a drunkard. But Shakespeare, argues Johnson, knows that kings love wine like other men. Johnson therefore concludes that Voltaire's criticisms are the 'petty cavils of petty minds; a poet overlooks the casual distinction of country and condition'. These criticisms are further qualified as 'minute and slender'. It is against this background that Voltaire's attacks on Shakespeare in the article 'Art dramatique' must be viewed. To prove his point, Voltaire shows how ridiculous Shakespeare appears when translated. The passages he translates are carefully chosen from *Julius Caesar*, *Antony and Cleopatra* and *Henry V*. The article 'Goût' from the *Questions sur l'encyclopédie* has the same limited objective in view. If Corneille has certain unhappy lines in plays such as *Pompée*, he is free from the extravagant words Shakespeare puts in the mouths of his heroes.[51] This time Voltaire translates passages from *Richard II* and *Henry IV part I*: he thereby shows that his repertory of plays has been extended.

James Rutlidge, an Irishman settled in France where he was known as Jean-Jacques Rutlèdge, had in his *Essay on the characters and*

---

[51] yet in the *Lettre à l'Académie française*, Voltaire suggests that the exposition in *Pompée* is much preferable to that of *King Lear*. His objection is particularly directed at the language of Gloucester who describes with relish how he begot his illegitimate son Edmund. Voltaire therefore asks for justice from the queen and princesses of France and from the daughters of so many heroes who know how such men should speak.

manners of the French (1770) praised the author of the *Lettres philosophiques* for having celebrated English achievements abroad. Dissatisfied with Voltaire's subsequent attitude, he published a comedy entitled *Le Bureau d'esprit* in April 1776. A second edition appeared in 1777 and in the preface to that edition, Rutlidge wrote that the errors and eternal bad faith of Voltaire were being demonstrated in the play. In act IV, scene viii, the Marquis d'Orsimont (Condorcet) reads a letter purporting to come from Voltaire who attacks Shakespeare and expresses fears that Le Tourneur's translation might reveal his own plagiarism. To prevent the decadence of French literature, the assembly decides to burn the translation. Did Rutlidge give Voltaire the idea of writing a proper letter to attack Shakespeare? What is certain is that Rutlidge was most provocative. For, by August 1776, he had produced a novel, *La Quinzaine anglaise*; its preface stated that the courageous translators of Shakespeare could show how Voltaire had fallen short of the Englishman in his imitation. In the eighth journey, which contains reflections on Shakespeare and Molière, a certain Bouillac talks to an English lord. He says that Shakespeare rid the English stage of shackles consecrated by antiquity; it was to him that the English certainly owed their superiority over the French in tragedy. To crown his attack, Rutlidge brought out in October 1776 his *Observations à messieurs de l'Académie française* where he sided with Le Tourneur against Voltaire.[52]

A further proof of Voltaire's widening knowledge of Shakespeare is to be found in his *Lettre à l'Académie française* (1776) which discusses Shakespeare's bad taste in plays not mentioned before such as *Romeo and Juliet* and *Troïlus*. In many other ways this *Lettre* appears to be merely a recapitulation of objections raised against Shakespeare during almost half a century from the days of the *Lettres philosophiques*, and the expression of his recently conceived dislike of Le Tourneur who had styled Shakespeare the god of tragedy. One point of particular interest, however, is that Voltaire openly quotes Thomas Rymer's *A Short view of tragedy* (1693) in support of his stand. He argues that many English men of letters had made the same observations he was now making. After accurately translating Rymer's 'There is not a Monky but understands Nature better; not a Pug in *Barbary* that has not a truer taste of things' as 'il n'y a point de singe en Afrique, point

---

[52] see André Genuist, *Le Théâtre de Shakespeare dans l'œuvre de Pierre Le Tourneur 1776-1783* (Paris 1971), p.47.

de babouin qui n'ait plus de goût que Shakespeare', he claims that he will follow a *via media* between Rymer and Le Tourneur. He also falls back on Rowe who in his edition of Shakespeare in 1709-10 had remarked that 'Shakespeare is indeed stored with a great many beauties, but they are in a heap of rubbish'. For in his letter to d'Argental, he speaks of 'perles dans son énorme fumier' (Best.D20220, 19 July 1776.) This letter circulated in Paris.

The recapitulation of objections is continued in the *Lettre à l'Académie française* (1777) which has certain affinities with the previous *Lettre* and which was indeed regarded by Voltaire and his contemporaries as a corollary to the first Academy discourse. It was in fact a reply to Elizabeth Montagu's book, *An Essay on the writings and genius of Shakespeare with some remarks upon the misrepresentation of m. de Voltaire* (1769), which was translated as *Apologie de Shakespear* (1777). It was printed as the dedication to the Académie française of Voltaire's last play, *Irène*. This second *Lettre* is more of a defence of French classical tragedy than a criticism of Shakespeare. Shakespeare's superiority over Corneille and Racine is, however, challenged. Voltaire's quarrel with mrs Montagu is that Shakespeare cannot be considered superior just because of the 'morceaux qui sont en effet naturels et énergiques, quoique défigurés presque toujours par une familiarité basse'. He argues that one should not be allowed to prefer two lines of Ennius to the whole of Virgil.

If the publication of two French translations of Shakespeare's plays, La Place's eight-volume *Théâtre anglais* (1746-49) and Le Tourneur's twenty-volume *Shakespeare traduit de l'anglois* (1776-82), can be conveniently described as historical landmarks in the evolution of Voltaire's stand against Shakespeare, the problem of assessing his reactions cannot be viewed solely from a literary angle. From the 1740s to the end of his career, the political element was always present in the background to his attacks. And it was only after 1768 when Voltaire had declared open war on England that his reactions can be associated with purely cultural nationalism. He did seek the help of distinguished Englishmen such as William Pitt, the prime minister, lord Bute, the lord high chancellor and Henry Fox to subscribe to his edition of Corneille (cf. Best.D9905, 19 July 1761, D9903, D9912, 25 July 1761). It is true that Voltaire resented the extension of English literary influence in France, the honours accorded to French anglophiles and the fact that he himself had played his part in vulgarising

English literature in his country. But it is equally true that he bitterly resented English colonial victories at the expense of the French. One might justifiably conclude that his outbursts would have been considerably toned down were it not for these military defeats. He finally proclaimed an absolute standard of good taste, by which he judged Shakespeare, but he was not, except in 1776, consistently against him despite his declaration of war in 1768.

To his visitors R. N. A. and R. A. G. Neville, Voltaire declared in 1772 that he was being vilified in London as an enemy of Shakespeare. He conceded that he was shocked and put off by Shakespeare's absurdities, but he was no less struck by his beauties. He even claimed that one would find after his death an edition of Shakespeare's works where he had marked the purple passages, and in great number.[53] This did not necessarily imply that one could get away with it simply by saying that Shakespeare was natural. In front of other visitors, John Moore and Douglas Hamilton, Voltaire rebuked an admirer of Shakespeare with this: 'Avec permission, Monsieur, mon cul est bien dans la nature, et cependant je porte des culottes' (p.164). He explained to Martin Sherlock in 1776 that love of Shakespeare had become a religion and that Shakespeare devotees were like religious fanatics (p.183).

One is no longer justified in dating Voltaire's anti-English feelings from 1760, although in that very year he had tried to distinguish between the English and their books when he told mme Du Deffand: 'J'aime autant les livres de cette nation que j'aime peu leurs personnes' (Best.D8764, 18 February 1760). His paradoxical nature would to a certain extent account for his ambivalent attitude towards Shakespeare and the English. Even if he were clearly anti-Shakespeare for a time, it does not automatically follow that he was opposed to English literature as a whole. Did he not, for instance, retain his admiration for Swift right up to the end?

iii. *Dryden, Otway and Voltaire*

The literatures of France and England were once treated as though they were completely apart and mutually exclusive. The English Restoration period, however, reversed this trend. Exaggerated claims

---

[53] *Voltaire's British visitors*, eds sir Gavin de Beer and André-M. Rousseau, Studies on Voltaire (1967), xlix. 157.

were even made to emphasize French influence on English literature after the 1660s. A more realistic attitude was adopted by those who thought in terms of an interpenetration of the two cultures. This was indeed the position of Lanson who was of the view that during the Restoration English and French critical ideas were close enough to allow a mutual influence. Lanson found in such an intellectual climate the real explanation for Voltaire's indebtedness to Dryden. He thought that Dryden gave Voltaire the idea of a 'drame plus violent'.[54]

Dryden is perhaps a perfect example of the interpenetration. Had he not acknowledged in the prologue to *Secret love: or the maiden queen* (1668), when he was in his most fairminded mood, that

> He who writ this, not without pains and thought,
> From French and English theatres has brought
> Th'exactest rules by which a play is wrought.
> The unities of action, place, and time;
> The scenes unbroken; and a mingled chime
> Of Jonson's humour, with Corneille's rhyme?

Yet in the *Essay of dramatic poesy* published almost simultaneously, the same Dryden was guilty of the most chauvinistic remarks ever made by an English writer. Eugenius, one of the speakers in the *Essay*, was ready to defend the honour of his country against the French, and to maintain that the English were as well able to vanquish them with their pens as their ancestors had been with their swords' (Watson, i. 43). Another speaker, Neander, who is Dryden himself, remarked (p.65):

We have borrowed nothing from them; our plots are weaved in English looms . . . for the verse itself we have English precedents of elder date than any of Corneille's plays: (not to name our old comedies before Shakespeare, which were all writ in verse of six feet, or alexandrines, such as the French now use).

Dryden wrote all this against the French at the very time when he was imitating Molière's *L'Etourdi* in his *Sir Martin Mar-All* (1668). The *Journal littéraire*, although alive to the reputation of Dryden[55] whom it described as 'un des plus estimés dans le genre dramatique',

[54] G. Lanson, *Histoire de la littérature française* (Paris 1894), p.692.

[55] A. Boyer, a French protestant refugee in London, had the highest praise for Dryden in his *Dialogues familiers* published some time before 1715. He put the following words in the mouth of an English speaker: 'Nous avons . . . un Sophocle et un Euripide en Shakespear, un Homère et un Virgile en Milton, et presque tous ces Poètes ensemble en Dryden seul.'

drew attention to his larceny. It complained how in his *Œdipus* Dryden had plundered whole scenes from the *Œdipe* of Corneille and had the effrontery to treat Corneille's works as whipped cream (ix. 198-99). Dryden was more severely criticised by the abbé J.-B. Le Blanc in his *Supplément du génie ou l'art de composer des poëmes dramatiques*, which he added to his *Lettres d'un Français* in 1745. Before censuring Dryden's jingoistic statements, Le Blanc ironically suggested that it was useless to follow the rules, as they were meant for fools: one had simply to take a Corneille or Racine play, change its title and the name of the characters and pass it off as one's own (pp.135-36). A. de La Chapelle castigated Dryden for pretending to have a great scorn for French writers 'qu'il pilloit néanmoins impitoïablement' (*Le Babillard* (Paris 1724), i. 71). This French version of *The Tatler* translated passages from Dryden's *Almanzor* and mentioned *All for love* in the same volume.

Despite a certain amount of chauvinism that prevailed on both sides of the Channel, it is sometimes possible to point to a common source of inspiration uniting English and French writers. Voltaire and Dryden, for instance, often drew inspiration from the same sources. One of these was Saint-Evremond with whose dramatic criticism Dryden agreed. All three writers complained of a lack of action on the French stage. In Voltaire's conception of tragedy is to be found an element which is entirely in accordance with the views of Dryden's friend. For in the *Appel à toutes les nations*, Voltaire quotes Saint-Evremond as having, *inter alia*, drawn attention to the lack of depth in French drama. He shares Saint-Evremond's view when he says that the latter 'a mis le doigt dans la plaie secrète du théâtre français' (M.xxiv.218). He concludes his remarks with the reminder that French plays are 'de belles conversations plutôt qu'une action' (M.xxiv.219). In his *Essay of dramatic poesy*, Dryden referred to Corneille's *La Mort de Pompée* and *Cinna* and made Neander remark that 'they are not so properly to be called plays, as long discourses of reason of State . . . their actors speak by the hour-glass, as our parsons do' (Watson, i. 60). There is thus a similarity of approach in dramatic criticism, stemming from a common source. Maillet was right in saying that when Voltaire's criticisms rise above petty considerations and when Dryden's observations are not blinded by patriotic fervour, there is a striking similarity between them.[56]

[56] A. Maillet, 'Dryden et Voltaire', *RLC* (1938), xviii. 280.

The extracts from Dryden's plays which are reproduced in the
Notebooks give some indication of Voltaire's interest in the English
writer. There are quotations from *All for love, Œdipus, Aureng-Zebe*
and *The Spanish friar*. However, an analysis of the 'Small Leningrad
notebook'[57] and the 'Leningrad notebooks' reveals that *The Indian
emperor* (1665) is Dryden's most frequently quoted work: once in the
former and four times in the latter group. In the former notebook,
Voltaire reproduced the following lines from *The Indian emperor*
(v, ii. 83-87; *Notebooks*, i.52):

> to prove religion true
> If either wit, or sufferings could suffice
> All faiths afford the constant, and the wise
> And yet ev'n they by education sway'd
> In age deffend what infancy obey'd.

In the latter notebooks, he reproduced line 9 from the same scene
spoken by a Christian priest, and added another line of his own to
emphasise the identity of the speaker (*Notebooks*, i.240):

> Down with him, kill him, merit heaven thereby.
> Discourse of a priest in the conquest of Mexico

before he gave a longer version consisting of a combination of the first
four lines from the 'Small Leningrad notebook' and the following two
lines from Dryden's *The Hind and the Panther* (ll.1685-86):

> The priest continues what the nurse began
> As thus the child imposes on the man.

Voltaire's translation reads (*Notebooks*, i.405-406):

> Cessez de nous vanter vos faibles avantages,
> Nous avons comme vous nos martirs et nos sages.
> Il en est en tout temps, il en est en tous lieux.
> Toute secte eut les siens, et tout peuple a ses dieux.
> Nous naissons ignorants; l'erreur de notre mére
> Succée avec le lait nous en devient plus chère.
> La nourrice commence, et le prêtre finit.

---

[57] this notebook dates from 1726 and the next year or two (*Notebooks*, i. 17). It was first
published by N. Torrey as 'Voltaire's English notebook' in *Modern philology* (1929),
xxvi. 307-25. In it Voltaire recorded his observations on English literature and quotations
from English writers. The volume of 'Leningrad notebooks' as a whole probably dates
very roughly from 1735 to 1750 (*Notebooks*, i. 29).

Au joug des préjugez le temps nous endurcit
On se fait de [l'erreur] une triste science.
L'âge mûr est encor la duppe de l'enfance.
La superstition qui commence au berceau
Tirannise la vie, et nous suit au tombau.

Voltaire's critical comments on Dryden in the mid 1730s appear ambivalent. His view in the *Letters concerning the English nation* is that Dryden was 'a Writer whose Genius was too exuberant, and not accompanied with Judgment enough' (p.175). He would have had a spotless reputation if he had produced only a tenth of his works. Voltaire nevertheless translates some lines from *Aureng-Zebe* (act IV, scene i) which he considers to be one of the purple passages in Dryden. This leads him to make some general remarks about English tragic writers. When he says that their style is too inflated, too unnatural and too closely copied from the Hebrew writers who 'abound so much with the *Asiatic* Fustian' (p.178), one is not certain whether he has Dryden in mind. His subsequent writings, however, make it clear that Dryden is included in the attack.

In his letter to Formont, Voltaire showed that he was aware of Prévost's translation of Dryden's *All for love*, that is, *Tout l'amour* (1735), although he had not yet read it. He thought that *All for love*, which he called *Cléopâtre*, was a monstrous work like most English plays. There was only one scene between Ventidius and Antony which was worthy of Corneille – a view, he added, which was shared by Bolingbroke, Addison and all good authors (Best.D942, 15 November 1735). Voltaire was very indignant against Dryden for having renewed his attack on French writers in the preface to *All for love* (1678). His reactions appear legitimate, since Dryden took the liberty of attacking not only the French dramatic tradition, but also Voltaire's idol, Racine. In Dryden's words, French playwrights and their heroes are (Watson, ii.224-25):

the most civil people breathing; but their good breeding seldom extends to a word of sense . . . they want the genius which animates our stage; and therefore 'tis but necessary, when they cannot please, that they should take care not to offend . . . while they affect to shine in trifles, they are often careless in essentials. Thus their Hippolytus is so scrupulous in point of decency that he will rather expose himself to death than accuse his stepmother to his father . . . He [Racine] has chosen to give him the turn of gallantry, sent him to travel from Athens to Paris, taught him to make love, and transformed the Hippolytus of Euripides into Monsieur Hippolyte.

The second dedicatory epistle to *Zaïre* (1736) provided Voltaire with the opportunity to refute strongly Dryden's preface. This retaliation developed into a lengthy attack on *All for love*. Your Dryden, who was a great genius, Voltaire said to Fawkener, put in the mouths of his amorous heroes 'ou des hyperboles de rhétorique, ou des indécences, deux choses également opposées à la tendresse' (M.ii.552). What better model than Racine by which to judge Dryden? Instead of the elegant language of Titus in *Bérénice*, Dryden makes Antony say:

Ciel! comme j'aimai! Témoin les jours et les nuits qui suivaient en dansant sous vos pieds ... un jour venait, et ne voyait rien qu'amour; un autre venait, et c'était de l'amour encore. Les soleils étaient las de nous regarder, et moi, je n'étais point las d'aimer.

Voltaire finds it hard to believe that Antony should have made such speeches to Cleopatra. As for the heroine herself, she complains that she has been deprived of Antony's caresses. By way of punishment for his cruelty, she says that she will leave on his lips the imprint of her ardent kisses. Voltaire remarks that it is very likely that Cleopatra often spoke in this manner, but one must not address a respectable audience in such indecent language. Some Englishmen may think that this is pure nature; Voltaire's reply is that it is precisely this type of nature that one must veil with care: for the 'honnêtes gens' there is no pleasure without decorum. The French, he concludes, recognized this rule before other nations not because they are without genius and daring, as the uneven and impetuous Dryden stupidly says, but because they are the most sociable and the most polished people on earth (M.ii.553).

All for love must have made some impact on Voltaire, however severe the judgement he passed on it, for he came back to it in the *Remarques sur Médée*. Corneille may have used strained and artificial metaphors,[58] but this failing was typical of the age when inflated

---

[58] Voltaire was not necessarily against the use of metaphor in drama. For in his letter to J. B. La Noue, author of the tragedy *Mahomet second*, Voltaire confessed that he liked a bold, metaphorical style, full of images. All other nations liked these striking images. However much he appreciated Racine's plays, he wished that the hero of *Bajazet* had a more sublime style. He was not claiming that one should go beyond nature: what he wanted was that it should be strengthened and made more beautiful (Best.D1966, 3 April 1739).

metaphors and false comparisons were the only ornaments used. Corneille was no worse than Dryden, as the latter compared Antony with an eagle carrying a wren on its wings. The wren which represented the emperor Augustus then rose above the eagle (Williams, ii.18).

It may be shown that far from being always hostile to Dryden in his criticism, Voltaire became more well-disposed towards him after 1736. The 1742 edition of the *Lettres philosophiques* reflects this change in attitude. The section on Dryden is increased by the addition of passages from *The Indian emperor* and *The Hind and the panther*.[59] What Voltaire has done is to reproduce with slight variations the translation he made in the 'Leningrad notebooks' (see above) and translate in addition the following conversation between Pizarro and Montezuma in *The Indian emperor*, act I, scene ii (*Lettres philosophiques*, ed. G. Lanson, ii.84):

> Pizarre dit à Montezume:
> L'envoyé du Très-Haut, le maître de ma loi,
> Le Pape a transporté ton Empire à mon Roi.
> L'Empereur Mexiquain répond:
> Le Pape est l'ennemi du Dieu qu'il représente,
> S'il autorise ainsi ton audace insolente;
> Et c'est un insensé s'il donne mes Etats,
> Dont il n'est point le maître, & qu'il ne connoit pas.

Voltaire uses his editorial discretion to emphasize in his introduction to this scene how Montezuma, the unhappy Indian king, refutes the arguments of the Christian priest. The priest's intention is to convert Montezuma so that he may be gently prepared for the torture intended for him. It should be pointed out how the first four lines of Montezuma's speech beginning with 'Cessez de nous vanter' (see above, p.51) are skilfully linked with the third letter on the Quakers. Had not Voltaire stressed the importance of martyrdom for the Quakers when he wrote the history of George Fox? Here Montezuma is using the same technique by maintaining that each sect has its saints and its wise men. Voltaire takes this opportunity to deflate the pretensions of the Christian religion, to denounce the priesthood and to attack superstition which follows one from the cradle to the tomb.

How ironical, but how typical of Voltaire, that in the very year when he was dedicating his tragedy *Mahomet* to pope Benedict XIV and

[59] see norman Torrey, 'Voltaire's English notebook', *MP* (1929), xxvi. 310, n.3.

trying to obtain by flattery his support for his candidature to the Académie française, he should be denouncing popery in such a flagrant manner! The themes – prejudice, superstition and imperialism – have been carefully chosen to suit Voltaire's taste. It is not surprising that he shows admiration for English daring and sometimes their licence.

In the 1756 edition of the *Lettres philosophiques*, Voltaire is ironical at the expense of the 'farce' *Don Sebastian* (1699) which Dryden calls tragedy. He nevertheless chooses the following conversation between Sebastian and Dorax-Alonso from act IV, scene iii (Lanson, ii. 98):

SEBASTIAN
...and know me for thy king.
DOR.
Too well I know thee, but for king no more.
This is not Lisbon; nor the circle this,
Where, like a statue, thou hast stood besieged
By sycophants and fools, the growth of courts;
Where thy gulled eyes, in all the gaudy round
Met nothing but a lie in every face;
And the gross flattery of a gaping crowd,
Envious who first should catch, and first applaud,
The stuff of royal nonsense

which he translates as (Lanson, ii. 85):

ALONZE
Qui, moi?
Je te connais fort bien, mais non pas pour mon Roi.
Tu n'es plus dans Lisbonne, où ta Cour méprisable,
Nourrissait de ton coeur l'orgueil insuportable.
Un tas d'illustres sots & de fripons titrés,
Et de gueux du bel air, & d'esclaves dorés,
Chatouillait ton oreille & fascinait ta vue;
On t'entourait en cercle ainsi qu'une statue.
Quand tu disais un mot, chacun, le cou tendu,
S'empressait d'applaudir sans t'avoir entendu;
Et ce troupeau servile admirait en silence
Ta royale sottise & ta noble arrogance:
Mais te voilà réduit à ta juste valeur.

Voltaire finds Alonzo's speech typically English. To the critics' question on how to reconcile so much ridicule with reason, such vulgarity with the sublime, Voltaire's answer is simply that one has

to bear in mind that these plays have been written by men. In defence
of the English theatre, Voltaire quotes the Spanish theatre which had
all the defects of the English stage without its beauties This leads him
to attack the Greek theatre for its 'puerilités si grossières'. Good taste
requires centuries to evolve. Racine had pure taste, but Voltaire takes
care to point out that it was in the great tragedies. Voltaire's restraint
in his criticism of Dryden's drama is worth noting, since his remarks
were made at a time when non-literary factors such as the colonial
struggle in the Seven Years War were beginning to influence his
judgement.

Whatever may have been Voltaire's reservations on Dryden as
a dramatist, this did not prevent him from using the latter's ideas
in his own plays as early as 1731. It is true that Dryden was an active
supporter of the royal cause against all internecine troubles, but like
Voltaire, he had anti-clerical feelings and considered religious bigotry
to be the main cause of civil wars. Dryden's thought may be illustrated
by reference to the following lines from *Tyrannic love* (1670):

> T'infected zeal you must no mercy show:
> For, from Religion, all Rebellions grow.[60]

Many passages dealing with religion in his plays are given a rational-
istic touch. Thus Bredvold[61] has remarked that in *Tyrannic love* st
Catherine does not go far beyond the principles of natural religion
when she converts Apollonius by showing the rational and ethical
superiority of Christianity. In the same way, we can detect deistic
feelings in Almahide, the heroine of Dryden's *The Conquest of Granada*
(1672), and in Voltaire's Zaïre. Almahide's words (*Dramatic works*,
iii. 149):

> Thou Pow'r unknown, if I have err'd forgive:
> My infancy was taught what I believe.

can be matched by Zaïre's (M.ii.560):

> les soins qu'on prend de notre enfance
> Forment nos sentiments, nos mœurs, notre croyance.

In fact, Voltaire may be drawing from Dryden's *The Indian emperor*,
and in particular from act v, scene ii, lines 86-87 which he had already reproduced in the 'Small Leningrad notebook' (see above, p.51).

[60] *Dramatic works*, ed. M. Summers (London 1931), ii. 347.
[61] L. I. Bredvold, *The Intellectual milieu of J. Dryden* (Michigan 1934), p.114.

Voltaire was no doubt stimulated by *The Indian emperor* when he published his tragedy, *Alzire*, in 1736. There are similarities in characterisation, in themes and incidents in both plays which are set in South America.[62] In *The Indian emperor*, there is a description of the torture of emperor Montezuma in act v, scene ii. Following French notions of *bienséance*, Voltaire does not actually show torture on stage, but simply mentions it in *Alzire* in act iv, scene iv, for instance. Some of the deistic theses that *Alzire* and *The Indian emperor* are made to prove are that a man's religion is insignificant and that all who worship God, whatever the manner, can understand one another. In both plays, the sham zeal of the Christian conquerors, who conceal their desire for gold behind lofty ideals of conversion, is denounced. The odds are generally weighted against the Christians who appear less noble then the native Americans, although Christian virtues are symbolized by Alvarez in *Alzire* and by Cortez in *The Indian emperor*.

Dryden's Indian hero is specifically mentioned by Voltaire in the article 'Espace' in the *Questions sur l'encyclopédie* in 1771. Voltaire uses him to refute Leibniz's contention that 'il n'y a point d'espace, point de vide'. He says that the Montezuma of Dryden's tragedy was sounder in his judgment, for Montezuma had asked: 'Que venez-vous me dire au nom de l'empereur Charles-Quint? il n'y a que deux empereurs dans le monde, celui du Pérou et moi' (M.xix. 1-2). Voltaire suggests that Montezuma was talking about things which he knew whereas we talk about two things – matter and spirit – of which we have no clear idea.

The testimony of the abbé Yart, an eighteenth-century specialist in English literature, is relevant here. In the *Idée de la poésie anglaise* (1753), with the English in mind, he asks whether it is not known that Voltaire confessed to having learnt 'à penser & à écrire vigoureusement dans l'étude de leurs livres, & à s'ouvrir, à leur exemple, un nouveau théâtre, en transportant comme Dryden la scène dans le nouveau monde' (iii. xxii).[63] It is to be remembered that Yart was an admirer of Voltaire. He bestowed lavish praise on Voltaire in his letter addressed to him (Best.D21097, 9 March 1778) and in his letter of the same date

[62] cf. Maillet's remark on the question of setting: 'C'est . . . à l'exemple de Dryden qu'est due l'une des réformes les plus heureuses réalisées par Voltaire: l'abandon du monde gréco-romain pour une scène plus vaste', in 'Dryden et Voltaire', p.279.

[63] see also T. W. Russell, *Voltaire, Dryden and heroic tragedy* (New York 1946), pp.96-100.

to the marquis de Villette where he calls Voltaire 'the first man in the world' (Best.D21098). However valuable Yart's assessment may be, it has its limitations, for Yart fails to mention other aspects of Dryden's works which stimulated Voltaire even more vigorously. Dryden's theatre no doubt appealed to Voltaire, but he was equally interested in Dryden's critical essays and in his satires. He drew much inspiration from these.

In his attempts to spread knowledge of the English drama among the French, Voltaire was not a lonely figure. At about the same time, Prévost gave his impressions on this topic in the *Mémoires d'un homme de qualité* (1731). Volume v of the *Mémoires* is taken up with an account of his journey to England by the marquis de Renoncour. The latter was so impressed by the performance of the actress mrs Oldfield that he began to appreciate the English theatre which he at first did not like. By choosing him as his spokesman, Prévost was able to place Otway's *The Orphan* and *Venice preserv'd* alongside *Hamlet* and Dryden's *Don Sebastian*. He thought that for the beauty of their sentiments, for that tragic form which stirs the depths of the heart and infallibly excites passions in the most torpid soul, he had seen nothing in Greek or in French to surpass the English stage. The plays quoted were rather disfigured by a mixture of buffooneries unworthy of the buskin, but that was a defect recognised by the English themselves.[64] Such views on English tragedy bring Voltaire fairly close to Prévost. However, it was Voltaire who made the greater impact on the French public.

Voltaire was not indifferent to Thomas Otway, one of the relatively successful Restoration dramatists, who was only thirty-three when he died in 1685. In the *Discours sur la tragédie*, he draws a parallel between La Fosse's *Manlius Capitolinus* (1698) and Otway's *Venice preserv'd* (1682). He claims that La Fosse (*c.* 1653-1708) took his subject from Otway who in turn based his play on the history of the conspiracy of Bedamar by the abbé de Saint-Réal.[65] In his view Saint-Réal is of the same standard as Sallust and his work is much superior to the plays of Otway and La Fosse. La Fosse was compelled by prejudice to conceal a well-known story behind Roman names, whereas Otway treated the subject in a natural manner, using real names. It did not appear

---

[64] *Mémoires et avantures d'un homme de qualité*, ed. Mysie E. Robertson (Paris 1927), v. 67-68.
[65] this was the *Conjuration des Espagnols contre la république de Venise* (1674).

ridiculous to an English dramatist that a Spanish ambassador should be called Bedamar and that conspirators should have names such as Jaffeir and Pierre. That alone could cause the failure of a play in France.

In his analysis of the English and French versions of the subject of the conspiracy, Voltaire points out that Otway is not afraid of grouping together all the conspirators. He emphasizes the importance of Renaud who assigns a role to every conspirator. He is particularly impressed by Renaud's speech to the conspirators, which he thinks is full of pathos, although he claims that it has been translated word for word from the abbé de Saint-Réal. In fact, it is Voltaire who has translated accurately the speech from act III, scene ii of *Venice preserv'd*:

> Never did so profound repose forerun
> Calamity so great: nay, our good fortune
> Has blinded the most piercing of mankind;
> Strengthened the fearful'st, charm'd the most suspectful,
> Confounded the most subtle; for we live,
> We live, my friends, and quickly shall our life
> Prove fatal to these tyrants:

as (M.ii.316):

Jamais repos si profond ne précéda un trouble si grand. Notre bonne destinée a aveuglé les plus clairvoyants de tous les hommes, rassuré les plus timides, endormi les plus soupçonneux, confondu les plus subtils: nous vivons encore, mes chers amis; nous vivons, et notre vie sera bientôt funeste aux tyrans de ces lieux, etc.

Voltaire criticises La Fosse because the latter is afraid of introducing a large number of characters on stage. La Fosse simply makes Renaud, under the name of Rutile, recite a weak section of the same speech which he says he has delivered to the conspirators. In Voltaire's opinion, it is obvious that this scene of *Venice preserv'd* is far superior to the scene in the French version, even if Otway's play is monstrous elsewhere.

It is not without significance that Voltaire's account of *Venice preserv'd* should precede his analysis of *Julius Caesar*. His interest in the former play was probably roused by his thorough knowledge of Shakespeare's tragedy which he imitated in *La Mort de César*. What must have attracted him to *Venice preserv'd*, although he nowhere acknowledges this, were the affinities between the English plays. These were to be found not only in the subject matter but also in the style. In the very scene which he had translated in part are speeches by Renaud and Pierre, which have a distinctly Shakespearian flavour. The quarrel between the two conspirators with its note of reconciliation at the end is very close to that between Brutus and Cassius in *Julius Caesar*. If Voltaire shows little trace of Otway's influence subsequently, it is because he consistently refuses to imitate an imitator. Having chosen to stress the positive qualities of Otway in the *Discours sur la tragédie*, he reserved himself the right to condemn him in a contemporary work.

In the *Lettres philosophiques*, after his attack on the grave diggers' scene in *Hamlet*, Voltaire expresses surprise that such stupidities should have been imitated in the reign of Charles II, which in his eyes stood for the reign of politeness and the golden age of the liberal arts. To illustrate his point, Voltaire refers to act III, scene i of *Venice preserv'd*: this takes place between the senator Antonio and the prostitute Aquilina. He bitterly complains that amidst the horrors of a conspiracy Antonio should have time for 'all the apish Tricks of a lewd, impotent Debauchee who is quite frantic and out of his senses' (p.169). Antonio bellows like a bull and barks like a dog, bites the legs of his mistress who kicks and then whips him. Voltaire perhaps read *Venice preserv'd* in the original and then watched a performance of it at Lincoln's Inn Fields Theatre either in 1727 or early in 1729[66] when this scene was expurgated. For he says that these buffooneries intended for the most vulgar mob were struck off by the players. It is true that La Place translated or adapted Otways' play under the title of *Venise sauvée*, but Voltaire cannot be referring to this version in the 1733 or 1734 edition of the *Lettres philosophiques* as it appeared only in 1747. He did, however, see La Place's adaptation performed on the 19th April 1749 shortly after the revival of *Zaïre* on the 14th April.[67] The role of Belvidera was played by the actress Jeanne Catherine Gaussin.

Three years later Voltaire mentioned *Venice preserv'd* in a letter to sir Everard Fawkener, repeating his point about the connection between the tragedy and Saint-Réal's book (Best.D4851, 27 March 1752). When he wrote to Keate, he stated that the poet James Thomson was rather icy. Otway was warmer, but although he took Shakespeare for his model, he did not come within an inch of him. Voltaire made it

---

[66] see Lanson's notes on the plays performed during Voltaire's visit to England (Lanson, ii. 91-95).

[67] see his letter to d'Argental, Best.D3898 (March/April 1749) and editorial notes.

clear that he could not tolerate a mixture of the tragic and the grotesque, as this seemed monstrous He did not claim that his judgement was sound, rather it was made in accordance with his own taste (Best.D8858, 16 April 1760).

Voltaire explicitly referred to La Place's version in the *Appel à toutes les nations*. The *Appel*, as he told the duc de La Vallière, had been written in favour of Corneille and Racine, and against Shakespeare and Otway (Best.D9754, 25 April 1761). Whereas in the *Lettres philosophiques* he seems to have welcomed the expurgation of the scene between Antonio and Aquilina, in the later work he sarcastically regrets that *Venice preserv'd* had not been faithfully translated, for we have been deprived of a senator's antics If the translator had been exact, we would have had the pleasure of seeing a scaffold, a wheel, a priest who wants to cheer up Pierre on his way to death and who is sent back like a tramp. The final lament is that there are a thousand traits of this nature which La Place has spared our false 'délicatesse' (M.xxiv. 206).

Since his avowed intention in the *Appel à toutes les nations* was to decry English literature, notwithstanding certain concessions made to Shakespeare, Voltaire had first directed his sarcasm at Otway's earlier tragedy, *The Orphan* (1680). He gave a lengthy account of its plot, and proceeding by means of antiphrasis, he remarked that Racine was worth very little when compared with the tender and elegant Otway. If *Hamlet* begins with two sentinels, *The Orphan* begins with two men-servants: for great men had to be imitated in every detail. Voltaire chose incidents in this tragedy of sensibility to prove that it is really not far above the level of Molière's *Amphitryon*. If he had wanted to be fair, he could, for instance, have quoted Monimia's dying speech which is well-known for its pathos. In this connection it has been observed that *The Orphan* is the most Racinian of Otway's tragedies, 'not because he approaches nearer the French in form, but because on certain sides the development of his sensibility seems to correspond with that of Racine'.[68] Voltaire, however, deliberately failed to notice that Monimia suffers the pangs of violent despair arising from the deception practised upon her by her brother-in-law, Polidore.

Voltaire preferred to harp on the doubtful manners of the play in great detail. In the 1764 edition of the *Appel à toutes les nations*,

[68] Bonamy Dobrée, *Restoration tragedy* (Oxford 1929), p.142.

before concluding his remarks on *The Orphan*, he observed that if such a theme, such speeches and such manners shock men of taste in Europe, they should forgive the author. For the latter was not aware that he had done anything monstrous since he had dedicated his play to the duchess of Cleveland with the same naïveté that he had written his tragedy (M.xxiv.208, n.1). Voltaire had no alternative but to suggest that Monime of Racine's *Mithridate* was superior to the heroine of Otway.

Perhaps Voltaire did not know that Otway had deliberately imitated Racine's *Bérénice* in his *Titus and Bérénice* (1676). Otherwise, he might have found material for a more justifiable comparison and he might have been less harsh in his reactions. Moreover, Otway had such a short career that Voltaire did not have much opportunity of commenting on him after the *Appel*.

iv. *Addison, Fenton and Voltaire*

Addison's tragedy of *Cato* won great success in England in the eighteenth century. A number of commentaries appeared in the year of its publication (1713). For instance, the author of *Cato examin'd*, John Pemberton or Charles Gildon, thought that the rules had been observed by Addison and concluded that there was much justice in the applause (pp.3-21). In his *Observations upon Cato*, G. Sewell felt that Cato's character and sentiments conformed not only to the true spirit of poetry, but to the best rules of criticism (p.3). John Dennis, however, condemned it severely in his *Remarks upon Cato*. He noted that the action which was not allegorical or universal carried no moral instruction with it 'for the Moral which is foisted in at the latter end of this Play, is wholly Foreign to it' (p.9). Cato himself is a stoic and therefore a very improper hero for tragedy (p.16). Judging the play by the rules of Aristotle and Boileau, Dennis says that he does not know one tragedy that has a hero so famous for wisdom or a conduct so 'notoriously indiscreet' (p.56).

These adverse comments did not prevent Abel Boyer from translating *Cato* in French prose and having it published by Jacob Tonson in London in 1713. François Deschamps also wrote *Caton d'Utique* which was performed and published in Paris in 1715.[69] The abbé Du

---

[69] see Russell, *Voltaire, Dryden and heroic tragedy*, p.64.

Bos translated various scenes of Addison's play in the *Nouvelles littéraires de la Haye* (1716), iv. 337-51. Later in the century Henri Panckoucke, a cousin of the publisher, wrote *La Mort de Caton* in imitation of Addison's *Cato*.

Voltaire first showed interest in Addison at the time of the *Essay on epick poetry*. In the 1727 *Essay* Addison was awarded the distinction of being the first 'who considered in their proper view the Materials which compos'd the Structure of the *Aeneid*' (White, p.93). In the section on Milton, Voltaire paid homage to Addison, 'the best Critick as well as the best Writer of his Age, [who] pointed out the most hidden Beauties of the *Paradise Lost*, and settled forever its Reputation' (p.134).

In the 'Discours préliminaire' to the *Poème de Fontenoy* (1745), written to celebrate the French victory at Fontenoy, Voltaire gave a balanced commentary on Addison's poem, *The Campaign* (1705).[70] His attitude deserves a special mention since Addison too had celebrated a famous victory – that of Blenheim. The fact that they were competitors in the same field did not prevent Voltaire from being fair to the man who had provided him with a model. He nevertheless rejects the view that Addison could have spoken more honourably of the king's household than the author of the *Poème* and claims that to one's great surprise one finds more insults than praise in Addison's work. However, far from refusing a very enlightened philosopher the praise that he deserves, Voltaire suggests that Addison would deserve more praise if he had spared crowned monarchs in his poem and if he had realised that eulogizing the vanquished simply adds to the laurel of the victors. He has no hesitation in describing Addison as a good poet and a judicious critic[71] who used in his poem less fable than he himself had done in the *Poème de Fontenoy*. Moreover, Addison's work was free from cold allegory which weakens the exploits of modern heroes: Addison did better, he stimulated the interest of all Europe in the action of his poem.

[70] in the *Siècle de Louis XIV* Voltaire describes *The Campaign* as being more permanent than Blenheim Palace: it is considered by the warlike and learned English nation to be one of the most honourable rewards of Marlborough (M.xiv. 367).

[71] under the heading 'Des beaux-arts en Europe du temps de Louis xiv' in the *Siècle de Louis XIV*, Voltaire wrote that Addison had not only won for himself everlasting fame by his *Cato*, but his other moral and critical essays 'respirent le goût: or y voit partout le bon sens paré des fleurs de l'imagination; sa manière d'écrire est un excellent modèle en tout pays' (M.xiv. 560).

Voltaire was already interested in Lucan's treatment of the character of Cato in *Pharsalia*. He particularly liked in book ix the speech of Cato who refuses to consult the oracle of Jupiter Ammon. He reproduced lines from Brébeuf's translation in the *Essai sur la poésie épique* (M.viii.328) and found in their deist message some support for didactic passages in *La Henriade* (see Taylor, pp.138-39). Since Voltaire was fascinated by the theme of *Pharsalia*, he was naturally drawn towards an author who had tackled the same theme, albeit in a different genre. It is therefore primarily as the author of the tragedy of *Cato* that Addison stimulated Voltaire's interest. In the section on Lucan in the *Essay on epick poetry*, Voltaire mentioned Addison's indebtedness to Lucan's *Pharsalia* in his *Cato*. He claimed that Lucan never received a greater honour than when he was imitated by Corneille and Addison, two men who were in every way superior to him (White, p.102).

This interest in Addison's drama lasted some fifty years. It is perhaps not so difficult to account for Voltaire's generally favourable attitude towards the Englishman. Voltaire must have appreciated the moral teaching of Addison in *Cato* – a teaching that harmonized with his own theory of tragedy and was forcefully emphasized in the very last lines of act v, scene iv, when Lucius says:

> From hence, let fierce contending nations know
> What dire effects from civil discord flow.
> 'Tis this that shakes our country with alarms,
> And gives up *Rome* a prey to *Roman* arms,
> Produces fraud, and cruelty, and strife,
> And robs the Guilty world of *Cato*'s life.

Pope had added his support for the didactic aim of tragedy in his *Prologue* to the play. Although he took the opportunity of appealing to Britons not to rely too heavily on French translations when writing tragedies, the prestige he enjoyed in the eyes of Voltaire must have been a contributory factor in the latter's positive reactions to *Cato*.

Addison seemed to Voltaire to represent an almost perfect amalgam of the best in the French and English traditions. It can be established that Voltaire shared the same critical outlook on *Cato* as John Breval, who said in 1717 in his *Epistle to Addison* (p.6):

> Here Bossu's Rules are mixt with Shakespeare's Fire,
> And critics rage, because they must admire.

He would certainly have agreed with the first line. What Voltaire writes in the 1730s explains further his admiration for Addison. In his preface to *Œdipe*, he shows that unlike La Motte, Addison has observed the unities, 'those fundamental rules of the theatre'. More important for an understanding of Voltaire's reactions is the *Discours sur la tragédie*. Voltaire says that in his play Addison was not afraid of making Cato bring the dead body of his son Marcus before the audience and of addressing it. Because of the way the French stage is made and the fact that it is full of seats for spectators who render any action impracticable, the French are incapable of introducing a dead body on stage. If they dared do this the groundlings would protest and the women would turn away their heads (M.ii.315). He asks why in plays heroes and heroines are allowed to commit suicide, but are prevented from killing anyone.[72] Would the stage appear less blood-stained by the death of Atalide, because she kills herself for her lover, than by Caesar's murder? If the sight of his dead son gives rise to an admirable speech from Cato, if that piece has been applauded in England and in Italy by those who are the greatest supporters of French *bienséance*, why would the French not get used to it? (M.ii.319).

Further in the *Discours* Voltaire emphasizes the differences between the English and the French stage: the English give more importance to action[73] than the French and they appeal to the eyes. The French set greater store by the elegance, the harmony and the charm of the verse.[74] Voltaire's aim here in showing the contrast is to reduce the merit of action, to belittle Shakespeare, Dryden and other tragic writers and to establish Addison's superiority over them. He has no hesitation in ruling that it is more difficult to write well than to show on stage murders, torture, racks, gallows, witches and ghosts (M.ii. 322). The appeal of Addison's *Cato*, the only tragedy in English well written from start to finish, clearly lies in its style, in its beautiful

[72] Voltaire insists on this point in the 'Cambridge notebook'. He asks why a person can be taken away dead from the stage and yet cannot be brought in dead. To support his contention, he quotes the example of Euripides's Hippolitus who appears wounded, while in Addison's *Cato*, Cato's son is brought in already murdered (*Notebooks*, i. 107).

[73] in the 'Cambridge notebook', Voltaire had written: 'You have the terror of the action peculiar to the Athenian theater, we have its elegance' (*Notebooks*, i. 106).

[74] here too Addison impresses Voltaire. He has this to say when writing about Greek tragedies in the *Dissertation sur la tragédie ancienne et moderne*: they are full of 'cette poésie d'expression et de cette élégance continue qui embellissent le naturel sans jamais le charger; talent que, depuis les Grecs, le seul Racine a possédé parmi nous, et le seul Addison chez les Anglais' (M.iv. 490).

poetry and in the bold and true sentiments expressed in harmonious verse.

Voltaire qualifies his praise of Addison in the first dedicatory epistle to Fawkener. Addison, the poet of the wise, had tried to improve on English plays by making his tragedy more credible and its imagery more elevated. But his manner was too studied and in his *Cato*, which has been praised so much, the daughters are certainly dull characters.[75] One should imitate only what is good in the great Addison (M.ii.539).

In the second dedicatory epistle to Fawkener, Voltaire points out how even the wisest of English writers became enslaved to custom.[76] He does not consider it reasonable that Addison should stick to the custom of ending every act with verses which are quite different in tone from the rest of the play. These verses included the inevitable metaphor. His remark on the obligatory use of comparison is particularly true of the first three acts, although the example he quotes of Cato comparing himself to a rock is not strictly accurate. What happens is that in the middle of act II, scene vi, Sempronius likens Cato to mount Atlas. (M.ii.549-50). Voltaire's point in this epistle is that metaphors are contrary to the laws of nature. This is perhaps why he liked *Zara*: the English author, as he put it to Thieriot, had been able to write *'without bombast! without similes at the end of acts!'* (Best.D1035, 16 March 1736).

The *Letters concerning the English nation* attempt a fair assessment of Addison: 'the first *English* Writer who compos'd a regular Tragedy and infus'd a Spirit of Elegance thro' every Part of it' (p.178). They echo the sentiment expressed in the *Discours sur la tragédie* about the excellence of the diction and the beauty of the verse in *Cato*. What is new is Voltaire's analysis of the characters: in his opinion Cato is far superior to Cornélie in Corneille's *La Mort de Pompée*, because Cato is great without being inflated whereas Cornélie, who is superfluous to the plot, tends to be bombastic at times.[77] Addison's Cato seems to be

---

[75] in his letter to Henri Panckoucke Voltaire again showed his dislike of these characters when he wrote: 'La partie carrée des deux filles de Caton, dans Addison, fait voir que les Anglais ont souvent pris nos ridicules' (Best.D14657, 8 January 1768). Voltaire is mistaken when he speaks of Cato's daughters: in fact, Cato has only one daughter, Marcia; Lucia is the daughter of the senator Lucius.

[76] in the same year, Addison was described by Voltaire in a letter to d'Olivet as one of the varied geniuses such as Pope, Leibniz and Fontenelle (Best.D946, 6 January 1736).

[77] yet Voltaire claimed in a letter to Hervey that the great French writers of the reign

the finest character on any stage. Blemishes exist, however, in the play. The other characters do not match. Such a well-written play is disfigured by a dull love plot casting over it a languor that quite kills it.

Voltaire could excuse any weakness in a play, except cold sentiments. Did he not criticise Corneille on this count (Best.D11727)? Addison seems to Voltaire to have spoiled a masterpiece while pandering to contemporary taste which insisted on a love story. Nevertheless a very interesting letter he wrote to sir George Lyttelton some years later makes it clear that Voltaire thought Addison had come within reach of perfection (Best.D4145, 17 May 1750):

Yr nation . . . is us'd to a wild scene, to a croud of tumultuous events, to an emphatical poetry mix'd with low and comical expressions, to murthers, to a lively representation of bloody deeds . . . all faults which never sullyd the greak, the roman or the french stage . . . T'is true we have too much of words, if you have too much of action, and perhaps the perfection of the Art should consist in a due mixture of the french taste and english energy. Mr Adisson, who would have reach'd to that pitch of perfection had he succeeded in the amourous part of his tragedy as well as in the part of Cato, warn'd often yr nation against the corrupted taste of the stage & since he could not reform the genius of the country, j am affraid the contagious distemper is past curing.

The 1751 edition of the *Lettres philosophiques* contains a longer section on Addison. The elegance which had been noted before now becomes an 'elegance male et énergique' of which Corneille was the first to give some fine examples in his unequal style. Voltaire believes that *Cato* is intended for an audience 'un peu philosophe et tres Républicain' (Lanson, ii.86n). He doubts whether French ladies and the 'Petits Maîtres' could like Cato in his dressing gown, reading Plato's *Dialogues* and reflecting on the immortality of the soul. But those who discard the customs, prejudices and weaknesses of their country, those who prefer philosophic elevation to professions of love would find a copy, albeit imperfect, of this sublime piece here. In Cato's fine monologue in act v, scene i, Addison seems to vie with Shakespeare. Voltaire says that he will translate Addison freely. Without that liberty one would be too far away from the original in one's desire to be close to it. He claims his translation is accurate in substance: if he

of Louis xiv had been the models of English writers. Addison, who had more taste than any other Englishman, was often indebted to them for his excellent critical opinion. Voltaire's conclusion was that *Cato*'s author owed his 'conduite & sa sagesse aux Corneilles, & aux Racines' (Best.D2216, *c.* 1 June 1740).

has added a few details, it is because he could not equal Addison
(Lanson, ii. 86-87):

> Oui Platon, tu dis vrai, notre ame est immortelle,
> C'est un Dieu qui lui parle, un Dieu qui vit en elle,
> Eh! d'où viendroit sans lui ce grand pressentiment,
> Ce dégoût des faux-biens, cette horreur du neant?
> Vers des siècles sans fin je sens que tu m'entraînes.
> Du monde et de mes sens je vais briser les chaînes,
> Et m'ouvrir loin d'un corps dans la fange arrêté,
> Les portes de la vie et de l'éternité.
> L'éternité! quel mot consolant et terrible!
> O lumière! ô nuage! ô profondeur horrible!
> Que suis-je? où suis-je? où vais-je et d'où suis-je tiré?
> Dans quel climat nouveau, dans quel monde ignoré,
> Le moment du trepas va-t-il plonger mon être?
> Ou sera cet esprit qui ne peut se connaître?
> Que me préparez-vous, abîmes tenebreux?
> Allons, s'il est un dieu, Caton doit être heureux.
> Il en est un sans doute et je suis son ouvrage.
> Lui meme au coeur du juste il empreint son image.
> Il doit vanger sa cause et punir les pervers.
> Mais comment? dans quel tems et dans quel Univers?
> Ici la vertu pleure et l'audace l'opprime;
> L'innocence à genoux y tend la gorge au crime:
> La fortune y domine et tout y suit son char.
> Ce globe infortuné fut formé pour César:
> Hatons-nous de sortir d'une prison funeste;
> Je te verrai sans ombre, o verité céleste!
> Tu te caches de nous dans nos jours de sommeil,
> Cette vie est un songe et la mort un réveil.

This translation was probably prompted by La Place's own version
which appeared in 1749 in volume viii of the *Théâtre anglais* and which
was closer to the English original. The English text reads:

> CATO
>
> It must be so – *Plato*, thou reason'st well! –
> Else whence this pleasing hope, this fond desire,
> This longing after immortality?
> Or whence this secret dread, and inward horror,
> Of falling into nought? why shrinks the soul
> Back on her self, and startles at destruction?

'Tis the divinity that stirs within us;
'Tis heaven it self, that points out an Hereafter,
And intimates eternity to man.
Eternity! thou pleasing, dreadful, thought!
Through what variety of untry'd being,
Through what new scenes and changes must we pass!
The wide, th'unbounded prospect, lyes before me;
But shadows, clouds, and darkness, rest upon it.
Here will I hold. If there's a pow'r above us,
(And that there is all nature cries aloud
Through all her works) he must delight in virtue;
And that which he delights in, must be happy.
But when! or where! – This world was made for *Caesar*.
I'm weary of conjectures – This must end 'em.
Thus I am doubly arm'd: my death and life,
My bane and antidote are both before me:
This in a moment brings me to an end;
But this informs me I shall never die.
The soul, secured in her existence, smiles
At the drawn dagger, and defies its point.
The stars shall fade away, the sun himself
Grow dim with age, and nature sink in years,
But thou shalt flourish in immortal youth,
Unhurt amidst the war of elements,
The wrecks of matter, and the crush of worlds.
     What means this heaviness that hangs upon me?
This lethargy that creeps through all my senses?
Nature oppress'd, and harrass'd out with care,
Sinks down to rest. This once I'll favour her,
That my awaken'd soul may take her flight,
Renew'd in all her strength, and fresh with life,
An offring fit for heaven. Let guilt or fear
Disturb man's rest: *Cato* knows neither of 'em,
Indifferent in his choice to sleep or die.

Voltaire was true to his ideal of imitation which he had defined in his letter to Asselin (Best.D937; see above, p.35).

Such was the impact of Cato's monologue on Voltaire that he thought it proper to reproduce it in the article 'Art dramatique' in the *Questions sur l'encyclopédie* in 1770. Its close proximity to his version of Hamlet's 'To be or not to be' soliloquy is a sure indication of its worth in Voltaire's eyes. This did not, of course, prevent Voltaire from criticising in the 1751 edition of the *Lettres philosophiques* other shortcomings he had noted in *Cato*. Despite the beauty of the monologue, *Cato* was not a beautiful tragedy because it had loosely connected scenes, which often left the stage empty, asides that were too long and without art, a conspiracy not necessary to the play, a certain Sempronius who appeared in disguise and was killed on stage. On account of such blemishes, French actors would never dare perform *Cato*[78] even if the French were to think like Romans or the English. The barbarism and irregularity of the English stage have even pierced through the wisdom of Addison.[79]

It may perhaps be pointed out that some of Voltaire's adverse comments on *Cato* in the later edition of the *Lettres philosophiques* are quite judicious. Although the asides found in the play are not, as Voltaire claims, too long, Addison seems to have used them too frequently. When Voltaire complains of a superfluous conspiracy, what he has in mind is the mutiny against the republican forces fomented by the machiavellian senator Sempronius and by Syphax, general of the Numidians. These two are the allies of Cato against Caesar and their mutiny is a secondary element in the plot and as such detracts from the main story. Moreover, Sempronius is utterly ridiculous, for he disguises himself as Juba, prince of Numidia, in an attempt to carry away Marcia, Cato's daughter, whom Juba loves. Voltaire's complaint against a dull love story also appears justified in that the sons of Cato, Portius and Marcus, happen to love the same woman, Lucia, while Portius conceals his love.

Voltaire came back to his criticisms which are explicitly made in the *Remarques sur les trois discours*. In his remarks on the third *Discours* it appears that Voltaire considers Addison's weakness to be due to a multiplicity of actions and plots and even more to the insipid, cold love episodes[80] and masked conspiracy in *Cato*. Otherwise Addison

[78] before Voltaire's début as a playwright, a tragedy vaguely reminiscent of *Cato*, by Deschamps, had in fact been performed in Paris; see above, p.62.

[79] cf. Voltaire's letter to Horace Walpole in which he says that Shakespeare lacked the elegance and 'pureté' which made Addison respectable. That letter made it clear that it was Shakespeare and not Addison that was devoid of regularity, decorum and art (Best.D15141, 15 July, 1768).

[80] this is a point Voltaire constantly harps upon. For instance, in his letter to Keate, he says that if Addison had put more warmth in his *Cato*, he would have been his man (Best.D8858, 16 April 1760). To the same correspondent he subsequently suggested that with more warmth and concern, *Cato* would in his view be the first in Europe (Best.D15024, 17 May 1768). In the article 'Goût' of the *Questions sur l'encyclopédie*

might have reformed the English theatre by the eloquence of his 'style noble et sage' (Williams, iii. 1050).

Addison's literary plans are discussed in Voltaire's preface to his *Socrate* (1759) (M.v.361-62), which purports to be a translation of an English play on the death of Socrates (by James Thomson). Addison is supposed to have long debated whether he would opt for Cato or a man who is simply virtuous, unscheming and without passion and who could not possibly have any appeal on stage. He apparently believed that Cato was the virtuous man who was needed, but that Socrates was even superior to him. He looked upon Cato as the victim of liberty and Socrates as the master of wisdom. Voltaire argues that Richard Steele persuaded Addison that Cato was more suitable to the English nation in troubled times. He further claims that *Cato's* success which had rendered Addison bolder, induced him to plan a three-act play on the death of Socrates. But, added Voltaire, as the office of secretary of state which he held soon after deprived him of the time he needed to complete this work, he gave his manuscript to his pupil Thomson.

With regard to Addison's proposed play on Socrates, Voltaire showed that he was well-informed. Such a play was indeed mentioned when Addison retired in 1718. It is known that he undertook some literary work that was never completed and that he left to Tickell the care of his work. There is no evidence, however, to substantiate Voltaire's assertion on the relations between Addison and Thomson: in any case, Thomson (1700-48) would have been too young to have had a literary friendship with Addison who died in 1719.

It was probably in the article 'Art dramatique' of the *Questions sur l'encyclopédie* (1770) that Voltaire gave the best explanation for Addison's impact on him. Addison appeared to him to possess a harmonious blend of taste and genius: he was the only English writer 'qui sut le mieux conduire le génie par le goût'. The clear implication was that Addison was superior to Shakespeare who had only one element in the blend, genius.[81] He combined propriety of style with an

(1771), Voltaire claims that if Addison had known how to treat passions, if the warmth of his soul had matched the dignity of his style, he would have reformed his nation. He explains the success of *Cato* in terms of party propaganda. However, once factions had died down, only some very fine verses and coldness were left of *Cato* and nothing contributed more to consolidate Shakespeare's empire (M.xix. 279).

[81] this point is reinforced in the conversation Voltaire had with Martin Sherlock in 1776. Voltaire is reported to have said: 'Cato is incomparably well written: Addison had much taste, but the abyss between taste and genius is immense. Shakespeare had an

imagination characterized by restraint, combined force with natural ease both in his poetry and in his prose. This friend of the *bienséances* and the rules wanted tragedy to be written with dignity and this is how his *Cato* is written. From the very first act, the lines are worthy of Virgil and the sentiments worthy of Cato. Voltaire presumably appreciates the epic tone of the play. There is no theatre, he adds, in Europe where the scene between Juba and Syphax was not applauded as a masterstroke of skill, of well-developed characters, of fine contrasts and of a pure and noble diction.[82]

However, Voltaire refuses to let *Cato's* weaknesses pass unnoticed. Its great success was due to its beauties of detail and the fact that it was topical in its allusions to contemporary quarrels in England. But once it lost its topicality, the verse appeared only beautiful, the maxims only noble and just. As the play was cold, only its coldness was felt and one went back to the 'irrégularités grossières mais attachantes de Shakespeare' (M.xvii. 405). This was precisely the point made by Johnson in his preface to *The Plays of W. Shakespeare* (1765). Johnson's reply to Voltaire, who wondered why the English put up with Shakespeare's extravagances, was that Addison spoke the language of poets, Shakespeare that of men. He added: '*Cato* affords a splendid exhibition of artificial & fictitious manners, and delivers just and noble sentiments, in diction easy, elevated and harmonious, but its hopes and fears communicate no vibration to the heart' (*Eighteenth-century essays on Shakespeare*, p.125). Voltaire would have found in Johnson a confirmation of his own views.

The article 'Goût' of the *Questions sur l'encyclopédie* provides the final explanation for Voltaire's liking for Addison. He states that of all those Englishmen who wrote in good taste and with wit and imagination, Addison was the most authoritative and his works were very useful. One would have wished that he did not too often sacrifice his own taste to the desire to please his own party and to provide *The Spectator* with a quick circulation.[83] Nevertheless, Addison was often

amazing genius, but no taste' (*Letters from an English traveller* (London 1780), pp.155-56).

[82] Dennis thought otherwise. In his *Remarks upon Cato*, he showed that the reconciliation scene between Syphax and Juba (act II, scene v) was a vulgar parody of that between Antony and Ventidius in Dryden's *All for love*.

[83] Voltaire seems quite well-informed of the situation prevailing in England in the reign of queen Anne. In fact Addison had written *The Campaign* on behalf of the Whigs at the suggestion of Godolphin, while Bolingbroke had approved of John Philips, the author of the rival Tory eulogy called *Blenheim*.

courageous enough to prefer the French stage to the English stage. He pointed out the defects of the latter and when he wrote *Cato*, he took care not to imitate Shakespeare's style (M.xix.279).

It is likely that Voltaire was influenced by Addison's tragedy in three of his plays. For it was natural that he should have been deeply interested in the way in which Addison, under the cloak of high-sounding phrases such as liberty, bravery and patriotism, was making political propaganda. *Cato* was, after all, applauded by all parties. Were not some of his own plays written on behalf of the *philosophes* – admittedly, not a very organized body – or as in the case of *L'Ecossaise*, written to satisfy a private vendetta? *Brutus* develops the tradition inaugurated in *Œdipe* where fundamental questions concerning kingship were discussed. Instead of isolated maxims, Voltaire here has recourse to sustained reasoning to compare the merits of the demo-cratic system represented by Brutus and the monarchy represented by Arons.[84] As in *Cato* Addison used Lucius to give a warning against the dangers of civil war, so in *Brutus* Voltaire broadcast the following message against revolution through Arons in act I, scene ii (M.ii. 330-31):

> Quel homme est sans erreur? et quel roi sans faiblesse?
> Est-ce à vous de prétendre au droit de le punir?
> Vous, nés tous ses sujets; vous faits pour obéir!...
> N'allez pas mériter un présent plus sévère,
> Trahir toutes les lois en voulant les venger,
> Et renverser l'Etat au lieu de le changer...
> Vous pouvez raffermir, par un accord heureux,
> Des peuples et des rois les légitimes nœuds,
> Et faire encor fleurir la liberté publique
> Sous l'ombrage sacré du pouvoir monarchique.

Faguet claimed that *Cato* served as a model for Voltaire's tragedies and that after his return from England he gave tragedy a dogmatic turn and an apostolic air, which originated not in Shakespeare, but in Addison.[85] Indeed, in *La Mort de César*, Voltaire celebrates the virtues of a just, enlightened, liberal monarchy which is hostile to repressive tyranny and revolutionary reaction. The play is full of

[84] see R. S. Ridgway, *La Propagande philosophique dans les tragédies de Voltaire*, Studies on Voltaire (1961), xv, chapter 3.

[85] E. Faguet, 'Jugements particuliers de Voltaire sur plusieurs grands écrivains', *Revue des cours et conférences* (Paris 1900), ix. 100.

references to Cato. Antoine pays tribute to Cato's character in act I, scene i, while in act II, scene iv, Cassius tells Brutus that it is time to imitate Cato, but Brutus replies (M.iii.336):

> Si Caton m'avait cru, plus juste en sa furie,
> Sur César expirant il eût perdu la vie;
> Mais il tourna sur soi ses innocentes mains;
> Sa mort fut inutile au bonheur des humains.
> Faisant tout pour la gloire, il ne fit rien pour Rome;
> Et c'est la seule faute où tomba ce grand homme.

In act III, scene ii (M.iii.346) Cassius reminds Brutus that Caesar is his father only from a biological point of view, for

> Caton forma tes mœurs, Caton seul est ton père;
> Tu lui dois ta vertu, ton âme est toute à lui.

Rome sauvée ou Catilina (1749) provided Voltaire with another opportunity of developing his interest in the character of Cato. Perhaps Addison's *Cato* had something to offer him. In the preface to his play, Voltaire commented on English daring in making a tragedy out of Catiline's conspiracy whereas the French thought that Cicero should not be represented on stage (M.v.209). Cicero is no doubt the hero of *Rome sauvée*, but Cato often appears in the play; his utterances and behaviour do justice to the lofty patriotism that emerged from Addison's tragedy.

This does not, however, mean that Addison's influence excludes any other influence on Voltaire. In *Rome sauvée* the impact of Ben Jonson's *Catiline* appears more important than *Cato*'s. In his preface, Voltaire specifically refers to Ben Jonson's attempt to turn Cicero's 'In Catilinam' speeches into a tragedy. He criticizes Ben Jonson for having made Cicero speak in prose: he points out that Cicero's prose and the verse used by the other characters offer a contrast worthy of the barbarian age of Ben Jonson. What he says of Cicero in Jonson's *Catiline* is not accurate, since Cicero often speaks in blank verse and sometimes in rhymed couplets. Despite his objections Voltaire seems to have used the English play. To make his own play more like a French classical tragedy, he reduced the considerable number of characters found in *Catiline*, from thirty-three to a mere ten in *Rome sauvée*. He gave a hint about what he had done to *Catiline* when he commented in the preface: 'D'ailleurs les représentations de *Catilina* exigent un trop grand nombre d'acteurs' (M.v.209). He claimed that he had suppressed the ambassadors of the Allobroges (who appear in Jonson's *Catiline*) because they did not deserve to appear on stage with Cicero, Caesar and Cato (M.v.210). In making Cicero the hero of *Rome sauvée*, Voltaire was probably following the lead of Ben Jonson. Both the Cicero and the Cato of *Rome sauvée* could have been inspired by the Cicero and the Cato of *Catiline*.

It would therefore be an exaggeration to insist, as Russell[86] does on the basis of remarks made by Villemain, Faguet and Lanson, that Shakespeare had nothing to offer Voltaire in *Brutus* and *La Mort de César*. It would not be difficult to show other examples of Voltaire's indebtedness to Shakespeare in *La Mort de César*. Brutus's soliloquy in act II, scene ii, for instance, is closely modelled on act II, scene i of *Julius Caesar*. On the other hand the speech in *Brutus* (act I, scene ii), when Brutus says in reply to Aron's proposal (M.ii.331),

> Arons, il n'est plus temps: chaque Etat a ses lois,
> Qu'il tient de sa nature ...

is faithfully imitated from Corneille's *Cinna* (act II, scene i). Voltaire's indebtedness to Corneille and Shakespeare is not perhaps so surprising since both of his predecessors showed a keen interest in political matters in their tragedies. Did not Voltaire himself suggest at the end of his translation of *Julius Caesar* in 1764 that it would be profitable to compare the conspiracy between Cinna and Emilie against Augustus with that between Brutus and Cassius against Caesar?

Even a minor figure like Elijah Fenton (1683-1730) succeeded in evoking a response from Voltaire. Fenton became better known in France for his 'Life of Milton' which prefaced his edition of *Paradise lost* (1725). The 'Life of Milton' reached a wider public on account of its incorporation in French in Dupré de St Maur's translation of *Paradise lost* in 1729. At the time of writing the biography Fenton had also collaborated with his friend Pope as a translator of the *Odyssey* (1725-26). Some two years before, he had his tragedy of *Mariamne* performed in London on the 22nd February 1723.[87] The play was published the same year.

---

[86] *Voltaire, Dryden and heroic tragedy*, pp.5, 89.

[87] see H. Fenger, 'Voltaire et le théâtre anglais', *Orbis litterarum* (Copenhagen 1949), vii. 171.

Voltaire was working on his own tragedy of *Mariamne* in March 1723. It is mentioned for the first time in a letter he wrote to the marquise de Bernières (Best.D148, 29 March 1723). He told Cideville that he had almost completed the first draft of his play and that however good the English version by Fenton was he could very well do without it (Best.D149, ? April 1723).

It is possible that under the influence of Fenton Voltaire made Mariamne drink a cup of poison on stage in the first version of his play.[88] For despite his affected indifference to Fenton in his letter to Cideville, he had concluded the letter with the request that Cideville should come to La Rivière-Bourdet with a copy of the English *Mariamne*. It appears that Fenton's influence produced negative results, for the death of Mariamne poisoned on stage was revolting to the spectators and the play failed miserably when it was performed in Paris for the first time on the 6th March, 1724. Voltaire nevertheless acknowledges that it was against his taste that he had had to describe Mariamne's death in the revised version of his play (M.ii.164). He would have liked to show it on stage. One can safely say that Voltaire's preference was influenced by English taste.

It is clear from the correspondence that Voltaire spent considerable time both before and after the first performance revising the text of *Mariamne*. In his letter to d'Argental, for instance, he said he wanted the text to be good before the performance. He was not going to hurry over the revision, as (La Motte's) *Inès de Castro* had shown that nothing good can be done in a short time: he was therefore working day and night on it, writing a few lines and rubbing out many (Best. D184, ? January 1724). To the marquise de Bernières he spoke of a new *Mariamne*: he was convinced that it had killed him! (Best.D208, c. 20 September 1724).

There are differences between Voltaire's and Fenton's versions of the death of Mariamne which is fully described in F. Josephus's *Jewish antiquities* and which formed the subject of *Mariamne*, a tragedy by Alexandre Hardy published in 1610. Voltaire had at first invented the character of Varus, a Roman praetor. But in 1762 he substituted it for Soheme. In Fenton's version there is a character called Flaminius, a Roman general, who loves Arsinoe, the chief attendant on the queen. There is no trace of this Flaminius in Voltaire.

[88] see K. H. Hartley, 'The sources of Voltaire's *Mariamne*', *AUMLA* (1964), xxi. 5-14.

However, there are certain similarities between Voltaire and Fenton. Sensibility is an important element in both plays: Fenton's play is full of reminiscences of *Hamlet*, *King Lear* and *Othello*. In act IV, Sohemus, the first minister who plots with Salome to poison Herod and cast the blame on Mariamne, says:

> But if these tears flow from the nobler source
> Of indignation, and the generous shame
> Of injur'd merit.

These lines are also reminiscent of *Paradise lost* where in book I Satan refers to his 'high disdain from sense of injured merit' (l.98). It would have been natural for Milton's biographer to echo such lines.

Hartley has suggested (p.12) that Voltaire obtained from Fenton the idea of making the tyrant Herod alternate with the lover. There is a harmonious blending of the two in act III, scene iv when Hérode says (M.ii.196):

> Mariamne a changé le cœur de son époux.
> Mes mains, loin de mon trône écartant les alarmes,
> Des peuples opprimés vont essuyer les larmes.
> Je veux sur mes sujets régner en citoyen,
> Et gagner tous les cœurs, pour mériter le sien.

Hartley went so far as to conclude that Fenton's attempt to propose this most unlikely candidate of all for the title of the Man of Feeling contributed to the dramatic effectiveness of Voltaire's tragedy.

Fenton's influence on Voltaire should not be pushed too far. It should be pointed out that at this stage of his career, Voltaire's knowledge of English could not have been extensive. Even if what he says to the abbé Duvernet later in life, that Thieriot brought him English books to read while he was in the Bastille for the second time (Best. D17553, 13 January 1772) is true, this familiarity with English could not have taken place long before 1723. On the other hand, some influence on Voltaire by the abbé Nadal whose *Mariamne* was performed on the 15th February 1725 is not to be dismissed. For example, Nadal had in the preface to his play criticised the rhyme in the following lines:

> Souviens toi qu'il fut prêt d'exterminer enfin
> Les restes odieux du sang asmonéen.

These lines subsequently disappeared from Voltaire's *Mariamne*. Voltaire made it a point to attend the performance of his rival's play (M.ii.159). Nadal attacked Voltaire in a preface to his play which was published in 1725. The preface was suppressed afterwards, but Voltaire wrote to Nadal using Thieriot's name (Best.D226, 20 March 1725). When Voltaire's *Hérode et Mariamne*, as the revised play came to be called, was performed on the 10th April, 1725, it was a complete success. People were struck *inter alia* 'et du portrait ressemblant des femmes et des fureurs touchantes d'Hérode', as Cideville reported to Voltaire (Best.D229, 13 April 1725).

What emerges from a study of Voltaire's reactions to English tragic dramatists is that when he was solely preoccupied with aesthetic considerations, Voltaire looked for the highest standard in tragedy. The ideal tragedy should be distinguished by that rare combination of French taste and English energy. It would not have occurred to Voltaire that he was pursuing a chimerical objective, but he was certainly not the only writer to be thinking along these lines. In England too, Colley Cibber in his prologue to *Zara* could not understand why

> nature never should inspire
> A Racine's judgement with a Shakespeare's fire!

It is the same lofty ideal, though indirectly formulated. Cibber followed it with the fantastic claim that Aaron Hill, who was only a second-rate writer after all, had given his public a taste of both Racine and Shakespeare.

In finding his perfect tragic poet, Voltaire came nearer than Cibber. Shakespeare never stood any chance of fulfilling that role since for all his energy, fire and genius, he had right from the start left Voltaire with the impression that he lacked taste. Moreover, Voltaire was no Chateaubriand to confess that he had looked at Shakespeare through classical perspectives and that tragedy written according to the rules was cold. Whereas with Chateaubriand the years seemed to widen the perspective, with Voltaire they tended in the opposite direction as far as drama was concerned. For reasons both literary and non-literary, the rules assumed an ever increasing importance as time went by. Dryden might have proved to be the dramatist after Voltaire's own heart: he knew the rules (even if he did not apply them), was endowed with the tragic fire and the right philosophical outlook. Yet he often lacked taste.

Otway and Fenton did not escape Voltaire's attention, but they were not important enough to capture his imagination permanently. It seems that in his search Voltaire left no stone unturned. In his eyes even James Thomson was worth considering as a candidate for the prize. In his letter to Saurin, the author of the play *Blanche et Guiscard* (1763) which was adapted from Thomson's *Tancred and Sigismunda*, Voltaire claimed that if there were more concern in Thomson's other plays and if he had been less rhetorical, Thomson would have reformed the English stage (Best.D11727, 28 February 1764). He made another interesting assessment of Thomson's tragedies in a previous letter to George Lyttelton. The latter had edited the *Works* of Thomson and sent them to Voltaire who gratefully acknowledged receipt. Voltaire said he was not surprised that England had done more justice to Thomson's poem, *The Seasons*, than to his dramatic performances. Although Thomson's tragedies seemed 'wisely intricated, and elegantly writ', yet they 'want perhaps some fire; and it may be that his heroes are neither moving nor busy enough' (Best.D4145, 17 May 1750). In both letters Voltaire claimed acquaintance with Thomson.

Voltaire might have been more generous towards Thomson as a playwright considering that the latter had sought inspiration in *Zaïre* for his tragedy of *Edward and Eleonora* (1738). But Lyttelton spoiled matters in connection with *Socrate* by publicly denying what Voltaire took pains to proclaim in the preface under the pseudonym of Fatema. The story was that the manuscript of *Socrate* had been sent by Thomson to Dodington and Lyttelton, then by Lyttelton to Fatema, the so-called translator. (M.v.362; see also André Michel Rousseau, *L'Angleterre et Voltaire*, i. 159-60).

After this process of elimination is applied, only Addison is left. The attention devoted to Addison by Voltaire might well appear out of proportion to his real importance in English literature. Voltaire was, however, acting in accordance with criteria chosen by himself. On the basis of one tragedy, he granted the prize to Addison who in his view had nearly reached perfection. On one occasion, he even claimed that Addison had combined genius with taste. Little did he realise that by making such a claim he was helping to destroy the myth of a dichotomy that was supposed to exist in English literature.

2

English comedy and Voltaire

i. *Voltaire on comedy*

RIGHT at the outset of his career Voltaire laments the decline of French comedy and seeks consolation in a good recital of excerpts from *Le Misanthrope*. He complains in a letter to mme de Mimeure that the stage has been taken over by very bad plays and by very bad actors; on the other hand, he has praise for mademoiselle de Montbrun because of her performance in comedies that are well-established, such as *Le Misanthrope* (Best.D28, *c.* 25 June 1715). When decades later, the same complaints are made in the correspondence, it cannot therefore be argued that Voltaire's attitude was simply prompted by the difficulties that beset his comedy of *Le Droit du seigneur*.[1] Voltaire asks d'Olivet whether he has noticed that since Regnard not one single comic writer knew how to make a valet speak as he should. He wonders how a nation which believes it is gay can have spread so much gloom over comedy (Best.D10287, 26 January 1762). When he writes to his friend Damilaville, complaining how *Le Droit du seigneur* has been 'castrated and mutilated', there is almost the suggestion that the French have gone out of their way to ban what is comic in comedy. To Voltaire this was an unmistakable sign of decadence: only a ridiculous age might frown upon laughter (Best.D10305, 4 February 1762).

Why does Voltaire come to such a depressing conclusion about the state of French comedy? It seems that in comedy as in the other genres, he looks back with nostalgic regret on the achievements and standards of taste of the previous century. Molière is described by Voltaire in his letter to *Le Nouvelliste du Parnasse* (Best.D415, 20 June 1731) as being

---

[1] Voltaire held the poor taste for 'bourgeois tragedies' to which writers without genius had recourse responsible for the exclusion of 'plaisanteries' from *Le Droit du seigneur* (see his letter to Thibouville, Best.D10289, 26 January 1762).

superior to Plautus and Terence, and subsequently in the *Siècle de Louis XIV* as the best comic writer of all nations who rescued comedy from chaos. He is the standard by which any comic writer, any type of comedy is judged. In the *Siècle de Louis XIV*, for instance, Destouches is compared to Molière. Destouches may not have known the human heart and achieved the comic excellence which sets Molière apart, but at least he avoided that type of comedy which is neither tragic nor comic;[2] such comedy is a 'monstre né de l'impuissance des auteurs et de la satiété du public après les beaux jours du siècle de Louis xiv' (M.xiv. 65). In his letter to Sumarokov Voltaire considers it is a blot on the French nation's reputation that the *comédie larmoyante* should have succeeded the only true comic genre which had been raised to the level of perfection by the inimitable Molière. Unfortunately for French comedy, Molière was followed by the creation of 'monsters', save for a brief spell when Regnard, who in Voltaire's view had a truly comic genius, came close to Molière (Best.D14524, 26 February 1769). Since Molière was held in such high esteem,[3] the reflections we have on him are likely to prove useful in a survey of Voltaire's conception of comedy.

Voltaire had not always been so hostile to the new genre of serious comedy and its slight variations known by the names of *comédie larmoyante*, *tragédie bourgeoise* and *drame*. He perhaps first came to recognize its potential in 1725 when he revealed in the preface to *Mariamne* how his play came under attack. The public's grievance was that a husband who was old and not gentle and who was refused conjugal rights could never be the subject of a tragedy (M.ii.167). This led him to reflect that plays such as *Britannicus*, *Phèdre* and *Mithridate* are based on passions which are felt by 'bourgeois' and princes alike and that their plots would suit both comedy and tragedy. If one forgot the titles of Racine's plays one would realise that their subject matter had indeed been treated by Molière: the story of *L'Avare*, for instance, is precisely the same as that of *Mithridate*. Both Molière and Racine were successful: 'l'un a amusé, a réjoui, a fait rire les honnêtes gens; l'autre a attendri, a effrayé, a fait verser des larmes.'

It was in the preface to his comedy *L'Enfant prodigue* (1738) that

---

[2] in the section on comedy in the article 'Art dramatique' of the *Questions sur l'encyclopédie*, Voltaire repeats his objection and accounts for the success of this mixed type of writing by the fact that it was interesting. His major grievance is that the pathetic took the place of the comic (M.xvii. 419).

[3] see W. H. Barber, 'Voltaire and Molière' in *Molière: stage and study*, eds W. D. Howarth and M. Thomas (Oxford 1973), pp.201-17.

Voltaire showed a genuine liking for the mixed genre and at the same time revealed some aspects of his theory of comedy. He claims that his play combines serious with witty parts, comedy with pathos. This variety it shares with life itself, which is full of contrast. By stressing this point, Voltaire is indeed destroying the barriers between the genres. It is not, however, suggested that a comedy must be made up of grotesque and pathetic scenes. There are very good plays where there is nothing but gaiety; some that are very serious, some that are mixed and some where the pathos leads to tears. No genre must be ruled out and the best genre is the one that has been best treated (M.iii.443). The justification for the *comédie larmoyante* is that there is always need for novelty in the theatre. Too much of a good thing spoils it: if Roman 'grandeur' always filled tragedies, one would become tired of it. All genres are good, provided they are not boring (p.445).

Voltaire then proceeds to examine the source of the comic. Very often one cannot explain what creates comedy, one can only feel it. Yet everyone laughs when the technique of mistaken identity is exploited in a play: to illustrate his point, Voltaire gives examples taken from Molière's plays. There are no doubt other techniques of comedy, but none gives rise to so much mirth when one is watching a play or when one is in a social gathering, as these examples of mistaken identity. Another source of comedy is to be found in ridiculous characters. When portrayed on stage, they please the spectator without necessarily causing him to burst into laughter. One is also entertained by the portrayal of social foibles and in this case the entertainment is serious. However, a dishonest man will never produce laughter because it is incompatible with scorn and indignation. One could easily trace the source of other emotions. It is up to dramatists to show us the development of their techniques. But they are more concerned with stirring the passions than with examining them. Passions are better than any definition or treatise.

Definitions of comedy do abound in Voltaire's writings, beginning from the 1730s. In the *Letters concerning the English nation*, true comedy is defined as 'the speaking Picture of the Follies and ridiculous Foibles of a Nation' (p.191). In an epistle dating from the same period, the *Lettre à un premier commis*, comedy is given a high status[4] and is

---

[4] comedy was perhaps most highly regarded during the Punic wars when it became a method of appeasing the gods. It was a very solemn religious act. See the *Appel à toutes les nations* (M.xxiv.213).

closely linked with tragedy.[5] Both genres are considered to be lessons in virtue, reason and decorum. Molière had founded the school of civil life. The moral and educational aims of plays are qualified since they cannot preserve the young from debauchery. Voltaire stressed the humanising influence of comedy in a letter he wrote to Albergati Capacelli years later. What is true comedy? he asks. 'It is', he replies, 'the art of teaching virtue and the *bienséances* by means of action and dialogue.' The eloquence of the monologue is cold by comparison. Destouches's *Le Glorieux* apparently turned a very proud man into a modest character. It is thanks to comedy that financiers are no longer coarse, courtiers no longer vain 'petits maîtres', doctors have given up their consultations in Latin and some pedants have become men[6] (Best.D9492, 23 December 1760).

It must not be imagined that Voltaire was in favour of explicit moral instruction in comedy. In the critical notes on *Le Médecin malgré lui*, accompanying *La Vie de Molière* which was intended to preface the Paris edition of Molière in 1734, but which was actually published in 1739, Voltaire acknowledged that 'on va plus à la comédie pour rire que pour être instruit' (M.xxiii.111). What he meant was that the message should be subtly conveyed in the play. His opposition to open preaching[7] is clearly expressed in the prologue to *L'Echange* (1747) where he engages in a dialogue with madame Du Tour (M.iii. 254):

VOLTAIRE

Aimez-vous mieux la sage et grave comédie
Où l'on instruit toujours, où jamais on ne rit,
Où Sénèque et Montaigne étalent leur esprit,
Où le public enfin bat des mains, et s'ennuie?

MADAME DU TOUR

Non, j'aimerais mieux Arlequin
Qu'un comique de cette espèce:

[5] in the preface to *Nanine* (1749), Voltaire argues that comedy and tragedy overlap only in the treatment of love; otherwise they are two completely different genres (M.v.9-10).

[6] in this respect, comedy appeared even better than a sermon. In *La Guerre civile de Genève* (1768), Voltaire wrote: 'Mieux qu'un sermon l'aimable comédie / Instruit les gens, les rapproche, les lie.' (M.ix.547).

[7] the preface to *L'Ecossaise* (1758) suggests that when moral teaching is combined with entertaining the *honnêtes gens*, then comedy becomes one of the most useful efforts of the human mind. It requires considerable talent to achieve this combination (M.v.411).

Je ne puis souffrir la sagesse,
Quand elle prêche en brodequin.

Madame Du Tour, who is obviously Voltaire himself, thinks that the moral teaching should flow from the action[8] and she defines the main characteristics of ideal comedy in terms that would have met with Boileau's approval. Such comedy should have a combination of subtle ridicule, finely sketched portraits and an easy, gay, lively and graceful style.

On the question of subtle touches to be achieved in comedy, Voltaire's position is most ambivalent. Although he thought so highly of Molière, he appeared in the 1730s to be reproaching him with a failure to show subtlety in plays that were written in the style of the 'bas comique'. In the earliest version of *Le Temple du goût*, Molière is given the role of adviser to Regnard, but in the second edition produced in Amsterdam in 1733, he is made to acknowledge his weakness thus: 'si je n'avois écrit que pour les Connoisseurs, j'aurois moins donné dans le bas Comique' (Carcassonne, p.169).[9] Shortly afterwards Voltaire excuses Molière's weakness on the grounds of economic necessity. In the critical notes on *Les Fourberies de Scapin* appended to *La Vie de Molière*, for example, he established a distinction between 'true' comedy and farce and defended Molière against Boileau's attack in *L'Art poétique* (M.xxiii.122):

On pourrait répondre à ce grand critique que Molière n'a point allié Térence avec Tabarin dans ses vraies comédies, où il surpasse Térence; que s'il a déféré au goût du peuple, c'est dans ses farces, dont le seul titre annonce du bas comique, et que ce bas comique était nécessaire pour soutenir sa troupe.

When he writes to Vauvenargues in 1745, Voltaire appears to have gone to the opposite extreme on the subject. He now says that subtle comedy can appeal only to a small number of 'esprits déliez'. The general public needs more sharply delineated traits. Voltaire continues (Best.D3062, 7 January 1745):

[8] Voltaire recognized that *Tartuffe* was devoted to open preaching. Yet in the *Vie de Molière* he had the highest praise for Cléante's speeches which seemed to him to constitute the most powerful and elegant sermon that existed in French. He even suggested that this very fact provoked the hostility of professional preachers who did less well in the pulpit than Molière in the theatre (M.xxiii.117).

[9] in the notes on *Monsieur de Pourceaugnac*, Voltaire admitted that all Molière's farces contained scenes worthy of the 'haute comédie' (M.xxiii.119).

De plus ces ridicules si delicats ne peuvent guères fournir des personnages de téâtre. Un défaut presque imperceptible n'est guère plaisant. Il faut des ridicules forts, des impertinences dans les quelles il entre de la passion, qui soient propres à L'intrigue. Il faut un joueur, un avare, un jaloux, etc. Je suis d'autant plus frappé de cette vérité que je suis occupé actuellement d'une fête pour le mariage de Mr le dauphin dans la quelle il entre une comédie, et je m'aperçois plus que jamais que ce délié, ce fin, ce délicat qui font le charme de la conversation, ne conviennent guère au téâtre.

It seems that his experience of the stage made Voltaire increasingly aware of practical problems such as those he had to face when writing *La Princesse de Navarre*, which he began in April 1744 and modified many times before it was performed in February 1745.[10] It was responsible for his change in attitude. The practising playwright even recognized his own shortcomings in *L'Indiscret* and wondered whether his comedy was not rather dull. That is why in his letter to d'Argens he quoted the following lines from Antoine Legrand's *L'Impromptu de la folie* (1726) to prove that an elevated style was unsuitable to comedy (Best.D9244, 20 September 1760):

Le comique écrit noblement
Fait bailler ordinairement.

In Voltaire's view the basic requirement in comedy is that it should provoke laughter. From the days of *Zadig* onwards, Voltaire held firmly to this view. When Zadig reached a position of influence in Babylon, he saw to it that the theatres performed comedies where one laughed: by reviving what had long grown out of fashion, he showed that he had good taste. The preface to *Nanine* points out that there is no objection to a comedy being full of passion and pathos provided it makes the *honnêtes gens* laugh. If a comedy lacked comic substance, then it would be a very 'vicious' and unpleasant genre (M.v.10). The correspondence emphasizes this basic need. When he writes to Thieriot, for instance, Voltaire states that the first law of comedy is that it must be comic, for 'sans guaité point de salut' (Best.D8946, 29 May 1760).[11]

---

[10] this *comédie-ballet* provides evidence of Voltaire's continued attempt to draw a distinction between 'pure' or 'true' comedy and other types of comedy. For in his 'avertissement', he describes the play as one of those works where one sees a mixture of opera, comedy and tragedy (M.iv. 274).

[11] cf. his letter to Thibouville: 'Sans comique, point de salut. Une comédie où il n'y a rien de plaisant n'est qu'un sot monstre' (Best.D10289, 26 January 1762); his letter to

Dramatic construction is another major requirement in comedy, as it is in tragedy. Voltaire sets so much store by dramatic structure that it appears to be the dominant feature in his analysis of Molière's plays in the *Vie de Molière*. Nearly all the plays discussed – *L'Etourdi*, *Le Cocu imaginaire*, *L'Ecole des femmes*, *Le Malade imaginaire*, even the masterpiece of 'haute comédie', *Le Misanthrope* – suffer from structural weaknesses, while *Le Dépit amoureux* betrays a lack of verisimilitude. The best denouement of all Molière's comedies is that of *L'Ecole des maris* because it is 'vraisemblable, naturel, tiré du fond de l'intrigue; et, ce qui vaut bien autant, il est extrêmement comique' (M.xxiii.102-103). The plot is 'fine, intéressante et comique'. This criticism is to be read in conjunction with the second edition of *Le Temple du goût* which sums up neatly Voltaire's general comment on the essential weakness of Molière: 'Si j'avois été le maître de mon tems, mes denouemens auroient été plus heureux, mes intrigues plus variées' (Carcassonne, p.169).

Similarly, other qualities to be sought in comedy can be indirectly inferred from Voltaire's own writings. With regard to his comedy of *L'Ecossaise*, Voltaire wondered in a letter to d'Argental why Murray could not see the heroine Lindane in a café and why she should bore the public with a description of the way in which she had met Murray. It is these 'petites misères, qu'on appelle en France bienséances' which cause the action of most French comedies to drag. That is why French comedies cannot be performed in Italy or in England where people expect plenty of action, excitement and movement on stage and frown on useless preliminaries (Best.D9062, 14 July 1760). Here too Voltaire makes no distinction between comedy and tragedy[12]: he attributes to French comedy a weakness that he has often stressed in French tragedy – a lack of action. What is rather remarkable is that Voltaire should consider French comedy to be unworthy of the English stage: although he had referred to French weaknesses in tragedy, he had never thought that French tragedy was in a similar position. It was

the d'Argentals: 'Je veux qu'une comédie soit intéressante, mais je la tiens un monstre si elle ne fait pas rire' (Best.D10373, c. 15 March 1762).

[12] to know in what respects comedy is considered inferior to tragedy, one must refer to Voltaire's comments on *Le Malade imaginaire* in the *Vie de Molière*. If even a masterpiece like *Tartuffe* cannot attract an audience, it is because the depiction of a person's ridiculous ways is not moving; the mind grows tired of witticisms, while the emotions never run dry. The language of comedy can entertain, but it cannot move and one goes to the theatre primarily to be moved (M.xxiii. 126).

only when he declared war on England that Voltaire communicated to Walpole his view that Paris was vastly superior to Athens in the field of comedy and that Molière and even Regnard were better than Aristophanes (Best.D15140, 15 July 1768).

Voltaire did not perhaps find English comic authors particularly useful in the formulation of his theory of comedy. He however admitted that French comedy was full of shortcomings and he could therefore be expected to turn his attention to England for inspiration. On the other hand, the very fact that comedy for all its merits never enjoyed in Voltaire's eyes the same high status as tragedy explains why he apparently devoted less time to it. From Voltaire's point of view, there was no harm done, because he had a better medium in which to exercise his comic talent – the *contes philosophiques* and the *facéties* which in the end brought him greater fame than the comedies he wrote.

ii. *English comic dramatists and Voltaire*

Despite his oft-repeated assertion that he was the first to have introduced English literature into France, it can be shown that Voltaire's claim is not justified as far as comedy is concerned. He had been forestalled in this field by writers such as Saint-Evremond, Muralt and Prévost. Voltaire, however, left no stone unturned in his attempt to convince the world that he was playing a leading role in familiarising a French public with English comedy. He engaged in a systematic denigration of most of his rivals' efforts in the same area. He does not mention Samuel Chappuzeau who completed *Le Théâtre françois* by 1673 and published it in 1674. This work contains *inter alia* some sections on comedy, one of which is entitled 'Difference de la comédie françoise d'avec l'Italienne, l'Espagnole, l'Angloise et la Flamande'. Voltaire does attack Samuel Sorbière in the 'Avertisement to the reader' which prefaces his *Essay on epick poetry*. He says that he has no intention of imitating 'the late Mr Sorbieres, who having staid three Months in this Country without knowing any Thing, either of its Manners or of its Language, thought fit to print a Relation which proved but a dull scurrilous Satyr upon a Nation he knew nothing of'.[13]

---

[13] in his *Observations on m. de Sorbière's voyage into England* (1665), Thomas Sprat described Sorbière's work as a 'Rude Satyr' (p.102).

Sorbière's *Relation d'un voyage en Angleterre* (1664) has one or two lines about English comedies being written in prose. However, neither Sorbière nor Chappuzeau made a genuine contribution to the dissemination of knowledge about English comedy in France. Despite his title, Chappuzeau hardly discusses English comedy in his attempt at comparative literature.

Voltaire made a shrewd calculation as to where the brunt of his attack should fall. It seems that he saw in Saint-Evremond a writer who competed with him in the field of French and English comparative literature. This is perhaps why he tried in his works to damage the reputation of his late rival. In the *Lettre de mr de V . . . à m de C . . .*, with which he prefaced his revised edition of the *Temple du goût* in June 1733, Voltaire says that all of Saint-Evremond's prose works should not have been published (Carcassonne, p.105). In a footnote to the text, Voltaire wrote that Saint-Evremond's comedies were even worse than his poetry.[14] But such was his reputation that Saint-Evremond was offered five hundred louis to publish his comedy of *Sir Politick would be* (p.132). Voltaire was aware that Saint-Evremond had imitated Ben Jonson's *Volpone* in his *Sir Politick would be* which was written as far back as the period 1662-65.[15] Yet in his preface to *La Mort de César*, he claimed that the author of *Sir Politick would be* knew absolutely nothing of English drama, not even the English language (M.iii. 309-10). In Voltaire's opinion, *Sir Politick would be* conformed neither to English taste nor to that of any other nation. Nevertheless, he admitted that Saint-Evremond wrote his play in order to acquaint the French with English comedy.

Between 1666 and 1667 Saint-Evremond wrote an essay entitled 'De la comédie angloise' which was published in 1668. In it he showed acquaintance with Jonson's comedies. Apart from *Volpone*, he referred to *Epicoene*, *The Alchemist*, *Every man in his humour* and *Bartholomew fair*. In a later addition to his essay, he also mentioned Shadwell's comedy, *Epsom Wells*. Like *Sir Politick would be*, Saint-Evremond's essay may to a certain extent be regarded as a pioneering work in comparative literature; it defended English flexibility in applying the rules and praised the variety of action to be found in English plays.

[14] the same disparaging remarks were made in the article 'Académie' of the *Questions sur l'encyclopédie* (1770): Voltaire, not forgetting the 'insipid' *Sir Politick*, condemned all of Saint-Evremond's works for their triviality (M.xvii. 53).

[15] see Saint-Evremond, *Œuvres en prose*, ed. R. Ternois (Paris 1966), iii. 32-40.

Perhaps more significant, it placed Molière on the same footing as Ben Jonson when in its concluding remark it stated: 'Notre Molière à qui les Anciens ont inspiré le bon esprit de la Comédie, égale leur Banjanson à bien représenter les diverses humeurs et differentes manieres des hommes, l'un et l'autre conservant dans leurs peintures un juste rapport avec le génie de leur Nation' (*Œuvres en prose*, ed. R. Ternois, iii. 60). Saint-Evremond, perhaps the first French dramatist to have imitated an English dramatist,[16] subsequently adapted Vanbrugh's *The Provok'd wife*. The comedy was published under the title of *La Femme poussée à bout* in 1726.

The Swiss B. L. de Muralt devoted the second of his *Lettres sur les Anglais* (written in 1695, but published in 1725) to the English theatre, to comedy in particular. He was rather hostile to English writers: he claimed that any person of taste who liked what is natural, anyone accustomed to Molière would not like English comedies 'qui le plus souvent sont remplies de Pointes d'esprit & d'Ordures, bien plus que de traits fins & qui fassent plaisir, ou de ce qui est de quelque usage' (ed. Charles Gould (Paris 1933), p.115). Ben Jonson was a good poet in certain respects, but his characters were mechanical and he was much inferior to Molière (p.116). Muralt, however, reserved his greatest contempt for Thomas Shadwell (?1642-92). He mercilessly exposed Shadwell's jingoism when he translated the preface, prologue and act I, scene i of *The Miser*, the latter's adaptation of *L'Avare* (pp.118-21). As is evident from the letter on comedy in the *Letters concerning the English nation*, Voltaire knew Muralt's work well, although he did not entirely agree with his views.

In his account of English drama in the *Mémoires d'un homme de qualité*, Prévost mentioned several tragedies and included Congreve and Farquhar in his list of tragic writers. When he came to comedy, he remarked that the English were no less successful in this genre. Apart from the question of regularity, he doubted whether one could find in any country anything more agreeable and more ingenious than their comedies such as *The Constant couple*, *The Recruiting officer*, *The Provoked husband*, *The Careless husband* and *The Way of the world*. In other words, Prévost was trying to draw the attention of the French public to the works of Farquhar, Vanbrugh, Cibber and Congreve respectively.

[16] cf. H. C. Lancaster, *A History of French dramatic literature in the seventeenth century* (Baltimore 1942), part v, p.26.

Strangely enough, Voltaire, who except in the *Appel à toutes les nations*, never let an occasion pass without criticising Saint-Evremond, did not provide much evidence to show that he knew Ben Jonson's comedies any better. This does not mean that he was indifferent to Ben Jonson altogether, for in the 'Small Leningrad notebook' he gave an inaccurate transcription of Jonson's poem, *On the countess dowager of Pembroke*, which was quoted in *The Spectator* of 11 March 1712 (*Notebooks*, i. 64). Voltaire also referred to Jonson's tragedy of *Catiline* in the 'Leningrad notebooks' (*Notebooks*, ii. 455). In the *Essai sur les mœurs* he acknowledged that after Shakespeare Jonson brought some improvement to the coarse drama of the English (M.xii. 56).

If Voltaire was not the first to draw the attention of the French to English comedy, few Frenchmen of the seventeenth and eighteenth centuries could claim to have read the subject as widely as he. He knew the works of Shadwell, Wycherley, Vanbrugh, Congreve and Cibber quite well and he was also interested in Steele. Although he attacked his competitor Saint-Evremond on many occasions, Voltaire must nevertheless have realised that the latter knew more about Ben Jonson's plays than he. It was this fact and the desire to be considered original that made him prudently focus attention on the English comic writers of later times – those of the Restoration and post-Restoration periods.

Voltaire appears on the whole well-disposed towards these writers in the *Letters concerning the English nation* and he discusses them in strict chronological sequence in this work. He says, however, that he will not give a detailed account of their plays which he is so fond of applauding (p.190). He had presumably read many of these authors by that date. For, in his letter to Thieriot, which he wrote in English, Voltaire said: 'You'll tell me whom you like best, Ben Jonson or Congreve or Vanbruk or Wicherly' (Best.D478, 14 April 1732). More than Muralt, Voltaire genuinely believed in the value of a comparative approach in stimulating taste and originality. As he remarked in the *Conseils à un journaliste* (1737; M.xxii. 257):

N'oubliez jamais, en rapportant les traits ingénieux de tous ces livres, de marquer ceux qui sont à peu près semblables chez les autres peuples, ou dans nos anciens auteurs . . . Les comparer ensemble (et c'est en quoi le goût consiste), c'est exciter les auteurs à dire, s'il se peut, des choses nouvelles.

It can further be argued that his conviction that the French were weak at comedy as much as the efforts of Saint-Evremond and others to promote an interest in English comedy in France stimulated Voltaire's own interest in English comedy.

In the nineteenth of the *Letters concerning the English nation*, Voltaire was critical of the 'judicious and ingenious' Muralt who in his essay on comedy had spent so much time on Shadwell and had compared his comedy, *The Miser*, with Molière's *L'Avare*. For Shadwell's plays – perhaps Voltaire included among these *The Virtuoso* (1676) with its frequent opening and closing of doors and hiding in boxes and closets, although he does not mention it specifically – had enjoyed favour with the general public for a while, but had been scorned by men of good taste. There were better dramatists than Shadwell to write about. What Voltaire says on Shadwell in the *Letters concerning the English nation* should be read in conjunction with his account of the English writer in the notes on *L'Avare* in the *Vie de Molière*. In the latter work, Voltaire recalls how Shadwell, described as being 'aussi vain que mauvais poète', gave his version of *L'Avare* in English in Molière's lifetime. Presumably basing himself on Muralt, Voltaire gives a French rendering of Shadwell's preface to *The Miser* (M.xxiii. 115):

Je crois pouvoir dire, sans vanité, que Molière n'a rien perdu entre mes mains. Jamais pièce française n'a été maniée par un de nos poëtes, quelque méchant qu'il fût, qu'elle n'ait été rendue meilleure. Ce n'est ni faute d'invention, ni faute d'esprit, que nous empruntons des Français; mais c'est par paresse: c'est aussi par paresse que je me suis servi de *l'Avare* de Molière.

He suggests that a man who does not have sufficient wit to conceal his vanity surely lacks the necessary wit to surpass Molière.

Wycherley (1640-1716) enjoyed a great reputation as a comic writer both in England and in France. In England, Dryden borrowed from Wycherley's *The Plain dealer* (1676) for his comedy *Mr Limberham or the kind keeper* (1679). Both comedies are strongly critical of contemporary life. In the preface to *The State of innocence*, Dryden declared that his friend Wycherley had in *The Plain dealer* 'obliged all honest and virtuous men by one of the most bold, most general, and most useful satires which has ever been presented on the English theatre' (Watson, i. 199). The two writers were alike in their use of extravagant details in constructing their stories. Voltaire, who was thoroughly acquainted with Dryden's works, had read his preface to *The State of innocence* for another reason (see below). If Dryden could

borrow from Wycherley, so could he. Steele may have equally stimulated Voltaire's interest in *The Plain dealer*, for in *The Spectator*
(no.266), he spoke highly of Wycherley's play. He referred to the
'ironical Commendation of the Industry and Charity' of procuresses
which 'makes up the Beauty of the inimitable Dedication to the
Plain dealer and is a Master-piece of Raillery on this vice'. Voltaire
had read *The Spectator* in the original and he must have been struck
by this remark. This may to a certain extent explain why he liked
Wycherley.

Additional reasons may be found in the *Letters concerning the
English nation* where Voltaire describes Wycherley as an excellent
author who spent his life in high society; he knew its vices and its
ridiculous ways perfectly well and depicted them 'with the strongest
Pencil, and in the truest Colours' (p.182). Referring to *The Plain
dealer*, Voltaire says that Wycherley had written a *Misanthrope* in
imitation of Molière's. He recognizes that the strokes are stronger and
bolder in Wycherley's play than in Molière's *Le Misanthrope*, although
they are less delicate and 'the Rules of Decorum are not so well
observed'.[17] Wycherley appeals to Voltaire because he is supposed to
have corrected the only defect[18] to be found in Molière's play, that is,
'the Thinness of the Plot, which also is so dispos'd that the Characters
in it do not enough raise our Concern' (p.183). Voltaire finds that the
English play affects us[19] and that the plot is ingenious. It is no doubt
too bold for French manners. Voltaire says that *The Plain dealer* also
includes its own litigious Countess Pimbesche, that is, a character
reminiscent of the countess in Racine's comedy of *Les Plaideurs*. By

[17] *Le Pour et contre* described Voltaire's remarks on the language of Wycherley as
'ce trait de satyre' (i.286).

[18] Voltaire has here provided a neat summary of the objections he raised against *Le
Misanthrope* in the *Vie de Molière*. He gave specific reasons there for the so-called
failure of *Le Misanthrope*: 'Si on osait encore chercher dans le cœur humain la raison de
cette tiédeur du public aux représentations du *Misanthrope*, peut-être les trouverait-on
dans l'intrigue de la pièce, dont les beautés ingénieuses et fines ne sont pas également
vives et intéressantes; dans ces conversations mêmes, qui sont des morceaux inimitables,
mais qui, n'étant pas toujours nécessaires à la pièce, peut-être refroidissent un peu
l'action, pendant qu'elles font admirer l'auteur' (M.xxiii. 110).

[19] in the 1748 and 1751 editions of the *Lettres philosophiques*, Voltaire remarked that
there were no hypocrites among the English 'this free and bold nation'; on the other
hand, England had more misanthropists than the rest of Europe. That is why *Le
Misanthrope* or *L'Homme au franc procédé* (Wycherley's *The Plain dealer*) is one of the
good comedies of the London stage. It was written at a time when Charles II and his
court were trying to rid the nation of its melancholy (Lanson, ii. 104).

this, he means Widow Blackacre who, in his opinion, is the most comical and the best character on stage. He therefore shares Du Bos's views on Wycherley. Du Bos, a keen anglophile who visited London in 1694, remarked that the first English authors who gave their version of Molière's comedies translated them word for word. Subsequently, English writers accommodated French comedy to English manners. By changing the setting and the incidents, they won greater acclaim. Du Bos quoted Wycherley and his adaptation of Molière to prove his point (*Réflexions critiques sur la poésie et sur la peinture* (Paris 1733), i. 168).

Wycherley's impact on Voltaire may be seen a few years later in his comedy of *La Prude* which was performed in 1747. It was written in 1740 and was at first entitled *La Dévote*, as is evident from his letter to Frederick (Best.D2149, 26 January 1740). Voltaire wanted to have d'Argental's reactions to its heroine, originally called Mme Prudize (Best.D2155, 1 February 1740). It was Frederick who made the desired comments on the play: he found it charming, the characters well-sustained, the plot well constructed and its denouement natural. He read it with great pleasure (Best.D2198, 15 April 1740).

In the 'Avertissement' to his play (M.iv. 390-91), Voltaire says that it is not so much a translation as a slight sketch of Wycherley's famous comedy of *The Plain dealer* which has in England the same reputation as *Le Misanthrope* in France. The plot of *The Plain dealer* is much more complex; it raises more concern and has more incidents. The satire to be found in it is more vehement and insulting: the manners depicted are so daring that the scene could be set in a place of ill-repute close to a guard-room. Wycherley did not hesitate to dedicate his play to the most famous 'appareilleuse' of London. In Voltaire's opinion it is unthinkable that 'les termes de gueuse, de p . . ., de bor . . ., de rufien, de m . . ., de v . . .' and kindred words should fill a comedy which was seen by a very cultured court. One is also amazed that in *The Plain dealer* such language should be allowed to co-exist with the most profound knowledge of the human heart, the most exact and brilliant sketches and the most subtle wit. Yet this is true of Wycherley's play. Voltaire does not know of any comedy among ancients and moderns where there is so much wit. But the wit is of a kind that evaporates as soon as it is translated into a foreign idiom. Voltaire claims that the French rules of decorum which are sometimes insipid have prevented him from imitating this play in every detail: he has had to omit some characters completely. Although his imitation is 'partout voilée de gaze', it is still so strong that one would not dare show it on a Parisian stage.

Why did Voltaire give such a lengthy account of the plot of *The Plain dealer* – only the accounts of the plots of *Hamlet* and Otway's *The Orphan*, as they are described in the *Appel à toutes les nations*, appear longer – in the *Letters concerning the English nation*? It was perhaps as much to familiarize it in France as to provide the groundwork for his own comedy of *La Prude*. Voltaire's work is very much indebted to *The Plain dealer* for its story and its extravagant incidents. There are, however, differences between the two plays, but these are mostly limited to the language. Voltaire frequently takes the trouble of pointing out these differences in footnotes, even when they are minor. In act I, scene i, for instance, he says in a footnote that in the English text the captain of the ship fought against the Dutch and not the Algerians. More significant are the changes which make Voltaire's adaptation of the English version conform to French ideas of decorum. Voltaire has suppressed certain indecent acts performed in the English play such as the incident when Vermish feels the breasts of the disguised Fidelia. In act III, scene vii of *La Prude*, Bartolin simply says to Dorfise and Madame Burlet (M.iv. 444):

> En vérité, pouvais-je présumer
> Que ce jeune homme, à ma vue abusée,
> Fût une fille en garçon déguisée?

In a footnote Voltaire took care to point out that it would not have been proper to give a literal translation. Vermish's attempted rape of Fidelia is also omitted in the French play. It seems that Voltaire by using a more refined, if less daring, language and reducing the number of characters in his play, was determined to show that he could improve upon Wycherley.

Le Babillard, edited by A. de La Chapelle in 1724, gave an account of a performance of Wycherley's *The Country wife*. The periodical likened Mrs Pinchwife to an Agnes who by degrees allows herself completely to forget her duty through naïveté. In depicting the anxieties and the jealousy of a fop who torments himself with the false maxims he had erected for his peace of mind, Wycherley achieved some subtle and comic strokes (p.87). In the *Letters concerning the English nation*, Voltaire also alludes to Wycherley's *The Country wife* which he says is copied from Molière: it is a play 'of as singular and bold cast . . . a kind of *Ecole des femmes*' (p.186).[20] He gives a brief account of the plot and concludes with the remark that Wycherley's play is not perhaps 'the School of good morals, but 'tis certainly the School of Wit and true Humour'. Voltaire's judgement is sound, for the 'china scene' in the play, although generally regarded as one of the most indecent passages in the whole of Restoration comedy, is very funny as well as being outrageous. *The Country wife*, however, was to prove of lesser significance to Voltaire than *The Plain dealer*[21] which he had in mind years later. For he mentioned Lady Blackacre again when he wrote to Algarotti (Best.D7843, 2 September 1758).

Sir John Vanbrugh (1664-1726), known for his translation of Molière's *Le Dépit amoureux* as *The Mistake* (1706), is the next comic author to be discussed in the *Letters concerning the English nation*. Voltaire observed that Vanbrugh wrote more entertaining, though less ingenious, plays than Wycherley: the general opinion was that 'he is as sprightly in his Writings as he is heavy in his Buildings' (p.187). Voltaire ridiculed the architect-dramatist who designed Blenheim Palace by translating the following epitaph, written by a certain dr Evans (Lanson, ii. 114):

> Under this stone, reader, survey
> Dead sir John Vanbrugh's house of clay.
> Lie heavy on him, earth, for he
> Laid many heavy loads on thee!

as 'on souhaitait que la terre ne lui fut point legère, attendu que de son vivant il l'avoit si inhumainement chargée' (Lanson, ii.108). Vanbrugh's imprisonment in France which took place between 1690 and 1692 is recalled. What struck Voltaire in particular was that the play Vanbrugh wrote during his imprisonment – in fact, he probably wrote two comedies, *The Relapse* (1696) and *The Provok'd wife* (1697) – bore no trace of his resentment against the country that had meted out such harsh treatment to him.

---

[20] in the *Supplément du génie*, the abbé Le Blanc used Wycherley in his attack against the English dramatists. Molière is too simple, he argued ironically, variety is required in the plot. That is why in *The Country wife*, all the successful scenes are taken from *L'Ecole des maris* and *L'Ecole des femmes*.

[21] Prévost kept Wycherley's memory alive in France, for in 1735 he translated Pope's letter (dated 21 January 1715-16) to Edward Blount on the death-bed marriage of Wycherley (*Pour et contre*, vii. 294-97).

The Relapse made a strong impact on Voltaire. There are indications, although one cannot be certain, that mme Du Châtelet was referring to *L'Echange*, a play which has affinities with *The Relapse*, when she told an unidentified correspondent that they were going to perform at Cirey a comedy that Voltaire had written for them (Best.D978, 3 January 1736). Two months later Voltaire and mme Du Châtelet mentioned to Thieriot that in the little comedy they had performed there was a role 'assez plaisant et assez neuf' for mademoiselle Dangeville. Voltaire added that although mme Du Châtelet's acting was outstanding, the play was nothing more than a farce and as such unworthy of the public (Best.D1033, 10 March 1736). It was in fact never performed in public under its original name. *L'Echange*, also known as *Le Comte de Boursoufle*, was perhaps composed at Cirey soon after 1734[22]: act II, scene vii, refers to the capture of Phillipsburg by the French in 1734 during the war of the Polish succession. In 1761 it was performed in Paris at the Comédie-Italienne under the name of *Quand est-ce qu'on me marie* and was described as a 'comédie traduite de l'anglais'.

There can be no doubt about the indebtedness of *L'Echange* to *The Relapse* (which was itself influenced by Cibber's comedy *Love's last shift; or, the fool in fashion*) with regard to characterisation and plot, in particular. Although the plot of *L'Echange* can be paralleled by that of many a seventeenth-century comedy, it is taken directly from *The Relapse*. It deals with a penurious younger son (Le Chevalier) who quarrels with his elder brother (the Comte de Fatenville). With the help of a witty rogue (Trigaudin), he impersonates his brother in order to marry the latter's fiancée (Gotton), the daughter of the Baron de la Canardière, and inherit a rich dowry. The fraud is discovered, but too late to prevent the marriage and to give rise to all the extravagances of a farce. The Comte de Fatenville is appropriately named after Lord Foppington[23] who is, however, more complex than his French counterpart: unlike Fatenville, Foppington has rakish inclinations. The Baron de la Canardière is a close replica of the country gentleman Sir Tunbelly Clumsey, as Trigaudin is of Coupler, a match-maker.

L'Echange and *The Relapse* differ in other respects. Voltaire shortened the lengthy five-act English comedy into a swift-moving play in three acts. He succeeded in maintaining unity of interest by

[22] see G. Bengesco, *Voltaire: bibliographie de ses œuvres* (Paris 1882-90), i. 21-23.
[23] Lord Foppington also appears in Cibber's *The Careless husband* (1704).

discarding the main plot in Vanbrugh's comedy as it centres on Loveless, his wife Amanda and her cousin Berinthia. He avoided the problem of having to strike a balance simply by concentrating on the story of Fatenville and his brother. Vanbrugh, on the other hand, has a persistent interest in the unhappy marriage, which he took up in *The Provok'd wife*. In *The Relapse*, Loveless's seduction of Berinthia proves that he has relapsed into his past follies and thus justifies the title of the play, *The Relapse or virtue in danger*. Vanbrugh is not able to maintain this level of seriousness in his comedy and he therefore devotes as much attention to the sub-plot concerning Lord Foppington.

Voltaire had Vanbrugh's second play, *The Provok'd wife*, in mind when he revised the *Lettres philosophiques* in 1748 and 1751. He may have seen a performance of the unexpurgated version during his English visit: the play was often performed on the London stage (see Lanson, ii. 111, n.2). The beginning of the nineteenth letter in the revised editions compares the bombastic tone of English tragedy with the natural style of English comedy. This natural style is described as being more appropriate for rakes than for gentlemen. English comic characters have no hesitation in calling a spade a spade. As an example Voltaire refers to a play where a drunkard 'se masque en prêtre, fait du tapage, est arrêté par le guét. Il se dit curé; on lui demande s'il a une cure: il répond qu'il en a une excellente pour la chaude pisse' (Lanson, ii. 103). In *The Provok'd wife*, act IV, scene iii, Sir John Brute, who is masquerading as a parson, is arrested for unruly behaviour while drunk and he is brought before a justice of the peace. The following incident then takes place:

JUST.

Pray where do you live, sir?

SIR JOHN

Here – and there, sir.

JUST.

Why, what a strange man is this! – Where do you preach, sir? have you any cure?

SIR JOHN

Sir – I have – a very good cure – for a clap, at your service.

(*Sir John Vanbrugh*, ed. W. C. Ward (London 1893), i.346)

A different version of this scene is also known to exist: it was performed at the Haymarket Theatre in January 1706 (Ward, i. 388).

Sir John Brute now passes off as Lady Brute and still behaves in an unruly manner, but the above dialogue is omitted from the scene. Voltaire was probably unaware of the existence of this modified scene, or perhaps he preferred to focus attention on the original version with its anti-clerical tendencies in places. Another strong possibility is that he was basing his remarks on Saint-Evremond's *La Femme poussée à bout* 'traduite de la pièce anglaise, intitulée *The Provok'd wife*'.[24] It is to be noted that Saint-Evremond could use only the original text for his translation, since he was dead by the time of the later version. In act IV, scene V, the Chevalier Brute replied to the justice of the peace: 'Oui, Monsieur, j'en ai une excellente . . . la meilleure Cure du monde pour la chaud . . .' (*Œuvres*, ed. Desmaizeaux (London 1753), vii. 196). Marivaux found in *La Femme poussée à bout* material for the creation of some of the characters in his comedy, *Les Sincères*.[25]

It is likely that Voltaire was thinking of Vanbrugh when composing 'la capilotade', destined to become book xviii of *La Pucelle*. He wrote to Thieriot: 'Cher correspondant vous me fournissez de bons reliefs pour la capilotade' (Best.D9211, 9 September 1760). There is a reference to a 'capilotade' in Vanbrugh's comedy of *The False friend* (1702), closely imitated from Le Sage's *Le Traître puni* (1700) – itself a translation of *La Traicion busca el castigo* by don Francisco de Rojas (Ward, ii. 3-4). In act III, scene ii of *The False friend*, Lopez, servant to Don John, overhears his master. The latter has treacherous designs on the wife of his friend Don Pedro who is absent. Thereupon Lopez exclaims (Ward, ii. 52):

Unfortunate Don Pedro! thou has left thy purse in the hands of a robber; and while thou art galloping to pay the last duty to thy father, he's at least upon the trot to pay the first to thy wife. Ah, the traitor! What a capilotade of damnation will there be cooked up for him!

A parallel can be established between what happens in *The False friend* and in book xviii of *La Pucelle* where Fréron, La Beaumelle and other enemies of Voltaire repay the kindness of having been freed from English captivity by stealing the clothes of their benefactors! The whole of book xviii of *La Pucelle* is rightly described as 'la capilotade', since it is a concoction against his enemies by Voltaire. The possibility

[24] a ten-volume edition of Saint-Evremond's *Œuvres* (1740) is listed in Voltaire's library at Leningrad.
[25] see Lucette Desvignes, *Marivaux et l'Angleterre* (Paris 1970), pp.74-78.

that he had a different play of Vanbrugh in mind cannot be ruled out altogether.[26] In *The Confederacy* (1705) based on Dancourt's *Les Bourgeoises à la mode*, Clarissa, the wife of a rich money scrivener called Gripe and an expensive, luxurious woman, loses her necklace. Mrs Amlet, a seller of all kinds of private affairs to ladies, says that she will dance at the wedding of Corinna, Gripe's daughter by a former marriage. The farcical situation provokes the following reaction from Flippanta, Clarissa's maid (act III, scene ii; Ward, ii. 178-79):

Flip. What – what – what does the woman mean? Mad! What a capilotade of a story's here! The necklace lost; and her son Dick; and a fortune to marry; and she shall dance at the wedding; and – she does not intend, I hope, to propose a match between her son Dick and Corinna?

The English comic dramatist who won by far the greatest applause from Voltaire was Congreve (1670-1729).[27] He is first mentioned in the section on Milton in the *Essay on epick poetry*. Voltaire at one stage leaves Milton in order to make the point that each nation should pay more attention to the taste and manners of its respective neighbours. Such a comparative approach would be mutually beneficial. For Voltaire is convinced that Italian comic playwrights would learn from Congreve and some other authors to prefer wit and humour to buffoonery (White, pp.135-36). No other English comic writer is considered worth a mention in the *Essay*. This praise does not, however, appear in the *Essai sur la poésie épique* where there is the suggestion that Congreve's plays are not properly comedies as the French understand the word. It is almost as if Voltaire is making a concession in calling them comedies: 'Ne disputons jamais sur les noms. Irai-je refuser le nom de comédies aux pièces de M. Congrève... parce-qu'elles ne sont pas dans nos mœurs?' (M.viii. 308).

Congreve is described in the most glowing terms in the twenty-fourth of the *Letters concerning the English nation* by being called the

---

[26] see Besterman's note on Best.D9211.

[27] in *Théâtre anglais*, La Place translated Congreve's *Love for love* (1695) as *Amour pour amour* (1745). In the seventy-seventh of the *Lettres d'un Français* (1745), the abbé Le Blanc stressed Congreve's indebtedness to Molière. He pointed out how *The Double-dealer* (1694) and *The Way of the world* (1700) were influenced by *Tartuffe* and *Le Misanthrope* respectively. He complained that Congreve would lift entire scenes which he translated word for word. The scene of M. Dimanche in *Le Festin de Pierre* (that is act IV, scene iii of *Dom Juan*) is transported into *Love for love*, but Congreve made no acknowledgement.

Molière of England. He is placed alongside authors for whom Voltaire had great admiration: Pope and Swift. As Voltaire explains, Congreve was to have been a member of the British Academy advocated by Swift in *A Proposal for correcting, improving and ascertaining the English tongue*: moreover, the members of this proposed academy included such names as Pope, Swift and Prior and they had produced works that would last as long as the English language (pp.235-36). A few lines later in this letter, Congreve is grouped with other distinguished English writers who would have been members of the academy, such as Dryden and Addison. All these would-be members are supposed to have 'fix'd the *English* Tongue by their Writings' (p.237): at any rate, they were vastly superior to the first members of the Académie française, who were a disgrace to the French nation and appeared so ridiculous.

Some of the reasons for Voltaire's high opinion of Congreve are given in the nineteenth letter. The Englishman who brought such distinction to comedy had written only a few plays, but they are all excellent of their kind (p.188). The laws of drama are strictly observed[28] and the plays are full of characters which are contrasted with the utmost subtlety. One does not have to put up with any coarse jokes and everywhere there is evidence of characters using the language of gentlemen, while behaving like rogues. This proves that Congreve knew his public well and that he lived in what may be called polite company. His comedies are among the wittiest and the most regular (p.189).

Voltaire's grievances against Congreve are mostly on the personal level. He says that Congreve was infirm and almost dying when he visited him. Congreve had one defect and that consisted in not holding in esteem his first profession of writer, although he owed his reputation and his fortune to it. Apparently Congreve talked of his plays as trifles, unworthy of him and he asked Voltaire during their first conversation to visit him on no other footing but that of a gentleman who led a life of plainness and simplicity. Voltaire replied that if Congreve were a mere gentleman like any other, he would not have come to see him. He was deeply shocked by such unreasonable vanity (p.189).

Goldsmith corroborates the above story in his *Memoirs of m. de Voltaire* which were written towards the end of 1758 and the beginning

---

[28] Voltaire was taking up a point he made in the preface to *Œdipe* in 1730.

of 1759 but published in 1761.[29] He adds that Congreve's behaviour 'was a meanness which somewhat disgusted the Frenchman ... he [Voltaire] therefore informed Mr Congreve, that his fame as a writer was the only inducement he had to see him, and though he could condescend to desire the acquaintance of a man of wit and learning, he was above soliciting the company of any private gentleman whatsoever' (*Works*, iii. 252). It seems that Congreve consistently avoided publicity and frowned upon hero-worship. He disliked court and coffee-house alike. Judging by the prefaces to his plays and his letter of 7 July 1719 to Giles Jacob, the editor of the *Poetical register*, Congreve liked to call his plays 'poor trifles'. He was therefore genuinely embarrassed by Voltaire's profuse flattery when he called on him in 1726. Illnesses may account for his curt remarks to Voltaire, who appears to have mistaken genuine humility for snobbery. Far from thinking that Congreve was vain, writers such as Dryden, Pope, Swift, Steele and Gay spoke of his 'modesty' and his humility 'in the height of envy'd honors' (see J. C. Hodges, *William Congreve, the man* (London 1941), pp.107-108).

Richard Steele (1672-1729) interested Voltaire in more ways than one. He is mentioned by Voltaire in his first dedicatory epistle to Fawkener in 1733. In a paragraph which bears a close resemblance to the thought in the twenty-third of the *Letters concerning the English nation*, he reminds his friend that the English have no need for 'des regards du maître' to honour and reward merit in any field. Steele and Vanbrugh were comic dramatists as well as being members of parliament (M.ii.543). In the nineteenth of the *Letters*, Steele is simply described as one of those good comic authors whom England has (p.190).

It is strange that Voltaire does not discuss Steele's comedies in greater detail in the 1733 or subsequent editions of the *Lettres philosophiques*. For in 1736 the *Pour et contre* (viii. 109-321) gave a full account and a complete translation of Steele's last comedy, *The Conscious lovers* (1722).[30] A French version appeared under the name of

---

[29] see *Collected works of Oliver Goldsmith*, ed. A. Friedman (Oxford 1966), iii. 225. Despite inaccuracies, Goldsmith's biography is not an imaginary work. Goldsmith probably turned to an undiscovered source written after 1750, to which he made additions. For his account of Voltaire's visit in England, he may have drawn from literary acquaintances – most probably from the ageing Edward Young known to both Voltaire and himself (p.226).

[30] see G. R. Havens, *The Abbé Prévost and English literature* (New Jersey 1921), pp.92-94.

L'Amour confident de lui-même. The author who may have been Prévost himself, says that *The Conscious lovers* was regarded as the best of Steele's comedies.[31] After the translation of the first act, he observes that there was 'plus d'ordre et de bienséance' than one would have expected from an English comedy: the surprising thing was that Steele's comedy was applauded in theatres where the most vulgar and indecent buffoonery were popular (viii. 186). His remarks at the end of the translation are equally interesting: he admits that Steele took some liberty with the rules, especially that of the unity of place, but he defends this infringement on the ground of verisimilitude which the French do not observe, since their interpretation of the rules is too narrow. He likes the variety of scenes in *The Conscious lovers* because it relieves the imagination more than it hinders it and obeys the rule of verisimilitude which is what matters most in a play (viii. 322-25).

Voltaire was not indifferent to Steele's drama although he seems to have remembered it mostly in connection with what he had read in *The Tatler* and *The Spectator*.[32] In the preface to *Socrate* (1759), for example, Voltaire says that Steele persuaded Addison that the subject of Cato was more worthy of the stage than that of Socrates. He quotes Steele as saying in *The Tatler* that one should choose as the subject of a play the vice that predominates most among the nation for whom one works (M.v. 361-62).

It seems that Voltaire read with pleasure what he found in *The Spectator*. The article 'Anecdote' of the *Questions sur l'encyclopédie* gave him another opportunity of quoting Steele (M.xvii.196). With evident glee, Voltaire refers to Steele's little tale about the merchant Inkle in *The Spectator* (No. 11). He claims that Steele wanted to pass this tale off as one of the real causes of the war involving the English in the Caribbean. In trying to prove that men are as fickle as women, Steele invented the story of Inkle. The latter was guilty of the most shocking ingratitude because he sold an Indian girl, Jarika (Yarico),

---

[31] Le Blanc thought that *The Conscious lovers* was one of the best comedies of the English theatre. He particularly liked the first scene of act v which he found extremely beautiful and said could have been written only by Steele. He translated it and sent it to La Chaussée (*Lettres d'un Français*, ii. 122).

[32] to Fawkener, Voltaire complained that England had 'sunk into romances, the time of ... Pope, Adisson, Steele, Swift is gone' (Best.D4851, 27 March 1752). In a letter to J. V. Delacroix who had revived Marivaux's *Le Spectateur français*, he claimed that he had once known many contributors to the English *Spectator*, adding that Delacroix seemed to be the heir of Addison and Steele (Best.D17651, 22 March 1772).

pregnant by him, to the highest bidder in Barbados. The same Jarika had saved him from death. Steele's treatment of the story in *The Spectator* became popular in England and France. Voltaire himself did not write a comedy out of this story: it was left to Chamfort to do so with his one-act play, *La Jeune indienne*, in 1764.

A more important merchant, who was frequently referred to in *The Spectator* by Steele, made a big impact on Voltaire. This was sir Andrew Freeport, described in *The Spectator* (no.2) as 'a Merchant of great Eminence in the City of *London*: A Person of indefatigable Industry, strong Reason, and great Experience. His notions of Trade are noble and generous.' Steele opposed Freeport to sir Roger de Coverley, the mouthpiece of the landed interests. In fact, Freeport's defence of trading interests in *The Spectator* (no.174) was used by Steele in his comedy of *The Conscious lovers*. In act IV, scene ii, for instance, Mr Sealand tells Sir John Bevil that 'we Merchants are a Species of Gentry, that have grown into the World this last Century, and are as honourable, and almost as useful, as you landed Folks, that have always thought yourselves so much above us'. The name of Freeport was often used later in the eighteenth century as a pseudonym by economic writers.[33] Voltaire, however, had found material for the creation of the character of Freeport in *L'Ecossaise* (1760).[34] In tapping *The Spectator* as a source, he had been preceded by Marivaux. For the social aspect of many a play by the latter shows the influence of the *Spectator* in translation and sometimes in the original. The paternalism of sir Roger de Coverley is reflected in the 'maîtres' of Marivaux's comedies.[35]

It is true that Freeport, described as a 'gros négociant de Londres' makes his first appearance only in act II, scene v of *L'Ecossaise* but he has been away on business in Jamaica. Although in the next scene, he bursts into a hotel room occupied by Lindane, what he does subsequently even surpasses the noble and generous features attributed to Andrew Freeport in *The Spectator*. For instance, he tells Lindane that his Jamaica trip has earned him five thousand guineas and that he has made it a principle – which should be that of every Christian – to give a tenth of what he earns to someone in need. Thereupon he throws the money on the table, saying that he wants neither thanks nor gratitude.

[33] cf. *The Spectator*, ed. Donald F. Bond (Oxford 1965), i. 10, n.4.
[34] I am indebted to professor Colin Duckworth for having drawn my attention to this point.
[35] Desvignes, *Marivaux et l'Angleterre*, pp.79-103, 246-50.

In act III, scene iv, when he learns that a Government messenger has come to arrest Lindane unless someone stands bail for her, he immediately offers his money for that purpose. Freeport's generosity never falters, for in the last scene of the play, when he realizes that Lindane is to be married to someone else, he accepts the situation gracefully and says that he is pleased.

Like Steele, Voltaire also used Freeport in *L'Ecossaise* to show the opposition between the landed and trading interests. In act IV, scene i, Freeport admits that he dislikes the great lords as much as he dislikes bad writers. In act V, scene vi, he cannot help expressing his objection to Lord Murray's appearance and airs. However, since one of the main objectives of *L'Ecossaise* is to denigrate Fréron, Freeport is made to act out of character and to join in the denigration in act II, scene v and in act IV, scene i.

It is not surprising that Voltaire should have appreciated the talents of Colley Cibber (1671-1757) as actor and dramatist. He probably saw this important theatrical figure of his time perform on the stage. W. R. Chetwood, prompter at Drury Lane and a friend of Cibber, remarked that Voltaire's acquaintance with Cibber brought him frequently to the theatre so that he quickly improved his knowledge of English (*General history of the stage* (London 1749), p.46n.). Cibber became poet laureate in 1730 and Voltaire refers to this appointment when he describes him in the *Letters concerning the English nation* as 'an excellent Player, and also Poet Laureate, a Title which how ridiculous it may be thought, is yet worth a thousand Crowns a Year, (besides some considerable Privileges) to the Person who enjoys it' (p.190).

Le Mary négligent, that is *The Careless husband* (1705), Cibber's best comedy, is mentioned in the 1748 and 1751 additions to the *Lettres philosophiques*. Voltaire chose it as an example to illustrate his point that even in this 'most decent' of comedies, vulgar expressions are not absent. In act I, Sir Charles Easy tells the maid Edging: 'Kiss me.' As she rebukes him, he exclaims: 'What an unlimited Privilege has this Jade got from being a whore.' In act V, the stage direction is as follows: 'the scene opens and discovers Sir Charles without his Periwig and Edging, by him, both asleep in two easy Chairs. And then enter Lady Easy.' Voltaire combines these two scenes and puts Easy's words into the mouth of his wife. This combination is as effective as the original. In Voltaire's terse account, the husband has his head scratched by a maid sitting next to him, whereupon his wife comes and exclaims: 'A quelle autorité ne parvient-on pas par être putain?' Voltaire roundly condemns these expressions since they can be defended only by cynics who lean on Horace. To a French audience, these images would gain by being veiled.

In assessing the impact of English literature on Voltaire, one must always take into account Voltaire's French background whatever be the genre one is discussing. This background is of special significance in the case of comedy. For instance, it should not be difficult to show that the Dorfise of *La Prude* recalls Arsinoé of *Le Misanthrope* and that both characters bear some resemblance to Tartuffe. Moreover, many of the English comic dramatists in whom Voltaire was interested had been influenced by French comedy, by Molière's plays in particular. But Molière himself appears to have drawn some benefit from an English writer like Joseph Hall, even if it was through a translation by Urbain Chevreau.[36] Such a state of affairs can only add further support to the idea of an interpenetration of English and French literature in the seventeenth and eighteenth centuries.

One can detect a consistent trend in Voltaire's reactions to those English playwrights whose works he knew. As a rule, he seems to have spoken highly of those writers who showed respect for Molière and who in his view had tried to improve on him. If he could establish that English writers had surpassed Molière, he could lay the foundation for his own achievement in comedy. In particular, would he not strengthen his claim to be regarded as Molière's successor in France? Besides, none of the English comic dramatists had ever enjoyed the reputation of a Shakespeare in France. So personal prestige was not at stake. It was natural that Voltaire should have castigated those who attacked Molière, as in tragedy he censured those who appeared to him to have fallen short of Racine's standard. Shadwell deservedly incurred his displeasure, although Voltaire did not give him too much importance. Had not Dryden and Muralt chastised Shadwell enough before him?

It is obvious that the English comic writers of the Restoration and post Restoration times had their own contribution to make – at any rate this is what Voltaire thought. As a practising dramatist Voltaire was always interested in the way authors used their sources. To Congreve went all the compliments, but it was Wycherley, Vanbrugh

---

[36] see H. G. Hall, 'Molière, Chevreau's *Ecole du sage*, and Joseph Hall's *Characters*', *French Studies* (1975), xxix. 398-410.

and Steele who stimulated Voltaire's interest most and provided him with material for his plays. They encouraged him to follow a comparative approach both in his critical remarks in the *Lettres philosophiques*, in the prefaces to plays and in some of the comedies he wrote in the 'goût anglais'. He might thus be considered to have surpassed Saint-Evremond as a 'comparatiste'. If he allowed himself to be influenced by English comedy, it was because he was convinced that there were weaknesses in French comedy from which even Molière, the greatest of French writers, was not exempt and that one could learn from the English how to remedy these weaknesses. What he achieved in his own comedy is a different story.

3

Voltaire and the English epic

i. *Voltaire and the epic*

ALTHOUGH Voltaire used Milton's *Paradise lost* not so much in the epic proper as in other types of writings, it is still necessary to know what he thought of the epic as a genre if we are to make a well-balanced assessment of his reactions to Milton. By producing *La Henriade* in 1724, Voltaire had taken up the challenge of N. Malézieu who is reported to have said that the French 'n'ont pas la tête épique'. A sign of his self-confidence can be seen from his letter to Thieriot to whom he writes that the epic is his *forte* or else he is grossly mistaken. It seemed to him that one is at ease in a field where one's rivals are Chapelain, La Motte and St Didier (Best.D253, 17 October 1725). One could reasonably expect the poet who had given France the epic she deserved, who had read, if not fifty, at least a good number of epic poems in French by 1727 to contribute to a theory of the epic himself.[1] It is possible that in the elaboration of his theory he wanted to practise what he preached to the reader of the *Essay on epick poetry*, that rules should be extracted from the various examples before his eyes and that one should be governed by good sense alone (White, p.88). A consistent approach to a theory of the epic is fortunately provided by the *Essay on epick poetry*, which is to be regarded as the basic source, the French version, the *Essai sur la poésie épique* and the article 'Epopée' of the *Questions sur l'encyclopédie*. Some letters and part of his preface to the

---

[1] Voltaire was no doubt interested in the views of English critics such as Dryden, Pope and Addison. They were useful to him in more ways than one, though not necessarily in formulating his theory of the epic. Generally speaking Voltaire preferred to draw his inspiration from the French who had produced the best theorists of the epic. The 'Dissertation sur la poésie anglaise' in the *Journal littéraire* made the categorical statement that the French were better at understanding the rules of the epic than putting them into practice, that they criticized the ancients very well without equalling them (ix. 177). See also Taylor, pp.123-24.

1730 edition of the *Henriade,* called *Idée de la Henriade,* complete the picture.

As a creative writer, Voltaire had nothing but scorn for the professional critic and in the *Essay on epick poetry* he reserved his contempt for critics such as Aristotle, whose *Poetics* he nevertheless liked (see below), Castelvetro, Dacier and Le Bossu. It was, however, almost inevitable that at the time of composing *La Ligue* (1718), as *La Henriade* was called in its first version, he should have been familiar with some of the arguments used by the opponents in the quarrel between ancients and moderns, then in its critical phase. He refused to be dogmatic, preferring to be governed by the principle of common sense. Such an attitude makes him appear rather neutral in the quarrel. He was, on the other hand, by no means indifferent to moderns such as La Motte and Perrault. Indeed, a close parallel can be drawn between La Motte's and Voltaire's views on Homer. In the *Discours sur Homère* added to *L'Iliade* (1714), La Motte pointed out that Homer's style was too metaphorical, too much like that of a barbarous period when imagination had the upper hand over reason and his imagery was too prolific. This is precisely what Voltaire thought of Homer's style.

Voltaire condemned blind admiration for the ancients.[2] Although he would not go as far as Perrault who in the preface to the *Parallèle des anciens et des modernes* claimed that modern writers had received from heaven considerable enlightenment and that the same had been denied to the whole of antiquity, he acknowledged that just respect for the ancients proved a mere superstition if it betrayed a rash contempt for one's neighbours and countrymen. His advice was: 'We ought not to do such an Injury to Nature, as to shut our Eyes to all the beauties that her Hands pour around us, in order to look back fixedly on her former Productions' (*Essay,* p.87). This explains why in the article 'Anciens et modernes' of the *Questions* Voltaire agreed with Perrault's judgment on Homer. He thought that Perrault could very well be mistaken about the meaning of a passage, but that nevertheless he was often right as to the contradictions, the repetitions, the monotony of the battles, the lengthy speeches, the indecencies and the inconsistent behaviour of the gods in the *Iliad* (M.xvii. 230).

---

[2] the conclusion of the article 'Anciens et modernes' (1770) of the *Questions sur l'encyclopédie* sums up accurately Voltaire's attitude to the quarrel: 'heureux est celui qui, dégagé de tous les préjugés, est sensible au mérite des anciens et des modernes, apprécie leurs beautés, connaît fautes, et les pardonne' (M.xvii.240).

To obtain a clear picture of Voltaire's conception of the epic, one has to take into consideration an approach which often appears more negative than positive. The discussion is not so much about what the epic is as what it should not be. This impression emerges from the very first page of the *Essay on epick poetry*. Voltaire is opposed to Le Bossu since in the *Traité du poème épique* (1675) he teaches that the foundation of epic poetry is to be sought in the excellent works of the ancients. Voltaire's argument is that by taking the rules of epic poetry from Homer the critics confused the beginning of an art with the principles of the art itself (White, p.81). He cannot accept the critics' tendency to impose on France the literary ideal of another age and another country. He clarifies his position in the section on Homer of the *Essay*, where in agreement with La Motte he suggests that very few can control their prejudices and 'transport themselves far enough into such a remote Antiquity as to become the Contemporaries of *Homer* when they read him: Good Sense bids them to make Allowances for the Manners of his Time, but 'tis almost impossible to bring themselves to a quick Relish of them' (White, pp.90-91).

In fact this negative approach to the epic is nowhere better illustrated than in the section on Homer. The judicious reader with whom Voltaire identifies himself there objects to the monotony of the *Iliad*, although he concedes that lengthiness is a characteristic it shares with other epic poems. Voltaire stresses the dangers of a lack of imagination and the excesses of a fertile imagination when he says that 'there is no Epick Poetry without a powerful Imagination, and no great Imagination without over-flowing' (p.91). A more serious defect is Homer's incapacity to stimulate interest in his heroes. Achilles is too boisterous, Paris contemptible and Agamemnon too proud. Only Hector is interesting: he has the best character, but he is hemmed in by so many heroes that a dispersal of interest follows. The construction of the poem is faulty too, since there is no logical connection between the books. As he points out in the *Essai sur la poésie épique*, Desmarets's *Clovis* and Chapelain's *La Pucelle* are much better from the point of view of composition (M.viii.318). Voltaire is also critical of Homer's gods: they are perhaps at once absurd and entertaining.

Voltaire takes a different view on the inclusion of gods in an epic poem in the section on Lucan of the *Essay*; he commends Lucan for having abandoned the gods in his *Pharsalia*. Their presence might be justified in the 'dark fabulous Ages' of Homer and Virgil, but they would be totally unsuitable to the civil wars of Rome. Though the gods added dignity to the modest beginnings of Rome, they would have debased the character of Caesar and heaped ridicule upon him. 'What a poor Figure would that Conqueror make in the Field of Pharsalia, should he be assisted by *Iris* or *Mercury?*' Voltaire asks (White, p.101). In his view this proves conclusively that the gods are not essential in an epic. It is not because of their absence that *Pharsalia* is not a masterpiece, but because Lucan is incapable of managing with art the affairs of men.

Voltaire found support for his stand in a letter Antonio Cocchi[3] (1695-1758) published in the *Mercure de France* of December 1733 (Best.D667, *c.* October 1733). In this 'Lettre sur la *Henriade*' which delighted Voltaire and which he subsequently had published in the 1737 edition of *La Henriade*, Cocchi wrote that Voltaire's masterpiece, unlike other epics, managed very well without the countless super-human agents. This confirmed Cocchi in his belief that if the imaginary, invisible and all-powerful agents were removed from an epic and were replaced, as in tragedies,[4] by real characters, the beauty of the poem would be greatly enhanced. He came to this conclusion when he noticed how in Homer, Virgil, Dante, Ariosto, Tasso and Milton the finest parts of their epic were not where they made their gods and the devil act or speak. On the contrary, such parts were often conducive to laughter without ever producing in the human heart those moving sentiments that arise from the representation of some remarkable action.

Yet Voltaire admits that one has to take into account man's per-manent need for the supernatural element. In the *Essai sur la poésie épique* he therefore makes some concession for the use of the super-natural in the epic, because 'plus l'action sera grande, plus elle plaira à tous les hommes dont la faiblesse est d'être séduite par tout ce qui est au delà de la vie commune' (M.viii.309). Out of respect for popular beliefs, Virgil allowed the presence of gods and mythology in the *Aeneid*, but he took care to justify the introduction of absurdities such as the metamorphosis of Aeneas's ships into nymphs by saying that it was an ancient tradition. In the same way, an English epic poet

[3] see Taylor, pp.312-19.

[4] in the 'Idée de la Henriade', Voltaire insists on the similarity between an epic and a tragedy. He points out that certain happenings in his epic have been cut off in order to comply with the rule of verisimilitude required by the epic. He has not only avoided Lucan's mistakes, but has done what usually obtains in tragedies where the action is subordinated to the rules of the drama (Taylor, pp.307-308).

writing on the subject of King Arthur may be excused the incantations of Merlin. But it would be better to avoid the supernatural element (White, p.95; M.viii. 323).

It is not to be inferred that Voltaire completely rules out the supernatural from the epic. His stand appears clearly in the preface to the 1737 edition of *La Henriade*, written at his request by his protégé Linant. Since his aim is to refute the critics, Linant refers to the bold and novel idea put forward by Cocchi, that the supernatural is not what gives most pleasure in epic poetry. He agrees that this may be true by pointing out that if the ancient epics had only the supernatural, they would be merely collections of pagan miracles. Nevertheless, unlike Cocchi, Linant-Voltaire does not believe that the supernatural should be banished: 'il doit seulement être employé avec sobriété dans une religion aussi sévère que la nôtre, et dans un siècle où la raison est devenue aussi sévère que la religion' (Taylor, p.324).

It is not, however, easy to use the supernatural which in modern epics tends to be of Christian origin. As Boileau remarked in book iii of the *Art poétique*, where he wrote:

> Et quel objet enfin à présenter aux yeux
> Que le diable toujours hurlant contre les cieux,

the Christian supernatural can easily become ridiculous. It must be used with restraint; in Voltaire's words: 'Le merveilleux même doit être sage; il faut qu'il conserve un air de vraisemblance, et qu'il soit traité avec goût' (M.viii. 359). The action of an epic poem should as far as possible be centred on earth. God should not intervene at all if possible; if he does it should be from a distance. The fallen angels are symbolic and should not be given anthropomorphic treatment (cf. Taylor, pp.134-35).

What Voltaire will not concede at all in the epic is the mixture of pagan mythology and Christian religion. Thus when he deals with Tasso, he condemns his practice of calling the evil spirits by the names of Pluto and Alecto (White, p.122). It is obvious that he wants to erect this prohibition into a general principle; he also notes that none of the modern epic poets is free from this defect.[5] Voltaire is here relying on Boileau in the *Art poétique*. The latter castigates those authors who:

[5] for instance, Voltaire says that nothing can excuse in Camoens, his injudicious mixture of heathen gods and Christian religion (White, p.109).

Pensent faire agir Dieu, ses saints et ses prophètes,
Comme ces dieux éclos du cerveau des poètes.

It is by no means certain whether Voltaire further agreed with Boileau
in the last part of his injunction which reads:

De la foi d'un chrétien les mystères terribles
D'ornements égayés ne sont point susceptibles.

Voltaire says 'that the Hell of the Gospel is not so fitted for Poetry
as that of *Homer* and *Virgil*' (White, p.123). But if he preferred the
pagan hell to the Christian hell, it was simply because the former was
more poetical than the latter. In the *Essai* he is all in favour of allegory
as it is 'une image sensible de la vérité' (M.viii.363). He expresses the
point differently in the English original: 'Fiction is nothing but Truth
in Disguise.' There are certain rules to be observed if an allegory is
to be successful: it must be short, decent and noble – an allegory
carried too far or too low is like a beautiful woman who always wears
a mask. Moreover, to speak metaphorically for too long must be
tiresome because it is unnatural (White, p.139). When these points
have been taken into consideration, it must be admitted that allegory can
help animate a poem; after all, an allegory is 'a long Metaphor'. It is
due to his imagery that Homer towered above Chapelain and Desmarets: it turned him into a sublime painter. To Voltaire, imagination
is at the very heart of poetry, and that is why La Motte's translation
of a Homeric simile destroys its beauty through exaggerated compression. He condemns La Motte's insensibility to beauty and suggests that
a few antitheses and suble turns are no substitute for these magnificent
poetic touches (M.viii.318-19).

Towards the end of the *Essai sur la poésie épique*, some reasons are
put forward to account for the failure of the French in epic poetry. If
it is more difficult for a Frenchman than for any other person to write
an epic poem, it is not because of rhyme or the poverty of the language.
It is because the French are the least poetical of nations. They insist
on a natural, simple, almost conversational style – certainly as far as
the drama is concerned. There is precision and elegance, but no elevation in French poetry. Any attempt at elevation has been checked by
'l'esprit géométrique' and the language, argues the *Essay*, is not as
'copious' as it should be, for the French have discarded a multitude of
old energetic expressions whose absence has impoverished the language

(White, p.149). The result is that 'la méthode est la qualité dominante de nos écrivains' (M.viii.362).

Considering the price that the French have had to pay for concision, Voltaire cannot approve of anything that militates against it. He therefore condemns digressions in an epic, although he excuses Milton's human frailty (White, p.137). Descriptions must neither be too detailed nor too technical. Voltaire's conception of the epic is partly influenced by the deficiencies of the French language. One of these accounts for the failure to express common things with felicity in the epic or to describe objects by their proper name or even express them by a paraphrase (White, p.145). In his translation of Homer Pope can describe precisely where a dart pierced through the body of a hero, whereas a similar attempt would be thought burlesque in French. French writers are reduced to translating the ancients in prose and when, like La Motte, they dare translate in verse, they have to resort to considerable compression: La Motte's *Iliad* is a short abridgment of the Greek and even that is considered too long (White, pp.146-47). In other words, the epic must be short.

Voltaire suggests ways in which brevity can be achieved: an epic poet can, for instance, do very well without the help of anatomical descriptions. He draws a parallel between the conceptions of history which cardinal de Retz and the earl of Clarendon had and his own conception of the epic. Both historians drew complete pictures of those responsible for civil wars in their respective countries. But neither of them wasted time giving elaborate details of trivial matters. 'Why, then', asks Voltaire, 'should an *Epick* Poet, lie under the Necessity of elaborating those little Descriptions, which every noble Historian avoids with Care?' (White, p.147).

The fact that Voltaire warns against the pitfalls to be avoided in epic poetry does not necessarily mean that he lacks a positive approach. Far from it. At the very beginning of the *Essay*, he defines the epic poem as a discourse in verse dealing with some great, awe-inspiring and interesting action. The action can be simple or complex; the poem can have unity of place as in the *Iliad* or the hero can wander all over the world as in the *Odyssey*; it can have a single hero or a great many and their rank can vary considerably. Its action can be set virtually anywhere. Such a flexible definition of the epic does not, however, reveal Voltaire's real views on the subject. For he wanted the action of an epic to be constructed in the same way as the plot of a

113

tragedy. In his remarks on the first book of *La Henriade* in 1723, Voltaire stated that an epic poet is allowed to alter history, because 'il n'y a jamais eu d'événement dans le monde tellement disposé par le hasard qu'on en pût faire un poème épique sans y rien changer; qu'il ne faut pas avoir plus de scrupule dans le poème que dans la tragédie où l'on pousse beaucoup plus loin la liberté de ces changements' (Taylor, p.267). The action of the epic should develop progressively as in tragedy. All nations agree that a single and simple action which develops easily and gradually will please more than a confused mass of monstrous adventures (M.viii.309). Failure to do this in the *Aeneid* prevented Virgil from reaching perfection (White, p.99):

> if the natural Chain of Events in the *Æneid* could have allow'd *Virgil* to rise by Degrees in point of Sentiments and Grandeur, his Poem had been as unexceptionable as the Bounds of human Talent will permit. In short his Fault lies in having reach'd to the utmost Pitch of the Art in the middle of his Course.

What is above all required of the epic poet is that he must appeal strongly to the readers' passions. Inspired no doubt by the classical theorists of tragedy, Aristotle and Horace in particular, Voltaire writes that all hearts want to be moved and a poem, however perfect in other ways, would be dull anywhere any time if it did not move (M.viii. 309). Like the tragic dramatist, the poet is required to 'excite our Passions, to unfold the most intricate Recesses of the Soul, to describe the Customs of the Nations, to mark the Differences which arise in the Characters of Men, from the different Governments they are born under, in short to speak the Language of the polite World; than to play the Surgeon, the Carpenter or the Joiner, though never so elegantly' (White, p.147). The poem itself must have a structure which is very close to tragedy through the logical development of the story and the importance attached to psychological analysis.

How is the hero to behave in an epic? In Voltaire's conception, the epic hero must act and act with dignity. He must be concerned with great interests, exploits and passions. 'The Design of a Match between *Aeneas* and *Lavinia* unknown and indifferent to each other, and a War rais'd about a Stag wounded by a young Boy, could not indeed command our concern as well as the burning of *Troy*, and the Love of *Dido*' (White, pp.98-99). Voltaire approves of Tasso's art in transforming the excesses of the crusaders into exploits of a band of heroes delivering the holy land from the infidels. Yet there are episodes which are not very lofty. What was the great exploit reserved for Renaud (Rinaldo)? It was simply that he was destined by Providence to cut down a few old trees from a forest (M.viii. 341, 343). The hero should not be a typical warrior. In the *Essay*, Voltaire says that Aeneas had the misfortune to pass as a pious man and not as a great warrior. The fault, however, was not in Virgil: rather it lay in the wrong conception most people have of courage. They appear to be dazzled by the boisterous fury of a wild Hero and Aeneas was not of that type (White, p.98). In the French version, almost contradicting himself, Voltaire says that Aeneas behaves like a barbarian: he appears more like the ravisher of Lavinia than her avenger (M.viii.325).

In his remarks on Homer and other epic poets, Voltaire clearly indicated his attitude to the epic. Monotonous battles, digressions and lengthy speeches are to be avoided in this *grand* genre which can allow the supernatural provided it is used with restraint. If the gods and the devils interfere too much, they are likely to provoke laughter. Attention should therefore be focused on human characters: they alone are capable of moving us. The epic should as far as possible be modelled on tragedy and it should appeal to the emotions. Unlike tragedy, however, the epic must use imagery because it is essential to its beauty, but here too moderation is necessary. Does Voltaire judge Milton strictly in accordance with the rules of the ideal epic?

ii. *Milton's impact on Voltaire*

It may be misleading to suggest that by 1728 Milton was known in France almost entirely as a political writer,[6] although it is certain that his support for Cromwell in his political writings, particularly the *Pro populo anglicano defensio* (1651), roused intense dislike for Milton as an anti-royalist propagandist and for a while harmed his reputation as a poet. Bayle's *Dictionnaire historique et critique* (1697) briefly drew attention to Milton's poetry. The article 'Milton' mentioned two poems in blank verse, *Paradise lost* and *Paradise regained*:

Le premier passe pour l'un des plus beaux Ouvrages de Poésie que l'on ait vu en Anglois. Le fameux Poëte Dryden en a tiré une Piece de Théatre, qui fut

[6] John Martin Telleen, *Milton dans la littérature française* (Paris 1904), p.ii.

extrêmement applaudi. L'autre n'est pas si bon à beaucoup près; ce qui fit dire à quelques railleurs, que l'on trouve bien Milton dans le Paradis perdu, mais non pas dans le Paradis recouvré.

The 1715 edition of the *Dictionnaire* reproduced Dryden's famous lines on Milton. In his *Discours de la poésie épique* which he appended to *Les Aventures de Télémaque* (1717), A. M. Ramsay noted how one English poet (Milton) had managed to liberate English versification from the shackles of rhyme and had even started using inversions with some success (p.xlviii). The 'Dissertation sur la poésie anglaise' in the *Journal littéraire* devoted some ten pages to Milton in 1717. It showed admiration for him and in particular for Adam's self-analysis in *Paradise lost*: it was, however, mostly concerned with a plan of the poem.

It is a pity that Dennis is known in France in the eighteenth-century mainly as the author who was wittily pilloried by Pope in the *Dunciad*, for he also proved to be a pioneer in Milton criticism in England. His remarks on Milton's sublimity in *The Advancement and reformation of modern poetry* (1701) and *The Grounds of criticism in poetry* (1704) struck by their originality. Renown was, however, reserved for Addison and his papers on *Paradise lost* published in *The Spectator* in 1712 were to attract considerable attention both in England and in France. Four volumes of the first translation of *The Spectator* in French appeared in 1716-18. In the preface to volume iii the first translator referred to Addison's 'critique fine et judicieuse du célèbre poëme de Milton'. He nevertheless refrained from translating the papers on the ground that the poem had never been and would no doubt never be translated into French.[7] Subsequent translations of *The Spectator* remedied the omission of the first editions, but it was not until 1729 that a complete translation of the Addison papers on *Paradise lost* appeared in French. Since Voltaire showed a knowledge of the comments in the *Essay on epick poetry* he had probably read them in the original. *The Tatler*, on the other hand, was available in French by 1724. In his translation of an article for April 1709, the author expressed admiration for Milton's inimitable description of Adam in book viii and observed that nothing could be more beautiful than lines 268-91 which he translated rather freely (pp.116-17). In his translation of a

---

[7] see J. G. Robertson, 'Milton's fame on the continent', in *Proceedings of the British academy* (London 1908), iii. 323-24.

later article, however, the editor commented unfavourably in a footnote on Milton's metaphysics and his obscurity, though he continued to pay homage to *Paradise lost* for the parts where it is natural (pp.413-14).

One might therefore reasonably assume that by the time Voltaire published his *Essay on epick poetry* interest in Milton the poet had at least been kept alive if it had not been growing. It might also be appropriate to note that Voltaire's interest in Milton started about 1722 through his association with Bolingbroke,[8] although his interest in English literature generally may have been aroused earlier by his contact with lord Stair, the British ambassador in Paris. He praised the latter for having reconciled the British and French nations, and he consulted him on the question of suppressing rhyme in French poetry (see Best.D.80, 20 June 1719). However, it was left to Bolingbroke to introduce him to Milton and literary cosmopolitanism. It appears from a letter to Thieriot that Voltaire was delighted by his visit to the residence of the Bolingbrokes at La Source. He had found in Bolingbroke the epitome of English scholarship and French politeness: Bolingbroke knew Virgil as thoroughly as Milton, he liked English, French and Italian poetry and took into consideration their different geniuses (Best.D135, 4 December 1722). There is no doubt that Voltaire is here referring to Milton the epic poet and not the political writer. One can also presume that the same Bolingbroke drew Voltaire's attention to the edition of *Paradise lost* by susbscription, sponsored by lord Somers in 1688. Voltaire refers to it in the *Essay* (White, p.134).

There is a gap of about five years between Voltaire's first mention of Milton and the next references to him in the 'Small Leningrad notebook'. It was probably Bolingbroke who told Voltaire the lighthearted corkscrew story involving Cromwell, Milton and Waller. In this notebook, Voltaire also reproduced line 556 of *Paradise lost*,

---

[8] his interest was further stimulated by Young during the English visit. When in a private discussion at Bubb Dodington's house at Eastbury Voltaire attacked the episode of Sin and Death in *Paradise lost*, Young defended Milton and made the following epigram on Voltaire: 'Thou'rt so ingenious, profligate and thin / That thou thyself art Milton's Death and Sin.' Young added that Voltaire's objection to that fine episode was that death and sin were non-existent. In 1752 Young referred to this incident in the dedication to Voltaire at the beginning of *Sea piece*: 'On *Dorset* downs, when MILTON's page, / With *Sin* and *Death* provok'd thy rage, / Thy rage provok'd, who soothe with gentle rhymes?' See J. Spence, *Observations, anecdotes and characters of books and men*, ed. J. M. Osborn (Oxford 1966), i. 344-45; A.-M. Rousseau, *L'Angleterre et Voltaire*, i. 120-23.

book ii: he thus showed that he had begun to read Milton in the original. Much more significant for an appreciation of Milton's impact on Voltaire is the latter's *Essay on epick poetry*.

Before coming to the section on Milton in the *Essay*, Voltaire took care to mention that the battle of the fallen angels in *Paradise lost* would not succeed with the French. He was thus paving the way for his future attacks on this episode in the poem. The French reader, argues Voltaire, would also be surprised by many passages in Milton and as an example he quotes lines 59-64 of book i.[9] Voltaire had no doubt read English critical comments on these lines, for he says that they have in England more 'Partisans than Criticks' (p.86).[10] In the section on Virgil which owes some debt to Addison's comments, Voltaire discusses Virgil's possible sources as a preliminary to his remark that 'some People say *Milton* hath stolen his Poem from an *Italian* Stroller call'd *Andreino*' (p.97). One is tempted to construe Voltaire's statement as a denigration of Milton. This, however, is too severe a judgment on Voltaire who is writing primarily for an English public in 1727 and is therefore prepared to be lenient: he goes so far as to question the usefulness of 'such a trifling Enquiry'. He distinguishes between a person and his work. Whatever the critics may say about Virgil's indebtedness to various authors, the fact remains that his work is the 'Delight of all Ages'. It is implied that the same criterion applies to Milton. In the section on Milton, Voltaire explains how Milton obtained the idea of his epic when travelling through Florence[11] in his youth. Milton saw a play on the fall of man called *Adamo* by Andreini and he 'took from that ridiculous Trifle the first Hint of the noblest Work, which human Imagination hath ever attempted' (White, p.131).

In Voltaire's opinion, the great achievement of Milton was to have shown daring and produced original beauty by taking up the challenge

[9] these lines are accurately translated in the French version of the *Essay* where Voltaire is more severe towards the 'darkness visible'. It is very clear, he says, that the French would not tolerate such liberties. It is not enough that the licence of these expressions can be excused; French punctilio does not admit anything which has to be excused (M.viii. 311).

[10] in his *Remarks upon m. Voltaire's Essay on the epick poetry of the European nations* (London 1728), P. Rolli said that 'one must needs have no Poetical Notions at all, not to find out the beauty of the Epithet *visible* transfer'd from the Spectators Eyes to that *Darkness*' (p.21).

[11] under the influence of Rolli's *Remarks*, Voltaire changed Florence into Milan in the French version (see M.viii. 352).

of a subject which only lends itself to ridicule among the French, however much they respect the 'Mysteries of the Christian Religion' (White, p.132). Milton treated his subject without bombast, described the gluttony and curiosity of Eve without flatness and brought 'Probability and Reason amidst the Hurry of imaginary Things belonging to another World'. To Voltaire, *Paradise lost* is 'the only Poem wherein are to be found in a perfect Degree that Uniformity which satisfies the Mind and that Variety which pleases the imagination' (pp.132-33).

Voltaire commends the 'sublime wisdom' Milton revealed in his description of God and is deeply impressed because God is not the tyrannical figure invented by Heathens, Jews and Christian priests: he is 'always a Creator, a Father, and a Judge, nor is his vengeance jarring with his Mercy, nor his Predeterminations repugnant to the Liberty of Man' (p.133). Such a picture of God elevates the soul and in this respect Milton is far above the ancient poets as the Christian religion is above heathen fables. For the last point, Voltaire is particularly indebted to *The Spectator* where Addison thought that Milton's 'survey of the whole Creation is . . . as much above that, in which *Virgil* has drawn his *Jupiter*, as the Christian Idea of the Supreme Being is more Rational and Sublime than that of the Heathens' (White, p.133, n.2).

If in 1727 Voltaire expressed genuine admiration for Milton's presentation of God, it was because five years earlier he had himself been seeking a god who was different from the one found in traditional Christianity. He revealed his intimate thoughts on God in a deist poem which he never intended to publish. This was the *Epître à Uranie*, also known as *Epître à Julie* or *Le Pour et le contre*. The *Epître* contained lines such as (M.ix.359-61):

> Viens, pénètre avec moi, d'un pas respectueux,
> Les profondeurs du sanctuaire
> Du Dieu qu'on nous annonce, et qu'on cache à nos yeux.
> Je veux aimer ce Dieu, je cherche en lui mon père:
> On me montre un tyran que nous devons haïr . . .
> Et quand, par sa fureur effaçant ses bienfaits,
> Ayant versé son sang pour expier nos crimes,
> Il nous punit de ceux que nous n'avons point faits!
> Ce Dieu poursuit encore, aveugle en sa colère,
> Sur ces derniers enfants l'erreur d'un premier père.

Voltaire finally made this famous remark in the poem (M.ix. 361):

Je ne suis pas chrétien; mais c'est pour t'aimer mieux.

Milton thus appeared to him to be proclaiming quite openly the virtues of a paternal God of love and mercy. Such a conception of God was close enough to Voltaire's own concception at the time. In the 1733 *Essai*, on the other hand, God strikes the reader as being most ineffective and lacking in foresight and power (M.viii.359).

Again drawing inspiration from Addison in *The Spectator* (White, p.133, n.3), Voltaire speaks highly of the treatment of Adam and Eve for which Milton is entitled to the unanimous admiration of mankind. In the love of the human characters, there is softness, tenderness and warmth without lasciviousness. Voltaire's enthusiasm for Adam and Eve is in keeping with his theoretical view that it is proper for an epic to stimulate interest in human characters. Milton 'soars not above human but above corrupt Nature, and as there is no Instance of such Love, there is none of such Poetry' (White, p.133).

In his critical appreciation of *Paradise lost* in the *Essay*, Voltaire used Addison for better and for worse, though never in a slavish fashion. He leaned on him[12] to condemn the frequent reference to heathen mythology, the digressions, and even mentioned his name to support the view that an author should not talk about himself in an epic, as Milton does. He did not, however, entirely agree with Addison who felt that shadowy figures such as Sin and Death, Sin and Chaos would have been intolerable if they were not allegorical (White, p.139). He argued that since a great part of the action lay in imaginary worlds, it must of necessity admit of imaginary beings. Sin springing out of the head of Satan seemed to Voltaire a beautiful allegory of pride. What he objected to was the incest between Satan and Sin and his objection was on the grounds of taste: 'Let such a Picture be never so beautifully drawn, let the Allegory be never so obvious, and so clear, still it will be intolerable, on the Account of its Foulness. That Complication of Horrors, that Mixture of Incest, that Heap of Monsters, that Loathsomeness so far fetch'd, cannot but shock a Reader of delicate Taste' (p.140). His attack was more severe on those parts that were not allegorical. He singled out the bridge built by Sin and Death, which,

[12] as he did on Dryden in the French version when he wanted to emphasize Milton's gross mistakes (M.viii. 359).

in his view, was useless: this time he relied on French critics (p.141).[13]

Unlike Addison 'whose Judgment seems either to guide, or to justify the Opinion of his Countrymen' (p.141), Voltaire criticised the war in heaven, again claiming that he was voicing the opinion of French critics. He was perhaps influenced by his friend, the francophile Chesterfield who had procured him the patronage of queen Carolien for his edition of *La Henriade*. Chesterfield afterwards spoke highly of Voltaire's epic to his son and at the same time made ironical remarks about Milton and *Paradise lost*: he pretended that he did not know much about angels and devils and their speeches.[14] So Voltaire in his turn objected to the lengthy descriptions of the angels and their equally long speeches. This seemed to him to be an injudicious imitation of Homer and some of the war episodes even had a Rabelaisian flavour. By and large Voltaire had set the tone for many French critics in the eighteenth century. His review of *Paradise lost* was well-balanced and it concluded with the remark that 'the severest Critick must however confess there are Perfections enough in *Milton*, to atone for all his Defects' (p.143).

Since Voltaire himself says in the 'Advertisement' to the *Essay* that he considers this work as a kind of preface or introduction to *La Henriade*, it might be appropriate to discover what impact *Paradise lost* had on the epic that was being reedited in England at the time of the *Essay*. This impact is not likely to be very great since *La Ligue* – known as *La Henriade* as from mid-1724 (Taylor, p.60) – was written before Voltaire had made a serious study of *Paradise lost*.[15] It can, on the other hand, be traced whenever the text of *La Henriade* shows significant changes from previous editions.

In this connection, the allusions to heathen gods in *La Henriade* may provide some indication.[16] In book v, for instance, there is a description of Moloch's nefarious activities (Taylor, p.473, ll. 87-90):

[13] Voltaire also argues that Pandemonium would have been "entirely disapprov'd of by Criticks like Boyleau and Racine" (White, p.138).

[14] see the *Memoirs of his life* by dr Maty in Chesterfield's *Miscellaneous works* (London 1779), i. 83; cf. above, p.13.

[15] for a different view see Jean Gillet, *Le Paradis perdu dans la littérature française, de Voltaire à Chateaubriand* (Paris 1975), p.43.

[16] see Gillet, p.45. As has been noted, in 1728 Voltaire, in accordance with a 'spirit of liberty' proclaimed in the dedication to the queen of England, replaced the 1723 invocation to the pagan Muse by one to Truth (book i, l.7).

C'est lui qui dans Raba, sur les bords de l'Arnon,
Guidait les descendants du malheureux Ammon,
Quand à Moloch, leur dieu, des mères gémissantes
Offraient de leurs enfants les entrailles fumantes.

In 1723, the text had the following lines (Taylor, p.472 n., ll. 85-90):

Cet enfant de la nuit, fécond en artifices,
Sait ternir les vertus, sait embellir les vices,
Sait donner, par l'éclat de ses pinceaux trompeurs,
Aux forfaits les plus grands les plus nobles couleurs.
C'est lui qui, sous la cendre et couvert du cilice,
Saintement aux mortels enseignent l'injustice.

In an explanatory note on line 87, in the 1730 edition of *La Henriade*, Voltaire wrote that this was the land of the Ammonites who threw their children into flames, to the sound of drums and trumpets, in honour of the divinity, which they adored under the name of Moloch (Taylor, p.488).

It is not unlikely that Voltaire was thinking of Milton's account of Moloch in *Paradise lost* book i, for there is a close resemblance between their accounts. This is how Milton described Moloch (ll. 392-96):

First, Moloch, horrid king, besmeared with blood
Of human sacrifice, and parents' tears,
Though, for the noise of drums and timbrels loud,
Their children's cries unheard, that passed through fire
To his grim idol.

It is more likely that the following lines describing Chaos, which did not exist in 1723 but were added to book vii of *La Henriade* in 1737 are modelled on *Paradise lost* (Taylor, p.517, ll. 127-37):

Henri dans ce moment, d'un vol précipité,
Est par un tourbillon dans l'espace emporté
Vers un séjour informe, aride, affreux, sauvage,
De l'antique chaos abominable image,
Impénétrable aux traits de ces soleils brillants,
Chefs-d'œuvre du Très-Haut, comme lui bienfaisants.
Sur cette terre horrible, et des anges haïe,
Dieu n'a point répandu le germe de la vie.
La Mort, l'affreuse Mort, et la Confusion,
Y semblent établir leur domination.
Quelles clameurs, ô Dieu! quels cris épouvantables!

From 1728, Voltaire follows Milton and places his Chaos between the world above and hell. As he explains in a note in 1730 (Taylor, p.538), hell does not have to be at the centre of the earth. This is what he had done in 1723 when he followed Virgilian precedents. Line 144 of the text then read: 'L'un et l'autre à ces mots descendent aux enfers.' From 1728 it reads: 'Ils marchent aussitôt aux portes des enfers.'

In book ii, lines 891-916, of *Paradise lost*, Satan and Sin are suddenly confronted by

> The secrets of the hoary deep, a dark
> Illimitable ocean, without bound,
> Without dimension; where length, breadth, and highth,
> And time, and place, are lost; where eldest Night
> And Chaos, ancestors of Nature, hold
> Eternal anarchy, amidst the noise
> Of endless wars, and by confusion stand . . .
> . . . Into this wild Abyss,
> The womb of Nature, and perhaps her grave,
> Of neither sea, nor shore, nor air, nor fire,
> But all these in their pregnant causes mixed
> Confusedly, and which thus must ever fight,
> Unless the Almighty Maker them ordain
> His dark materials to create more worlds.

Professor Taylor points out the likelihood of Voltaire's indebtedness to Milton partly because he used the adjective 'abominable' frequently to describe the allegory of Sin and Death, as for example in the *Essai sur la poésie épique* (M.viii. 358). Milton's impact on Voltaire is also to be sought in the transformation of the material found in *Paradise lost*. In the above passage, Milton argues that the elements forming part of the realm of Chaos must engage in an incessant battle unless God orders them to create more worlds. This is perhaps what becomes in *La Henriade*: 'Dieu n'a point répandu le germe de la vie.'

Voltaire's interest in Milton was to last throughout his literary career. In 1728 he began the translation of the *Essay on epick poetry* for the *Almanach royal*. In his letter to Thieriot written from England (Best.D333, 2 May 1728), Voltaire remarked in English that his

little pamphlet could not succeed in France without being dressed in quite another manner. What j say of Milton cannot be understood by the french unless j give a fuller notion of that author. The stile besides is after the english fashion, so many similes, so many things which appear but easy and familiar here, would seem to low to yr wits of Paris.

It may well be that Voltaire's original intention was to bring about just a few changes dealing mainly with style, to the French version. What is certain is that when the *Essai sur la poésie épique* appeared in 1733, the changes went well beyond stylistic considerations. A number of factors[17] would help to explain the difference in approach to Milton. Moreover, Voltaire himself made a distinction between the two essays. In another letter he sent to Thieriot, he wrote that the 'english essay was but the sketch of a very serious work . . . in french' (Best.D336, 25 June 1728).

At the very time that Voltaire was writing to Thieriot and telling him that he disapproved of Desfontaines's intention of translating his English essay, Desfontaines's inaccurate version, the *Essay sur la poésie épique*, had appeared in Paris. Moreover *La Henriade's* popularity in England was limited to the English francophiles who had subscribed to the great edition; the majority of English readers did not like it and preferred *Paradise lost*.[18] In France, the *Journal de Trévoux* published in June 1731 an anonymous account of *La Henriade* under the title 'Lettre critique sur le poëme de m. de Voltaire'. This review is interesting, for it provides a useful indication of the reception Voltaire's epic had among the French and draws a parallel between Voltaire and Milton, to the advantage of the Englishman. It saw little merit in *La Henriade* and thought it remarkable that Milton, whom it described as a Calvinist, should speak in his admirable *Paradise lost* of free will and grace in a manner that was both 'serrée & catholique' while Voltaire who professed to be a Catholic spoke only like the Calvinists. It suggested that Voltaire was perhaps trying to win popularity with some other Christian sect, and denounced the sectarian tendency of a writer who was trying to achieve immortality. Its final

---

[17] among these must be included Dupré de St Maur's translation of *Paradise lost* in 1729 (it ran into several editions in the century and assured the author's election to the Académie française in 1733) and Rolli's *Remarks*, the aim of which was to censure Voltaire for 'condemning many of the sublimest Places of the divine English poem'. Constantin de Magny in the *Dissertation critique sur le Paradis perdu* (1729) and Bernard Routh in the *Lettres critiques sur le Paradis perdu et reconquis de Milton* (1731) tried to check Milton's progress in France, but they only succeeded in stimulating interest in him (see Robertson, p.327). C. Rollin gave a balanced commentary on *Paradise lost* in his *Traité des études* (1730).

[18] see Taylor, pp.76-77.

advice was that Voltaire should worship the English a little less (Best.D410). A certain La Bruyère had a reply published in the *Journal* in October 1731. He congratulated Voltaire on having avoided Milton's technique of making the angels fight with cannon, condemned the conceits and false ideas in Milton and rejected the current tendency of raising the status of Fénelon's *Télémaque* to that of an epic (Best. D436).[19] The elevated status of *Télémaque* was a sore point with Voltaire. He referred to it in the conclusion to the *Essai sur la poésie épique* where he described it as a moral novel. He claimed that even if *Télémaque* were written in beautiful verse, it would be a dull poem because of its long discourses on politics and economics (M.viii. 361).

These circumstances perhaps explain why the emphasis henceforth was not so much on the beauties of Milton's poetry as on its defects. In the *Stances sur les poètes épiques*, addressed to mme Du Châtelet in 1731, Voltaire devoted the first three stanzas to a rapid enumeration of the beauties and defects to be found in Homer, Virgil and Tasso. The last two stanzas were about Milton and himself (M.viii. 505-506):

> Milton, plus sublime qu'eux tous,
> A des beautés moins agréables;
> Il semble chanter pour les fous,
> Pour les anges, et pour les diables.
>
> Après Milton, après le Tasse,
> Parler de moi serait trop fort;
> Et j'attendrai que je sois mort,
> Pour apprendre quelle est ma place.[20]

Some of the significant changes which appear in the *Essai sur la poésie épique* can also be accounted for by Voltaire's desire to contribute something original to the Milton section[21], and at the same time to reduce the merit of Dupré de St Maur's work on Milton. He claims to have discovered some details in Milton's biography that had been omitted in Dupré's version of Fenton's *Life of Milton* and were unknown to the public. This is why he expands the passage on the

[19] on the assumption that *Télémaque* could be considered an epic, the *Journal littéraire* thought that the French had produced something 'de plus estimable dans le genre héroïque' ('Dissertation sur la poésie anglaise', pp.177-78).

[20] the last stanza was reproduced in a letter published in the *Mercure* where Voltaire says that he is not merely Milton's biographer (Best.D424, ? 10 August 1731).

[21] see Gillet, pp.58-59.

Adamo which he had briefly mentioned in the English text. He now says that Milton first planned to make a tragedy out of Andreini's comedy, that he had even written an act and a half. Voltaire mentions as the source of his information some men of letters: they in turn had obtained it from Milton's daughter who died while he was in England (M.viii.353).[22] Voltaire is so keen to dispel the impression that he was relying too much on secondary sources that he tries to be precise: he adds that Milton's tragedy began with Satan's monologue in book iv, which he translates. While Milton was working on this tragedy, he expanded his ideas and the epic took shape.

Pope doubted whether Milton ever intended to write a tragedy on the fall of man. He was wrong. For the Cambridge manuscript of *Paradise lost* shows that Milton planned to write a drama or even an opera out of the material. There is no record of performances of *Adamo* during 1638-39, but Milton might have seen a copy of the printed version (see J. Spence, *Anecdotes*, ed. J. M. Osborn, i. 198).

Other changes in the *Essai* aim at diminishing Milton and his work. Voltaire took delight in describing Milton's political and polemical activities which Fenton in his biography and Dupré de St Maur in his translation had passed over. By stressing the fact that Milton used his pen to defend regicide, Voltaire revived the old antipathy the French had to Cromwell's secretary. The reference to Milton's polemics with Claude Saumaise, the French classical scholar who was commissioned by Charles ii to write the *Defensio regia* (1649) against the English regicide government, enabled Voltaire to laugh at the man whom the English considered to be a divine poet, but who was just a very bad prose writer (M.viii. 355).[23]

In the French edition some of the characters of *Paradise lost* are made to appear as ridiculous as the author. Even Adam does not escape censure: rather like the Memnon of Voltaire's *conte*, he is deceived by the devil and his wife in one day (M.viii.306). Voltaire claims that critical opinion in France agrees unanimously that Satan speaks too

[22] Voltaire's *Essay* was the first work to have mentioned an Italian source of *Paradise lost*. A number of English writers became indebted to Voltaire in their investigation of Milton's sources. See A.-M. Rousseau, *L'Angleterre et Voltaire*, ii. 531-34.

[23] Voltaire had a further opportunity of denigrating Milton in the section on Saumaise in the *Siècle de Louis XIV*. Milton – the author of a 'poème barbare, quelquefois sublime, sur la pomme d'Adam, et le modèle de tous les poèmes barbares tirés de l'Ancien Testament' – refuted Saumaise in the same way as a wild beast fights against a savage (M.xiv. 133).

often and for too long on the same subject.[24] The episode of Sin and Death in book ii of *Paradise lost* which was viewed with sympathy and understanding in the English version now appears completely grotesque. So does the war in heaven. Voltaire, placing himself in the position of a Christian reader, says that one wants to laugh at the detailed descriptions of Nisroth, Moloch and Abdiel. The laughter gains in momentum 'lorsque je ne sais quel ange a coupé en deux je ne sais quel diable, les deux parties du diable se réunissent dans le moment' (M.viii. 359). Voltaire's summary of the speech of Sin (*Paradise lost*, ll. 727-810) is pure caricature. The *Essai* represents Voltaire's first[25] attempt to turn the seriousness of the epic into the mock heroic, to take up the challenge which he had thrown in the original version where he stated: 'Methinks the true Criterion for discerning what is really ridiculous in an Epick Poem, is to examine if the same thing would not fit exactly the Mock heroick' (White, p.139). His last word on *Paradise lost* in the *Essai*, which purports to represent the view of a majority of French critics, is that it is more strange than natural, more imaginative than graceful and its subject does not appear to be meant for man.[26]

Although *Paradise lost* had only a limited influence on Voltaire the epic poet, it does not necessarily mean that it left him indifferent. After 1733, it is worth investigating whether Milton's impact is absent in genres having little or no connection with the epic proper. Boileau may well have sustained Voltaire throughout the latter's long literary career and it is true that no French writer would choose to ignore Boileau's mock heroic poem *Le Lutrin*. But *Paradise lost* proved equally useful to Voltaire for polemical purposes. Had not Dryden and Pope, whose works he knew so well, shown Voltaire the way by consciously parodying the great English epic? With such good precedents[27], Voltaire repeatedly used *Paradise lost* to satirise

[24] Voltaire stood by what he said here. Many years later when he wrote to George Gray, the author of *A Turkish tale*, a parody of *Paradise lost* in five books, he said he preferred the servant Vixen to a boring angel Gabriel and an ugly devil who always repeated the same story (Best.D16511, 13 July 1770).

[25] see D. Williams, *Voltaire: literary critic*, p.232 and below p.144.

[26] Voltaire conceded that there were beauties of detail in Milton. In his letter to Vernet, for instance, he said that without such beauties Virgil and Chapelain, Racine and Campistron would be equals. So would Milton and John Ogilby, a seventeenth-century printer who translated Virgil and Homer (Best.D653, 14 September 1733).

[27] Voltaire was also familiar with the burlesque poem, *The Splendid shilling*, by John Philips (1676-1709). He referred to Philips in his *conte*, *Les Oreilles du comte de Chesterfield*.

people and institutions. The satirical poem *La Crépinade* (1736) attempts to prove that Satan created J. B. Rousseau, one of Voltaire's earliest enemies, in his own likeness. Rousseau was described as an 'animal dont l'âme et la figure / Fût à tel point au rebours de la nature' that the most stupid person recognized in him a portrait of the devil. Voltaire concluded his satire with the following advice (M.x. 79):

> Monsieur Satan, lorsque vous voudrez faire
> Quelque bon tour au chétif genre humain,
> Prenez-vous-y par un autre chemin.
> Ce n'est le tout d'envoyer son semblable
> Pour nous tenter: Crépin, votre féal,
> Vous servant trop, vous a servi fort mal:
> Pour nous damner, rendez le vice aimable.

In the same year the optimist writer, fresh from his denunciation of Pascal's pessimism in the *Lettres philosophiques*, wished to resume his sarcasm at the expense of an austere life and austere moralists such as Fénelon. He therefore nicknamed him 'Monsieur du Télémaque' in his poem *Le Mondain* (M.x.87). In his attack he found it appropriate to parody Milton when he wrote (M.x.85):

> Mon cher Adam, mon gourmand, mon bon père,
> Que faisais-tu dans les jardins d'Eden?
> Travaillais-tu pour ce sot genre humain?
> Caressais-tu madame Eve, ma mère?
> Avouez-moi que vous aviez tous deux
> Les ongles longs, un peu noirs et crasseux,
> La chevelure un peu mal ordonnée,
> Le teint bruni, la peau bise et tannée.
> Sans propreté l'amour le plus heureux
> N'est plus amour, c'est un besoin honteux.
> Bientôt lassés de leur belle aventure,
> Dessous un chêne ils soupent galamment
> Avec de l'eau, du millet, et du gland;
> Le repas fait, ils dorment sur la dure:
> Voilà l'état de la pure nature.

Milton had painted a completely different picture of Adam and Eve in *Paradise lost*. Milton's elegant lines run as follows (book iv, ll. 301-306)

> ... and Hyacinthin Locks
> Round from his parted forelock manly hung

Clustring, but not beneath his shoulders broad:
Shee as a vail down to the slender waste
Her unadorned golden tresses wore
Dissheveld.

Even more grotesque than the anti-heroic suggestion that Adam
and Eve must have had dirty finger-nails and dishevelled hair is the
animal behaviour attributed to the human pair. Voltaire's imagination
ran riot: it turned Adam and Eve into monkeys, as is evident from a
variant to these lines written in 1737 (M.x. 85):

Mon cher Adam, mon gourmand, mon bon père,
Je crois te voir, dans un recoin d'Eden,
Grossièrement forger le genre humain,
En secouant[28] madame Eve, ma mère:
Deux singes verts, deux chèvres pieds fourchus,
Sont moins hideux au pied de leur feuillée.
Par le soleil votre face hâlée,
Vos bras velus, votre main écaillée,
Vos ongles longs, crasseux, noirs, et crochus,
Votre peau bise, endurcie, et brûlée,
Sont les attraits, sont les charmes flatteurs,
Dont l'assemblage attire vos ardeurs.
Bientôt lassés, . . .

Le Mondain must likewise have taught Voltaire how to degrade
Milton's Satan in whom he had found touches of the sublime in the
Essays. For in book v of *La Pucelle*, nothing is left of the awe-inspiring
Satan: he has simply become 'le roi cornu de la huaille noire'. *Le
Mondain* ended on this light-hearted note (M.x.88):

C'est bien en vain que, par l'orgueil séduits,
Huet, Calmet, dans leur savante audace,
Du paradis ont recherché la place:
Le paradis terrestre est où je suis.

The theme of earthly paradise was of great interest to eighteenth-
century writers. Mme A. M. Du Bocage, for example, imitated Milton's
Paradise lost in her poem entitled *Le Paradis terrestre* which won the
prize of the Rouen academy in 1748. Before dedicating the following
lines to her (M.x.543-44):

[28] Voltaire at first wrote 'en secouant', then 'en tourmentant' before finally settling
for 'caressais-tu'. See his letter to d'Argens (Best.D1277, 2 February 1737).

129

En vain Milton, dont vous suivez les traces,
Peint l'âge d'or comme un songe effacé;
Dans vos écrits, embellis par les Grâces,
On croit revoir un temps trop tôt passé.
Vivre avec vous dans le temple des muses,
Lire vos vers, et les voir applaudis,
Malgré l'enfer, le serpent et ses ruses,
Charmante Eglé, voilà le *Paradis*.

Voltaire wrote to mme Du Bocage to say that she would have to put up with 'quelque grande diable d'ode fort ennuyeuse où je mettrai à vos pieds les Sapho, les Milton et les amours' (Best.D3991, 21 August 1749). On 12 October, Voltaire told her that the late mme Du Châtelet and he had together read 'her Milton' with the English text. (Best. D4034).

As he had shared with mme Du Châtelet an idyllic existence which was at the same time highly conducive to intellectual pursuits of a varied kind,[29] it was natural that Voltaire should have looked on Cirey as an earthly paradise.[30] It is also likely that in the last line of *Le Mondain* Voltaire was thinking of Satan's speech after his survey of the scene in hell. For Satan proclaimed (*Paradise lost*, book ii, ll. 254-55):

The mind is its own place, and in itself
Can make a Heav'n of Hell, a Hell of Heav'n.

There are other parts of *Paradise lost* on the subject of heaven and hell which could have evoked a response from Voltaire. In book ii, for instance, Mammon advertised the excellence of Hell when he observed (ll. 270-73):

[29] mme Du Châtelet must have stimulated Voltaire not only in his scientific, but also in his Miltonic studies. For in the *Eloge historique de mme Du Châtelet* (1752), Voltaire acknowledged that Tasso and Milton were familiar to her as well as Virgil (M.xxiii. 520). In this respect, mme Du Châtelet's role could be regarded as complementary to the formative influence of Bolingbroke in the early 1720s. Both were highly cultured.

[30] in his *Réponse à m. de Formont*, written in 1735 on behalf of mme Du Châtelet, in which he invited Formont to Cirey, Voltaire described Cirey as a 'véritable Eden' (M.x. 506). In this poem, Voltaire remains firmly attached to the earth. He seems to regret the fact that he cannot soar like Milton and Newton. In the sixth of the *Discours en vers* (1737) he writes: 'Pour moi, loin des cités, sur les bords du Permesse / Je suivais la nature, et cherchais la sagesse; / Et des bords de la sphère où s'emporta Milton, / Et de ceux de l'abîme où pénétra Newton, / Je les voyais franchir leur carrière infinie' (M.ix. 420).

... This Desart soile
Wants not her hidd'n lustre, Gemms and Gold;
Nor want we skill or art, from whence to raise
Magnificence; and what can Heav'n shew more?

Milton remains constantly in Voltaire's thoughts in the late 1730s. Voltaire must have discussed the English poet with his relative Etienne Mignot de Montigny, for Montigny expressed admiration for the astounding energy to be found in Pope and Milton, in the latter particularly. Montigny said that Voltaire himself had spoken of that energy (Best.D1443, 4 February 1738). After his serious studies in Newton, Voltaire relaxed by reading Milton. At any rate, this is what he told his correspondent Formont (Best.D1652, 11 November 1738). In this period, Voltaire seemed to make a distinction between a scientific work and one he claimed to be of pure imagination, by setting Newton against Milton. In his letter to Helvétius, he referred to his friend's mention of Milton to him. He had no doubt that his imagination would be as fertile as Milton's, but it would also be more pleasant and more controlled. Voltaire regretted that Helvétius's knowledge of Milton was restricted to his reading of the *Essai*, the unhappy rendering of the English version, as he put it (Best.D1997, 29 April 1739).

It was for good reasons that Voltaire took such an interest in the various attempts of other writers on the subject of temptation and the fall of man in plays. Apart from those of Andreini and Milton himself, there was Dryden's opera *The State of innocence and fall of man*, composed in 1673, but published only in 1677, three years after Milton's death. Voltaire probably learnt of the existence of Dryden's adaptation of *Paradise lost* from Bayle's *Dictionnaire* and it was also mentioned by *Le Babillard* in 1724 (i. 116-17). Judging by some of the comments made in the *Essay on epick poetry*, Voltaire must also have known the 'Author's apology for heroic poetry and poetic licence' prefaced to Dryden's opera, although he did not share Dryden's views on the place of 'fustian' in the epic. The ageing Milton had, according to Aubrey, given Dryden 'leave to tag his verses' that is, put them into rhyme.

Now came Voltaire's turn to attempt a dramatisation of the theme of temptation. It is possible that Milton's tragedy of *Samson agonistes* may have prompted Voltaire to write his libretto of *Samson* in 1731 at a time when he had become deeply immersed in Milton. But there are significant differences in the two writers' treatment of the biblical theme. Milton's Delilah, for example, is closer to the deceitful character of the Bible than the Dalila of Voltaire's opera, who has been transformed into a tragic heroine.[31]

With increasing confidence Voltaire dealt with the fall of man in *Pandore*. When he wrote to Berger, he spoke of mme d'Aiguillon's comment that *Pandore* was an opera 'à la Milton' (Best.D2219, *c.* 4 June 1740). He had no doubt read Milton's description of Eve (*Paradise lost*, book iv, ll. 714-19):

> More lovely than *Pandora*, whom the Gods
> Endowd with all thir gifts, and O too like
> In sad event, when to the unwiser Son
> Of *Japhet* brought by *Hermes*, she ensnar'd
> Mankind with her faire looks, to be aveng'd
> On him who had stole *Joves* authentic fire.

There are a number of similarities between *Pandore* and *Paradise lost*. In act i, scene ii of the opera, the countryside setting gives way to chaos and the infernal gods make the following sinister suggestion in connection with the destruction of man (M.iii. 577):

> Nous attendons
> Dans nos gouffres profonds
> La race faible et criminelle
> Qui n'est pas née encore, et que nous haïssons.

This is precisely the advice given by Beelzebub to the assembly of the fallen angels in hell in *Paradise lost*, where he says (book ii, ll. 345-58):

> ... There is a place
> (If ancient and prophetic fame in Heav'n
> Err not) another World, the happy seat
> Of some new Race called *Man*, about this time
> To be created like to us ...
> Thither let us bend all our thoughts, to learn
> What creatures there inhabit, of what mould,
> Or substance, how endu'd, and what thir Power,
> And where thir weakness, how attempted best,
> By force or suttlety.

[31] see W. H. Barber, 'Voltaire at Cirey: art and thought', *Studies in eighteenth-century French literature*, eds J. H. Fox *et al.* (Exeter 1975), pp.5-6.

The Jupiter of *Pandore* plays the role of Pandore's seducer in act III and in some respects resembles Eve's tempter in *Paradise lost*. Jupiter tries to flatter Pandore and bids her enjoy divinity and immortality. But he is rebuffed and denounced as a jealous tyrant and the temptation succeeds only in the last act when Némésis disguised as Mercure deceives her in the name of Prométhée.[32] According to the stage directions, when Pandore opens the box, night spreads over the theatre and a subterranean noise is heard. This is Voltaire's transformation, in a minor key, of the cosmic repercussions which follow Eve's eating of the apple in *Paradise lost*. In Milton's poem (book ix, ll. 782-84):

> Earth felt the wound, and Nature from her seat
> Sighing through all her Works gave signs of woe,
> That all was lost.

Prométhée does not at first see Pandore; he sees only that

> ... de l'infernale rive
> Les monstres déchaînés volent dans ces climats.
> (M.iii. 598)

He learns that death has made itself a passage on Earth. Voltaire is recapitulating briefly what happens in book x of *Paradise lost*. Sin tells Death (ll. 254-60):

> ... let us try
> ... to found a path
> Over this Main from Hell to that new World
> Where Satan now prevailes, a Monument
> Of merit high to all th'infernal Host,
> Easing their passage hence.

Satan rejoices at the sight of the bridge that paves the way between Hell and Earth. And God says (ll. 616-17):

> With what heat these Dogs of Hell advance
> To waste and havoc yonder World.

---

[32] Voltaire told d'Argental that he might not like the scene which shows Mercure's deceit in persuading Pandore to open the box, but Mercure's function was that of the serpent who persuaded Eve. If Eve had eaten simply out of greed, the play would have been cold, but the speech with the serpent warms up the story (Best.D2158, 2 February 1740). To the same correspondent, Voltaire talked of 'Pandore-Eve' two months later (Best.D2194, 1 April 1740).

In fact, Voltaire's *Pandore* borrows heavily, though in less detail, from Milton's war in heaven.

Not long after composing *Pandore*, Voltaire took the opportunity of using his knowledge of *Paradise lost* in a flattering letter he sent Frederick (Best.D2573, 22 December 1741). He showed the great distance that separated Frederick both in intellect and in rank from the millions of two-legged, featherless animals who people the earth. To make his point he reproduced what he described as a fine line from Milton: 'Amongst unequals no society.' He must have been quoting Adam's speech to Raphael from memory, for the lines actually read (book viii, ll. 383-84):

> Among unequals what societie
> Can sort, what harmonie or true delight.

In the same year, Voltaire wrote a poem entitled *Sur les disputes en métaphysique* which reads thus (M.x.526):

> Tels, dans l'amas brillant des rêves de Milton,
> On voit les habitants du brûlant Phlégéton,
> Entourés de torrents de bitume et de flamme,
> Raisonner sur l'essence, argumenter sur l'âme,
> Sonder les profondeurs de la fatalité,
> Et de la prévoyance et de la liberté.
> Ils creusent vainement dans cet abîme immense.

It illustrates how Voltaire adapts part of book ii of *Paradise lost* where Milton describes the activities of the fallen angels after the debate in Pandemonium. At lines 580-81, Milton refers to 'fierce *Phlegeton* / whose waves of torrent fire inflame with rage'. Some of the angels who retire on a hill (ll. 558-61):

> In thoughts more elevate, and reason'd high
> Of Providence, Foreknowledge, Will, and Fate,
> Fixt Fate, free will, foreknowledge absolute,
> And found no end, in wondring mazes lost.

To appreciate Voltaire's skill in the exploitation of this poem,[33] it is to the *Courte réponse aux longs discours d'un docteur allemand*

---

[33] the article 'Epopée' (1771) of the *Questions sur l'encyclopédie* again exploited the same lines. Milton is attacked because the most thorny problems of the most tiresome scholasticism are discussed in the very terms of the schoolmen (M.xviii. 582).

(1744) that one must refer. Martin Kahle, professor of philosophy at Göttingen and prominent among Wolff's disciples, had in his *Vergleichung* shown how absurd Voltaire's interpretation of pre-established harmony was in the *Métaphysique de Newton*. Instead of replying to Kahle in the *Courte réponse*, Voltaire shuns the specific issues raised and prefers to launch into a general attack on metaphysics. He, *inter alia*, invents a doctor who pontificates and proclaims nonsensical opinions in a loud voice. The doctor says that it has recently been discovered that what exists is possible, and that the essence of things does not change (M.xxiii.195). Voltaire pounces upon the word 'essence' and uses it out of context to make fun of the Schoolmen: 'Ah! plût à Dieu que l'essence des docteurs changeât.'

He finds it most appropriate to conclude the discussion on grounds that are familiar to him. However remote from everyday experience the physical setting of Milton's *Paradise lost* may be, for him it is a kind of *terra cognita*. In order to prove how futile metaphysics is, he establishes a parallel between the metaphysicians and the fallen angels who waste their time in endless speculation. The satire is apparently directed against the whole of mankind. Men are transformed into the fallen angels, 'ces diables que Milton nous représente dévorés d'ennui, de rage, d'inquiétude, de douleur, et raisonnant encore sur la métaphysique au milieu de leurs tourments' (M.xxiii.196). Voltaire does not merely suggest the resemblance: he takes some pains to reproduce the French version he had given of Milton's poetry in *Sur les disputes en métaphysique* and to quote accurately some lines from the English text. He is therefore making better use of the poem *Sur les disputes en métaphysique* by merging it with a piece of personal polemics. The reference to those who argue about being and the soul makes it clear that it is the schoolmen who are being attacked and not mankind in general. It may be pointed out that Voltaire's version is a fairly accurate rendering of lines 558-61 of book ii of *Paradise lost*.

It is true that some of Voltaire's harsh criticisms of Milton can be traced back to the *Essai sur la poésie épique* and that he nevertheless gave a hint to Titon Du Tillet of *La Henriade's* weakness when compared with the poems of Tasso and Milton. Titon Du Tillet proposed to include Voltaire in the 1755 supplement of his work, *Le Parnasse françois*, normally reserved for deceased writers. But Voltaire declined the honour, saying that his tragedies were of little account and that 'even the *Henriade* – the only work by which I am at all known among foreigners – is hardly a poem with which France can identify itself in order to place it by the side of Tasso and Milton'.[34]

Yet a hardening of Voltaire's attitude to Milton can be detected from the 1750s onwards. Presumably the same non-literary factors that modified his judgment of Shakespeare may equally be invoked to explain the change with regard to Milton. Voltaire is not, however, systematically opposed to all English writers from a particular period. He singles out for special treatment the two writers who have enjoyed the highest reputation in the world: Shakespeare and Milton. In *Le Siècle de Louis XIV*, for instance, he states in his review of Europe's achievements that he will not repeat what he had already said elsewhere about Milton. He however does just that while suggesting that the attacks have really been made by other critics. He again uses the caricatural technique of the *Essai sur la poésie épique*: he now mixes a passage from *Paradise lost*, book ii, ll. 940-42, where Milton describes the conflict of the four elements, with a passage from book x, ll. 272-78 where Death is likened to 'ravenous fowl lur'd with scent of living carcasses'. He concludes his long list of Milton's defects with the remark that Milton remains England's glory and admiration. The English place Milton above Dante, but this is no compliment to Milton since Dante's imagination is even more bizarre than his. The section on Milton seems heavily weighted against the English poet. The denigration stands out more conspicuously amidst the lavish praise showered on Addison and Pope in the same section (M.xiv.560). The 'Catalogue des écrivains français' of this work quoted Nicolas Gédoin, translator of Quintilian, who apparently thought that *Paradise lost* was 'un poème barbare et d'un fanatisme sombre et dégoûtant, dans lequel le diable hurle sans cesse contre le Messie' (M.xiv.76). Voltaire's attitude to Milton in the *Lettres philosophiques* is quite revealing. Milton is only indirectly referred to in the 1730s in connection with the princess of Wales's generosity to his impoverished daughter (letter xi). When Voltaire does mention Milton's epic in the 1756 addition on *Hudibras*, in letter xxii, it is to elevate Butler at Milton's expense (Lanson, ii. 148).

One is not justified in concluding from Voltaire's adverse comments that Milton ceases to influence him from that period. On the contrary, the impact of *Paradise lost* is as strong as ever on him. It is to be

[34] Voltaire's letter is available only in the English translation; see Best.D5131 (1752/1753) and editorial notes.

sought in a different type of writing such as *La Pucelle*. The textual history of Voltaire's burlesque epic is complex on account of the long period of its composition, the various manuscripts that went into circulation and the pirated editions to which it gave rise, especially between 1755 and 1756. Begun in 1730, ten books had already been written by August 1735; fifteen books were published in the Louvain edition of 1755, while 'la capilotade', that is book xviii, was completed by January 1761 and published with the authorized edition of *La Pucelle* in 1762. 1773 saw the publication of a twenty-one book edition of the poem.[35] These factors explain the difficulty of treating *La Pucelle* as if it belonged to a particular year.

Voltaire's borrowings from *Paradise lost* can be grouped into two categories in *La Pucelle*: those to which he himself draws attention and those which he does not acknowledge. The episode of the poetry competition in book xvi between the French represented by Saint Denis and the English represented by Austin is of a different order. Saint Denis is really Voltaire and Austin is not unlike Milton by the nature of his wild imagination, which is also of Old Testament inspiration. As could be expected, the Englishman is booed by the celestial audience and Voltaire-Saint Denis, the champion of French taste and of New Testament poetry at its best, wins the prize.

In the first category of borrowing may be placed the description of the 'palais de la Sottise' in book iii (Vercruysse, p.300):

> Devers la lune où l'on tient que jadis
> Etait placé des fous le paradis,
> Sur les confins de cet abîme immense,
> Où le chaos, et l'Erèbe, et la nuit
> Avant les temps de l'univers produit
> Ont exercé leur aveugle puissance,
> Il est un vaste et caverneux séjour
> Peu caressé des doux rayons du jour.

Voltaire wrote a note in 1762 to the effect that the souls of fools and small children who had died without baptism were placed in this paradise or limbo situated near the moon and he added: 'Milton en parle; il fait passer le diable par le paradis des sots: *the paradise of fools.*'

[35] see Vercruysse, pp.13-22, 59-62.

In book xi Voltaire is critical of Milton even while using him to justify his account of the mock-heroic fight between Saint Georges and Saint Denis. He asks (Vercruysse, p.446):

> N'a-t-on pas vu chez cet Anglais, Milton[36]
> D'anges ailés toute une légion
> Rougir de sang les célestes campagnes,
> Jeter au nez quatre ou cinq cents montagnes,
> Et qui pis est avoir du gros canon?
> Or si jadis Michel et le Démon
> Se sont battus, messieurs Denis et Georges
> Pouvaient sans doute à plus forte raison
> Se rencontrer et se couper la gorge.

In a note added in 1762, Voltaire summarised the war between Michael and the fallen angels which is described in *Paradise lost*, book vi, lines 512-669. He mistook book v for book vi and concluded with the sarcastic remark that this was 'un des morceaux des plus vraisemblables de ce poème'.

It would appear from book xx of *La Pucelle* that Voltaire was thinking both of the Old Testament and of Milton when he described the attempted seduction of Jeanne by Satan in the form of a donkey. He left it to the 'abbé' Tritême to reflect on the power of the Devil such as it is illustrated in the popular story of the seduction of Eve. God's rival

> séduisit autrefois
> Ma chère mère un soir au coin d'un bois
> Dans son jardin. Ce serpent hypocrite
> Lui fit manger d'une pomme maudite,
> Même on prétend qu'il lui fit encore pis.
> (Vercruysse, pp.562-63)

This episode gave Voltaire the opportunity of attacking Milton in a footnote dating from 1762. In his opinion, the gloomy and fanatical Milton, the detestable secretary of the Rump, and detestable apologist of the assassination of Charles I can sing of hell, describe the devil disguised now as a cormorant, now as a toad and hold the devils reduced to the size of pygmies[37] in Pandemonium as much as he likes:

---

[36] in the 1755 and 1756 editions of *La Pucelle*, Voltaire refers to the 'wise' Milton.

[37] this idea exerted a strange fascination on Voltaire at the time. In his letter to J. R. Tronchin, Voltaire complains that the latter is laughing at him in wishing to reduce his

such disgusting, horrible and absurd fancies could appeal only to a few fanatics like himself. These 'facéties abominables' are repugnant to him. However fierce his denunciation of Milton, Voltaire still enjoyed describing with witty relish – almost in the same breath – the transformation of Satan into a donkey and his abortive, but nearly successful, attempt at seduction. It needed a combination of Saint Denis, Jeanne and Dunois to save the day.

At times Voltaire loudly proclaims his source – too loudly perhaps for him not to have an ulterior motive, which is to divert attention from the real source. In book xi Saint Georges utters words 'dans le vrai goût d'Homère'. In a footnote dated 1762, Voltaire goes to the length of saying that the entire speech to Denis is clearly imitated from Homer, but when it comes to Milton, he often maintains complete silence. In book v, for example, Gribourdon, who has been thrown into hell for his attempted rape of Jeanne, contemplates the scene (Vercruysse, p.348):

> Puis d'un air morne il jette au loin la vue
> Sur cette vaste et brûlante étendue,
> Séjour de feu qu'habitent pour jamais
> L'affreuse mort, les tourments, les forfaits.

There is no doubt that Voltaire is here parodying Milton in book i of *Paradise lost*, for as Satan looks at hell, his thoughts torment him and (ll. 56-62):

> . . . round he throws his baleful eyes
> That witness'd huge affliction and dismay
> Mix'd with obdurate pride and stedfast hate:
> At once as far as Angels kenn he views
> The dismal Situation waste and wilde,
> A Dungeon horrible, on all sides round
> As one great Furnace flam'd.

The same Voltaire had been impressed by this passage described as 'un des plus sublimes endroits du poème singulier de Milton': he had quoted and literally translated it in the *Essai sur la poésie épique* (viii. 310-11). At the time he recognized that the sublime could emanate from evil and that this type of the sublime suited the English imagination (viii. 353).

actors to a height of two and a half feet like Milton's devils who became pygmies (Best.D8425, 10 August 1759).

In book xii of *La Pucelle*, Voltaire describes the chaplain who follows Agnès and has designs on her (Vercruysse, p.450):

> Cet aumônier ardent, insatiable,
> Arrive aux murs du logis charitable.
> Ainsi qu'un loup qui mâche sous sa dent
> Le fin duvet d'un jeune agneau bêlant,
> Plein de l'ardeur d'achever sa curée,
> Va du bercail escalader l'entrée...
> ... l'aumônier ravisseur
> Allait cherchant les restes de sa joie
> Qu'on lui ravit lorsqu'il tenait sa proie.

The inspiration comes from a simile in book iv of *Paradise lost* where Milton describes Satan's journey uphill before he enters paradise. Satan refuses to enter by a proper entrance, instead he chooses to leap over the gate (ll. 183-87):

> ... As when a prowling Wolfe,
> When hunger drives to seek new haunt for prey,
> Watching where Shepherds pen their Flocks at eeve.
> In hurdl'd Cotes amid the field secure,
> Leaps o're the fence with ease into the Fould.

The chaplain who in book x of *La Pucelle* had been successful in his attempt at rape was stopped this time by a raised drawbridge, whereupon he cursed God. In a variant to the text (Vercruysse, p.451), the chaplain was likened to Adam driven away from paradise and to Lucifer who was likewise chased from heaven with a fork, but they appeared less grotesque than this 'worm'.

The denigration of Fréron in book xviii of course formed part of a wider campaign against the arch enemy. After he had turned Fréron into a donkey, Voltaire progressively degraded him and made a Satanic snake of him. In a letter to the d'Argentals, he wrote: 'On dit que Satan était dans l'amphitéâtre sous la figure de Fréron, et qu'une larme d'une dame était tombée sur le nez du malheureux, fit psh psh, comme si ç'avait été eau bénite' (Best.D9207), *c.* 8 September 1760). The 'psh, psh' of Fréron recalls to a certain extent the 'dismal hiss' that greeted the triumphant Satan on his return to Pandemonium when his followers were turned into snakes (*Paradise lost*, book x, l.508).

In his attack on Fréron in the 'capilotade' Voltaire also has recourse to imagery which is of unmistakably Miltonic inspiration. The function of these images is to belittle Fréron and make him appear more despicable: they are suggestive of guile and treachery. Fréron is first compared with 'un dogue au regard impudent / Au gosier rauque, affamé de carnage' which at the sight of its master

> . . . rampe doucement,
> Lèche ses mains, le flatte en son langage
> Et pour du pain devient un vrai mouton.
> Ou tel encor on nous peint le démon
> Qui s'échappant des gouffres du Tartare,
> Cache sa queue et sa griffe barbare,
> Vient parmi nous, prend la mine et le ton,
> Le front tendu d'un jeune anachorète
> Pour mieux tenter sœur Rose ou sœur Discrète.[38]
>
> (Vercruysse, p.535)

This mixture of the familiar and the unknown is not simply due to the fact that *La Pucelle* is a burlesque epic. In *Paradise lost*, Milton changes the 'rarefied' images of hell, such as those used to convey an impression of the great size of Satan in book ii, lines 195-210, into more homely ones involving the countryside.

In the case of *Candide*[39] too, Milton's impact on Voltaire can be examined in two ways. There are the direct references to Milton in chapter xxv, where Candide on seeing a Milton[40] text in Pococurante's library, asks him whether he did not consider Milton to be a great man. This was a manner of introducing a virulent attack on Milton, in which the old grievances listed in the *Essai sur la poésie épique* are taken

[38] cf. *Paradise lost*, book ix, lines 503-505: '. . . pleasing was his shape / And lovely, never since of Serpent kind / Lovlier'.

[39] not long before, Voltaire seems to have been obsessed with the idea of hell and the devil. In a letter to d'Alembert, for example, he said he was annoyed that Jaucourt, author of the article 'Enfer' in the *Encyclopédie*, should have written about hell being part of Moses's doctrine and he added 'cela n'est pas vrai, de par tous les diables . . . L'enfer est une fort bonne chose . . . C'est ce monde-ci qui est l'enfer' (Best.D7267, 24 May 1757). In November of that year, he told Bottens that the devil was in Germany (Best.D7463, c. 15 November 1757).

[40] cf. Voltaire's letter to George Keate (Best.D8367, 20 June 1759) where he says that Keate's text will become very precious to him since Keate has been the owner and that he would conserve it as a monument of his friendship. For closeness of vocabulary, one may compare Candide's 'un Milton' with the letter's 'votre Milton'. Morize in his edition of *Candide* suggests that a recent reading of Keate's copy of *Paradise lost* and Louis Racine's translation of the poem in 1754 explain Voltaire's reactions to a certain extent (p.192, n.2). As in the case of Shakespeare, non-literary factors such as Voltaire's dislike of English colonial successes must not be excluded.

up again. Yet Voltaire does not restrict himself to the criticisms made in the *Essai*. He exploited in *Candide* some of the lines on Milton which he had added to the *Epître sur la calomnie* in 1760. These lines which he was to reproduce in the *Honnêtetés littéraires* in 1767 read (M.x. 288):

> Ne voit-on pas, chez cet atrabilaire
> Qui d'Olivier fut un temps secrétaire,
> Ange contre ange, Uriel et Nisroc
> Contre Ariac, Asmodée, et Moloc,
> Couvrant de sang les célestes campagnes,
> Lançant des rocs, ébranlant des montagnes;
> De purs esprits qu'un fendant coupe en deux,
> Et du canon tiré de près sur eux:
> Et le Messie allant, dans une armoire,
> Prendre sa lance, instrument de sa gloire?

In *Candide*, Milton is *inter alia* a vulgar imitator of the Greeks 'qui défigure la création, & qui . . . fait prendre un grand compas par le Messiah dans une armoire du Ciel pour tracer son ouvrage' (ed. Morize, Paris 1957, p.194). What Voltaire says on Milton in the *Epître sur la calomnie* is itself a development of the earlier attack made in book xi of *La Pucelle*. The 1761 edition of *Candide* also contains more disparaging remarks on the author of *Paradise lost*. Voltaire-Pococurante now condemns his long description of a hospital which is good only for a grave digger. In the 1759 edition, Voltaire had made Candide like Milton without any reservation; in 1761 Candide just likes him a little.[41] Voltaire had no doubt been encouraged in this hostile attitude by mme Du Deffand. In her letter to him, she said how pleased she was to find in *Candide* all the ill he speaks of Milton. She imagined that she had entertained similar thoughts, for she had always held Milton in horror. Her conclusion was that she and Voltaire had a complete identity of views (Best.D8559, 28 October 1759).

Morize pointed out that for the beginning of chapter iii of *Candide* where the peak of the satire against war is reached, Voltaire drew on his general recollection of the *Poème de Fontenoy* and on Veiras's *L'Histoire des Sévarambes* (p.14, n.2). The latter's influence may with some

---

[41] see Morize, pp.lxxxvi and 194. It appears that up to December 1760 Voltaire had left intact Candide's liking for Milton, for in a fragment torn from a longer letter he sent to Gabriel Cramer, Voltaire had written: 'Candide était affligé de ces discours [Pococurante's], il respectait Homère, il aimait Milton.' This passage was suppressed from Candide in 1761. See Best.D9269 (? December 1760) and editorial notes.

justification be invoked in respect of the destruction caused by cannon musketry and resulting in the 'boucherie héroïque'. But Voltaire himself by mentioning hell, albeit unobtrusively, in the second sentence of the chapter has given us a clue as to the real source of his inspiration in the description of the opposing armies. He was certainly thinking of Milton when he wrote: 'Les trompettes . . . les canons, formaient une harmonie telle qu'il n'y en eut jamais en enfer.' In *Paradise lost* Milton raises the fallen angels from time to time, only to knock them down with a tremendous crash. They wave banners with 'orient', that is, bright colours (book i, ll. 549-62):

> . . . Anon they move
> In perfect phalanx to the Dorian mood
> Of flutes and soft recorders; . . .
> . . . Thus they,
> Breathing united force with fixed thought,
> Moved on in silence to soft pipes that charmed
> Their painful steps o'er the burnt soil.

Further on (ll. 711-12) Milton says that Pandemonium

> Rose like an exhalation, with the sound
> Of dulcet symphonies, and voices sweet.

Voltaire of course knew books i and ii of *Paradise lost* very well, and judging by the number of times he refers to them, they must have made the biggest impact on him. He claims that the music and the sounds of cannon produced by the two armies in *Candide* were even more impressive than those of hell. He follows the Miltonic precedent of demolishing the superficial beauty of the armies, but the weapon he uses is the savage irony of grim reality.[42]

[42] another Englishman, Edward Keith, had no doubt stimulated Voltaire's imagination when from Chemnitz he gave him a brief but vivid account of an episode in the Seven Years War. He wrote: 'vous ne voiez pas du moins toutes les horreures que nous comtons; six battailles dans une année, des provinces riches et florissantes ruinées et dépeuplées; de la façon que nous allons on croirait que nous voulons exterminer la race allemande . . . l'hiver ne ralentit pas notre ardeur et tout enrûhmés que nous sommes, courons autravers des neiges pour nous entreégorger' (Best.D7503, 8 December 1757). That Voltaire was discreetly using his English background is again proved at the end of chapter iii of *Candide*. He had complained to Thieriot (Best.D305, 26 October 1726) about his difficult position in London. Fawkener, however, made life easier for him, as the anabaptist Jacques did for Candide. Like Fawkener, Jacques had a business interest in cloth which came from the east (cf. André Michel Rousseau, *L'Angleterre et Voltaire*, i. 79).

Milton is very much in Voltaire's mind in the 1760s. There is even some admiration for him in the correspondence. To Keate, who had just published *The Alps*, Voltaire wrote: 'Vous rendez l'horreur agréable', adding that it seemed that Milton's soul had passed into his body (Best. D11323, 26 July 1763). He also told d'Alembert that if Clairault (who had died on the 17 May 1765) had been to see Newton, he would soon 'faire humblement ma cour à Milton' (Best.D12617, 27 May 1765).

The *Dictionnaire philosophique* provides him with yet another opportunity of turning the seriousness of *Paradise lost* into the mock heroic. In the *Essay on epick poetry* he had made the point that if part of an epic can be accurately treated in a mock heroic manner, then that part betrays its ridiculous nature. He went on to give an example of this by observing 'that nothing is so adapted to that ludicrous way of writing, as the Metamorphosis of the Devils into Dwarfs' (White, p.139). Voltaire waited nearly forty years before he used this particular example. In the article 'Résurrection' of the *Dictionnaire*, he states categorically that on the day of Resurrection all the dead will walk underground like moles, then he adds: 'On sera fort pressé dans cette vallée; mais il n'y a qu'à réduire les corps proportionnellement, comme les diables de Milton, dans la salle de Pandémonium.'[43] Voltaire uses the imagery of book i, lines 772-80 of *Paradise lost* to belittle Jews, and by implication, Christians too. It cannot be flattering for them to be turned into the devils of hell. As Voltaire had then entered the most militant phase of his attack on 'l'infâme', who could illustrate his argument about the mock heroic better than Jews and Christians?[44] He finds it appropriate to place them in this preposterous situation.

It seems that in the last ten years of his life Voltaire was determined, as part of his war against England, to deal a final and crushing blow to Milton. He proceeded in a round about way by showing the indebtedness of Biblical mythology to Indian mythology which in his view was the subject of *Paradise lost*. He therefore insinuated that *Paradise lost* was an imitation of an imitation.[45] In *Dieu et les hommes* (1769), Voltaire recalled how in the first century of the Christian era a very

[43] eds Benda and Naves (Paris 1961), p.374.
[44] the wrath of Amasis against Amaside in *Le Taureau blanc* is another illustration of the mock heroic style used by Voltaire to make fun of Milton (*Romans et contes*, ed. H. Bénac (Paris 1960), p.582).
[45] cf. Gillet, p.88.

skilful forger, who could have been a Jew or a half-Jew and a half-Christian, learnt something about the religion of the Brahmins and subsequently fabricated a writing which he attributed to Enoch. In his sarcastic conclusion, Voltaire wrote: 'C'est enfin sur ce fatras du livre prétendu d'Enoch que Milton a bâti son singulier poème du *Paradis perdu*' (M.xxviii.138).

In this period, Voltaire took great care to stress that the Indians were the first nation to have developed the mythology of the serpent and that of the rebellion in heaven. He discussed the question in the *Fragments historiques sur l'Inde* (1773) (M.xxix.173), *Le Taureau blanc* (1773) (Bénac, p.577), and the correspondence[46] and finally in 1776 in the *Lettres chinoises, indiennes et tartares* (M.xxix.479-82). All his discussions invariably tended to discredit Milton, and he even quoted scripture to make his point! In the *Fragments*, Voltaire made the following observation: Milton came from a nation renowned for the mathematical sciences, but did he not transform our devil into a toad, into a cormorant and into a serpent, although the holy scripture definitely says the opposite? (M.xxix.176).

The *Précis du siècle de Louis XV* (chapter xxix), the *Fragments* and the *Lettres chinoises* owe much to Holwell's *Interesting historical events relative to the provinces of Bengal* (1766) which was sent to him by a mr Peacock in 1767. Voltaire thought that Holwell's book was instructive and discussed it with Peacock (Best.D14579, 8 December, 1767). He used it for his description of the Bengali paradise in the *Lettres chinoises* (M.xxix. 486-87) and for the Indian background of the *Princesse de Babylone*. John Moore found him reading Holwell again in 1773 (*Voltaire's British visitors*, p.172).

In the article 'Epopée' of the *Questions sur l'encyclopédie* (1771), Voltaire sets out to destroy the reputation not only of Milton, but also of Milton's translator, Dupré de St Maur. Milton is now deemed guilty of having failed to use rhyme in *Paradise lost* which is also marred by the fanatical spirit that prevailed in Cromwell's time. Further it is Voltaire's intention to elevate the merit of other epic writers. In his attempt to discredit Milton, Voltaire at one point completely leaves the epic aside and dwells on Milton's political activities and his personal

---

[46] cf. Voltaire's letter to mme Du Deffand where he at first pays tribute to the Indians to whom he says we owe our first principles of geometry. But from them also we obtained fables: 'celle sur laquelle Milton a bâti son singulier poëme, est tirée d'un ancien livre indien écrit il y a plus de cinq mille ans' (Best.D18511, 13 August 1773).

polemics with Saumaise (M.xviii.587). One of the essential aims of the article is to represent Milton as a vulgar imitator who ransacked a number of authors: the point about imitation is highlighted by the fact that the last section of the article is entitled 'Du reproche de plagiat fait à Milton'. In the main part of the article, Voltaire states that an episode in Tasso has become the subject of the whole poem of *Paradise lost*, which is based on the fourth book of *Gerusalemme liberata*.[47] Unlike Milton, Tasso has the merit of concentrating the interest on human characters and passing quickly over the episode of the devil (M.xviii.580-81). For the first time, Voltaire attributes the origin of the war in heaven to Claudian's *Gigantomachy*. The imitation of the war of the giants and the fable of rebellious angels against God are to be found in the apocrypha attributed to Enoch. Milton's use of cannon is derived from Ariosto who, however, preserves some decorum (M.xviii.582). To the same Ariosto, Milton owes Adam's vision, but Ariosto's vision is at least characterized by more verisimilitude than his imitator (p.586).

In the last section of the article, Voltaire defends Milton against William Lauder's accusation of plagiarism[48] and exposes the fraud (pp.590-91). He at first suggests that Milton borrowed from Hugo Grotius's *Adamus exsul* and the Jesuit Masenius's *Sarcotis*, but that there was no shame in that since Euripides and Virgil had borrowed from Homer. In modern times, Molière borrowed from Cyrano de Bergerac: no one would dream of accusing Molière of plagiarism. This fairmindedness is however more apparent than real. It is clear that Voltaire's intention is to emphasize Milton's indebtedness to Masenius (Jacopo Masenio), thus denying him any originality. Milton borrowed from Masenius the exordium, the invocation, the description of the garden of Eden, the portraits of Eve and Satan. It is the same subject, the same story, the same ending. Voltaire says that the Satan of Milton in wishing to take revenge on man for the wrong done to him by God has the same purpose as Masenius's Satan, as if Milton never knew the book of Genesis! Milton obtained from Masenius countless other

---

[47] in the *Essai sur la poésie épique*, Voltaire had explained Milton's inferiority to Tasso by suggesting that the English language lacked the harmony of Italian poetry. He later claimed that he himself was alive to the harmony of English sounds and rhythms (*Voltaire's British visitors*, p.184).

[48] Lauder was supported by Samuel Johnson. On this controversy, see *Milton*, ed. Shawcross, ii. 27-29.

episodes such as the description of luxury, pride, avarice and greed. What above all, says Voltaire, convinced readers of Milton's plagiarism was the perfect resemblance of the beginning of the two poems. At one stage, Voltaire says that Milton could have borrowed a maximum of two hundred lines and at the same time he refers to so many features borrowed from Grotius and Masenius. He does agree that these borrowings are lost 'dans la foule des choses originales, qui sont à lui' (p.592). One does not see any instance of originality quoted in this article where *Paradise lost* is wittily described as 'cet ouvrage, moitié théologique et moitié diabolique' and its author as having sacrificed to the devil (p.588).

Rather late in the day, Voltaire in the 'Epopée' article tries to reduce the value of Dupré de St Maur's work by suggesting that it is not a faithful translation of Milton, although it at first appears to be so. He condemns Dupré's alterations and omissions. Then he gives a fairly accurate translation of ll. 385-452 of book v of *Paradise lost*. It is a most careful piece of engineering. For he has selected just those lines that are likely to bring out the mock heroic possibilities of Milton's epic and to heap ridicule on him. These lines include the following rendering (M.xviii.583):

Bonjour, mère des hommes, dont le ventre fécond remplira le monde de plus d'enfants qu'il n'y a de différents fruits des arbres de Dieu entassés sur la table. La table était un gazon et des siéges de mousse tout autour, et sur son ample carré d'un bout à l'autre tout l'automne était empilé quoique le printemps et l'automne dansassent en ce lieu par la main. Ils firent quelque temps conversation ensemble sans craindre que le dîner se refroidît.

Voltaire jubilantly adds in a footnote to the last sentence that he has given a word for word translation of 'No fear lest dinner cool'. This translation preserves the mock heroic and familiar tone of the passage dealing with Satan's encounter with Sin, which Voltaire had already dealt with in the *Essai sur la poésie épique* and the apostrophes to Adam in *Le Mondain*. The height of comedy is reached towards the end by a combination of literalism and transliteration where 'And to thir viands fell' becomes 'tombèrent sur les viandes'. Voltaire continues (p.584):

et l'ange n'en fit pas seulement semblant; il ne mangea pas en mystère, selon la glose commune des théologiens, mais avec la vive dépêche d'une faim très réelle, avec une chaleur concoctive et transsubstantive: le superflu du dîner transpire aisément dans les pores des esprits; il ne faut pas s'en etonner, puisque l'empirique alchimiste, avec son feu de charbon et de suie, peut changer ou croit pouvoir changer l'écume du plus grossier métal en or aussi parfait que celui de la mine.

Yet in the same article, Voltaire translates the beginning of *Paradise lost* literally without producing mock-heroic banter. This was a further attempt to prove his superiority over Dupré de St Maur. He now points out the difficulty of establishing who the author really was (p.588),[49] although he had no doubt that the two authors (Dupré de St Maur and Chélon de Boismorand) had failed to produce an accurate translation. As in the case of Hamlet's 'To be or not to be' soliloquy, Voltaire must have been impressed[50] by some purple passages such as Satan's monologue to the sun in book iv of *Paradise lost*: for he had many years before translated some of the lines freely in the *Essai sur la poésie épique*.[51] Admittedly, he had turned Satan into a disgraced courtier lacking the grandeur of Milton's Satan (Gillet, p.67). He here adds a further eleven lines to his translation (p.589).

The fact that Voltaire kept coming back to Milton only to emphasize certain passages of *Paradise lost* reveals his fragmented view of the poem. However, it provides a reliable indication of the latter's impact on him. Voltaire found it convenient to invoke the rules in his attack on Milton, the epic poet. He nevertheless drew inspiration from him in a number of writings. Indeed, few English writers were openly

---

[49] in his *Lettre à l'Académie française* (1776), Voltaire claimed that many years before he had urged Dupré de St Maur to learn English and translate Milton (M.xxx.351). Considering that he had urged Thieriot to learn English and translate *Gulliver*, this is not impossible. It is unfortunate that St Maur's correspondence with Voltaire has not survived. Three letters from Voltaire about him have survived. In the first addressed to Du Resnel, translator of Pope, Voltaire claims that St Maur and he corresponded (Best.D771, 21 July 1734). It appears from the last two (Best.D1981, 7 October 1739 and Best.D2409, ? December 1741) addressed to the same correspondent that St Maur was among those who had dinner and supper with Voltaire. In Best.D2409, St Maur is referred to as the translator of Milton.

[50] as he was by the 'very fine blank verse set amidst countless harsh and obscure lines'. See the article 'Marie Magdeleine' (1772) of the *Questions sur l'encyclopédie*. This article also condemned Milton for having made a novel out of the New Testament in his *Paradise regained* where the blank verse often resembles very bad prose, and where Satan proposes to Christ to sit down and eat (M.xx. 34-35).

[51] David Durand, who wrote an epic poem in seven books entitled *La Chute de l'homme* (1729) and the anonymous *Connaissance des beautés* thought Voltaire's version was better than Louis Racine's because it had more warmth and life (see M.xxiii. 421).

discussed and often discreetly used by the Frenchman to the same extent as Milton. The significance of Milton must be judged by Voltaire's reactions which appear in one form or another in works as varied as the following: the essays on epic poetry, *La Henriade*, poems such as *Le Mondain*, the play *Pandore*, the *contes philosophiques*, the *Dictionnaire philosophique*, the *Questions sur l'encyclopédie*, not to mention the correspondence.

A study of Voltaire's reactions to Milton in distinct phases, as was the case with Shakespeare, does not commend itself, despite the parallel one can draw between Voltaire's attitude to the two English poets. No doubt non-literary factors play some part in Voltaire's comments on Milton from the 1750s. On the other hand, one cannot point to a period when Voltaire can be said to be unreservedly in favour of Milton. He probably made the fairest assessment at the time of the *Essay on epick poetry*, but even then he had major reservations against Milton and these were of an entirely literary nature. If he subsequently emphasized Milton's weaknesses, Voltaire would appear consistent and to be acting in accordance with the literary principles found in his theory of the epic. It also seems that Voltaire was less influenced by the politics and religion of Milton, in spite of his malicious occasional references to these aspects in his writings.

The personal element was probably more important in Voltaire's reactions to Milton. His professional jealousy of Dupré de St Maur is understandable. Granted that his *Essay on epick poetry* was meant for an English public, the fact remains that a French translation of the *Essay* by Desfontaines had appeared in France in 1728, so Voltaire cannot be denied the honour of having been the first to introduce *Paradise lost* to his countrymen. Previous attempts in this field by Bayle, Ramsay, the *Journal littéraire* and *Le Babillard* cannot be placed on the same level as Voltaire's comprehensive critical work. Yet it was Dupré de St Maur who won all the glory and the reward with his translation of the poem in 1729. This perhaps explains why the first editions of the *Lettres philosophiques* maintain a strange silence about *Paradise lost*. It may also explain why some forty years later Voltaire was still obsessed with undoing St Maur's reputation. In the interval, all his efforts towards making *La Henriade* France's national epic seem to have failed miserably, since he himself admitted to Titon Du Tillet that France could not identify itself with his work which was inferior to those of Tasso and Milton. *Paradise lost* proved so popular in France that the abbé

La Baume intended his prose poem, *La Christiade* (1753), to be a sequel to it. Voltaire must have been stung by Fréron who not only gave a good review of *La Christiade* in the *Année littéraire* of 1754, but saw fit to add that *Paradise lost* was above any epic in the French language (vii. 170).

4

English Augustan satirists and Voltaire

i. *Voltaire's attitude to satire*

It is generally assumed that Voltaire took an unfavourable view of satire.[1] But more often than not this conclusion is based on remarks made by Voltaire in a few letters and published works appearing at odd intervals. Yet Voltaire had a long literary career and non-literary factors such as the polemical and intellectual issues in which he was involved must certainly have influenced his literary judgements. It is these factors which make it so difficult to know his taste. Now with regard to the latter, Naves pointed out that if all Voltaire's writings which were strictly critical were pieced together, they might not exceed one eighth of the whole of his output, but all the same the critical writings were countless and the importance of taste in his thought should be measured in the light of this multiplicity and frequency (*Le Goût de Voltaire*, p.187). If a similar task were undertaken in connection with Voltaire's pronouncements on satire, these would appear to constitute only a small fraction of a more important fraction. Nevertheless, this exercise is essential if we want to know what Voltaire really thought of satire. Besides, it would be interesting to know what the leading satirist of the eighteenth century had to say on a type of writing that made his reputation in later times. A chronological approach alone will reveal whether any sort of evolution or any consistency may be traced in Voltaire's attitude to the subject.

In his letter to the *Nouvelliste du Parnasse*, we have one of the earliest indications of Voltaire's contempt for satire when he writes: 'Depuis l'âge de seize ans, où quelques vers un peu satiriques, & par conséquent très condamnables, avaient échappé à l'imprudence de mon

[1] Voltaire uses the word in the sense of the Latin *satura*, that is, a medley, of which the variety might lie in the subjects chosen and in the form which can be dialogue, fable, anecdote, precept, verse, prose or a combination of verse and prose (cf. *The Oxford companion to classical literature*, ed. P. Harvey (Oxford 1962), p.382).

âge . . . je me suis imposé la loi de ne jamais tomber dans ce détestable genre d'écrire' (Best.D415, 20 June 1731).[2] He claims that he had never composed any satirical writing in verse or prose since his childhood nor had he ever applauded any of those writings whose only merit lay in flattering human spitefulness. Further on he associates satire with envy: the more he loves truth, the more he hates and despises satire which has always been the language of envy. Shortly afterwards, Voltaire writes to the *Mercure de France* and does not hesitate to call those who wrote works such as the satire *J'ay vu* 'auteurs de ces lâches ouvrages'.[3] The periodical is also praised for having never accommodated any satire. It should be pointed out that Voltaire's judgement was probably influenced by the knowledge that these letters were going to be published.

The *Temple du goût* where prose alternates with verse,[4] is severe towards those critics who rely essentially on satire. They are turned away from the temple because in their 'démangeaison de se faire connoître', they insult well-known authors and secretly write a bad review of a good work; they are little insects about whose existence we know simply from the efforts they make to bite (Carcassonne, p.71).

Voltaire gives an example of what he considers to be satire in the *Lettre de m. de V . . . à m. de C . . .* which he later inserted in the 'édition véritable' of the *Temple* published in Amsterdam in 1733. In his view Boileau's lines:

Si je pense exprimer un auteur sans défaut,
La raison dit Virgile, et la rime Quinault.

constitute satire and rather unjust satire at that, whatever be the respect due to his great predecessor. Voltaire establishes a connection between satire and invective and if anything, invective is worse than satire whereas criticism itself could have a positive quality. This is how he

---

[2] Voltaire had written a literary satire entitled *Le Bourbier* (1714) against Houdar de La Motte and the Moderns. In his letter to the *Mercure de France* (Best.D416, 30 June 1731), Voltaire reemphasizes his stand by challenging slanderers to dare maintain that he had ever written or approved of any satirical work.

[3] Best.D416. *J'ay vu* was by Antoine Louis Lebrun. It was falsely attributed to Voltaire and was partly responsible for his imprisonment.

[4] to Voltaire, verse satire was not, as was the case with Boileau, an end in itself. It was a means to a wider end. See R. Mortier, 'Les formes de la satire chez Voltaire', *Documentatieblad werkgroep 18ᵉ eeuw* (1972), pp.43-64. Mortier's article, which is primarily concerned with Voltaire's practice of satire, shows well the variety of forms his satire assumes.

expresses these subtle distinctions: 'Tous les honnêtes-gens qui pensent sont critiques; les malins sont satiriques; les pervers font des libelles' (Carcassonne, p.107). The best criticism is, however, inferior to the creative act. As he puts it in the *Mémoire sur la satire* (1739), the writer's ideal should be: 'ne critiquer qu'en essayant de mieux faire'.

At about the same time, mme Du Châtelet is warned about the dangers of satire in the *Epître sur la calomnie*, which was composed in 1733 and published in 1736 (M.x.283):

> Quiconque en France avec éclat attire
> L'œil du public, est sûr de la satire.
> Un bon couplet, chez ce peuple falot,
> De tout mérite est l'infaillible lot.

Voltaire then recalls how Eglé's reputation was attacked by everyone, including the poet Roy.[5] The Virgin Mary too, he adds, was not spared A variant to the text reads (M.x.283, n.3):

> Des chansonniers comme une autre a souffert.
> Certain lampon courut longtemps sur elle . . .
> C'est de tout temps ainsi que la satire
> A de son souffle infecté les esprits.

Voltaire claims that the whole world is governed by satire:

> Jérusalem a connu la satire.
> Persans, Chinois, baptisés, circoncis,
> Prennent ses lois: la terre est son empire;
> Mais, croyez-moi, son trône est à Paris.

He describes these Parisian satirists in the most contemptuous terms (p.284):

> Jeunes oisons, et bégueules titrées.
> Disant des riens d'un ton de perroquet, . . .
> Blondins y sont, beaucoup plus femmes qu'elles,
> Profondément remplis de bagatelles.

If, by chance, someone with better taste who has read good literature dares express an opinion before them

---

[5] in a note added in 1756, Voltaire described Roy as a 'poète connu en son temps pour quelques opéras, et par quelques petites satires nommées calottes, qui sont tombées dans un profond oubli'. He has more to say about 'calottes' in the *Mémoire sur la satire*, see below, p.155

Tout aussitôt leur brillante cohue,
D'étonnement et de colère émue,
Bruyant essaim de frelons envieux,
Pique et poursuit cette abeille charmante.

However satire can sometimes have a positive role to play. Thus in
the *Conseils à un journaliste*, Voltaire insists that the journalist should
not remain passive, for satire can be used to exact vengeance on behalf
of good writers: 'Faites vous toujours un mérite de venger les bons
écrivains des zoïles obscurs qui les attaquent; démêlez les artifices de
l'envie' (M.xxii.258). Even in this work, the negative aspect of satire
comes out clearly. In Voltaire's mind, satire is inextricably linked with
slander and a mercenary spirit.

It is the *Mémoire sur la satire* that represents Voltaire's lengthiest
essay on satire. The *Mémoire* would at first sight appear to embody all
his thoughts on the subject. But the method adopted by Voltaire, a
history of satire from Boileau to Desfontaines, prevents him from
writing a proper theory. Voltaire expresses the pious hope that the
young who read his essay will learn to hate satire and that those who
indulge in this type of writing will feel ashamed: he even thinks that
his essay will be regarded as a petition made on behalf of all honest
people to check an intolerable abuse (M.xxiii.48). He reminds his
readers that the first rule in education in all countries is not to say
anything that might slight anyone and that, in this respect, the French
are superior to other nations. While standing up for truth, one has no
need to hurt people's feelings. Voltaire deplores the fact that it took
the French so long to establish in their literature what had always
prevailed in daily intercourse between men and that they should be so
late in realising that insults are not reasons (M.xxiii.49).

Voltaire first pays homage to Vaugelas on whom he bestows lavish
praise as a critic who did not merely teach the French language, but
politeness as well. Vaugelas, Voltaire claims, criticizes thirty authors,
but he does not name one: he even takes the trouble to change their
sentences leaving only what he condemns, for fear lest those censured
should be identified. The aim of the seventeenth-century writer was to
set an example and not to offend and, by refusing to attack people's
reputation, he certainly won greater fame than if he had taken delight
in leaving insults behind him. We may note, in Voltaire's remarks on
Vaugelas, an ideal indirectly preached, namely that criticism or satire

should be a school of instruction. This was in line with traditional views of satire which at its best had moral and didactic aims. Such aims were being lost sight of in the first half of the century.

In Voltaire's eyes modern satire has few achievements and it may well expose the satirist to grave risks.[6] He sarcastically asks in connection with Boileau's satires: 'Est-ce à ses satires qu'on doit la perfection où les muses françaises s'élevèrent? Pour lors Molière et Corneille n'avaient-ils pas déjà écrit?' (M.xxiii.52). He wonders whether they have been of any use: it seems that they succeeded only in ridiculing ten or twelve writers, in making two men who had never offended him die of sorrow and finally in rousing enemies who chased him until his death (M.xxiii.53). However, while attacking him in the *Mémoire sur la satire*, Voltaire pays homage to Boileau's qualities as a satirist. He is against the introduction of personal matters in satire and has to admit that however cruel his satires may have been, Boileau always spared the private life of those whom he tore to pieces, whereas his successors took greater liberties.

In the section entitled 'Des Satires nommées calottes', Voltaire claims that there has been only a change of fashion in the art of slander, the alexandrine being replaced by the couplet. He makes 'calotte' satire responsible for the decadence in taste: a sure sign of decadence is the enthusiasm shown for these productions, which is accompanied by a poor joke 'toujours répétée, toujours retombant dans les mêmes tours, sans esprit, sans imagination, sans grâce' (M.xxiii. 56).

Although the *Mémoire sur la satire* purports to deal with principles governing the theory and practice of satire, it is abundantly clear that the author pays lip service to such principles in this very work. After having made a further point about satire, that man's taste cannot be reformed by it, but by works which are aesthetically pleasing, Voltaire devotes the rest of the *Mémoire* to attacks on his enemies. The vocabulary, tone and spirit of the essay change and there is no doubt at all that Desfontaines or J. B. Rousseau did not appreciate Voltaire's 'civilité', let alone approve his polemical writing. It was inevitable that his personal enemies should have been mentioned in this general discourse: after all, the *Mémoire* was written 'à l'occasion d'un libelle de l'abbé Desfontaines contre l'auteur' (M.xxiii.47).

[6] it is possible that Voltaire read about the assault by Rochester's men on Dryden in 1679. The violent antagonism between Dryden and Rochester was described in the *Journal littéraire* ('Dissertation sur la poésie angloise', p.172).

Whatever his own practice was, Voltaire could not help giving advice to others on how to write satire. For instance, in the *Conseils à m. Racine sur son poème de la Religion* (1742), he asks Louis Racine not to use invective against fellow writers because 'cette indécence n'est plus d'usage; les honnêtes gens la réprouvent. Il faut imiter la plupart des physiciens de toutes les académies, qui rapportent toujours avec éloge les opinions de ceux même qu'ils combattent' (M.xxiii.184). He reminds Racine that Boileau himself would condemn his first satires if he came back to the world.

The *contes philosophiques* are as important as his other writings in a survey of Voltaire's theory and practice of satire. In *Le Monde comme il va* which was probably composed in 1742, Babouc invited a few men of letters to dinner. Their behaviour was disgusting and as soon as he got rid of them, he started reading a few new books. He was roused to indignation by these 'gazettes de la médisance, ces archives du mauvais goût, que l'envie, la bassesse et la faim ont dictées; ces lâches satires où l'on ménage le vautour et où l'on déchire la colombe' (Bénac, p.75). He was so disappointed that he threw these hateful writings into the flames.

Envy can turn the most innocent writing into satire which can be produced in unexpected ways. Sometimes it merely suffices to put together sections of a poem provided they are out of context. This is what 'L'Envieux' did in *Zadig*. He found the sheet of paper on which Zadig's poem was written (Bénac, p.12):

Elle avait été tellement rompue que chaque moitié du vers qui remplissait la ligne faisait un sens, et même un vers d'une plus petite mesure; mais, par un hasard encore plus étrange, ces petits vers se trouvaient former un sens qui contenait les injures les plus horribles contre le roi.

The 'Envieux' dispatched the satire to the king.

Voltaire's private correspondence which was not meant for publication is also revealing. As Fréron had criticised Marmontel's tragedy *Aristomène* in the *Lettres sur quelques écrits de ce temps* (1749) (ii. 289-321), Voltaire wrote a letter of encouragement to his friend saying that satire takes no account of whatever is good. He quoted Racine as saying that satires disappear, while the good works attacked remain. These satires are not completely forgotten: they pour hatred and contempt on their authors. And Voltaire concluded in these terms: 'Quel indigne métier mon cher ami! Il me semble que ce sont des malheureux condamnés aux mines qui rapportent de leur travail un peu de terre et de cailloux sans découvrir l'or qu'il fallait chercher' (Best. D4075, December 1749). Here, however, there is some pity for satirists on account of their incapacity to distinguish between good and bad.

It would therefore appear that much of what Voltaire has to say on satire is influenced by his personal relationships with contemporary writers and critics. Attention has been drawn to the strong emotional overtones in many of Voltaire's comments on satire and professional critics (Williams, *Voltaire: literary critic*, p.116). The polemics in which Voltaire was involved with a number of persons were bound to make him look on satire in an entirely unfavourable light. In his letter to the *Journal encyclopédique*, for instance, he pointed out that satire in verse, even in beautiful verse, was decried and even more so satire in prose especially because 'on y réussit d'autant plus mal qu'il est plus aisé d'écrire en ce pitoyable genre' (Best.D8696, *c.* 5 January 1760). Voltaire reinforced his point about satire being an easy genre when in the *Parallèle d'Horace* (1761), he observed how difficult it was to write a tragedy, whereas a satire and an epistle required no effort. It was therefore blasphemy to put a Racine and a Boileau on the same footing (M.xxiv.227). Voltaire's strictures against satire must also be viewed against a wider socio-political background in which the writer had a precarious status, was constantly threatened by denunciation in both his public and private life, faced prison or exile and often depended on the goodwill of a civil servant like Malesherbes.[7]

If we are interested in a fresh approach to satire, nothing is more rewarding than Voltaire's review of the poems of Charles Churchill[8] in the *Gazette littéraire* in 1764 (M.xxv.168). There is an attempt at classification and the emphasis is on political satire. Voltaire first claims

[7] see R. Mortier, 'La Satire, "ce poison de la littérature"': Voltaire et la nouvelle déontologie de l'homme de lettres', in *Essays in the age of Enlightenment in honor of I. O. Wade*, ed. J. Macary (Geneva 1977), p.242.

[8] R. Mortier believes that the whole of Voltaire's doctrine on satire may be found in these few lines. He points out how Voltaire reproached Churchill with having violated 'toutes les lois de la bienséance et de l'honnêteté sociale'. See his article 'La Satire, "ce poison de la littérature"', p. 238. I agree with many of his arguments. My only reservation is that however interesting Voltaire's review may be, it needs to be supplemented by other writings, for a single work cannot explain Voltaire's theory of satire completely. Professor Mortier's earlier article, 'Les formes de la satire chez Voltaire', seems to corroborate this point. There Mortier argues (p.60) that to understand what Voltaire means by satire one must look at the *Epître à Boileau*.

that the nature of satire varies according to that of governments. He subsequently tries to account for the tone of satire in various countries. He seems to equate satire with freedom of expression: this should be greater wherever the people have some share in legislation. His survey is both historical and geographical. This leads him to state that satire is a kind of public censorship in harmony with the principles of democracy. That is why it was so violent in ancient Greece where it was used only in the theatre. It was toned down when aristocratic principles began to have the upper hand over those of democracy. Voltaire's conclusion is most interesting. He maintains that in England the law gives every individual the right to attack any man in his public life, but everywhere it must protect the reputation and private life of a citizen. If the law is silent, then it is up to the public to 'venger les droits de la société outragée' (M.xxv.168). Here Voltaire draws closer to Dryden, who in his *Discourse concerning satire*, commented on the private and public aspects of satire (see below, p.189).

It is perhaps a foolhardy attempt to restrict the movements of our Protean genius, for between 1767 and 1772, Voltaire resumes his negative attitude towards satire. In his letter to Pezay, he writes (Best.D14025, 9 March 1767):

Toute satire en attire une autre, et fait naître souvent des inimitiés éternelles... Je ne connais aucune satire qui soit demeurée sans réponse. Les familles, les amis entrent dans ces querelles, c'est le poison de la littérature.

In the preface to the 1768 edition of *Les Scythes*, Voltaire observes that what is universally appreciated at one time loses popularity in another age. Nevertheless there are constants in literature, at any rate in this limited field (M.vi. 274):

Il n'est qu'un seul genre pour lequel le jugement du public ne varie jamais, c'est celui de la satire grossière, qu'on méprise, même en s'en amusant quelques moments; c'est cette critique acharnée et mercenaire d'ignorants qui insultent à prix fait aux arts qu'ils n'ont jamais pratiqués, qui dénigrent les tableaux du Salon sans avoir su dessiner ... misérables bourdons qui vont de ruche en ruche se faire chasser par les abeilles laborieuses !

Thus contempt for satire remains true for all times: it is also directed against those who fail to produce any creative work. The mercenary satirists are denigrated by the animal imagery: the insinuation is that like the drones they only make a noise while others work hard.

A subsequent judgment on satirists in the article 'Amplification' in the *Questions sur l'encyclopédie* (1770) emphasizes not so much their negative attitude as their superficial nature: 'les satiriques se contentent d'une plaisanterie, d'un bon mot, d'un trait piquant: mais celui qui veut s'instruire et éclairer les autres est obligé de tout discuter avec le plus grand scrupule' (M.xvii.191). In the same article, Voltaire shows how positive he himself has been as a critic when he declares: 'Quand j'ai fait ces critiques, j'ai tâché de rendre raison de chaque mot que je critiquais.' Implied in this statement is his contempt as a creative artist for the professional critic.

The influence of the personal element in Voltaire's judgement on satire is never absent for long from the private correspondence and the published writings. An equally strong attack may be seen in a letter to La Harpe. Clément, the author of the verse epistle *Boileau à m. de Voltaire* (1772), had attacked a number of writers, including La Harpe. Voltaire calls the poem a 'satire grossière' and its author 'un jeune écolier'. He claims that the young man 'verra qu'un satirique qui ne couvre pas par des talents éminents ce vice né de l'orgueil et de la bassesse, croupit toute sa vie dans l'opprobre, qu'on le hait sans le craindre, qu'on le méprise sans qu'il fasse pitié, que toutes les portes de la fortune et de la considération lui sont fermées, que ceux qui l'ont encouragé dans ce métier infâme sont les premiers à l'abandonner et que les hommes méchants qui instruisent un chien à mordre ne se chargent jamais de le nourir' (Best.D17702, 19 April 1772). The advice is that every young writer should steer clear of this hated genre. Further on in the letter Voltaire argues that satire is justified occasionally when one is attacked. The example he quotes is that of Fontenelle who had been criticised by Racine and Boileau. Although Fontenelle succeeded only in producing a few mediocre epigrams against them, there is still a strong case for engaging in a defensive war.[9] Satirists are metamorphosed into spiders, for 'ces araignées croyent saisir les abeilles dans leurs filets, mais les abeilles en passant déchirent leur toile, percent de leur aiguillon l'animal abominable et vont continuer à faire leur miel et leur cire. C'est une chose plaisante à considérer que tous ces bas satiriques qui osent avoir de l'orgueil' (Best. D17702).

---

[9] in the *Honnêtetés littéraires* (1767), Voltaire rejected the advice that he should show indifference to his opponent La Beaumelle although the latter was a nonentity (M.xxvi. 134).

Here Voltaire is simply reinforcing the new offensive launched against satirists in 1771 in the *Epître à monsieur d'Alembert* (M.x.428-34). After having talked of 'folliculaires' such as La Grange and La Beaumelle, Voltaire gives vent to a passionate outburst:

> Ces serpents odieux de la littérature,
> Abreuvés de poisons et rampant dans l'ordure,
> Sont toujours écrasés sous les pieds des passants.

By means of repulsive images he then denounces the petty satirists who cannot learn an honourable trade, but try to

> . . . sur les dons des dieux porter leurs mains impies;
> Animaux malfaisants, semblables aux harpies,
> De leurs ongles crochus et de leur souffle affreux
> Gâtant un bon dîner qui n'était pas pour eux.

The period 1769-72 is also noteworthy for some major fluctuations in Voltaire's attitude to satire. His *Epître à Boileau* (1769) widens the scope of satire and gives it a much more significant social role. Voltaire abandons the attack against the Cotins of his time and devotes his energy to defending the oppressed and fighting for justice (M.x. 400-401):

> Non, ma muse m'appelle à de plus hauts emplois.
> A chanter la vertu j'ai consacré ma voix . . .
> Du fond de mes déserts, aux malheureux propice,
> Pour Sirven opprimé je demande justice . . .
> Je fais le bien que j'aime, et voilà ma satire.

He now appears more enthusiastic. To d'Alembert, he writes: 'Une satire doit être piquante et gaie' (Best.D17634, 12 March 1772). He does not make much difference between satire and irony, for in both types of writing, he insists on the need for 'guaité'. He makes his position clear in a letter to d'Argental (Best.D17747, 18 May 1772):

On a suivi entièrement le conseil de l'ange très sage, dans la petite réponse à mr le Roy. Point d'injure; baucoup d'ironie et de guaité. Les injures révoltent; l'ironie fait rentrer les gens en eux-mêmes, la guaité désarme.

Later in the year when he writes to Duvernet he comes out with a positive statement on satire: 'La louange endort, la satire réveille; et le monde est si rassasié de vers, que la satire même a cessé d'être amusante' (Best.D17781, c. June 1772).

Voltaire's attitude to satire certainly gives rise to a remarkable sense of irony. On the one hand, there is his lofty disdain of the genre, proclaimed both publicly and privately. On the other hand, there is the fact that a major part of his literary career is devoted to writing satire and that he scores considerable success in the very field of literature which he despises. This dichotomy is perhaps not difficult to understand. Despite his intentions, he may have been forced to come back to satire by circumstances hostile to the 'philosophes'. It is also likely that Voltaire did not want to steer a lonely course when nearly everyone else was against satire. If he had passionately held a contrary opinion, he would of course have dared to stand apart. To many French writers, satire appeared an upstart genre and it did not seem worthwhile to go against the current for its sake. At first Voltaire did not perhaps know that it was satire that would guarantee his future fame. Indeed, he had entertained high hopes for his painstaking and ambitious efforts in other genres. To posterity, however, these have proved less successful than his satire. Towards the end of his career,[10] when his reputation seemed secure, Voltaire may have felt free to express views he secretly believed in, but which he had not dared communicate even in private letters to friends. He finally admitted that satire could be intellectually stimulating. Whereas in his *Discours de réception à l'Académie française* in 1746 Voltaire had deplored the fact that Boileau had started his career by writing satires because satire dies with its victims, in the article 'Académie' of the *Questions sur l'encyclopédie* (1770) he took a different view. Unlike Saint-Evremond's comedies, Boileau's 'good' satires were now considered to be everlasting (M.xvii.53).

Another impression that emerges is that in the correspondence and in the published works from the *Temple du goût* to the *Epître à d'Alembert*, Voltaire often relies on stock animal imagery in his attempt to denigrate satirists and their writings. It follows that in this aspect of his satirical technique, Voltaire has strong affinities with earlier French satirists. For, in spite of all the theorists who frown upon metaphors, animal imagery has a permanent place among the polemical devices of seventeenth-century writers. It seems that the turning of one's opponents into crows is the most familiar polemical device of the century, from Mathurin Régnier to La Bruyère.

[10] it may be remembered that Dryden gave his positive views on satire in his famous *Discourse concerning satire* only in 1692, some eight years before his death and after he had produced the bulk of his works.

Since Voltaire was also familiar with many English satirists and their works, did he gain anything from this intercourse? Did he find any inspiration in English criticism in particular? On the whole, it does not seem that English critical writings on satire made a great impact on Voltaire's own theory, although the English polemical tradition can certainly be shown to have influenced his practice of satire. This is perhaps because the French, who had drawn considerably from the works of Italian writers such as Vida, Scaliger and Castelvetro since the Renaissance, had by the end of the seventeenth century their own critics. They did not need the assistance of foreigners until late in the eighteenth century.[11]

In some ways, English and French writers differed in their attitudes to satire. The former always gave it a high status. In *An Apology against a pamphlet*, Milton who was no doubt following Roman precedents wrote: 'A Satyr as it was borne out of a Tragedy, so ought to resemble his parentage, to strike high, and adventure dangerously at the most eminent vices among the greatest persons' (*Complete prose works*, i. 916). Butler defined satire thus: 'A Satyr is a kinde of Knight Errant that goe's upon Adventures, to Relieve the Distressed Damsel Virtue, and Redeeme Honour out of Inchanted Castles, And opprest Truth, and Reason out of the Captivity of Gyants or Magitians' (*Characters and passages from note-books*, p.496). Nevertheless Dryden appears to have made some impact on Voltaire's conception of satire. Such differences as existed between the English and the French were mainly confined to theory. When it came to writing satire, they were strikingly similar.

ii. *Butler, Rochester and Voltaire*

An important source of inspiration to Voltaire was the *Hudibras* of Butler (1612-80). Before Voltaire wrote on *Hudibras*, Butler's merit had already been established by the *Journal littéraire*. In the opinion of this influential periodical, Butler's reputation was not inferior to Scarron's, but as a writer he was preferable to the latter as he had a fixed aim and thanks to a surprising effort of his imagination he succeeded in leading his readers to his goal while entertaining them ('Dissertation sur la

[11] cf. Naves, *Le Goût de Voltaire*, p.119.

poésie angloise', p.165). Prévost was equally enthusiastic: he described *Hudibras* as 'une des plus singulières productions de l'esprit humain et le chef-d'œuvre d'un genre dans lequel les Anciens ne nous ont point laissé de modèles' (*Pour et contre*, xiii. 290). In letter xxiii of the *Letters concerning the English nation*, Voltaire had high praise for *Hudibras*, mingled with slight criticism. He writes (pp.212-13):

There's one *English* Poem especially which I should despair of ever making you understand . . . the Principles and Practice of the Puritans are therein ridicul'd. 'Tis *Don Quixot*, 'tis our *Satyre Menippée* blended together. I never found so much Wit in one single Book as in that, which at the same Time is the most difficult to be translated. Who wou'd believe that a Work which paints in such lively and natural Colours the several Foibles and Follies of Mankind, and where we meet with more sentiments than Words, should baffle the Endeavours of the ablest Translator? But the Reason of this is; almost every Part of it alludes to particular Incidents. To explain this a commentary would be requisite, and *Humour* when explain'd is no longer Humour.

In the 'Leningrad notebooks', Voltaire reproduces lines from *Hudibras*: they are mostly taken from the first part, canto i. The quotation entitled 'Hudibras of Butler' starts with (*Notebooks*, i. 240):

> Which made some take him for a tool
> The knaves do work with call'd a fool.

In *Hudibras* (ed. J. Wilders (1967), part I, canto i, lines 32-36), the lines read:

> But howsoe're they make a pother,
> The difference was so small, his Brain
> Outweigh'd his Rage but half a grain:
> Which made some take him for a tool
> That Knaves do work with, call'd a Fool.

Voltaire selects certain aspects of the poem, such as fanaticism and burlesque methods of settling disputes, which appeal to him particularly (*Notebooks*, i.240-41):

> For he was of that noble crew
> Or errant saints whom all men grant
> To be the true church militant,
> Such as they build their faith upon
> The holi text of Pike and gun

Decide all controversy
By infallible artillery
And prove their doctrine ortodoxe
By apostolik blows and knoks[12] ...
But Hudibras gave him a twitch
As quick as ligthning on the breech.
Just in the place where honour's lodg'd
As wise philosophers have judg'd;
Because a kik in that part more
Hurts honour than a wound before.[13]

The French satirist must have been delighted with the imagery of the last six lines above. For it is the type that produces laughter as well as deflation. Wilders is right in saying that the imagery of *Hudibras* is 'either so homely and commonplace that it deflates its subject or so fantastically learned and pedantic that it mocks itself by its own excess' (p.xl). Hudibras is indeed denigrated by the animal imagery, for

Mighty he was at both of these,
Any styl'd of *War* as well as *Peace*.
(So some Rats of amphibious nature
Are either for the Land or Water.)
(*Hudibras*, I, i, ll. 25-28)

His knowledge is satirised by another animal image (ll. 51-52):

Beside 'tis known he could speak *Greek*,
As naturally as Pigs squeek.

Whenever he wanted to belittle someone, Voltaire could draw on the stock of homely and burlesque imagery he had found in *Hudibras*. He used similar techniques in his burlesque poem *La Pucelle*. In book iv, for example, Hermaphrodix is slapped for trying to rape Jeanne (Vercruysse, pp.335-36):

Jeanne, qu'anime une chrétienne rage,
D'un bras nerveux lui détache un soufflet
A poing fermé sur son vilain visage.
Ainsi j'ai vu, dans mes fertiles champs
Sur un pré vert une de mes cavales

[12] cf. Wilders, p.7, part I, canto i, lines 190-98, which show some variations from the Voltaire quotation.
[13] cf. Wilders, p.183, part II, canto iii, lines 1065-70.

Au poil de tigre, aux taches inégales,
Aux pieds légers, aux jarrets bondissants,
Réprimander d'une fière ruade
Un bourriquet de sa croupe amoureux,
Qui dans sa lourde et grossière embrassade
Dressait l'oreille et se croyait heureux.

Grimm had no doubts about the influence of *Hudibras* on *La Pucelle* when he observed in April 1755: 'On dit que la lecture de *Hudibras* n'a pas nui à l'auteur de *La Pucelle*; qu'il en a tiré quantité de traits ingénieux et plaisants qu'il a ensuite ajustés à sa mode, et qui n'y ont sûrement pas perdu' (*Correspondance littéraire*, ed. M. Tourneux (1877), iii. 6).

In a letter to Bertrand in 1755, Voltaire wrote: 'Il est vrai, mon cher philosophe, que je badinais à trente ans. J'avais traduit le commencement de cet Hudibras, et peut-être cela était-il plus plaisant que celui dont vous me parlez. Pour cette pucelle d'Orléans, je vous assure que je fais bien pénitence de ce péché de jeunesse' (Best.D6522, 30 September 1755). He may have started a translation years before, but it was in the 1756 addition to the *Lettres philosophiques* that it appeared. What is significant in the letter to Bertrand is that Voltaire himself should link together *Hudibras* and *La Pucelle*.

Voltaire's view on *Hudibras* underwent a slight change in the 1756 addition to the *Lettres philosophiques* (Lanson, ii. 148-49):

Le poème d'Hudibras . . . semble être un composé de la *Satire Ménippée* et de Don Quichotte; il a sur eux l'avantage des vers; il a celui de l'esprit: la *Satire Ménippée* n'en approche pas; elle n'est qu'un ouvrage très médiocre. Mais à force d'esprit l'auteur d'*Hudibras* a trouvé le secret d'être fort au-dessous de *Don Quichotte* . . . *Don Quichotte* est lû de toutes les Nations, et *Hudibras* n'est lû que des Anglais . . . Pour faire connaître l'esprit de ce Poeme unique en son genre, il faut retrancher les trois quarts de tout passage qu'on veut traduire; car ce Butler ne finit jamais. J'ai donc réduit à environ quatre-vingt vers les quatre cent premiers vers d'*Hudibras*, pour éviter la prolixité.

The rendering included some of the *Hudibras* lines quoted in the notebooks. These lines heaped ridicule on Presbyterian militants who are described as follows (Lanson, ii. 150):

La meilleure secte du monde,
Et qui certes n'a rien d'humain;
La vraye Eglise militante,

Qui prêche un pistolet en main,
Pour mieux convertir son prochain
A grands coups de sabre argumente.

In part I, canto i, lines 239-78 of *Hudibras*, the security of the state
is closely linked with the preservation of Hudibras's beard. Voltaire
gives the following rendering (p.151):

Au nez du Chevalier critique
Deux grandes moustaches pendaient,
A qui les Parques attachaient
Le destin de la République.
Il les garde soigneusement,
Et si jamais on les arrache,
C'est la chute du Parlement:
L'état entier, en ce moment,
Doit tomber avec sa moustache.

To listen to Voltaire one would think that *Hudibras* was a greater
work than *Paradise lost*. In his view, Butler enjoys a better reputation
than Milton because *Paradise lost* was very gloomy. Moreover, Butler
was more entertaining. Voltaire goes to the length of saying that the
fights in *Hudibras* were better known than those in Milton's epic. That
Voltaire should have stressed the fights in *Hudibras* was not at all
fortuitous for he exploited them in the countless similar episodes that
take place in *La Pucelle*. The fights in both *Hudibras* and *La Pucelle*
are to the discredit of those taking part in them. Voltaire cleverly
uses the grotesque idea that the security of state depended on a man's
beard in *Hudibras* by making the destiny of France depend on the
virginity of a woman in *La Pucelle*. While the English are ravaging
France, the patron saint of the French, Denis, announces to the French
leaders at Orleans that he proposes to look round for a virgin who will
liberate the country.

As Voltaire's aim in revising some letters of the *Lettres philosophiques*
in the 1750s is not merely to familiarise the French public with English
literature, but to suit his own polemical purposes, it is quite possible
that he may have found the lines at the beginning of *Hudibras* relevant.
These could have been used not only in *La Pucelle*, but in many other
works such as *Le Monde comme il va*. Butler starts his poem in the
following manner (Wilders, p.1):

When *civil* Fury first grew high,
And men fell out they know not why;
When hard words, *Jealousies* and *Fears*,
Set Folks together by the ears,
And made them fight, like mad or drunk,
For Dame *Religion* as for Punk,
Whose honesty they all durst swear for,
Though not a man of them knew wherefore.

It may be noted that in 1734 *Hudibras* impresses Voltaire by its wit and by the ridicule with which it portrays mankind. In the 'Leningrad notebooks', however, it becomes clear that the fanaticism described in the poem has a greater appeal for him. From this point the progression appears natural: it culminates in the attack on sectarian wars in the 1756 addition to the *Lettres philosophiques*. Both Anglicans and Puritans are belittled in lines such as (Lanson, ii. 149):

Lorsqu'Anglicans et Puritains
Faisaient une si rude guerre,...
Que partout, sans savoir pourquoi,
Au nom du ciel, au nom du Roi,
Les gens d'armes couvraient la terre.

Before making his 1756 addition to the *Lettres* Voltaire might have taken the opportunity to exploit some parts of *Hudibras* at a deeper level in *Le Monde comme il va*. In the earlier *conte philosophique*, the Persian soldier betrayed complete ignorance as to the causes of the war, for he gave the following reply to Babouc (Bénac, p.66):

Par tous les dieux, dit le soldat, je n'en sais rien. Ce n'est pas mon affaire: mon métier est de tuer et d'être tué pour gagner me vie.

But the brunt of the attack is reserved for later years.

1756 sees the beginning of the Seven Years War and the lesson of that foolish war is reflected in Voltaire's correspondence. In a letter to Thieriot, Voltaire says: 'Je ne sçai s'il y a dans ce tableau baucoup de traits plus honteux pour l'humanité que de voir deux nations éclairées se couper la gorge en Europe pour quelques arpens de glace et de neige dans l'Amérique' (Best.D6755, 29 February 1756). He makes a similar protest to Moncrif: 'On plaint ce pauvre genre humain qui s'égorge dans notre continent à propos de quelques arpens de glace en Canada' (Best.D7215, 27 March 1757). Voltaire had more scope to elaborate on the follies he had seen in *Hudibras*, which must have still remained fresh in his mind after his revision of the *Lettres philosophiques*. In chapter xxiii of *Candide* as the hero does not know England, he asks whether people are as mad there as in France. The target is cleverly arranged: Martin eagerly grasps the opportunity offered him. He informs the ignorant Candide about this 'autre espèce de folie' and he adds 'vous savez que ces deux nations sont en guerre pour quelques arpents de neige vers le Canada, et qu'elles dépensent pour cette belle guerre beaucoup plus que tout le Canada ne vaut' (Bénac, p.199).

In his 1756 rendering of *Hudibras*, Voltaire had singled out the militant Puritan church (Lanson, ii. 150-51):

> Qui promet les célestes biens
> Par le gibet & par la corde,
> Et damne sans miséricorde
> Les péchés des autres Chrétiens,
> Pour se mieux pardonner les siens;
> Secte qui toujours détruisante
> Se détruit elle-même enfin.

He did not specifically mention Puritans in *Candide*, but he made the satire against religious sects equally biting there. In chapter iii after his escape Candide approaches a man who had lectured on charity for one hour in a great assembly. Because Candide does not follow up the preacher's suggestion of denouncing the pope as anti-Christ, he is treated in the most uncharitable manner: 'Tu ne mérites pas d'en manger [du pain] . . . va, coquin, va, misérable, ne m'approche de ta vie' (Bénac, p.143). The preacher's wife adding insult to injury, 'lui répandit sur le chef un plein . . .'. Voltaire keeps us guessing as to the nature of the thing poured over Candide. After his burlesque attacks against Maupertuis in the *Histoire du docteur Akakia* and after having relished similar burlesque techniques in the works of Butler and Pope, Voltaire probably had excremental possibilities in mind. He intervenes personally to deliver a sharp attack: 'O ciel! à quel excès se porte le zèle de la religion dans les dames!' The preacher's unchristian behaviour contrasts strikingly with that of the Anabaptist Jacques.

The concluding remark on *Hudibras* in the 1756 edition of the *Lettres philosophiques* is typical of Voltaire. He says that 'un homme qui aurait dans l'imagination la dixième partie de l'esprit comique, bon ou mauvais, qui régne dans cet ouvrage, serait encore très-plaisant: mais il se donnerait bien de garde de traduire *Hudibras*' (Lanson, ii. 152). Having exploited *Hudibras* as much as he wanted, he saw fit to reduce its merit and stick to the position he had adopted in 1734. Fréron, in a twenty-five page article devoted to *Hudibras*, refuted Voltaire's opinion that the poem could not be translated and announced a translation by an 'English gentleman who knew as much French as English' (*Année littéraire* (1755), iii. 48). The translation appeared in 1757.

Voltaire remembered Butler years later. In his remarks on Corneille's *Horace*, he wrote: (Williams, ii. 243):

Il n'est pas toujours vrai que dans notre poésie il y ait continuellement un vers pour le sens, un autre pour la rime, comme il est dit dans *Hudibras*:

> For one for sense, and one for rhyme,
> I think sufficient at a time.
> C'est assez, pour des vers méchants,
> Qu'un pour la rime, un pour le sens.

In the *Epître au roi de la Chine* (1771) in which he satirises the French literary scene, Voltaire again draws attention to Butler's opinion with which he does not agree. For he complains of

> cette loi si dure
> Qui veut qu'avec six pieds d'une égale mesure
> De deux alexandrins côte à côte marchants,
> L'un serve pour la rime et l'autre pour le sens.
>
> (M.x.414)

In the article 'Bouffon, burlesque, bas comique' of the *Questions sur l'encyclopédie* (1770), Voltaire had nothing but praise for Butler. He described him as one of the three or four Englishmen who excelled in this genre and he added: 'Hudibras est autant au-dessus de Scarron qu'un homme de bonne compagnie est au-dessus d'un chansonnier des cabarets de la Courtille' (M.xviii.27-28).

Butler's fellow satirist, Rochester (1647-80), the notorious rake and patron of poets such as Dryden, was mentioned in the second edition of Bayle's *Dictionnaire* (1702). He was described in the section 'Eclaircissement sur les Manichéens' as a man 'qui s'etait distingué par son esprit et par des compositions de plume pleines de sel et d'agrémens et l'un de ces Athées qui vivent selon leurs principes; car il se plongea dans les plus affreux excès de l'ivrognerie et de l'impudicité'. Bayle added that Rochester was converted by Gilbert Burnet, bishop of Salisbury.

Voltaire too was interested in Rochester. He wrote a few lines on him in the 'Small Leningrad notebook' under the heading 'Verses of the earl of Rochester extempore'. The lines quoted are from Rochester's poem *The King's epitaph* (*Notebooks*, i. 61):

> Here is the health to our pleasant witty king
> Whose word no man relies on,
> Who never said a foolish thing
> Or ever did a wise one.

Pope may have established in Voltaire's eyes the reputation Rochester enjoyed as a wit. In his edition of Mulgrave's works in 1723, Pope took considerable pains to omit Mulgrave's famous line against Rochester. Mulgrave wrote: 'Rochester I despise for his mere want of wit.' Pope's version read: 'Last enters Rochester of sprightly wit' (*Rochester*, ed. D. Farley-hills (London 1972), pp.14-15). Rochester's wit must have made a great impression on Voltaire, for he quoted *The King's epitaph* to Martin Sherlock about fifty years later. In an early part of the 'Cambridge notebook' and in the 'Leningrad notebooks' (*Notebooks*, i. 237) he even quotes more lines which are apparently not by Rochester, though attributed to him. Later in the 'Cambridge notebooks' (*Notebooks*, i. 98) he gives his version of Rochester's *Satire against mankind*.

In letter xxi of the *Letters concerning the English nation*, Voltaire tries to rehabilitate Rochester who has too often been portrayed as 'the Man of Pleasure, as one who was the Idol of the Fair' (p.197). He wants to show him rather as a man of genius and a great poet. After having recalled that Boileau wrote on the same subject, he adds: 'I don't know any better Method of improving the Taste than to compare the Productions of such great Genius's as have exercis'd their Talent on the same Subject' (p.198). This remark is important, because whatever be Voltaire's later pronouncements against English taste in literature, it reveals his firm belief in the usefulness of the comparative approach to an appreciation of literature and its importance in matters of style. Voltaire's contribution to comparative literature would no doubt have been enriched if he had known that Rochester's disciple, John Oldham (1653-83), had also written against man. Even here, however, Voltaire tries to make excuses for any English literary influence to which he may be subjected by arguing that 'the Delicacies of the *French* Tongue, will not allow a Translator to convey into it the licentious Impetuosity and Fire of the *English* Numbers' (p.200).

The lines of the 'Cambridge notebook' entitled 'Traduction de la satire de l'homme de mylord Rochester' (*Notebooks*, i. 98):

> Ouy je sais ta raison cette esclave orgueilleuse,
> Des brutes ses égaux rivale dédaigneuse,
> Qui croit entre eux et l'ange occuper le milieu
> Et pense être icy bas l'image de son dieu.
> Vil atome importun qui croit, doute, dispute,
> S'élève, rampe, tombe, et nie encor sa chute,
> Qui vous dit, je suis libre, en nous montrant ses fers
> Et dont l'œil tout troublé croit percer l'univers.
> Allez révérends fous dont les soins sophistiques
> Ont compilé l'amas de vos riens scolastiques,
> Pères de visions, et d'énigmes sacrez,
> Autheurs du labirinthe ou vous vous égarez,
> Inventez, arrangez, expliquez vos mistères,
> Et courez dans l'école adorer vos chimères

became in the *Letters concerning the English nation* (pp.200-201):

> Cet Esprit que je haïs, cet Esprit plein d'erreur,
> Ce n'est pas ma raison, c'est la tienne, Docteur,
> C'est la raison frivôle, inquiette, orgueilleuse,
> Des sages Animaux rivale dédaigneuse,
> Qui croit entr'eux & l'Ange occuper le milieu,
> Et pense être ici bas l'image de son Dieu.
> Vil atôme importun, qui croit, doute, dispute,
> Rampe, s'éleve, tombe & nie encor sa chute,
> Qui nous dit je suis libre, en nous montrant ses fers,
> Et dont l'œil trouble & faux croit percer l'Univers;
> Allez, révérends Fous, bien-heureux Fanatiques,
> Compilez bien l'Amas de vos Riens scolastiques;
> Pères de Visions, & d'Enigmes sacréz,
> Auteurs du Labirinthe où vous vous égarez,
> Allez obscurément éclaircir vos mistères,
> Et courez dans l'école adorer vos chimères.

The later draft is a slight improvement on the earlier one; it already shows what the attack against doctors such as Kahle and Pangloss is likely to be. From both drafts can be seen something of the technique that will be used to satirise the smallness of man in *Micromégas* and the stupidity of schoolmen and system builders in the *Courte réponse*.

Voltaire took pains to use Rochester's ideas as well as the manner in which he expressed them in the *Satire against mankind*. It may be seen from a close reference to the quotations in the 'Cambridge notebook' and the *Letters* that Voltaire improves upon his model by changing the order of Rochester's lines and by freely adapting them. Rochester had written:

> Blest glorious Man, to whom alone kind Heav'n
> An everlasting Soul hath freely giv'n;
> Whom his great Maker took such care to make,
> That from himself he did the Image take,
> And this fair Frame in shining Reason drest,
> To dignifie his Nature above Beast.
> Reason, by whose aspiring Influence,
> We take a flight beyond material Sense,
> Dive into Mysteries, then soaring pierce
> The flaming limits of the Universe, . . .
> And 'tis this very Reason I despise,
> This supernat'ral Gift, that makes a Mite
> Think he's the Image of the Infinite; . . .
> This busie puzling stirrer up of doubt,
> That frames deep Mysteries, then finds 'em out,
> Filling with frantick crowds of thinking Fools,
> The reverend Bedlams, Colleges and Schools,
> Born on whose Wings, each heavy Sot can pierce
> The limits of the boundless Universe: . . .
> But Thoughts were giv'n for Actions Government;
> Where Action ceases, Thought's impertinent.
> Our sphere of Action is Lifes happiness,
> And he that thinks beyond, thinks like an Ass.
> Thus whilst against false reas'ning I inveigh,
> I own right Reason, which I would obey, . . .
> 'Tis not true Reason I despise, but yours.
> (*Poetical works of John Wilmot, earl of Rochester*,
> ed. Q. Johns (1933), pp.61-63)

In order to make his point about the importance of the comparative method in the *Conseils à un journaliste*, Voltaire referred to Rochester whom he described as a very successful satirist. He noted the pleasure which a reader with refined taste would have on seeing 'ce que Despréaux a rendu d'une manière si correcte; ce que Dryden et Rochester ont renouvelé avec le feu de leur génie' (M.xxii. 257). Voltaire thought that parallels in literature were like comparative anatomy which helped one to know nature better. It is thanks to these parallels that one is able to show not only what an author has said, but what he might have said. There is no doubt about the high regard in which Rochester is held, placed as he is in the company of Boileau and Dryden, the leading satirists of the seventeenth century in France and England.

Crown prince Frederick of Prussia kept Rochester alive in Voltaire's mind in the same period. In an obvious allusion to Rochester's poem, *The King's epitaph*, Frederick wrote to him: 'On disoit de ce prince qu'il ne lui étoit jamais échappée de parolle qui ne fût bien placée, et qu'il n'avoit jamais fait d'action qu'on pût nomer louable' (Best. D1392, 19 November 1737).

In an attempt to minimise his indebtedness to Rochester, Voltaire had concluded his remarks on the English man in the *Letters* by saying that whether the ideas expressed in the text quoted were true or false, ' 'tis certain they are express'd with an Energy and Fire which form the poet' (p.203). The author of the article on English poetry in the *Journal littéraire* had expressed himself in a different way. In his view Rochester in his satires bites and tears to pieces in cruel and pitiless fashion: he displays the same licence which became manifest in his life. With regard to the *Satire against mankind* on the other hand, he finds that if Rochester is inferior to Boileau from the point of view of style and the beauty of the poetry, he is at least equal to him where imagination and thought are concerned (p.171).

There is not a long interval between the time Voltaire made his remarks on Rochester in the *Lettres philosophiques* and used Rochester's ideas about man's littleness, conceit, stupidity, idle speculation and lack of action in his works. In *Micromégas* which was probably composed in 1739,[14] a few years after the *Lettres philosophiques*, he delivers his onslaught on men simply by varying the angle of his camera and by changing those who look through it. After having himself laughed at our 'petite fourmilière', Voltaire looks at the globe from the point of view of the Saturnian and the Sirian: they recognize 'cette mare, presque imperceptible pour eux, qu'on nomme la Méditerranée, et cet autre petit étang qui, sous le nom du grand Océan, entoure la

---

[14] the dating of this *conte* poses many problems. See my article 'A propos de la date de composition de *Micromégas*', *Studies on Voltaire* (1975), cxl. 73-83.

taupinière' (Bénac, p.103). It follows almost logically that if mountains on earth are but 'petits grains pointus dont ce globe est hérissé', the inhabitants themselves will appear insignificant: therefore 'le microscope, qui faisait à peine discerner une baleine et un vaisseau, n'avait point de prise sur un être aussi imperceptible que des hommes' (p.105).

The denigration of man in *Micromégas* proceeds with their metamorphosis into 'insectes invisibles' (p.108) and finally into 'animalcules' and 'petites mites' (pp.112, 113). The only redeeming trait in mankind is that it is made up of 'atomes intelligents, dans qui l'Etre éternel s'est plu à manifester son adresse et sa puissance' (p.109). There is no doubt that for the vocabulary as for the thought, *Micromégas* is to a certain extent indebted to the *Satire against mankind*. The camera focuses not only on the physical smallness of man, but also on other aspects of his insignificance and stupidity. Sufficient examples are produced to drive home the satire which has now become very vehement. It must be pointed out, however, that *Micromégas* owes even more to Swift's *Gulliver's travels* (see below, p.249).

The next work in which Voltaire could have used Rochester was the *Courte réponse*. To be in a better position to appreciate its full impact, it is perhaps helpful to consider it as one of the climaxes in the series of controversies centring on Leibniz. The field of Leibnizian controversy has been conveniently split up under three headings: Liebnizian systematic metaphysics, as professed by Wolff and his disciples; the problem of human free-will; and the question of optimism.[15] Before the *Courte réponse*, Voltaire had written a very outspoken criticism of Wolff and the new scholasticism in a letter to Maupertuis. He did not distinguish between Wolffian and Leibnizian metaphysics and referring to Wolff in the letter he remarked (Best.D2526, 10 August 1741):

Cet homme là ramène en Allemagne toutes les horreurs de la scolastique surchargées de raisons suffisantes, de monades, d'indiscernables, et de touttes les absurditez scientifiques que Leibnits a mis au monde par vanité, et que les allemans étudient parce qu'ils sont allemans.

Personal animosity developed between Voltaire and Jean Deschamps, the most fervent supporter of Wolff and the translator and populariser of his works. In the *Cours abrégé de philosophie wolffienne* which he published in 1743, Deschamps had digressed from a serious discussion

[15] see W. H. Barber, *Leibniz in France: from Arnauld to Voltaire* (Oxford 1955), p.177.

of 'Des élements des corps' to make abusive personal remarks about Voltaire. Moreover, convinced that Kahle refutes Voltaire so well in the *Vergleichung*, he persuaded Gautier de Saint-Blancard to translate the German work. The French translation by Saint-Blancard appeared under the title of *Examen du livre intitulé 'La Métaphysique de Newton'* in 1744.

When due consideration is given to the circumstances surrounding this quarrel, one cannot help feeling that Voltaire must have also been encouraged in his stand by the violence he had noted in Rochester's attack on mankind in general and schoolmen and system builders in particular. After a courteous beginning in a letter he wrote to Kahle, Voltaire insists that Kahle knows little or nothing about monads and preestablished harmony (Best.D2945, ? March 1744). The irony at Kahle's expense is produced both by the challenge Voltaire throws at him to solve the problem of free-will and by the phrase 'vous me ferez plaisir de m'en avertir' which is reemphasised in the following sentence in a slightly different formula: 'Quand vous aurez ainsi demontré, en vers ou autrement, pourquoi tant d'hommes s'égorgent dans le meilleur des mondes possibles, je vous serai très obligé.' This second challenge helped to throw ridicule on Leibnizian optimism. It was but a passing attack, as the concentrated attack took place in the 1750s, notably in *Candide*.

However, even in the *Courte réponse* one can appreciate the tone of Voltaire's biting sarcasm. Voltaire achieves his satirical effect by using imagery that belittles metaphysics and by an insistent harping on its chimerical nature. In addition to Kahle, he hits at another system-atizer, Malebranche, the Cartesian philosopher. Malebranche is contemptuously treated as a man who

ne concevant rien de beau, rien d'utile que son système, s'exprime ainsi: "Les hommes ne sont pas faits pour considérer des moucherons; et on n'approuve pas la peine que quelques personnes se sont donnée de nous apprendre comment sont faits certains insectes, la transformation des vers, etc. Il est permis de s'amuser à cela quand on n'a rien à faire, et pour se divertir." (M.xxiii.194).

Voltaire suggests that empirical knowledge is useful and constructive while Malebranche has wasted forty years studying reactionary *a priori* theories like Descartes's vortices. He is here reinforcing a point he made in *Micromégas* where the 'philosophe malebranchiste' spoke of his vision of God. It was a grotesque picture of man reduced to the condition of passive onlooker: 'C'est Dieu qui fait tout pour moi: je vois tout en lui, je fais tout en lui; c'est lui qui fait tout sans que je m'en mêle' (Bénac, p.112). Rochester had suggested the opposite, that 'thoughts are given for Actions Government'. Voltaire concludes the *Courte réponse* with an ironical remark at the expense of those who can understand things that are so incomprehensible and who can see a different world from the one in which we live.

Rochester is remembered by Voltaire long afterwards. In the *Questions sur l'encyclopédie* (1770), Voltaire refers to him thus in the article 'Amour': 'Si tu réfléchis sur ces prééminences, tu diras avec le comte de Rochester: "L'amour, dans un pays d'athées, ferait adorer la Divinité!" ' (M.xvii.173).

Five years later, Rochester's extreme philosophy is reaffirmed when the atheist Birton is compared with him in the *Histoire de Jenni*. In Voltaire's words, Birton was 'un caractère à peu près dans le goût du feu comte de Rochester'. He was extreme in his dissipation, in his courage, in his ideas, in his expressions, in his Epicurean philosophy, attracted to nothing unless it was extraordinary, which he very soon got tired of, having the kind of spirit which takes likeness for demonstration; wiser and more eloquent than any other young man of his period but never giving himself the trouble of going into anything deeply (Bénac, p.523).

There is no doubt that Voltaire appreciated and exploited the works of Butler and Rochester, *Hudibras* and the *Satire against mankind*, in particular. At times he even tended to exaggerate the importance of Butler at the expense of Milton. One can appreciate his stand: Butler must have appeared less of a rival than Milton. Moreover, he could be enjoyed on two levels: as a light-hearted writer and as one who could stimulate serious thought. There was the same mixture of wit and seriousness in Rochester which appealed to Voltaire. However, the influence of Butler and Rochester on Voltaire has to be set against that of other Augustan satirists if a sense of proportion is to be maintained.

iii. *Dryden's satirical influence on Voltaire*

Perhaps more significant than either Butler or Rochester to Voltaire was Dryden (1631-1700). It was the author of the 'Dissertation sur la poésie anglaise' who was probably responsible for the French pre-

judice against Dryden as a satirist, although he briefly referred to
Dryden's extraordinary talent for satire.[16] He thought poorly of
English satirists. He found Boileau vastly superior to all of them,
claiming that in Boileau's satires there was 'pas un seul mot qui puisse
alarmer la pudeur la plus scrupuleuse' (*Journal littéraire*, (1717) ix.
170). With reference to Dryden's satirical masterpiece, *Absalom and
Achitophel*, he observed (p.171):

Les mœurs licencieuses de la Cour de Charles II ne fournissaient que trop de
matière au libertinage de cette plume, qui a bien osé jetter tout son venin sur
ce Prince, sur ses favoris et ses favorites, sans prendre d'autre précaution que
de cacher Charles, Monmouth et Londres, sous les noms de David, d'Absalom
et de Jérusalem. Il y a dans cette pièce du feu infiniment, des pensées fort
neuves, mais en récompense bien de l'obscénité et de profanation.

The importance of this article, however ambiguous in its attitude to
Dryden's merit, lies in the fact that it emphasizes Dryden's role as a
satirist.

Like his contemporary Rochester, Dryden was indebted to French
writers. Indeed, it has been argued that the pamphleteers who attacked
Shaftesbury, including Dryden, looked to French works for hints that
could help them in writing their own lampoons and satires, since
d'Urfé's *L'Astrée* had set the pattern for numerous allegories with
political significance in France (Ian Jack, *Augustan satire* (1966),
p.55). However, Van Doren observed that Dryden's debt was to
French criticism and to French ideals exquisitely expressed rather than
to any French poetry that he read (*The Poetry of J. Dryden* (1931),
p.98). Dryden himself did not think highly of French heroic poetry.
In the dedication to the *Aeneis* (1697), he claimed that 'the affected
purity of the French has unsinewed their heroic verse. The language
of an epic poem is almost wholly figurative: yet they are so fearful of a
metaphor that no example of Virgil can encourage them to be bold
with safety' (Watson, ii. 247-48). Dryden's attack on the French may
partly explain the unfavourable judgment passed on him by the
Journal littéraire. In this way a myth was created that Dryden could
never have had a satirical influence on Voltaire.

---

[16] it is likely that Voltaire read the essay: he was then on good terms with its author,
Saint-Hyacinthe, who watched a performance of *Œdipe* by his side. See J. Gillet, *Le
Paradis perdu dans la littérature françoise*, pp.25, 27, nn.25, 26; see also P. Van Tieghem,
La Découverte de Shakespeare, p.13.

177

The connection between Dryden and Voltaire starts in a strange way. Companions in misfortune, they were both assaulted by aristocrats: Dryden by Rochester's men in 1679, and Voltaire by the chevalier de Rohan's men in 1726. Dryden was suspected of having helped John Sheffield, earl of Mulgrave in a passage in his *Essay upon satire* which was circulated in manuscript in 1679. (See above, p.170). This unhappy coincidence, however, played a small part in the connection. For Voltaire must have felt a deeper affinity with Dryden on account of the similarity of their outlook on some aspects of religion. One is not, however, justified in saying that Voltaire was interested in Dryden only as a playwright who had accomplished the poet-philosopher role to which he himself aspired or that he thought of Dryden, as he did of English literature in general, in terms of the drama (Russell, pp.66, 148). Russell appears to be supporting traditional French attitudes to Dryden.[17]

The position is rather different. Voltaire was interested in Dryden in other ways. At the request of Charles ii, Dryden translated the Jesuit Maimbourg's *Histoire de la Ligue* in 1684. This translation could not have left the author of the epic *La Ligue* indifferent. Moreover, Maimbourg was the very man whom Bayle had attacked in the *Critique générale de l'histoire du Calvinisme* (1682). It is generally recognised that Voltaire showed great admiration for Bayle most of his life and that he had read the *Critique générale*.[18] His interest in Maimbourg and Bayle no doubt prompted his interest in Dryden. The catalogues of Voltaire's library at Leningrad and at Ferney are not particularly useful where Dryden is concerned, since they list only his *Essay of dramatick poesy*, his translations of *Fables ancient and modern* and the *Dramatic works*. Yet Voltaire proved that his acquaintance with Dryden extended well beyond these works. *The Spectator* directed his attention to Dryden's *Absalom and Achitophel*. For Addison spoke highly of the character *Zimri* and quoted some famous lines from the poem about him (no.162). Steele repeated the eulogy and the quotation (no.222), while Addison described *Absalom* as 'one of the most popular poems that ever appeared in *English*' (no.517).

In his dedication to the translation of the *History of the League*, Dryden compares the French and English religious conflicts. In his

---

[17] e.g. in *Le Babillard* and *Le Pour et contre*, A. de La Chapelle and Prévost respectively stressed the style of Dryden's tragedies.

[18] see H. T. Mason, *Pierre Bayle and Voltaire* (Oxford 1963), p.6.

view there never was 'a plainer parallel than of the troubles of France and of Great Britain; of their leagues, covenants, associations, and ours; of their Calvinists and our Presbyterians: they are all of the same family'.[19] Voltaire shows similar sentiments in *La Henriade*. Towards the end of the first book, the future Henry IV visits England, 'ce sanglant théâtre où cent héros périrent' (l.297). Queen Elizabeth, whose peoples forgot their losses in her reign, asks Henry for an account of the troubles of France. At the beginning of the second book, Henry replies (Taylor, p.391):

> C'est la religion dont le zèle inhumain
> Met à tous les Français les armes à la main.
> Je ne décide point entre Genève et Rome.
> De quelque nom divin que leur parti les nomme,
> J'ai vu des deux côtés la fourbe et la fureur.

Voltaire shows an intimate knowledge of Dryden's satires and this knowledge was not necessarily restricted to the satires quoted in the notebooks or elsewhere. For the chevalier de Boufflers, who was staying with Voltaire at Ferney, wrote to his mother, the marquise de Boufflers: 'Il est venu chez lui un Anglais qui ne peut pas se lasser de l'entendre parler anglais, & reciter tous les poèmes de Driden, comme papa récite la *Jeanne*' (Best.D12274, *c.* 30 December 1764). The English visitor was Boswell. That very year, in his review of Churchill's poems in the *Gazette littéraire*, Voltaire left no doubt as to his esteem for Pope and Dryden as satirists. He also made it clear that he had read their works (M.xxv.168).

Dryden's satire, *The Medal* (1682), is twice quoted in the notebooks, with minor alterations: once in the 'Small Leningrad notebook' and once in the 'Leningrad notebooks'. In the former, the title of the item is 'Dryden about Religion' and in the latter, it becomes 'Dryden in a tragedy'. Voltaire chooses lines that appeal to him in particular (*Notebooks*, i. 52):

> The common cry is ever religion's test
> The Turk's at Constantinople best
> Idols in India, Popery at Rome
> And our own worship only true at home
> And true but for the time, tis hard to know

---

[19] *The Works of John Dryden*, ed. W. Scott, revised by G. Saintsbury (London 1892), xvii. 89.

How long we please it shall continue so
This side today, and that tomorrow burns
So all are God a'mighty in their turns.[20]

The above passage and other Dryden quotations were probably taken from E. Bysshe's *Art of poetry* under the heading 'Religion'. Bysshe's work was first published in 1702 and frequently after this. Voltaire does not seem to have made much use of these lines subsequently, although with regard to thought some parallel can be drawn between the first four lines and the famous lines spoken by the heroine of *Zaïre* in act I, scene i (M.ii.560):

La coutume, la loi plia mes premiers ans
A la religion des heureux musulmans...
J'eusse été près du Gange esclave des faux dieux,
Chrétienne dans Paris, musulmane en ces lieux.

It is not surprising that Voltaire should have used an English satirical source for religious propaganda in a play: it is a permanent aspect of his technique to exploit a source in a different genre. He also reproduced the last two lines of the quotation in the article 'Blasphème' in the *Questions sur l'encyclopédie* in 1770. There he wrote that Dryden had said (M.xviii.5):

This side today and the other to morrow burns,
And they are all God's almighty in their turns.

He translated the lines as

Tel est chaque parti, dans sa rage obstiné,
Aujourd'hui condamnant, et demain condamné.

The error in the later quotation may be due to the fact that Voltaire was relying on his memory.

However, the rest of *The Medal* may have proved useful to Voltaire in satirising J. B. Rousseau in the *Temple du goût*. In Dryden's poem, Shaftesbury's supporters are denigrated by means of animal imagery (cf. above, p.164). They are turned into 'bellowing Renegado Priests' and 'puny Sects'. The animal imagery further trivializes them in the lines (ll. 304-305):

And frogs and toads, and all the tadpole train,
Will croak to Heav'n for help from this devouring crane.

20 see *The Poetical works*, ed. G. Noyes (Cambridge, Mass. 1950); ll. 103-10.

In the Kehl edition of the *Temple*, Rousseau is still allowed the merit of a skilled versifier, but new ways of exacting vengeance upon him have been found. He is now turned into the frog about which he wrote in *Le Rossignol et la grenouille* (Carcassonne, p.123):

> Qui du fond d'un petit thorax
> Va chantant, pour toute musique,
> Brekeke, kake, koax, koax, koax.

'La Critique' cannot help exclaiming: 'Quel horrible jargon'. Puzzled as to who that could be, she is told that it is Rousseau 'dont les Muses avaient changé la voix, en punition de ses méchancetés' (p.124). The dual influence of the English and French satirical traditions is evident here. With his reading of Dryden and other English satirical writers fresh in his mind, Voltaire must have remembered the treatment meted out to Shaftesbury's supporters in Dryden's *The Medal*. Nor had he forgotten the French satirists' delight in metamorphosing their enemies into crows.

It is not simply as a writer with sceptical, deist and anti-fanatical views that Dryden interests Voltaire. In the 'Cambridge notebook' where he is talking of the theatre, it is significant that Voltaire should link Dryden's name with Shadwell. For Shadwell is the very man whom Dryden mercilessly satirised in 1682 in *Mac Flecknoe*. Voltaire remarks: 'Remember Smith, and Euripides Hippolitus, with Shadwell and Dryden' (*Notebooks*, i. 107). There is no doubt that Voltaire had read or heard of Dryden's successful attempt to pile contempt on Shadwell. The latter's reputation never recovered from the onslaught of *Mac Flecknoe*.[21] In the *Letters concerning the English nation*, Voltaire wondered why Muralt should speak of an author who 'was held in pretty great Contempt in his time, and was not the Poet of the polite Part of the Nation' (p.181). As he knew Pope's *Dunciad* very well, it is likely that Voltaire would have been interested in *Mac Flecknoe*, which probably inspired the 1728 *Dunciad*. Both poems describe the succession of one dunce to another on the throne of Dullness.

Dryden began *Mac Flecknoe* in high style with a grave sententia (ll. 1-2):

> All human things are subject to decay,
> And when fate summons, monarchs must obey.

---

[21] see A. Beljame, *Le Public et les hommes de lettres en Angleterre au XVIIIe siècle*, translated by E. O. Lorimer (London 1948), p.175.

Epic associations of grandeur are used to make Shadwell helplessly ridiculous, 'but the effect, though disastrous for the enemy, is very different from that of the humour which merely belittles ... Dryden continually enhances: he makes his object great, in a way contrary to expectation; and the total effect is due to the transformation of the ridiculous into poetry' (T. S. Eliot, *Homage to J. Dryden* (1924), p.15). Dryden's method is thus different[22] from Butler's in *Hudibras*, which was rather that of straightforward diminution: the quarrels which were followed by the civil war are represented as being as insignificant as any petty dispute for a whore. Yet Butler is the satirist for whom Dryden had the highest praise in the *Discourse concerning satire*, despite the criticism that the double rhyme of *Hudibras* 'is not so proper for manly satire; for it turns earnest too much to jest, and gives us a boyish kind of pleasure' (Watson, ii. 147).

The contempt Dryden shows for Shadwell is expressed with the denigration of a lampoon (ll. 16-24).

> Mature in dulness from his tender years;
> Shadwell alone of all my sons is he
> Who stands confirmed in full stupidity.
> The rest to some faint meaning make pretence,
> But Shadwell never deviates into sense.
> Some beams of wit on other souls may fall,
> Strike through and make a lucid interval;
> But Shadwell's genuine night admits no ray,
> His rising fogs prevail upon the day.

These lines derive their destructive force from the fact that outwardly they have the veneer of an eulogy. They reveal a Dryden who does not hesitate for a moment to refer to his adversary by name. His constant harping on the name and his use of words like dullness, stupidity, strengthened later by 'tautology' also mean that he is quite unwilling to beat about the bush. His practice is therefore quite at variance with his theory as expressed in the *Discourse concerning satire* where he had observed (Watson, ii. 137):

[22] in much the same way as Boileau's mock heroic *Le Lutrin* is different from Scarron's burlesque *Le Virgile travesti*. For his own mock heroic, *Mac Flecknoe*, Dryden had sought a model in *Le Lutrin* which he had described thus: 'the most beautiful, and most noble kind of satire. Here is the majesty of the heroic, finely mixed with the venom of the other; and raising the delight which otherwise would be flat and vulgar, by the sublimity of the expression' (Watson, ii. 149).

How easy it is to call rogue and villain, and that wittily! But how hard to make a man appear a fool, a blockhead, or a knave, without using any of those opprobrious terms! To spare the grossness of the names, and to do the thing yet more severely, is to draw a full face, and to make the nose and cheeks stand out, and yet not to employ any depth of shadowing.

When he writes satire, Dryden finds the direct method at times superior to all subterfuge. The attack is not always on a high plane, particularly in lines 102-103:

> Much *Heywood*, *Shirly*, *Ogleby* there lay,
> But loads of *Sh*– almost choakt the way.

There is no doubt about what Dryden is implying by leaving a blank after Sh in the last line. Voltaire quoted Dryden among those who identified their victims only by the initial letters of their names. This is simply not true: Dryden and Pope often clearly named their opponents. Perhaps Voltaire did not need to refer to Dryden when defending his practice of satire, since he could quote Pope (see below, p.225). He may well have been inspired by Dryden when he exploited to the full the potential offered by proper names. The repetition of names such as La Beaumelle, Fréron and Berthier with their variants proved most effective in Voltaire's polemical writings.

In his attack against his enemy La Beaumelle in the *Supplément au siècle de Louis XIV* published in 1753, Voltaire writes (M.xv. 102-103):

C'est La Beaumelle qui daigne enseigner la langue française à Voltaire; c'est La Beaumelle qui décide sur les auteurs; c'est La Beaumelle qui se mêle de condamner Louis xiv; c'est La Beaumelle qui dit qu'*on se gâte à Potsdam;* c'est La Beaumelle qui, sans daigner jamais apporter la moindre raison de ses décisions, parle avec la même modestie que s'il avait un roi d'Angleterre à faire.

The despised name of La Beaumelle stands out conspicuously in the *anaphora*. Voltaire's technique of paying an ironical compliment goes hand in hand in the *Supplément* with the older technique of rhetoric which puts the emphasis on passion. Indeed, Voltaire's apostrophe to La Beaumelle produces all the effects of a seventeenth-century tirade. Lanson noted how Voltaire exploited the sound effects of his enemies' names. This was particularly noticeable in the *Relation du jésuite Berthier* (1759) where proper names 'renvoyés comme à la raquette – frère Berthier, frère Coutu; dit Berthier, dit Coutu, – croisent, compliquent le dessin sonore du morceau' (*L'Art de la prose* (1908), p.158).

1760 also sees the publication of *Les Fréron* in the *Recueil des facéties parisiennes*. Although this poem contains allegations about Fréron's doubtful morals in the lines (M.x.565):

> L'autre jour un gros ex-jésuite,
> Dans le grenier d'une maison,
> Rencontra fille très-instruite
> Avec un beau petit garçon.
> Le bouc s'empara du giton.
> On le découvre, il prend la fuite

it is on the whole less insulting than the remarks made in the other satirical writings of the same year against Fréron. Much of its effect is derived from the name Fréron which appears at the end of each of the seven stanzas like a kind of refrain. It is almost goodnatured fun: even children are brought in to chant 'C'est Fréron'. There is also some of the humour of *Candide* in the repetitive phrase 'C'est du Fréron, c'est du Fréron' which echoes Candide's 'mangeons du jésuite, mangeons du jésuite!' (Bénac, p.172)

Although *The Indian emperor* is the most frequently quoted work of Dryden in the 'Leningrad notebooks', it is the satires *The Medal* and *Absalom and Achitophel* that are the most lengthily quoted – eight lines each. Voltaire chooses the beginning of *Absalom and Achitophel* (ll. 1-4, 7-10; *Notebooks*, i. 243):

> In ancient times ee'r priestcraft did begin
> Before poligamy was taught a sin
> When man on many multiplied his kind
> Eer, one to one, was cursedly confin'd, [. . .]
> Then Israels monarch after heaven's own heart
> His vigorous warm did variously impart
> To wives and slaves, and wide as his command
> Scatter'd his maker's image through the land.

It would be a mistake to assume that Voltaire was quoting these lines simply for the sake of quoting. He may have found here another technique for satirising the Jews. The fact that he had many sources for his views on Jews such as Maillet, Fréret, Bolingbroke and Toland[23] does not exclude Dryden from being an additional source. He did

---

[23] Voltaire mentions these names in *La Défense de mon oncle* (1767), (M.xxvi. 423). See H. Mason, *Pierre Bayle and Voltaire*, p.30.

laugh at Jewish customs in the *Traité de métaphysique* and the *Dictionnaire philosophique*. In the former work, Voltaire insinuates that the Jews lack initiative. Using superlatives, he describes the Old Testament as follows: 'le plus ancien livre qui soit au monde, conservé par un peuple qui se prétend le plus ancien peuple . . . ce livre m'apprend que Dieu a autrefois donné aux Juifs les lois les plus détaillées que jamais nation ait reçues; il daigne leur prescrire jusqu'à la manière dont ils doivent aller à la garde-robe' (ed. T. Patterson (1937), p.36). In the article 'Abraham' in the *Dictionnaire* the satire against the Jews and those who believe in their history is couched in authoritative terms: 'C'est un singulier exemple de la stupidité humaine, que nous ayons si longtemps regardé les Juifs comme une nation qui avait tout enseigné aux autres, tandis que leur historien Josèphe avoue lui-même le contraire' (ed. Benda and Naves, p.5). In the article 'Carême' he has the opportunity of ridiculing the Jewish habit of fasting and wonders whether they took this custom from the Egyptians whose rites they imitated 'jusqu'à la flagellation et au bouc émissaire' (p.64).

Imagery has a crucial role to play in *Absalom and Achitophel*: it is strongly reminiscent of *Paradise lost*. It is consistently applied to those who have risen against the king or who are plotting a new uprising (ll. 144-45):

> Some had in courts been Great and thrown from thence
> Like Fiends were harden'd in Impenitence.

The epic association of the poem does not merely give it dignity: it is a powerful instrument used in a serious manner by Dryden to denigrate his adversaries. The epic grandeur serves only to make the fall of Satan (Shaftesbury) the greater.[24] In *La Pucelle*, Voltaire must have remembered the interesting precedent set by Dryden in *Absalom and Achitophel* and taken up by Pope in *The Dunciad* (book iii, ll. 23-26) for he used epic imagery to deflate and denigrate his principal opponent, Fréron. Boileau's *Le Lutrin* might have served the same purpose, but there is not much trace of its imagery in the attack on Fréron.

There is evidence of a general English influence on Voltaire in the early 1730s. In the *Discours sur la tragédie*, Voltaire confessed to his

---

[24] Hoffman's comment is most apposite here: 'with all its mitigations, all its fairness at the level of representation of a gifted man, the judgment that the portrait holds over its subject is that he is the intrepid devil himself emerging from Hell to destroy Eden and to devote man to death'. See A. W. Hoffman, *J. Dryden's imagery* (1962), p.80.

friend Bolingbroke that on his return to England, where he had spent
nearly two years studying English continuously, he felt embarrassed
when he wanted to write a tragedy in French. He had almost become
used to thinking in English and he added: 'Je sentais que les termes
de ma langue ne venaient plus se présenter à mon imagination avec
la même abondance qu'auparavant. C'était comme un ruisseau dont
la source avait été détournée' (M.ii. 311-12). This being the case, some
individual writers must have had a greater impact on Voltaire than
others. Dryden must have been among those whom he esteemed most.
The ode entitled *La Mort de mlle Lecouvreur* (1730) provides some
evidence of Dryden's status in Voltaire's eyes. Dryden is given a place
of honour along with other celebrities in the temple of memory
(M.ix. 370):

> Le sublime Dryden, et le sage Addison,
> Et la charmante Ophils, et l'immortel Newton,
> Ont part au temple de mémoire.

Despite the hatred for satire shown in his letter to the *Nouvelliste
du Parnasse* in 1731, this letter is significant for an assessment of a direct
English influence on Voltaire's satirical writings at this stage of his
literary career. In it he also looks at the positive aspects of criticism:
his conclusion is that authors who wish to teach others to think should
set examples of politeness as well as eloquence and unite social decorum
with decorum in style. We can see the influence of Dryden's decorum
here – a decorum which is also the ideal of French classicism – and the
role of the dual tradition in Voltaire's works. Voltaire refers to his
English visit and England must surely be one of those foreign countries
he mentions which think that the French are not fair to their contemporaries. It is England that prompts Voltaire to be fair to other
French writers and to do something about the bad reputation the
French have with regard to their treatment of contemporaries. There
is a similarity between Voltaire's attitude and Dryden's in the *Discourse
concerning satire* and the *Essay of dramatic poesy*. In the first essay,
Dryden had written: 'It had been much fairer if the modern critics
who have embarked in the quarrels of their favourite authors, had
rather given to each his proper due' (Watson, ii. 117).

It is not unlikely that Dryden's fairmindedness influenced Voltaire
in this period as Pope's vituperation did later. For Voltaire used the
best and the worst in English satire as the occasion demanded. He

certainly shows generosity in his handling of the *Œdipe* controversy with La Motte about tragedies written in prose. The polemics of the preface to *Œdipe* may have been vigorous, but it was courteous and gave him much satisfaction. In a letter to Porée, he wrote (Best.D392, 7 January 1731):

J'écris avec tant de civilité contre lui, que je l'ai demandé lui même pour examinateur de cette préface où je tâche de lui prouver son tort à chaque ligne, & il a lui même approuvé ma petite dissertation polémique. Voilà comme les gens de lettres devraient se combattre.

He corroborates this account in the *Mémoire sur la satire* where he stresses the extraordinary nature of the event, namely that a royal censor should have approved a work written against himself (M.xxiii. 49). It is the same sort of satisfaction Dryden felt about Zimri in *Absalom*: 'The character of Zimri in my *Absalom* is, in my opinion, worth the whole poem: 'tis not bloody, but 'tis ridiculous enough. And he for whom it was intended, was too witty to resent it as an injury' (*Discourse concerning satire*, Watson, ii. 137). La Motte himself says in the 'approbation' to this preface that in it Voltaire made many observations that were opposed to his views, but 'elles m'ont paru polies et même obligeantes par les égards personnels, agréables et spécieuses par les raisons' (M.ii. 47, n.1).

The treatment of Fontenelle in the *Temple du goût* does not appear grossly unfair[25] for Voltaire appreciates his merit. Although the 'sage' Fontenelle of the Rouen edition becomes the 'discret' Fontenelle of the Kehl edition, he is endowed with positive qualities which are held before Rousseau's eyes as examples worth imitating. He is described (Carcassonne, p.78) as a man who

> ... par les Beaux Arts entouré,
> Répandait sur eux, à son gré,
> Une clarté pure et nouvelle.

---

[25] contemporaries held a different view of Voltaire's tactics in the *Temple*: e.g. Cideville wrote to Voltaire: 'En général cet ouvrage a charmé les juges équitables par son heureux invention, par sa varieté, et son stile, mais il a blessé par La critique amère que vous y faites de deux gens vivans tel que mr. de Fontenelle et mr. Rousseau ... il est en vérité indigne de vous de vous répandre en injures et d'estre satirique' (Best. D582, 28 March 1733). cf. the tone of La Bruyère's attack on Fontenelle who was referred to as Cydias in *Les Caractères* and Théobalde in the *Discours à l'Académie* in *Les Caractères*, ed. R. Garapon (Paris 1962), pp. 175-77, 493.

Voltaire pays homage to the varied genius of Fontenelle when he writes:

> D'une main légère il prenait
> Le compas, la plume et la lyre.

He then uses Rousseau as an instrument of disparagement: this technique is all the more remarkable since Rousseau's first objections to Fontenelle's presence in the temple could well be his own genuine objections to a writer against whom he had written epigrams. However, the objections put into Rousseau's mouth are really Voltaire's. Dryden had pointed out in the *Discourse concerning satire* how hard it was to make a man appear a fool without using the word. In the *Essay of dramatic poesy*, he used Neander as his mouthpiece to attack French drama, while in *Absalom* he used Jews and allegorical characters to satirise the English people and the opposition to Charles II led by Shaftesbury in 1681. He himself appeared as the mouthpiece of the King's party. Through Rousseau, Voltaire is able to hit out at the author of the *Lettres du chevalier d'Her*, the tragedy of *Aspar*, and Fontenelle's other mediocre productions without having to use the word mediocre. This is an achievement worthy of Dryden at his best. Then through 'La Critique' Voltaire mentions those works of Fontenelle which appeal to him. He here reaffirms the position he took towards Fontenelle regarding these works in the letter to the *Nouvelliste du Parnasse*.

The eulogy of Fontenelle in the *Temple* is continued with the remark that Fontenelle shows 'cette compassion filosofique qu'un esprit éclairé et étendu ne peut s'empêcher d'avoir, pour un homme qui ne sait que rimer; et il alla reprendre paisiblement sa place entre Lucrèce et Leibnitz' (Carcassonne, p.79). It is true that Voltaire later looks on Fontenelle with modified rapture.

It seems that there is in Voltaire's treatment of Fontenelle something of the spirit which had prevailed at the time of the *Œdipe* controversy with La Motte, and that when he is not too aggressively provoked, Voltaire can show a certain amount of fairness to his opponent. Because of this apparent fairness to Fontenelle in the *Temple du goût*, Voltaire's criticism here appears less personal than it is in writings involving other opponents or even Fontenelle himself later on. It is at the same time most effective.

Like *Absalom and Achitophel*, the *Temple du goût* is written on various levels. Generosity is not maintained throughout and Voltaire's handling of the Rousseau episode is far from generous. Jean Baptiste Rousseau succeeded only in obtaining from 'La Critique' a 'demi-pardon dédaigneux après avoir subi les plus cuisantes réprimandes' (Carcassonne, p.10). But his metamorphosis is treated in a light vein. In the *Temple*, Voltaire does not think it necessary to heap abuse on his adversary. Indeed the whole Rousseau episode may be considered as a huge joke: it is when he appears so lighthearted that Voltaire can excel as a satirist. Voltaire is not grossly unfair to Rousseau. Bouhier, for instance, struck the right note when in a letter to Ruffey he showed no surprise at what Voltaire had said of Rousseau 'lequel paroissant l'avoir attaqué le premier, a mérité quelques représailles. C'est véritablement agir de corsaire à corsaire' (Best.D578, 24 March 1733). Voltaire could have been fairer to Rousseau had the latter been less prejudiced against him and less aggressive. Despite his attitude towards Voltaire, Rousseau is included in the general amnesty Voltaire offers his enemies in 1733. In his treatment of Rousseau at this stage, there is a trace of the English influence we noted earlier on in the case of Fontenelle, less pronounced perhaps on account of Rousseau's lack of detachment when compared with Fontenelle's.

It must be remembered that Dryden was *inter alia* dramatist, lyric poet, satirist and critic. Voltaire possibly knew Dryden's critical works. However good the French were at criticism, a practical writer like Voltaire must have realised that there was something to gain by studying an English critic who had made such an intelligent use of his French sources. It is likely that Voltaire read Dryden's *Discourse concerning satire*, for the *Discourse* certainly recalls some of his pronouncements on satire. With reference to personal satire, Dryden had stated in the *Discourse* that

we have no moral right on the reputation of other men. 'Tis taking from them what we cannot restore to them. There are only two reasons for which we may be permitted to write lampoons. The first is revenge, when we have been affronted in the same nature, or have been any ways notoriously abused, and can make ourselves no other reparation. And yet we know, that in Christian charity, all offences are to be forgiven, as we expect the like pardon for those which we daily commit against Almighty God . . . the second reason which may justify a poet when he writes against a particular person; and that is when he is become a public nuisance (Watson, ii.125-26).

He believed much more in fine raillery (pp.136-37):

yet still the nicest and most delicate touches of satire consist in fine raillery . . .
A witty man is tickled when he is hurt in this manner, and a fool feels it not . . .
yet there is still a vast difference betwixt the slovenly butchering of a man,
and the fineness of a stroke that separates the head from the body, and leaves
it standing in its place.

There are indications that Voltaire had read Dryden's dedication to
the *Aeneis* (1697) before writing his *Essay on epick poetry*. In the *Essay*
he showed great surprise at Dryden's attitude to Milton, for 'the same
Mr. *Dryden* in his Preface upon his Translation of the *Aeneid*, ranks
Milton with *Chapellain* and *Lemoine* the most impertinent Poets who
ever scribbled. How he could extol him so much in his verses, and
debase him so low in his Prose, is a Riddle which, being a Foreigner,
I cannot understand' (White, p.134). These remarks prove that he had
read Dryden's famous 'Lines on Milton'. Dryden had written:

> Three *Poets*, in three distant *Ages* born,
> *Greece*, *Italy*, and *England* did adorn.
> The *First* in loftiness of thought Surpass'd;
> The *Next* in Majesty; in both the *Last*.
> The force of *Nature* cou'd no farther goe:
> To make a Third she joynd the former two.
> (*The Poems and fables of John Dryden*, ed.
> J. Kinsley (1970), p.424).

In the French version of the *Essay*, Voltaire takes a different line with
regard to Dryden's stand. He now appreciates Dryden's views and
accounts for them by the existence in *Paradise lost* of many defects:
'C'est ce grand nombre de fautes grossières qui fit sans doute dire à
Dryden, dans sa préface sur *L'Enéide*, que Milton ne vaut guère mieux
que notre Chapelain et notre Lemoyne' (M.viii.359). He hastens to
add: 'Ce sont les beautés admirables de Milton qui ont fait dire à ce
même Dryden que la nature l'avait formé de l'âme d'Homère et de
celle de Virgile.' Not satisfied with his paraphrase of Dryden's eulogy,
Voltaire subsequently reproduced the last two lines in the 'Leningrad notebooks' under the title 'Dryden sur Milton' (*Notebooks*,
i. 335).

In the 'Small Leningrad notebooks' an item dealing with the origin of
the romance languages seems to originate from a passage in Dryden's
Essay of dramatic poesy. Voltaire wrote (*Notebooks*, i. 65):

From the rubishes of the roman empire, several great kingdoms are formed, and grounded upon its ruines. In the same manner, italian tongue, the french, the spanish arose from the ruines of the roman language.

Dryden had written (Watson, i. 83):

But when by the inundation of the Goths and Vandals into Italy, new languages were brought in, and barbarously mingled with the Latin (of which the Italian, Spanish, French and ours (made out of them and the Teutonic) are dialects) a new way of poesy was practised.[26]

Voltaire's hostility to Dryden seems to have been restricted to the drama although he was not consistently hostile. In other fields, he had nothing but praise for the English writer in the 1740s and subsequently. On 3 November 1743, he was elected as a member of the Royal Society. After his election, he wrote to Martin Ffolkes, president of the society and paid homage to English writers, Dryden among them: 'My first masters in yr free and learned country were Shakespear, Adisson, Dryden, Pope' (Best.D2890, 25 November 1743).

In the *Siècle de Louis XIV*, Voltaire bestows lavish praise on Dryden (M.xiv.560):

Dans le grand nombre des poëtes agréables qui décorèrent le règne de Charles II, comme les Waller, les comtes de Dorset et de Rochester, le duc de Buckingham, etc. on distingue le célèbre Dryden, qui s'est signalé dans tous les genres de poésie: ses ouvrages sont pleins de détails naturels à la fois et brillants, animés, vigoureux, hardis, passionnés, mérite qu'aucun poëte de sa nation n'égale, et qu'aucun n'a surpassé. Si Pope, qui est venu après lui, n'avait pas, sur la fin de sa vie, fait son *Essai sur l'homme*, il ne serait pas comparable à Dryden.

The Wife of Bath's tale seems to have attracted some attention in France in the eighteenth century.[27] The *Journal étranger* published a translation based on Dryden's version in June 1757. The *Année littéraire* published its own translation in January 1764. Shortly before that Voltaire's tale in verse, *Ce qui plaît aux dames*, appeared in print. Voltaire was against the publication of this 'conte à dormir debout' (Best.D11523, 1 December 1763), as he described it in a letter to Damilaville, at the same time as the serious *Traité sur la tolérance*, because he felt that the lighter work might harm the latter. He added in another letter to his friend (Best.D11574, 19 December 1763):

[26] see Torrey, 'Voltaire's English notebook', pp.310, n.2, 322, n.1.
[27] see Alfred C. Hunter, 'Le "Conte de la femme de Bath" en français au XVIIIe siècle', *RLC* (1929), ix. 117-40.

ne dira-t-on pas que ces deux écrits sont des jeux d'esprit, et qu'un homme qui traitte à la fois de la religion et des fées est également indiférent pour ces deux objets? cette réflexion ne peut elle pas faire quelque tort à la tolérance qu'on attend des plus honnêtes gens du royaume, et des mieux disposés?

There is no doubt that *Ce qui plaît aux dames* was influenced by Dryden's version of Chaucer's work. Voltaire, who knew nothing about Chaucer, acknowledged in the letter to Damilaville: 'Ce qui plait aux Dames est tiré en partie d'un vieux roman, et a même été traitté en anglais par Driden. Tous les autres seront de ma façon, et n'en vaudront pas mieux' (Best.D11574). What he borrowed from Dryden he certainly altered. Dryden had gibed at priests whose prayers made the goblins disappear while (ll. 36-38)

> The Midnight Parson posting o'er the Green,
> With Goun tuck'd up to Wakes; for Sunday next,
> With humming Ale encouraging his Text.

Voltaire continued along similar lines and satirised 'l'infâme', but he did this in a very lighthearted manner. He set the scene of the action in Rome and France instead of King Arthur's Britain. This provided him with the opportunity of passing disparaging remarks (M.x. 9) on

> Rome la sainte,
> Qui surpassait la Rome des Césars

and ecclesiastics who take all the money at the expense of others. Worse, they are even guilty of petty thieving, for the knight who carries indulgences but little money is robbed of his horse in burlesque fashion by a monk from St Denis. Or, as Robert, having recourse to a typical Voltairean antiphrasis, says (M.x.14):

> Un moine noir a, par dévotion,
> Saisi le tout quand j'assaillis Marthon.

Marthon complains to King Dagobert about her rape; he sends her to queen Berthe. From this point up to Robert's justification, the tale follows Dryden. Robert is forced to marry an old witch as he had promised to do anything she wanted in return for his life. The court of queen Berthe had decided to save Robert's life if within eight days he could tell them what ladies liked most and the old witch alone told him the secret. Fortunately for the Knight the witch became a young beauty in the end. Voltaire's tale has the same ending as Dryden's.

In fact *Ce qui plaît aux dames* follows the English tale fairly closely except in matters of detail. For instance, the French knight is given eight days, whereas the English knight is given a year to save his life. Voltaire realised how tedious the long medieval sermon on poverty could be in Dryden's *The Wife of Bath her tale*, particularly as it was delivered on the Knight's wedding night. So he improved his *conte* by making the witch deliver her sermon before the court and not on her wedding night. He also avoided Dryden's digressions.

Prévost had translated Dryden's poem, *Alexander's feast*, in the *Pour et contre* (xi. 49-62). He prefaced his translation with these remarks:

Veut on lire un chef-d'œuvre de nos voisins, et goûter du moins une partie du plaisir qu'il a causé dans sa langue naturelle? Il faut commencer par se défaire du préjugé national, et croire un moment que le bon goût de la poésie n'est pas borné à la France.

Prévost's judgement is shared by Voltaire, for in 1771 in the article 'Enthousiasme' of the *Questions sur l'encyclopédie* he showed the highest regard for the poem. He wrote (M.xviii. 555):

De toutes les odes modernes, celle où il règne le plus grand enthousiasme qui ne s'affaiblit jamais, et qui ne tombe ni dans le faux ni dans l'ampoulé, est le *Timothée*, ou la fête d'Alexandre, par Dryden: elle est encore regardée en Angleterre comme un chef-d'œuvre inimitable, dont Pope n'a pu approcher quand il a voulu s'exercer dans le même genre. Cette ode fut chantée; et si on avait eu un musicien digne du poëte, ce serait le chef-d'œuvre de la poésie lyrique.

He did not alter his view: in 1772 he described Dryden's work as 'la plus belle Ode écrite depuis Pindar' to his visitors, the Nevilles. He wished it had been well set to music. Voltaire described Pope's attempt on the same subject 'comme d'un carosse coupé, trainé par deux petits chevaux noirs, fort jolis, suivant de loin un char triomphant, attelé de six chevaux blancs' (*Voltaire's British visitors*, p.155).

The above remarks on Dryden's poem, *Alexander's feast*, may give the impression that Dryden had a bigger impact on Voltaire than Pope. In one sense this is true, because Dryden impressed Voltaire both as a dramatist and as a satirical writer. Pope, on the other hand, was no dramatist, however influential he may have been in his poetry. However, whether Voltaire openly acknowledged it or not, it was Dryden's satires which proved of greater significance to him. The influence of *The Medal, Mac Flecknoe* and *Absalom and Achitophel* in particular spreads across a number of Voltaire's works.

iv. *'Minor' English satirical poets and Voltaire*

It would have been natural for Voltaire to show some interest in sir Samuel Garth (1661-1719), for the latter had in 1699 written a burlesque poem in the manner of Boileau's *Le Lutrin* entitled *The Dispensary*. In the preface, Garth proudly acknowledges his indebtedness to Boileau, although he maintains that he copied Boileau in one line in canto I and in two or three lines in the complaint of 'Molesse' in canto II. In the 'Leningrad notebooks' Voltaire quotes the following lines from canto III of *The Dispensary* (ll. 244-47; *Notebooks*, i. 239):

> By Garth
> The wise trough thought the insult of death defy,
> The fool through bless'd insensibiliti.
> T'is what the guilti fear, the pious crave;
> Sought by the wretch, and vainquish'd by the brave.

Voltaire's interest in *The Dispensary* was probably roused by his earlier interest in *The Rape of the lock* which was equally indebted to *Le Lutrin* (see below). That he was also generally interested in the mock-heroic as a genre may be shown by his reference to Butler and Scarron in his writings and by his own contribution, *La Pucelle*. It was only in the *Questions sur l'encyclopédie* that he put together his thoughts on this genre and made a systematic review of writers, French and foreign, who produced burlesque works. He may very well have used Garth earlier in his career, since in *The Dispensary* Garth deals with a subject of such a nature as to appeal to him: a quarrel between doctors and apothecaries. He had successfully exploited basically similar and futile quarrels in *Hudibras* and we also know how much he appreciated the ridiculous in Moliéresque comedy.

Voltaire waited until the article 'Bouffon, burlesque et bas comique' of the *Questions sur l'encyclopédie* before he mentioned Garth specifically. But he then placed him above Boileau, for he believed that *The Dispensary* had more imagination, variety and naïveté than *Le Lutrin*. What was more surprising to Voltaire was that the profound erudition

found in the English poem was embellished by 'la finesse et les grâces'.
He gave his own version of the beginning of canto I (M.xviii. 28):

> Muse, raconte-moi les débats salutaires
> Des médecins de Londres et des apothicaires.
> Contre le genre humain si longtemps réunis,
> Quel dieu pour nous sauver les rendit ennemis?
> Comment laissèrent-ils respirer leurs malades,
> Pour frapper à grands coups sur leurs chers camarades?
> Comment changèrent-ils leur coiffure en armet,
> La seringue en canon, la pilule en boulet?
> Ils connurent la gloire; acharnés l'un sur l'autre,
> Ils prodiguaient leur vie, et nous laissaient la nôtre.

This rendering was, however, quite different from the original
which reads as follows (ll. 1-6, 11-16):

> Speak, Goddess! since 'tis Thou that best canst tell,
> How ancient Leagues to modern Discord fell:
> And why Physicians were so cautious grown
> Of others Lives, and lavish of their Own;
> How by a Journey to th' Elysian Plain
> Peace triumph'd, and old Time return'd again ...
> There stands a Dome, Majestick to the Sight,
> And sumptuous Arches bear its oval Height;
> A golden Globe plac'd high with artful Skill,
> Seems, to the distant Sight a gilded Pill:
> This Pile was, by the Pious Patron's Aim,
> Rais'd for a Use as Noble as its Frame.

In the article 'Caractère' of the *Questions sur l'encyclopédie*, Voltaire
again referred to *The Dispensary* which he described as a 'petit poëme
très-supérieur aux *Capitoli* italiens, et peut-être même au *Lutrin* de
Boileau' (M.xviii. 50). Garth also helped Voltaire to define 'le caractère'.
In canto I, he described how Goddess Nature to the 'learn'd unveils her
dark disguise', noting (ll. 42-47):

> How the dim Speck of Entity began
> T'exert its primogenial Heat and stretch to Man.
> To how minute an Origin we owe
> Young *Ammon*, *Caesar*, and the Great *Nassau*.
> Why paler Looks impetuous Rage proclaim,
> And why chill Virgins redden into Flame.

Voltaire, showing firm approval of Garth, translated these lines in the following manner (M.xviii.50-51):

> Un mélange secret de feu, de terre et d'eau
> Fit le cœur de César et celui de Nassau.
> D'un ressort inconnu le pouvoir invincible
> Rendit Slone impudent et sa femme sensible.

Not long afterwards when he was visited by the Nevilles, Voltaire tried to diminish the merit of Boileau and *Le Lutrin*. It was only to increase that of Garth's poem. His visitors observed that *The Dispensary* came off in great triumph. Apparently Voltaire went to the length of telling them that the English poem owed nothing to *Le Lutrin*. After repeating some passages of Garth, Dryden and others, he mentioned that he read only other people's poetry. With regard to his assessment of Boileau and Garth, the British visitors concluded that it was a flagrant instance of the force of jealousy in rival writers (*Voltaire's British visitors*, p.155).

Matthew Prior (1664-1721) was described as one of the best English poets of the times by the *Journal littéraire* in 1717. The author of the 'Dissertation sur la poésie anglaise' was impressed by Prior's *Poems on several occasions* and his 'stile enjoué et galant' (ix.170). In the *Mémoires d'un homme de qualité* Prévost mentioned Prior as a major English poet along with Addison and Thomson, just after he had referred to Milton and Spenser (p.69). It is certain that Diderot looked on Prior in quite a different light. Some chapters of his novel *Les Bijoux indiscrets* (1748) on the metaphysics of the soul were probably inspired by Prior's *Alma: or, the progress of the mind* (1718). In view of the importance of the concept of the soul in Diderot's thought, the discussion on the location of the soul which takes place in *Les Bijoux indiscrets* may be regarded as a basis for development in future works which culminated in the *Rêve de d'Alembert*.[28]

Prior appealed to Voltaire in many ways. It is hardly surprising that he should have been impressed by someone whose career offered some similarity with his own. Diplomat in Holland and France, Prior was secret agent in Paris in 1711 when he negotiated the treaty of Utrecht for the Tories. Some years before Voltaire's official mission to Frederick in 1743, there was a lampoon in circulation on his departure

[28] see Otis Fellows, 'Metaphysics and the *Bijoux indiscrets*: Diderot's debt to Prior', *Studies on Voltaire* (1967), lvi. 509-40.

from Cirey. The text of the lampoon is available in a note to his letter
to d'Argental (Best.D1221). In this letter Voltaire says he will go and
see prince Frederick who had asked him to come to his court. He
claims that his aim is to put a great distance between himself and envy.
But the author of the lampoon concluded as follows (Best.D1221,
9 December 1736, n.2):

> Et ma manie est d'être
> Un ministre d'état,
> Des princes le maître;
> Au moins ambassadeur
> Comme feu Prieur.

Voltaire might have wished to emulate Prior in his dealings with
Frederick of Prussia on behalf of the French government in 1743.
France wanted Prussia to join the war against Austria. When he told
Frederick 'Je n'ambitionne point du tout d'être chargé d'affaires
comme des Touches et Prior, deux poètes qui ont fait deux paix entre
la France et l'Angleterre' (Best.D2859, *c.* 8 October 1743) Voltaire
must not be taken too literally. His negotiation with Frederick was not
a failure as was once thought. It may even have helped him in winning
a seat at the Académie française subsequently.[29]

Moreover, the very appointment of Prior as Ambassador appeared
to him in the 1730s as proof that England knew how to reward men
of merit and talent. That is why Voltaire put him alongside men whom
he admired in the twenty-third of the *Letters concerning the English
nation* (p.225). Lack of space meant that Voltaire could only mention
Prior briefly in letter xxii. Prior was described as 'one of the most
amiable *English* poets, whom you saw Plenipotentiary and Envoy
Extraordinary at *Paris* in 1712' (p.211). Prior indeed went back to
Paris with Bolingbroke in 1712 and remained there after Bolingbroke's
return to England, exercising the powers of a plenipotentiary. The description is considerably lengthened in the 1756 edition where the diplomat's loss of popularity in England is recorded. Voltaire says that people
in France never thought that Prior was a poet. He adds that France was
to adopt the same policy towards England: cardinal Dubois sent
Destouches as ambassador to London, but Destouches did not appear
more of a poet to the English than Prior to the French (Lanson, ii. 133).

[29] see Jean Sareil, 'La mission diplomatique de Voltaire en 1743', *Dix-huitième
siècle* (1972), pp.271-99.

What made the greatest impact on Voltaire was Prior's *Alma*. In the 1756 edition of the *Lettres philosophiques*, he writes: (Lanson, ii. 133):

cette histoire est la plus naturelle qu'on ait faite jusqu'à présent de cet être si bien senti & si mal connu. L'ame est d'abord aux extrémités du corps, dans les pieds & dans les mains des enfans; de là elle se place insensiblement au milieu du corps dans l'âge de puberté: ensuite elle monte au cœur, & là elle produit les sentiments de l'amour & de l'héroïsme: elle s'élève jusqu'à la tête dans un âge plus mûr; elle y raisonne comme elle peut, & dans la vieillesse, on ne sait plus ce qu'elle devient: c'est la sève d'un vieil arbre qui s'évapore, & qui ne se répare plus.

Voltaire criticises Prior's work on the ground that it is too long, claiming that every joke should be short and that even a serious piece of writing should be short as well. His remark could have been more justifiably applied to *Hudibras* which is a much longer poem. Nevertheless, he fully exploited parts of *Alma* subsequently.

It is not difficult to explain why Voltaire felt attracted towards Prior. Having already enjoyed and used Butler's *Hudibras*, Voltaire was charmed by the poetry of another master of the mock-heroic. For Prior's *Alma*, a dialogue in three cantos, was written in the metre and manner of *Hudibras*. We do not know for certain when Voltaire first became interested in *Alma*, but there is no doubt that its subject matter was of considerable interest to him. In one sense, the poem is a satire on metaphysical systems and is a burlesque attempt to explain the location of the soul and its progress upwards from the legs in childhood to the head in maturity. Such an attempt could not leave Voltaire indifferent as he was himself trying to refute all speculation on the soul in the 1720s and 1730s. In the 'Cambridge notebook', he writes (*Notebooks*, i. 88):

We do not know what a soul is, we have no idea of the thing, therefore we ought not to admitt it. We are not of another gender than the beasts but of another species.

Further on in the same work, he expands the subject, putting the emphasis on what is really important to man. He writes (p.95):

Je ne sçaurois comprendre ce que c'est que la matière, encore moins ce que c'est qu'esprit.

S'il y a un dieu, s'il n'y en a point, si le monde est fini ou infini, créé ou éternel, arrangé par intelligence ou par loix phisiques, encor moins par hazard.

Je ne saurois comprendre

> comment je pense,
> comment je retiens mes pensées,
> comment je remue.

Les premiers principes aux quels mon existence est attachée sont tous impénétrables. Ce n'est donc pas cela qu'il faut chercher mais

> ce qui est utile, et dangereux, au corps humain,
> les loix par les quels il se meut, non pr quoy il se meut,
> l'art d'augmenter les forces mouvantes, non les principes du mouvement.

In accordance with Cartesian philosophy such as it is defined in the thirteenth of the *Letters concerning the English nation* 'the Soul, at its coming into the Body, is inform'd with the whole Series of metaphysical Notions . . . in a Word, completely endued with the most sublime hights, which it unhappily forgets at its issuing from the Womb' (p.98). Voltaire takes up this point in *Micromégas* (Bénac, p.111). *Alma* is also a satire on the vanity of worldly concerns. Prior's appeal must have been irresistible to Voltaire who was to attack the vanity of metaphysics in his correspondence, in the *Courte réponse* and in *Candide*.

Another likely source of inspiration to Voltaire was Prior's poem in three books entitled *Solomon on the vanity of the world* (1708). In his preface, Prior spoke of 'the Noble Images and Reflections, the profound Reasonings upon Human Actions' found in the book of *Ecclesiastes* and of his intention to group together 'the Proof of that great Assertion, laid down in the beginning of the *Ecclesiastes*, ALL IS VANITY'. Towards the end of his account of Prior in the 1756 edition of the *Lettres philosophiques*, Voltaire notes how 'notre Plénipotentiaire finit par paraphraser en quinze-cent vers ces mots attribués à Salomon, que *tout est vanité*. On en pourrait faire quinze mille sur ce sujet. Mais malheur à qui dit tout ce qu'il peut dire.' Now in the edition of this poem by H. B. Wright and M. K. Spears, *Solomon* runs into some 2652 lines. It is possible that Voltaire took a special interest in the first two books dealing with knowledge and pleasure respectively and numbering some 1762 lines, although the third book on power which fills 890 lines did not perhaps leave him indifferent.

The passage in the 1756 edition of the *Lettres philosophiques* quoted above (Lanson, ii. 133) is an interesting attempt by Voltaire to summarize part of the first canto of *Alma*. In the dialogue (ll. 237-47) between Matthew and Richard in this canto, Matthew observes that the different systems of the metaphysicians were formed only to produce disagreement. He proposes to steer a middle course and he puts forward a scheme which would reconcile Aristotle with Gassendi, knowing full well that it would be unintelligible to the majority. Thereupon he outlines his own 'system' as follows (ll. 252-65):

> My simple *System* shall suppose,
> That ALMA enters at the Toes;
> That then She mounts by just Degrees
> Up to the Ancles, Legs, and Knees:
> Next, as the Sap of Life does rise,
> She lends her Vigor to the Thighs:
> And, all these under-Regions past,
> She nestles somewhere near the Waste:
> Gives Pain or Pleasure, Grief or Laughter;
> As We shall show at large hereafter.
> Mature, if not improv'd by Time
> Up to the Heart She loves to climb:
> From thence, compell'd by Craft and Age,
> She makes the Head her latest Stage.[30]

The exploitation of the first canto takes place in the very first chapter of *Candide*. In his critical edition of *Candide*, A. Morize pointed out in the notes how Voltaire used Pangloss to rail at the methods and ideas of Wolff, Hartsoecker and Pluche (pp.4-6). Pangloss said:

Il est démontré que les choses ne peuvent être autrement: car tout étant fait pour une fin, tout est nécessairement pour la meilleure fin. Remarquez bien que les nez ont été faits pour porter des lunettes, aussi avons-nous des lunettes. Les jambes sont visiblement instituées pour être chaussées, & nous avons des chausses. Les pierres ont été formées pour être taillées, & pour en faire des Châteaux; aussi Monseigneur a un très beau Château; le plus grand Baron de la province doit être le mieux logé: & les cochons étant faits pour être mangés, nous mangeons du porc toute l'année.

[30] *The Literary works of Matthew Prior,* eds H. B. Wright and M. K. Spears, (Oxford 1971), i. 477.

It is not unlikely that Voltaire was also putting to good use material
he had come across in the course of his revision of the *Lettres philosophiques* in 1756. Prior perhaps sharpened his skill in satirising the
a priori philosophers. For he must have been struck by the satirical
technique of Matthew in canto 1. Matthew said to Dick (ll. 270-73):

> First I demonstratively prove,
> That Feet were only made to move;
> And Legs desire to come and go:
> For they have nothing else to do.

In the third canto, Prior put damaging confessions in Matthew's
mouth. Matthew, who is as naïve as Voltaire's characters, proudly
declares (ll. 330-41):

> We *System*-makers can sustain
> The *Thesis*, which, You grant, was plain;
> And with Remarks and Comments teaze Ye;
> In case the Thing before was easy.
> But in a Point obscure and dark,
> We fight as LEIBNITS did with CLARK:
> And when no Reason we can show,
> Why Matters This or That Way go;
> The shortest Way the Thing We try,
> And what We know not, We deny:
> True to our own o'erbearing Pride,
> And False to all the World beside.

Voltaire must have enjoyed this tremendously and soon afterwards
he produced the *Relation du jésuite Berthier* (1759). Through the
dialogue between the Jesuit Berthier and the author of the Jansenist
periodical, the *Nouvelles ecclésiastiques*, Voltaire succeeded in satirising
both Jesuits and Jansenists in this pamphlet. The first priest at hand
refused to confess the dying Berthier. By means of careful engineering
the Jesuit was placed in the hands of the worst enemy of his order for
confession. Berthier admitted that Jesuits and Jansenists acted with
the same pride and were more interested in pursuing their selfish ends
than in keeping the peace of the world.

In part of the article 'Ame' of the *Dictionnaire philosophique*, Voltaire
moves away from Prior when he gives burlesque explanations of the
formation and disappearance of souls. Some system-builders maintain
that God forms them as and when the need is felt and that they arrive

at the time of sexual intercourse. Then follows a lively, witty dialogue to expound the various theories:

"Elles se logent dans les animalcules séminaux, crie celui-ci. – Non, dit celui-là, elles vont habiter dans les trompes de Fallope. – Vous avez tous tort, dit un survenant: l'âme attend six semaines que le fœtus soit formé, et alors elle prend possession de la glande pinéale; mais si elle trouve un faux germe, elle s'en retourne, en attendant une meilleure occasion." La dernière opinion est que sa demeure est dans le corps calleux; c'est le poste que lui assigne La Peyronie; il fallait être premier chirurgien du roi de France pour disposer ainsi du logement de l'âme.[31]

These ideas are nowhere to be found in Prior. But earlier in the article 'Ame', Voltaire draws closer to Prior. In book i of *Solomon*, Solomon discourses on vegetables, animals and man. In his discourse, he finds 'a thousand Doubts oppose the searching Mind' (l. 55). He puts many questions to which there is no satisfactory answer. For instance, he asks (ll. 74-77):

> Why does the fond *Carnation* love to shoot
> A various Colour from one Parent Root;
> While the fantastic *Tulip* strives to break
> In two-fold Beauty, and a parted Streak?

Voltaire asks a similar question: 'Si une tulipe pouvait parler, et qu'elle te dît: "Ma végétation et moi nous sommes deux êtres joints évidement ensemble", ne te moquerais-tu pas de la tulipe?' (p.8). Towards the end of book i, Solomon castigates his Rabbins and Logicians because they never stop quarrelling

> And Sculk behind the Subterfuge of Art.
> Divide the Simple, add the Plain define;
> Fix fancy'd Laws, and form imagin'd Rules,
> Terms of their Art, and Jargon of their Schools,
> Ill grounded Maxims by false Gloss enlarg'd,
> And captious Science against Reason charg'd.

He is forced to conclude that 'human Science is uncertain Guess'. No one can tell him whether 'Thought can climb beyond the Bounds of Matter, what is Space or Time'. Metaphysical speculation is mercilessly derided for (ll. 701-702):

[31] *Dictionnaire philosophique*, eds Benda and Naves (Paris 1961), p. 10.

> . . . whence Things arose, or how
> They thus exist, the Aptest nothing know.

In his *Dictionnaire* article Voltaire was to come to nearly the same conclusion. After having scoffed at the jargon of St Thomas, 'l'ange de l'école', on the definition of the soul, Voltaire explains that God gave man understanding so that he may behave properly and not go into the essence of things he had created (Benda and Naves, p.14):

C'est ainsi qu'a pensé Locke et, avant Locke, Gassendi, et avant Gassendi une foule de sages; mais nous avons des bacheliers qui savent tout ce que ces grands hommes ignoraient.

Various fragments or sections were grouped together under the heading 'Ame' and published in 1770 in the *Questions sur l'encyclopédie*. The third of these sections entitled 'De l'âme des bêtes, et de quelques idées creuses' specifically mentions Prior by name (*Dictionnaire philosophique*, p.429).[32] Voltaire pours contempt on extreme schools of thought: 'l'une . . . ôte le sentiment aux organes du sentiment, l'autre . . . loge un pur esprit dans une punaise.' Nor has he any sympathy for those who explain away everything by instinct. He says he will agree with those whose philosophy begins and ends with doubt. But when they make categorical statements, he will tell them what Prior, with whom he is in complete agreement, says in his poem on the vanity of the world. In book i of *Solomon*, Prior seeks an explanation for the variations in the behaviour of animals and insects, as they puzzle him. He would like to know in particular why the fox hates man and spends his time plundering, whereas the spaniel or the hound, which looks like the fox is so friendly to man. He confesses that it is hard to know the cause. He finds or thinks he finds that there is some similarity of principles between man and animals. Like us, they love or hate and their actions seem to be guided by thought. Prior therefore concludes in these terms (ll. 231-36):

> Then vainly the Philosopher avers,
> That Reason guides our Deed, and Instinct their's.
> How can We justly diff'rent Causes frame,

[32] that Voltaire may have had Prior in mind at the beginning of this section which speaks of 'l'étrange système qui suppose les animaux de pures machines sans aucune sensation' (p.428) is confirmed by canto III of *Alma*. There Matthew tells Dick that he seems to him to mean 'That ALMA is a mere machine' (1.305).

When the Effects entirely are the same?
Instinct and Reason how can we divide?
'Tis the Fool's Ign'rance, and the Pedant's Pride.

Voltaire interprets Prior in his own manner and asks (Benda and Naves, p.429):

Osez-vous assigner, pédants insupportables,
Une cause diverse à des effets semblables?
Avez-vous mesuré cette mince cloison
Qui semble séparer l'instinct de la raison?
Vous êtes mal pourvus et de l'un et de l'autre.
Aveugles insensés, quelle audace est la vôtre!
L'orgueil est votre instinct. Conduirez-vous nos pas
Dans ces chemins glissants que vous ne voyez pas?

It is obvious that in the article 'Ame' as it appears in the *Dictionnaire philosophique* proper and in sections of the *Questions sur l'encyclopédie*, Voltaire uses Prior in conjunction with Locke to give additional weight to his attack on pretentious philosophizing, which was initiated under the auspices of Locke in the 1730s.

Voltaire comes back to Prior in the article 'Bouffon, burlesque, bas comique' of the *Questions sur l'encyclopédie*. He now wishes to conclude his impressions in a lighter vein, in keeping with the nature of the article. Prior is styled mediator between the philosophers who argue about the soul. Voltaire claims that *Alma* is written in *doggerel rhyme* and in the *stilo Bernesco* of the Italians. He selects the very beginning of the poem to line 89 in order to suggest to his readers a different seat for 'Alma'. According to Prior, Aristotle defines 'Alma' as being all in all and this is the belief of the Oxford wits. The Cambridge wits, on the other hand, disagree: they maintain that 'Alma' sits 'Cock-horse on Her Throne, the Brain' and (ll. 72-79):

A thousand little Nerves She sends
Quite to our Toes, and Fingers Ends;
And These in Gratitude again
Return their Spirits to the Brain;
In which their Figure being printed
(As just before, I think, I hinted)
ALMA inform'd can try the Case,
As She had been upon the Place.

'Alma's' position naturally suggests to Prior a legal imagery where the Judge waits for the barristers to bring evidence to him for judgement. Voltaire is not interested in this. What appeals to him is the next image used by Prior (ll. 84-89):

> The POPE thus prays and sleeps at ROME,
> And very seldom stirs from Home:
> Yet sending forth his Holy Spies,
> And having heard what They advise,
> He rules the Church's blest Dominions;
> And sets Men's Faith by His Opinions.

The basic material is moulded by Voltaire and takes the following shape (M.xviii. 28):

La grande question est d'abord de savoir si l'âme est toute en tout, ou si elle est logée derrière le nez et les deux yeux sans sortir de sa niche. Suivant ce dernier système, Prior la compare au pape qui reste toujours à Rome, d'où il envoie ses nonces et ses espions pour savoir ce qui se passe dans la chrétienté.

He once more describes the system put forward by Matthew (Prior), such as he had mentioned it in the 1756 edition of the *Lettres philosophiques*.

Towards the end of his article, Voltaire points out the similarity between Fontenelle and Prior. Fontenelle wrote: 'Il est des hochets pour tout âge' while Prior's lines run thus (canto III, ll. 534-35):

> Would FORTUNE calm her present Rage,
> And give us Play-things for our Age.

Voltaire insists that they wrote without any mutual influence on each other, since Prior's work was written twenty years before Fontenelle's and Fontenelle knew no English. Prior concludes his poem as follows (ll. 600-13):

> For PLATO's Fancies what care I?
> I hope You would not have me die,
> Like simple CATO in the Play,
> For any Thing that He can say?
> E'en let Him of *Ideas* speak
> To Heathens in his Native GREEK.
> If to be sad is to be wise;
> I do most heartily despise
> Whatever SOCRATES has said,
> Or TULLY writ, or WANLEY read.

Dear DRIFT, to set our Matters right,
Remove these Papers from my Sight;
Burn MAT's DES-CART', and ARISTOTLE:
Here, JONATHAN, Your Master's Bottle.

In Voltaire's inimitable rendering, these lines read (M.xviii.29):

Je n'aurai point la fantaisie
D'imiter ce pauvre Caton,
Qui meurt dans notre tragédie
Pour une page de Platon.
Car, entre nous, Platon m'ennuie.
La tristesse est une folie:
Etre gai, c'est avoir raison.
Çà, qu'on m'ôte mon Cicéron,
D'Aristote la rapsodie,
De René la philosophie;
Et qu'on m'apporte mon flacon.

The end of *Alma* made a particularly strong impression on Voltaire. This is because he found it to be a 'poemë singulier, rempli de vers ingénieux et d'idées aussi fines que plaisantes'. May not one be entitled to regard Voltaire's remark as an admission that there was really no dichotomy between the quality of English *thought* and English *literature*?

Even a less important satirist such as Charles Churchill (1731-64) did not escape Voltaire's attention. Voltaire had in his library at Leningrad two volumes of the *North Briton* edited by John Wilkes and Churchill and published in 1763. In volume i he could read of Churchill's attack on Hogarth. The article claimed that all objects were painted in a grotesque manner on Hogarth's retina (i. 158). What must also have pleased Voltaire was the reference to Dryden and his *Absalom and Achitophel* in the periodical.

In a review of Churchill's *Poems* published in the *Gazette littéraire de l'Europe* of 18 April 1764, Voltaire notes that these are satires full of bitterness and passion and that judging by his principal objective one might think that Churchill wrote neither for foreigners nor for posterity. The description of a few comedians, a quarrel with journalists, a ghost story, a private broil with Hogarth, etc – all this could not be of interest outside London and beyond the particular circumstances of the time (M.xxv.167).[33] Despite this criticism, Voltaire must have

[33] Voltaire's judgement seems to be corroborated by professor Humphreys who observed that Churchill 'is too attached to his time now to be much read, yet his energy

been interested in Churchill's personal satire on actors in *The Rosciad* in 1761 and on Hogarth in 1763. Hogarth was among the spectators when Churchill's friend, Wilkes, was brought into court. The latter had in the *North Briton* denounced George iii's speech closing parliament in April 1763. Hogarth took the opportunity to make a caricature sketch in May 1763. This prompted Churchill to publish an *Epistle to William Hogarth* in June.[34]

Inevitably, Voltaire is led to compare Churchill with the more famous Augustan satirists. He continues his review with the comment (M.xxv.168):

M. Churchill passe pour un des plus grands poëtes, et peut-être pour le premier des poëtes satiriques que l'Angleterre ait produits. Il ressemble moins à Pope qu'à Dryden, qu'il paraît aussi avoir plus étudié. Il n'est pas aussi pur, aussi correct que Pope, mais il a plus d'originalité dans sa manière; et son style, quoique avec une élégance moins continue, a une harmonie plus abondante et plus variée.

Here Voltaire is practising what he had often preached concerning the usefulness of the comparative approach in matters of taste and style.

Near the end of the review, Voltaire's judgment becomes more severe towards Churchill and he reverses the position in favour of the great English and French satirists (pp.168-69):

M. Churchill nous paraît avoir violé toutes les lois de la bienséance et de l'honnêteté sociale. Livré à l'esprit de parti, il prodigue la louange ou le blâme, suivant les préjugés qu'il a adoptés ... Pope, Dryden, et d'autres satiriques anglais, se contentaient de désigner leurs victimes par les lettres initiales de leurs noms; M. Churchill dédaigne même d'employer le voile le plus léger. Despréaux, qui quelquefois a outrepassé lui-même les bornes légitimes de la satire, est, auprès du satirique anglais, le plus doux et le plus poli des hommes.

How ironical that Voltaire should criticise Churchill for openly satirising his victims! Yet his assessment of Churchill would have been shared by T. S. Eliot in the twentieth century. The latter remarked that 'the blundering assaults of ... Churchill – a man of by no means poor abilities – do not make poetry; Churchill gives us an occasional

reminds us that force was a prized Augustan quality and his bite of phrase is not entirely outdone by Dryden or Byron' ('The literary scene', *Pelican guide to English literature*, (1968), iv. 86).

[34] see *The Poetical works of C. Churchill*, ed. D. Grant (Oxford 1956), p.xxvii and pp.213-30.

right line, but never a right poem' ('Poetry in the eighteenth century', in *Pelican guide*, iv. 276).

When compared with writers such as Shakespeare, Milton, Dryden, Addison and Pope, all the satirists discussed in this section might be regarded as 'minor'. But from the point of view of their impact on Voltaire, a distinction must certainly be made between Garth, Prior and Churchill. Garth's impact appears limited and there is little justification for the reputation he enjoyed at Boileau's expense. The explanation of the Nevilles for Voltaire's preference is plausible. Churchill appears as a foil to the greater satirists, Pope, Dryden and Boileau. He was useful in the sense that he allowed Voltaire to exercise his talent in comparative literature and to prove once more his knowledge of Dryden as a satirist. On a more personal level, Voltaire must have been touched by Churchill's lines on him in *The Apology* (1761). Churchill found a fellow-sufferer in Voltaire and defended him against his English opponents when he wrote:

> UNHAPPY Genius! plac'd by partial Fate,
> With a free spirit in a slavish state; . . .
> In vain thy dauntless fortitude hath borne
> The bigot's furious zeal and tyrant's scorn.
> Why didst thou safe from home-bred dangers steer,
> Reserved to perish more ignobly here?
> (*The Poetical works of C. Churchill*, ed. D. Grant,
> p.39)

As far as Prior is concerned, one may not perhaps follow Voltaire's reactions to him in as wide a variety of writings as in the case of Milton. Yet he meant more to Voltaire than has hitherto been recognized. It may even be that he had the same significance for him as he had for Diderot. Besides, Voltaire allowed him to join forces with Addison in destroying the myth of a dichotomy which was supposed to exist between English taste and genius.

v. *Pope's satirical impact on Voltaire*

Pope was highly thought of in France in the eighteenth century. The author of the article on English literature in the *Journal littéraire* paid a glowing tribute to Pope and his mock-heroic poem, *The Rape of the lock*. In his opinion, Pope equalled all the English poets of his time in inventiveness and in imagination; he surpassed most of them by his correct and judicious expressions. As for the poem, 'toute l'ordonnance en est entièrement neuve, les pensées vives et brillantes, le stile soutenu par tout, la versification aisée, & la rime plus riche que dans la plupart des Poëmes Anglois'. The remark about Homer, that everything he touches changes into gold, could equally apply to Pope. The only quarrel the journalist had with Pope was that his style was from time to time 'lacking in modesty' and that he lowered himself by using 'équivoques' (pp.174-75). Desfontaines who translated *The Rape of the lock* as *La Boucle de cheveux enlevée* in 1728 wrote in the preface that the translation would help to show the error into which prejudice could lead the French, namely that the English could write only about the serious and could not aspire to refinement of wit, delicate satire, and elegant badinage. For the poem had invention, design, order, the supernatural, fiction, images and thought; in a word, what constitutes true poetry. Moreover, the comedy was far removed from insipid burlesque, the satirical allusions did not offend, the witticisms were not too free and the raillery on the fair sex was delicate.[35]

These favourable judgements on Pope were confirmed by Voltaire. Even before his stay in England contacts were established between Voltaire and Pope through Bolingbroke. It was probably Bolingbroke who laid the foundation for the mutual esteem that developed between the two poets subsequently. In a letter to Pope dated 18 February 1723/1724, Bolingbroke said that he was reading Voltaire's tragedy *Mariamne*. He claimed that his 'Imagination [resided] in that of Voltaire' and that Pope would find in the play 'that Art which Racine put into the Conduct of his Pieces, and that delicacy which appears in his diction, with a Spirit of Poetry which he never had, and which flags in the best of Corneilles Tragedys' (*Correspondence of Alexander Pope*, ed. G. Sherburn (Oxford 1956), ii. 221-22). Voltaire, Bolingbroke added, would introduce himself to Pope and he intended to send him *Mariamne*.

After reading Voltaire's *La Henriade*, Pope commented on it in a letter to Bolingbroke on 9 April 1724. He modestly acknowledged that he could not judge with any exactness of the beauties of a foreign language which he understood but imperfectly and that he could

[35] cf. *Pope*, ed. J. Bernard (London 1973), p.110.

speak only of the design and the action of the poem. He nevertheless went on to say that Voltaire's 'Characters and Sentences are not like Lucans, too profess'd or formal and particularised but full, short, and Judicious . . . It seems to me that his judgment of Mankind, and his Observation of human Actions in a lofty and philosophical view, is one of the principal Characteristics of the Writer, who however is no less a Poet for being a man of sense . . . I conclude him at once a Freethinker and a Lover of quiet; no Bigot, but yet no Heretick' (Sherburn, ii. 228-29).

Pope seems to have corresponded directly with Voltaire after this; unfortunately no letter from him to Voltaire has survived. What we have is correspondence between Pope and intermediaries. However, Pope himself said in a letter to Caryll on the 25th December 1725: 'I have read *Marianne* before our friend sent it, having formerly had some correspondence (about the poem on the League) with its author' (Sherburn, ii. 354)[36]. There is therefore no reason to suppose that Pope never wrote to Voltaire. On the other hand, two letters from Voltaire to Pope have been preserved. In the second letter, written in English, Voltaire asked Pope to translate four lines from the *Henriade* (Best. D337, *c.* 1728). Pope did not respond, perhaps because he knew that Richard Towne had begun a translation: he apparently liked it so much that he assured Charles Mordaunt that he would examine it carefully if Towne were to publish it (Best.D342, 14 November 1728). There is no doubt that contacts between the two writers increased during Voltaire's visit to England,[37] though they were not very intimate.[38]

Many scholars have overemphasized the fact that Voltaire was interested in the 'thought' of Pope, as if he could not also have been stimulated by Pope in other ways. In his *Essay on epick poetry*, for instance, Voltaire showed how much he appreciated Pope's style as a translator of Homer. For he wrote (White, pp.89-90):

[36] in a note on this letter Sherburn says that Pope's statement about a correspondence before 1725 is surprising. But see Besterman's commentary on Pope's letter to Bolingbroke above (Best.D187).

[37] in his *Memoirs of m. de Voltaire*, Goldsmith gave an account of Voltaire's impressions of Pope during his first interview with him. Voltaire was apparently moved with compassion by the physical appearance of Pope. 'But when Pope began to speak, and to reason upon moral obligations, and dress the most delicate sentiments in the most charming diction, Voltaire's pity began to be changed into admiration and at last into envy. It is not uncommon with him to assert, that no man ever pleased him so much in serious conversation' (*Works*, iii. 253).

[38] see R. Pomeau, *La Religion de Voltaire* (Paris 1956), p.128.

As to Homer, those who cannot read him in the Original, have Mr Pope's Translation; they may discern the Fire of that Father of Poetry, reflected from such a polish'd and faithful Glass. I will neither point out his Beauties, since none of them are lost in this Translation.

For this remark, incidentally, Voltaire was indebted to Pope's own comment in the *Preface to the Iliad* where he wrote: 'This fire is discerned in Virgil, but discerned as through a glass, reflected from Homer.' Likewise Nestor's speech in the *Iliad* (book i, ll. 254-81) which Voltaire summarizes in the *Essay* (p.127) draws heavily from Pope's *Iliad* (i, ll. 358-64) (White, p.127, n.5).

It is evident that even in the *Discours en vers* with its marked analogies as regards thought with Pope's *Essay on man*, Voltaire was interested in Pope's style. In this connection, professor Pomeau noted that when Voltaire remade the *Essay on man* in the *Discours*, Pope's poem provided him with a model which he imitated for its form rather than for its content, for ideas common to Voltaire and Pope had previously been expressed in the *Remarques sur les Pensées de Pascal* independently of Pope's influence (Pomeau, p.129). In a letter he wrote to Thieriot, Voltaire said (Best.D635, 24 July 1733):

dites à mr Pope que je l'ay très bien reconnu in his essay on man. T'is certainly his stile. Now and then there is some obscurity, but the whole is charming.

In this period Voltaire was favourably disposed towards the *Essay on man*.[39] But he gradually showed his opposition to the philosophy of 'Whatever is, is right', as proclaimed at the end of the first epistle. It is clear from his letter to mme Du Deffand (Best.D1039, 18 March 1736) that he objected to epistle IV in particular. What he disliked was Pope's use of words like *amour social*. He thought that Pope's works swarmed with such obscurities. He nevertheless conceded that there were 'cent éclairs admirables qui percent à tout moment cette nuit'.

Voltaire discussed both the matter and manner of the *Essay on man*. Although his comment is unfavourable, he shows his preoccupation with the style of the *Essay* in his letter to d'Argental: 'Pourquoy ne sera t'il pas permis à un Français de dire d'une manière guaie, et sous l'envelope d'une fable, ce qu'un Anglais a dit tristement et sèchement dans des vers métaphisiques traduits lâchement?' (Best.D1746, c. 6

[39] for Voltaire's reactions to the *Essay on man*, see R. G. Knapp, *The Fortunes of Pope's* Essay on man *in eighteenth-century France*, Studies on Voltaire (1971), lxxxii. 79-122.

January 1739). Yet while querying the notion of 'Tout est bien' in the *Parallèle d'Horace* (1761), describing it as a Platonic idea, a chaos like other systems, he also added: 'mais on l'a orné de diamants' (M.xxiv. 224-25). That was a striking homage to the brilliance of Pope's language in the *Essay on man*.

Pope's satirical impact on Voltaire may be seen during the latter's visit to England. In the first of his letters to Pope in this period, Voltaire expressed regret on learning of the coach accident Pope had had (Best.D301, September/October 1726):

Is it possible that those fingers which have written the rape of the lock and the Criticism . . . should have been so barbarously treated? Let the hand of Dennis, or of your poetasters be cut off . . . Rely your accident concerns me as much as all the disasters of a master ought to affect his scholar.

He confirmed his high regard for Pope in a letter that he wrote to Thieriot soon afterwards. He said he considered Pope to be the best poet of England and even of the whole world (Best.D303, 26 October 1726):

J hope you are acquainted enough with the English tongue, to be sensible of all the charms of his works. For my part j look on his poem call'd the essay upon criticism as superior to the art of poetry of Horace; and his rape of the lock, la boucle de cheveux, (that is a comical one) is in my opinion above the lutrin of Despréaux. J never saw so amiable an imagination, so gentle graces, so great varyety, so much wit, and so refined knowledge of the world, as in this little performance.

Thus in Voltaire's judgement Pope was even superior to his model, Boileau.[40] Thieriot apparently showed this letter to Francis Atterbury who was living in exile in France. Atterbury in turn quoted extracts to his son-in-law Morice in London. More important, Pope had the satisfaction of reading this eulogy through the Atterbury circle (see A.-M. Rousseau, *L'Angleterre et Voltaire*, i. 65).

In the 'Small Leningrad notebook', Voltaire compared Bolingbroke with Pope (*Notebooks*, i. 61):

I think oft. of Mr. B. and Mr. P. They are both virtuous and learned; of equal wit and understanding, but quite contrary in their wais . . . B is a dark

[40] for Pope's indebtedness to French writers, Boileau in particular, see E. Audra, *L'Influence française dans l'œuvre de Pope* (Paris 1931). There is, however, hardly a mention of Boileau's sources in Audra. For this one may consult J. Marmier, *Horace en France au dix-septième siècle* (Paris 1962).

lanthorn; tho' it is illuminated within, it affords no manner of light, or advantage to such, as stood by it.

As suggested by Besterman, the reference to the second B. is really to P., that is Pope. The *Letters concerning the English nation* enabled Voltaire to give public approval to feelings privately expressed about Pope. The most elegant, the most correct, and even more important, the most harmonious poet that England ever had, 'mellow'd the harsh Sounds of the *English* Trumpet to the soft Accents of the Flute. His Compositions may be easily translated, because they are vastly clear and perspicuous; besides, most of his Subjects are general, and relative to all Nations' (pp.215-16).

Voltaire's remarks on Pope are significant because they reveal his keen interest in Pope's works, particularly his satires, and because they are an acknowledgement of his debt to a writer whom he regards as a master in the field of satire. His intimate knowledge of Pope's *Essay on criticism* and *The Rape of the lock* is apparent from his quotations in the *Notebooks*. In the 'Small Leningrad notebook' he jotted down lines 687-92 of the *Essay on criticism* as follows (*Notebooks*, i. 58):

> With tyranny then superstition joyned
> As that the body, this enslave the mind.
> Much was believ'd, but little understood
> And to be dull, was constru'd to be good.
> A second deluge Learning thus o'er run
> And the monks finish'd what the goths begun.

The same lines were reproduced in the 'Leningrad notebooks' at page 239. The importance of this quotation lies in the fact that Voltaire chose lines which are fairly close in form and content to *The Dunciad* (see below).

Voltaire wrote a letter in English to Du Resnel on 11 November 1729 (Best.D367), in which he made critical comments on the manuscript of the latter's translation of the *Essay on criticism*. Du Resnel's translation was to appear in 1730. Voltaire also made general remarks on the notes which Du Resnel inserted in his translation. He went to the length of giving advance notice of the publication of Du Resnel's translation in the *Letters concerning the English nation* (p.216). Pope's *Essay* had been translated by Robeton in 1717, but this was not satisfactory. When Du Resnel sent him a copy of the first edition of his *Essai sur la critique*, Voltaire showed how pleased he was with it and he praised the translator for having embellished Pope; he also said that he liked the spirit of tolerance in the work (Best.D391, end of 1730). Nearly forty years later Voltaire claimed in a letter to Thibouville that as he had written half of Du Resnel's verses, he had too much modesty to speak about it (Best.D15481, 20 February 1769). After due allowance is made for the exaggeration, one cannot deny the value of Voltaire's help to Du Resnel, especially in view of the authoritative and confident tone in which Best.D367 and D391 are written.

In the 'Small Leningrad notebook', Voltaire also quoted lines 19-34 from canto IV of *The Rape of the lock* (*Notebooks*, i. 63):

> No chearful breeze this sullen region knows,
> The dreaded east is all the wind that blows.
> Here in a grotto sheltered close from air
> And screen'd in shades from day's detested glare
> She sighs for ever on her pensive bed,
> Pain at her side, and megrim at her head.
> Two handmaids wait the trhone, alike in place
> But differing far, in figure, and in face.
> Here stood ill nature, like an ancient maid
> Her wrinkled form in black and white array'd,
> With stores of prayers for morning nights and noons
> Her hand is fill'd, her bosom with lampoons.
> There affectation with a sickly mien.
> Shows in her cheek the roses of eighteen
> Practisd to lisp, and hang the head a side,
> Faints into airs, and languishes with pride.

He first made a free translation of the passage in the 'Cambridge notebook' (*Notebooks*, i. 102):

> Umbriel à l'instant, vieux gnome rechigné,
> Va d'une aile pesante et d'un air renfrogné
> Chercher en murmurant la caverne profonde
> Où, loin des doux rayons que répand l'œil du monde,
> La déesse aux vapeurs a choisi son séjour.
> Les enfants d'Aquilon y siflent à l'entour
> Et le soufle mal sein de leur aride haleine
> Porte aux environs la fièvre et la migraine.
> Sur un riche sopha derrière un paravant,
> Loin des flambeux, du bruit des parleurs et du vent,
> La quinteuse déesse en soupirant repose,

Le cœur gros de chagrins sans en savoir la cause,
N'ayant pensé jamais, l'esprit toujours troublé,
L'œil chargé, le teint pâle et l'hipocondre enflé.
La médisante envie est assise auprès d'elle,
Vieux spectre féminin, décrépite pucelle,
Avec un air dévot déchirant son prochain
Et chansonant les gens l'évangile à la main.
Sur un lit de fleurs négligemment penchée
Une jeune bauté non loin d'elle est couchée.
C'est l'affectation qui grasseye en parlant,
Ecoute sans entendre et lorgne en regardant,
Qui rougit sans pudeur et rit de tout sans joye,
De cent maux différents prétend qu'elle est la proie
Et pleine de santé sous le rouge et le fard
Languit avec tendresse et se pâme avec art.

Voltaire then used this translation in the *Letters concerning the English nation* (pp.216-18). It is basically the same rendering as in the notebooks, but the variants to the text clearly show how Voltaire was adapting his material. Apart from changes in spelling in the two versions, one may note how 'les enfants d'Aquilon', 'en soupirant repose', 'languit avec tendresse' of the 'Cambridge notebook' became in the *Letters concerning the English nation* 'les tristes Aquilons', 'incessamment repose' and 'se plaint avec molesse' respectively. In his comments on the *Lettres philosophiques* in the *Pour et contre* in the latter part of 1733, Prévost described Voltaire's translation of *The Rape of the lock* as 'fort supérieure à l'original' (i. 299).

Why did Voltaire take such pains with Pope's works? It has been argued that he admired the *Essay on criticism* for its neo-classical style and the overall spirit of tolerance and moderation which pervades the poem.[41] The poem could certainly be enjoyed on various levels. General principles on the art of writing or criticism very quickly give way to attacks on individuals and the *Essay* is full of contemporary allusions to Pope's enemies or those of his friends, to bad poets and bad critics. All this is done in the name of literary taste which Pope sets out to preserve. The most famous allusion is perhaps that relating to Dennis in lines 582-87. This is how Pope denigrates his bitter and inveterate critic (Butt, p.162):

[41] R. G. Knapp, p.23.

Fear not the Anger of the Wise to raise;
Those best can *bear Reproof*, who *merit Praise*.
  'Twere well, might Criticks still this Freedom take;
But *Appius* reddens at each Word you speak,
And *stares*, *Tremendous*! with a *threatning Eye*,
Like some fierce Tyrant in Old Tapestry!

As hostilities between Dennis and Pope became protracted, Pope finally delivered his devastating onslaught on his enemy in *The Dunciad* The poem was first published in three books in 1728, although it was composed earlier. Pope might even have shown it to Voltaire in manuscript form.[42] This would certainly have been an appropriate way to return the courtesy Voltaire had shown him earlier by sending him his play. From the Mount of Vision in book iii of *The Dunciad*, the ghost of Settle shows the king Great Britain as he passes in review a number of people who are described 'each by his proper figure, character and qualifications'.[43] With regard to Dennis, Pope has this to say (Butt, pp.410-11):

> Ah Dennis! Giddon ah! What ill starv'd rage
> Divides a friendship, long confirm'd by age?
> Blockheads with reason wicked wits abhor,
> But fool with fool is barb'rous civil war.
> Embrace, embrace my Sons! be foes no more!
> Nor glad vile Poets with true Criticks' gore.

Voltaire could normally be expected to show some interest in the revenge a fellow satirist like Pope was taking on Dennis, but there were additional reasons to explain his enjoyment at seeing Dennis torn to pieces. For Dennis is the very man who had attacked the French in the most chauvinistic terms in a letter dated 15 October 1688. The letter described his journey to France and was published in *Miscellanies in verse and prose* in 1693. Dennis says that before he begins he will use plain dealing, 'a thing which they [the French] never did yet with any one'. He admits that he mortally hates them for 'they have so long made sport for their neighbouring Nations by extravagant and absurd Commendations of their own that to endeavour to bring proofs of their vanity, would be something more *ridiculous* than that . . . The

---

[42] see Dédéyan, *Voltaire et la pensée anglaise*, p.68.
[43] 'The Dunciad variorum: arguments', in *The Poems of Alexander Pope*, ed. J. Butt, p.348.

French then are affected and impudent, which are but the necessary effects of that National Vice, their Vanity. *But then they have one good quality, which proceeds from the same Vanity. And that is their extraordinary civility to Strangers. For they are civil not for our satisfaction, but their own, not as they imagine it a duty, but an accomplishment . . . Tis to please himself that a Frenchman is officious to me'* (quoted in Lanson, ii. 267-68).

In his 'Projet d'une lettre sur les Anglais', the first part of which was probably written in December 1727,[44] Voltaire begins by noting how he came across a bad book by 'un nommé Dennis, car il y a aussi de méchans écrivains parmi les Anglais' (Lanson, ii. 256). He then gives a translation of Dennis's above quoted letter which enables him to illustrate very clearly the latter's jingoism. But he lets him off lightly, maintaining a tone of serene detachment and simply saying that not all the English think like Dennis and that he has not the slightest wish to imitate him. For tactical reasons, Voltaire probably felt at this stage of his career that Dennis had better be chastised by an Englishman.

The portrait of envy in *The Rape of the lock* is likely to have appealed to Voltaire very much because it has the same quality as *Hudibras*'s true church militant. It was easy for him to substitute 'l'évangile à la main' in his translation of *The Rape of the lock* for 'un pistolet en main' which he had already used in *Hudibras*. Both images revolve around fanaticism. The English poems and Boileau's *Le Lutrin*, all mock-heroic poems, were useful for *La Pucelle*. Moreover, Voltaire exploited the theme of envy in the *Discours sur l'envie* in 1738 when he attacked enemies such as J. B. Rousseau and Desfontaines. The latter was also satirised in the comedy of *L'Envieux* which dates from the same period. Voltaire no doubt relished the description of *Sir Plume*, that is, sir George Browne, in canto IV: he was singled out for his 'earnest Eyes, and round unthinking Face' (l. 125).

Voltaire again showed his appreciation of Pope's style in the letter published in the *Nouvelliste du Parnasse* in 1731. He placed Pope together with the most famous authors ancient and modern. In a reference to Campistron, he wrote (Best.D415):

il manque à cet auteur, d'ailleurs judicieux & tendre, ces beautés de détail, ces expressions heureuses, qui sont l'âme de la poésie, & qui font le mérite des

[44] see A.-M. Rousseau's complementary note 2, Lanson, ii. 310.

Homeres, des Virgiles, des Tasses, des Miltons, des Popes, des Corneilles, des Racines, des Boileaux.

A year later he was telling Thieriot (Best.D492, 26 May 1732):

J hope sr Homer Pope and sr Ovid Gay will be so kind as to forgive my boldness. You know j entertain for 'em the sense of the highest esteem. J admire their works, j love their persons, j would with all my heart live with them.

The Dunciad proved very popular in France in the eighteenth century. The extent of its popularity may be judged by the fact that Palissot, the enemy of the 'philosophes', decided to imitate it by calling his mock-heroic poem *La Dunciade*.[45] Long before Palissot, Voltaire had been interested in *The Dunciad* which perhaps exerted the greatest influence on him. Its influence may be seen in the *Temple du goût*, although it is not necessarily restricted to it. Carcassonne argued at some length in favour of various European influences on the *Temple*, without mentioning Pope's. But the *Temple* can be shown to have been directly inspired by *The Dunciad*. Sonet indicated that it was probably while reading *The Dunciad* that Voltaire became convinced that Swift was the English Rabelais (p.29). In *The Dunciad*, book i, Pope wrote (Butt, p.351):

> O thou! whatever Title please thine ear,
> Dean, Drapier, Bickerstaff, or Gulliver!
> Whether thou chuse Cervantes' serious air,
> Or laugh and shake in Rab'lais' easy Chair.

In many of his other writings, Voltaire used the phrase 'English Rabelais' to describe Swift, in the *Siècle de Louis XIV* (M.xiv.560), for instance. There is no doubt that he borrowed from Pope and his friends of the Scriblerus Club the name of Scriblerus when he wrote in the *Temple*: 'Nous rencontrâmes sur le chemin, Baldus . . . Scriblerius, une nuée de Commentateurs qui restituoient des passages, et qui compiloient de gros volumes à propos d'un mot qu'ils n'entendoient pas' (Carcassonne, pp.65-66). Swift, Arbuthnot, Pope, Gay and

---

45 *La Dunciade* was published in three books in 1764, then in ten books in 1771. In it Diderot and the contributors of the *Encyclopédie* were described as minions of the goddess of stupidity. In the preface to the 1764 edition, Palissot mentioned that the model for this immortal poem did not exist in any other nation. He particularly liked the singular mixture of bold, sometimes bizarre pictures, the delicacy of raillery accompanied by a sustained gaiety and the frequent witticisms.

Parnell founded the Scriblerus Club in 1713 with the aim of ridiculing all bad taste in learning. Martin Scriblerus appears frequently in the introduction and in footnotes by Pope to *The Dunciad*. In 1714, Arbuthnot had also written *Memoirs of the extraordinary life, works and discoveries of Martinus Scriblerus*.

In the *Temple* can be found another verbal echo of *The Dunciad*. Before publishing *The Dunciad*, Pope spoke of his aims in the poem in a letter he wrote to Swift on 23 March 1727/28. 'This Poem will rid me of these insects: the next felicity is to get rid of fools and scoundrels; which I can't but own to you was one part of my design in falling upon these Authors' (Sherburn, ii. 481). In the *Temple* Voltaire wrote of those 'petits insectes dont on ne soupçonne l'existence, que par les efforts qu'ils font pour piquer' (Carcassonne, p.71).

The Dunciad and the *Temple du goût* have similar themes. In both works, bad poets and bad taste are wittily pilloried. In *The Dunciad* poets who have attacked Pope and pedants are given rough treatment by being shown in ridiculous situations and grotesque attitudes. The tone, however, is generally cruder than in the *Temple*. In *The Dunciad* Curl, one of the booksellers competing in the game that marks the coronation of Tibbald, is placed in a burlesque posture (Butt, p.377):

> Obscene with filth the Miscreant lies bewray'd,
> Fal'n in the plash his wickedness had lay'd.

There is nothing in the *Temple* that can be compared with this situation. Yet Curl and Lintot are the kind of booksellers that one comes across in both writings. They help Dulness extend her empire.

It was not without significance to Voltaire that the bookseller should be made to run after a phantom in *The Dunciad*. The Goddess Dulness was responsible for its creation (Butt, p.373):

> She form'd this image of well-bodied air,
> With pert flat eyes she window'd well its head
> A brain of feathers, and a heart of lead
> And empty words she gave, and sounding strain
> But senseless, lifeless! Idol void and vain!

Voltaire uses this information in his description of a 'fripon de Libraire' (Carcassonne, pp.67-68) who

> Des beaux esprits écumeur mercenaire,
> Vendeur adroit de sottise et de vent,

En souriant d'une mine matoise
Lui mesuroit des livres à la toise.

There is certainly more invective in *The Dunciad* than in the *Temple*.
At the beginning of book i (Butt, p.354), the Goddess Dulness looks
at the 'Chaos dark and deep' and sees

How Hints, like spawn, scarce quick in embryo lie,
How new-born Nonsense first is taught to cry.
Maggots half-form'd, in rhyme exactly meet,
And learn to crawl upon poetic feet.

The satire of critics in the *Temple*, on the other hand, is rather mild in
tone (Carcassonne, p.66):

Le Goût n'est rien . . . Nous avons l'habitude
De rédiger au long de point en point,
Ce qu'on pensa; mais nous ne pensons point.

Differences of techniques between *The Dunciad* and the *Temple du
goût* do exist. Although Voltaire's work was condemned as satire by
friend and foe alike, it is mild and fair when compared with *The
Dunciad*. For Pope has recourse to systematic denigration and allows
his opponents little merit. Yet it is Pope who probably gave Voltaire
the idea of writing his own *Dunciad*. Like *The Dunciad*, the *Temple
du goût* has the same origin: they are both society jokes. Perhaps with
the precedent of the Scriblerus Club in mind, Voltaire explained in the
Lettre de mr de V . . . à m. de C . . . how his work arose (Carcassonne,
p.105):

Vous avez vu, et vous pouvez rendre témoignage, comment cette bagatelle
fut conçue et exécutée. C'étoit une plaisanterie de société. Vous y avez eu
part comme un autre; chacun fournissoit ses idées; et je n'ai guère eu d'autre
fonction que celle de les mettre par écrit.

In that letter, Voltaire also said that many changes were made to the
Temple du goût and these gave rise to seven or eight *Temples*. Pope
himself appeared in one of them, but his name was subsequently
omitted. As Voltaire acknowledged, this was a matter for regret.

In 1742 appeared *The New Dunciad* in which Pope aimed 'to declare
the Completion of the Prophecies' mentioned at the end of book iii.
In book iv of *The New Dunciad*, there is a parody of a degree ceremony.
Dulness proceeds to grant degrees, but before she is able to give her

blessings to all, her speech is interrupted by a tremendous yawn which becomes contagious (Butt, pp.797-98):

> All nature nods:
> What mortal can resist the Yawn of Gods?
> Churches and Chapels instantly it reach'd;
> (St. James's first, for leaden Gilbert preach'd)
> Then catch'd the Schools; the Hall scarce kept awake;
> The Convocation gap'd, but could not speak:
> Lost was the Nation's Sense, nor could be found,
> While the long solemn Unison went round:
> Wide, and more wide, it spread o'er all the realm;
> Ev'n Palinurus nodded at the Helm:
> The Vapour mild o'er each Committee crept;
> Unfinish'd Treaties in each Office slept;
> And Chiefless Armies doz'd out the Campaign;
> And Navies yawn'd for Orders on the Main.

It is quite likely that this episode of the yawn in *The Dunciad* inspired a similar episode in Voltaire's *Relation du jésuite Berthier* where Berthier starts yawning, followed by Coutu. Then the coachman 'se retourna, et les voyant ainsi bâiller, se mit à bâiller aussi; le mal gagna tous les passants: on bâilla dans toutes les maisons voisines' (*Dialogues et anecdotes philosophiques*, p.54). Although he had used *The Dunciad* more than once, Voltaire did not hesitate to tell Thieriot that 'La Dunciade de Pope me parait un sujet manqué' (Best.D9044, 7 July 1760). He could not help betraying the source of his attack against enemies such as Gauchat and Chaumeix in the eighteenth book of *La Pucelle* when, about a month later, he asked d'Alembert for the following information (Best.D9137, 13 August 1760):

Quelques anecdotes vraies sur Gauchat et Chaumeix, quels sont leurs ouvrages, le nom de leurs libraires . . . J'attends ces utiles mémoires pour mettre au net une Dunciade.

Despite the fact that Voltaire had borrowed from Milton for his description of the 'palais de la Sottise' in book iii of *La Pucelle* and had acknowledged his borrowing (see above p.137), his indebtedness to Pope appears even greater. Whereas Milton quickly passes over the 'Paradise of Fools', Pope gives more detail about this paradise, queen Dulness and her attendants. At the beginning of book iii of *The Dunciad* (Butt, p.402), Tibbald

hears loud Oracles, and talks with Gods.
Hence the Fool's paradise, the Statesman's scheme,
The air-built Castle, and the golden Dream
The Maid's romantic wish, the Chymist's flame.
And Poet's vision of eternal fame.

This is how Voltaire describes some of the attendants at the court of queen Sottise in *La Pucelle* (Vercruysse, p.301):

Sa cour plénière est à son gré fournie
De gens profonds en fait d'astrologie...
C'est là qu'on voit les maîtres d'alchimie
Faisant de l'or et n'ayant pas un sou.

At the beginning of book ii of *The Dunciad* (Butt, p.372), Dulness

summons all her sons: An endless band
Pours forth, and leaves unpeopled half the land;
A motley mixture! in long wigs, in bags,
In silks, in crapes, in garters, and in rags;
From drawing rooms, from colleges, from garrets,
On horse, on foot, in hacks, and gilded chariots,
All who true dunces in her cause appear'd.

Voltaire uses the idea in book iii of *La Pucelle* through an invocation to Sottise (Vercruysse, p.309):

O toi, Sottise! ô grosse déité!
De qui les flancs à tout âge ont porté
Plus de mortels que Cibèle féconde
N'avait jadis donné de dieux au monde:
Qu'avec plaisir ton grand œil hébété
Voit tes enfants dont ma patrie abonde,
Sots traducteurs et sots compilateurs,
Et sots auteurs, et non moins sots lecteurs.

The goddess is further asked for the names of her most cherished sons in this huge crowd and for the names of those who have been most prolific in producing clumsy and insipid works and who have been most constant in shying and braying. Voltaire adds that he is aware that the goddess has lavished her tenderest attention on the author of the *Journal de Trévoux*. He obviously means the editor, Berthier. In *The Dunciad*, book i, Dulness liked Prynn, Eusden, Philips and Dennis. But her minion was Tibbald (Butt, p.359):

In each she marks her image full exprest,
But chief, in Tibbald's master-breeding breast.

The illness of Berthier in the *Relation* also recalls that of Dennis, in
The Narrative of Dr. Robert Norris (1713). *The Narrative* is about 'one
Mr. Dennis, an officer of the custom-house, who was taken ill of a
violent frenzy last April.[46] The patient's ravings became so violent that
he had to be bound to the bedstead. A so-called apothecary cut the
critic's bandages. In the *Relation*, the diagnosis of Berthier's illness
reveals that he too suffers from poisoning and the coachman is asked
whether he has any packet for the apothecaries. The poison turns out
to be two dozen copies of the *Journal de Trévoux* (p.55). In the
Narrative of Dr. Robert Norris, the cause of Dennis's illness was
Addison's *Cato*. Pope took a medical revenge on another opponent,
Curll, when in 1716 he published a *Full and true account of a horrid and
barbarous revenge by poison on the body of mr. Edmund Curll*. In the
Account, Pope and Curll, supposedly reconciled, drink to each other,
'yet it was plain, by the pangs this unhappy stationer felt soon after,
that some poisonous drug had been secretly infused therein.[47] It is
also forecast that the poison 'will infallibily destroy him by slow
degrees in less than a month' (p.468).

In addition to *The Dunciad*, Voltaire also liked Pope's moral essay
Of the use of riches which was the original title of the *Epistle to
Bathurst*. For in 1733, he wrote to Thieriot: 'Je viens de recevoir et de
lire, le poème de Pope sur les richesses. Il m'a paru plein de choses
admirables' (Best.D608, *c.* 10 May 1733). The poem satirised the
behaviour of Peter Walter and Francis Chartres, fraudulent South Sea
Company directors and governors of the Charitable Corporation.
Voltaire, who later developed the habit of inserting explanatory
comments on the enemies he attacked in poems like *La Pucelle*, must
have enjoyed Pope's abundant footnotes on these public wrongdoers.
His admiration for the Englishman continued when he placed him
alongside Addison and Fontenelle. In a letter to d'Olivet, he said that
he knew few people whose genius was as varied as that of Pope,
Addison, Machiavelli, Leibniz and Fontenelle (Best.D980, 6 January
1736).

[46] *The Works of Alexander Pope*, eds Elwin and Courthope (London 1871-89),
x. 451.
[47] Elwin and Courthope, x. 463.

By coincidence, in the same letter (Best.D608) where Voltaire mentions Pope's moral essay, he also asks Thieriot to send him lady Mary Wortley Montagu's poems. The name of Mary Montagu is associated in eighteenth-century English literary history with those of Pope and Hervey. Voltaire knew all of them. He had met lady Mary in England in 1727, probably through Fawkener,[48] and had asked her for her views on the Milton section of his *Essay on epick poetry*. She had not been complimentary: nevertheless Voltaire was not vindictive towards her. On the contrary, he never stopped admiring her.[49]

One must remember that lady Mary was a writer not only of charming verses and letters, but also a collaborator with lord Hervey in attacks upon Pope. Her *Verses to the imitator of Horace* ran into six editions in 1733. If he knew of her *Court poems*, renamed *Town eclogues*, only one volume of which had appeared and that as far back as 1716,[50] Voltaire may very well have known the more recent *Verses*. He would have been aware of the hostilities between Pope and lady Mary, especially as she was collaborating with another friend of his, lord Hervey. Anticipating the attack in *An Epistle to dr. Arbuthnot* (1735), Pope composed in the same period an epigram entitled *To ld. Hervey & lady Mary Wortley*, which was published only in 1950. It ran as follows (Butt, p.820):

> When I but call a flagrant Whore unsound,
> Or have a Pimp or Flaterer in the Wind,

[48] cf. Norma Perry, *Sir Everard Fawkener, friend and correspondent of Voltaire*, Studies on Voltaire (1975), cxxxiii. 38.

[49] see R. Halsband, *The Life of lady Mary Wortley Montagu* (Oxford 1956), p.120. James Caldwell, who met lady Mary in Toulouse in 1746 told Montesquieu that she did not like Voltaire, thought poorly of *La Henriade* and found the *Essay* 'effroyable'. See A.-M. Rousseau, *L'Angleterre et Voltaire*, i. 100. In the eleventh of the *Lettres philosophiques* lady Mary is praised for her introduction of inoculation against smallpox in England. She must have verbally communicated to Voltaire such information as she had acquired in Turkey about inoculation. In 1758 Voltaire asked Algarotti to send his regards to lady Mary who was then settled in Venice (Best.D7843, 2 September 1758). The highest praise was perhaps reserved for her in Voltaire's article in the *Gazette littéraire* of the 4th April 1764, where she was called 'la Sévigné d'Angleterre'. Voltaire went on: 'c'est une élégance charmante, nourrie d'une érudition qui ferait honneur à un savant, et qui est tempérée par les grâces. Il règne surtout dans l'ouvrage de milady Montagu un esprit de philosophie et de liberté qui caractérise sa nation ... Les lettres de ces deux Françaises [mme de Sévigné and mme de Maintenon] n'intéressent que leur nation; les lettres de milady Montagu semblent faites pour toutes les nations qui veulent s'instruire' (M.xxv.163, 166).

[50] see Best.D608, n.2.

Sapho enrag'd crys out your Back is round,
    Adonis screams – Ah! Foe to all Mankind!

Thanks, dirty Pair! you teach me what to say,
    When you attack my Morals, Sense, or Truth,
I answer thus – poor Sapho you grow grey,
    And sweet Adonis – you have lost a Tooth.

Not only did Voltaire familiarise himself with Pope's satirical writings, but he seems to have been equally well-informed of attacks against Pope and to have been sufficiently interested in some of these. In *Des mensonges imprimés* published after *Sémiramis* in 1749, Voltaire speaks of more than a hundred libels written against Pope by his enemies. He adds: 'Pope eut quelquefois la faiblesse de répondre; cela grossit la nuée des libelles. Enfin il prit le parti de faire imprimer lui-même un petit abrégé de toutes ces belles pièces . . . J'ai été tenté d'avoir beaucoup de vanité, quand j'ai vu que nos grands écrivains en usaient avec moi comme on en avait agi avec Pope' (M.xxiii.436).

Voltaire had other opportunities of justifying his own practice of satire by quoting Pope as a precedent. He liked to compare himself with the Englishman for better or for worse. He told mme Denis once that a man of letters always runs the risk of being bitten by hack writers and denounced by 'dévots'. He then added: 'Demandez à Pope; il a passé par les mêmes épreuves; et s'il n'a pas été mangé, c'est qu'il avait bec et ongles' (Best.D5595, 20 December 1753). His admiration for Pope's stand is so strong that when he decides to attack Fréron in his play *L'Ecossaise*, he writes in the 'Avertissement' in 1761 (M.v. 418):

il n'y a plus d'autre moyen de rendre les lettres respectables que de faire trembler ceux qui les outragent. C'est le dernier parti que prit Pope avant que de mourir: il rendit ridicules à jamais, dans sa *Dunciade*, tous ceux qui devaient l'être; ils n'osèrent plus se montrer, ils disparurent; toute la nation lui applaudit.

There is no doubt that Voltaire used against his enemies the worst features of eighteenth-century polemical techniques common to both England and France. His familiarity with Pope's attacks against his enemies and the latter's attacks against Pope may have encouraged Voltaire in this tendency to a certain extent. In 1716 in *A True character of mr. Pope*, Dennis had transformed Pope into Satan when he wrote: 'By his constant and malicious Lying, and by that Angel Face and

Form of his, 'tis plain that he wants nothing but Horns and Tayl, to be the exact Resemblance, both in Shape and Mind, of his Infernal Father.'[51] The author of the poem *The Blatant-beast* (1742) drew on the same inspiration for the metamorphosis of Pope into Satan.[52] Such literary techniques would certainly have appealed to Voltaire who was never short of enemies.

Polemical devices of a less literary kind were also being used in eighteenth-century England. Voltaire could have seen on the title page of *The Dunciad variorum* of 1729 the picture of an ass loaded with books bearing the names of prominent dunces.[53] In the pamphlet entitled *Pope Alexander's supremacy and infallibility examin'd: and the errors of Scriblerus and his man William detected*, published in the same year, the frontispiece represents Pope with the body of a rat, leaning on a pile of books on a pedestal, a pen clutched in his paw and another paw holding his pensive head. A note entitled *A Letter to the publisher* is attached to the ear of an ass standing close to the pedestal. At the foot of the pedestal is the inscription: MARTINI SCRIBLERI VERA EFFIGIES.[54]

In April 1759, Voltaire had indicated that he was working on something that was not 'à l'eau rose' but 'quelque chose de plus fort' (Best.D8249, 6 April 1759). This strong stuff which went through many revised versions was his play *Tancrède*, produced in September 1760. It did not contain any attack against Fréron, with whom he was then preoccupied, but it appeared with a print representing a donkey braying in front of a lyre which was suspended from a branch. Beneath the 'portrait' were the following lines (M.v. 402-403):

> Et ce monsieur qui soupire,
> Et fait rire,
> N'est-ce pas Martin F....?

Some commentators believed that the print was intended to serve as a frontispiece to *L'Ecossaise*. When Fréron himself heard about it he proclaimed that *L'Ecossaise* was to be published 'ornée du portrait de l'auteur'.[55] The engraving commissioned from Gravelot and Voltaire's

---

[51] quoted in J. V. Guerinot, *Pamphlet attacks on Alexander Pope 1711-1744* (London 1969), pp. xxxii-xxxiii.

[52] Guerinot, p.306.

[53] there is a reproduction in an edition by the Scolar Press, Leeds, 1966.

[54] reproduced in Guerinot, opposite p.166.

[55] F. Cornou, *Trente années de luttes contre Voltaire et les philosophes du dix-huitième siècle: E. Fréron (1718-1776)* (Paris 1922), p.256. In *Fréron contre les philosophes* (Genève 1975), J. Balcou has nothing to say on this matter or on *Le Pauvre diable*.

verses were really meant for *Tancrède*. When these appeared in Cramer's edition of *Tancrède* in February 1761, Voltaire told Algarotti that the engraving had been well drawn, adding 'il y a un portrait qui est d'après nature' (Best.D9643, 22 February 1761).[56] Voltaire's comment is *mutatis mutandis* almost a faithful translation of the inscription in *Pope Alexander's supremacy*. It was made in the same year as his own attack on Pope in the *Parallèle d'Horace, de Boileau, et de Pope.*

There seems to be a change in Voltaire's attitude to Pope after the Lisbon earthquake in 1755, but he is still courteous towards him and appreciative of his works. He does him justice in the *Préface au Poème sur le désastre de Lisbonne* and states in a letter to Cideville: 'Comme je ne suis pas en tout de l'avis de Pope, malgré l'amitié que j'ay eüe pour sa personne et l'estime sincère que je conserverai toutte ma vie pour ses ouvrages, j'ay cru devoir luy rendre justice dans ma préface' (Best.D6821, 12 August 1756). However, Voltaire did not keep the promise he made with regard to his lifelong esteem for Pope's works. In the *Parallèle d'Horace, de Boileau, et de Pope* (1761), he strongly criticised some of Pope's works, the *Epistle to dr. Arbuthnot* in particular. He suggests that Pope is much inferior to Horace and Boileau (M.xxiv. 225):

Quant aux autres *Epîtres* de Pope qui pourraient être comparées à celles d'Horace et de Boileau, je demanderai si ces deux auteurs, dans leurs *Satires,* se sont jamais servis des armes dont Pope se sert? Les gentillesses dont il régale milord Harvey, l'un des plus aimables hommes d'Angleterre, sont un peu singulières.

He then gives what he calls a word for word translation of the deadly lines against Sporus in Pope's *Epistle*:

Que Harvey tremble! Qui cette chose de soie!
Harvey, ce fromage mou fait de lait d'ânesse!
Hélas! il ne peut sentir ni satire ni raison.
Qui voudrait faire mourir un papillon sur la roue?
Pourtant je veux frapper cette punaise volante à ailes dorées,
Cet enfant de la boue qui se peint et qui pue . . .
Ainsi, l'épagneul bien élevé se plaît civilement
A mordiller le gibier qu'il n'ose entamer . . .
Soit que, crapaud familier à l'oreille d'Eve,
Moitié écume, moitié venin, il se crache lui-même en compagnie . . .

[56] see J. S. Henderson, *Voltaire's* Tancrède, Studies on Voltaire (1968), lxi. 119-20.

Ainsi les rabbins ont peint le tentateur
Avec face de chérubin et queue de serpent;
Sa beauté vous choque, vous vous défiez de son esprit;
Son esprit rampe, et sa vanité lèche la poussière.

The climax of his denigration of Pope and English taste is reached in his conclusion (p.226):

Les lecteurs pourront demander si c'est Pope ou un de ses porteurs de chaise qui a fait ces vers. Ce n'est pas là absolument le style de Despréaux. Ne conclura-t-on pas de ce petit écrit que la politesse d'une nation n'est pas la politesse d'une autre?

Voltaire also enjoyed translating at the same time the episode in the second book of *The Dunciad* where Curll is splashed in filth. He claimed that the difference in taste between the two neighbouring countries was so great that he could do no better than give a faithful translation of 'un des plus délicats passages' of *The Dunciad* to make his point:

Au milieu du chemin on trouve un bourbier
Que madame Curl avait produit le matin:
C'était sa coutume de se défaire, au lever de l'aurore,
Du marc de son souper, devant la porte de sa voisine...
Le mécréant Curl est couché dans la vilainie,
Couvert de l'ordure qu'il a lui-même fournie, etc.

In his opinion, the portrait of 'La Mollesse' in *Le Lutrin* is of another kind; but then each nation has its own taste.

While recording Voltaire's strictures against Pope, it is necessary to remind oneself of his own satirical practice. Voltaire does not hesitate to fall back on the same burlesque technique used by Pope in *The Dunciad*, to attack his opponent Maupertuis, in one of the *Akakia* pamphlets. In the *Réponse d'un académicien de Berlin à un académicien de Paris* published in the *Bibliothèque raisonnée* on 18 September 1752, Voltaire counters Maupertuis's threat to kill him with 'je ne pourai que vous jetter à la tête ma seringue et mon pot de chambre'. Like Pope who exploited the physical characteristics of his enemies, particularly their faces[57] in works such as the *Essay on criticism* and *The Rape of the lock*, Voltaire disfigured his critics. In the epigram, the *Anti-giton*, Desfontaines was described as having 'l'œil louche et le mufle effronté' (M.ix.563). The foulest attack ever made against an enemy was, of

[57] Tillotson, *On the poetry of Pope*, p.34.

course, reserved for Fréron in 1760 in *Le Pauvre diable*. He there became a 'vermisseau né du cul de Desfontaines' (M.x.103).

For all his complaints against the Englishman's lack of taste, Voltaire could very well have used Pope's animal imagery against Hervey when he attacked Fréron, first in the private correspondence, then in his published writings. For instance, in a letter to Thieriot Voltaire wrote: 'il se trouve toujours... des Frérons qui mordent. Je vous prie de m'envoyer... la malsemaine dans laquelle Fréron répand son venin de Crapaud' (Best.D8655, 15 December 1759). Voltaire's satire against Fréron continues in the same vein in another letter to Thieriot where the arch enemy receives the following treatment: 'cet autre animal de Fréron... Ce Fréron saisit la chose comme un dogue affamé qui ronge le premier os qu'on luy présente' (Best.D8694, 4 January 1760). In her monologue in *L'Ecossaise*, Lady Alton while referring to Fréron says that 'nos dogues mordent par instinct de courage; et lui, par instinct de bassesse' (M.v.438). Fréron is described in the preface to *L'Ecossaise* as 'un crapaud, un lézard, une couleuvre' (M.v.410). Is it not also legitimate to conclude that the imagery used against him in the 'capilotade' is partly derived from the last four lines against Sporus in the *Epistle to dr. Arbuthnot* and translated in the *Parallèle d'Horace* (see above, p.227)? Had Voltaire not exploited the animal imagery of Butler and Dryden against other persons? (see above, pp.164, 180, 181).

It is even possible that Voltaire once took up an offensive remark made against Pope by his enemies. To counteract Pope's denigration of Hervey in the *Epistle to dr. Arbuthnot*, Voltaire observed in 1764: 'Quand on songe que c'était un petit homme contrefait, bossu par devant et par derrière, qui parlait ainsi, on voit à quel point l'amour-propre et la colère sont aveugles' (M.xxiv. 225, n.1). Although Pope's physical deformity was common knowledge, it is strange to hear this type of criticism from a man who had never been his enemy, for Voltaire's attack is more reminiscent of Dennis who in 1711 in his *Reflections critical and satyrical upon a late rhapsody call'd an Essay upon criticism* had called Pope a 'hunch-back'd Toad'.[58] In *The Difference between verbal and practical virtue* (1742), attributed to lord Hervey, the author complained that Pope's mind was more deformed than his body.[59]

---

[58] *The Critical works of John Dennis*, edited by E. N. Hooker (Oxford 1939), i. 415.
[59] see W. L. MacDonald, *Pope and his critics* (London 1951), p.71.

Voltaire's defence of Hervey and condemnation of Pope in the *Parallèle d'Horace, de Boileau, et de Pope* can easily be explained. Apart from his later unsuccessful attempt to resist English literary fashions which he had been among the first to encourage himself in the earlier part of his career, personal factors are involved. Here Voltaire is in some way repaying Hervey for his support as a subscriber to the English edition of the *Henriade* and showing him a mark of his friendship.[60] He maintained contact with the Herveys after his return to France and Hervey visited him in Paris in 1729 after his trip to Italy. In a letter to Hervey in 1732, Voltaire spoke of the 'high sense of respect and gratitude which j entertain for yr lordship and mylady Hervey' (Best.D455, ? January 1732) and referred to his boldness in attempting a translation of Hervey's account of his journey to Italy,

or rather a loose imitation for french poetry is not strong enoug to stik closely to your.

> Trhougout all Italy beside
> What does one find, but want and pride,
> Forces of superstitious folly,
> Decay, distress and melancoly, etc.

Voltaire translated Hervey's account in full in the 'Cambridge notebook' (*Notebooks*, i. 101), incorporated the translation with changes in the *Letters concerning the English nation* (pp.195-96) and reproduced the English original in the later 'Leningrad notebooks' (*Notebooks*, i. 238).

The friendship between Hervey and Voltaire continued for many years. Voltaire affirmed in a letter to Hervey: 'De tout ce que j'ay vu en Angleterre, Mylord c'est vous dont j'ay gardé le souvenir le plus cher' (Best.D652, 14 September 1733). He congratulated him on his appointment as lord privy seal in 1740 (Best.D2216, *c.* 1 June 1740). It is clear from the correspondence of both men that literary matters cemented their friendship. Hervey for his part told Henry Fox that he liked Voltaire's verses[61] and in his letter to Algarotti in September 1737, he mentioned having received a letter and 'a vast packet of verses' from Voltaire (*Lord Hervey and his friends*, p.273). He did not hesitate to give friendly advice in French to Voltaire who, in his view, had made

[60] see 'Voltaire's correspondence with lord Hervey: three new letters', ed. T. J. Barling, *Studies on Voltaire* (1968), lxii. 13-27.

[61] see *Lord Hervey and his friends 1726-1738*, ed. the earl of Ilchester (London 1950), p.179.

indiscreet attacks on religion in the *Lettres philosophiques*: 'réfléchissez dont combien D'amitié je devrois avoir pour vous quand je tâche de vous guérir d'un mal que j'avoue en même tems m'a tant diverti' (Best.D1110, 4 July 1736). One can therefore understand Voltaire's feelings on seeing Pope's attacks on Hervey. It is true that Hervey himself somewhat mistrusted Voltaire and thought poorly of his dedication of *Zaïre* to Fawkener. Warm at the outset, relations between them became cool and bitter towards the end. (See A.-M. Rousseau *L'Angleterre et Voltaire*, i. 166-70).

Important as Voltaire's sarcastic remarks on Pope are, the fact remains that they are confined to a limited period. For most of his life Voltaire admired Pope's works. When he chose to, he could even attack the reputation of other famous polemicists in order to increase the merit of Pope. Thus in 1737 in the *Sixième discours sur l'homme*, he did not hesitate to write (M.ix. 415):

> Despréaux et Pascal en ont fait la satire;
> Pope et le grand Leibnitz, moins enclins à médire,
> Semblent dans leurs écrits prendre un sage milieu.

In 1748 in the *Epitre à mme Denis*, Voltaire had the highest praise for Pope (M.x.349):

> L'ombre de Pope avec les rois repose;
> Un peuple entier fait son apothéose,
> Et son nom vole à l'immortalité.

Even after the *Parallèle d'Horace, de Boileau, et de Pope*, he acknowledged the qualities of Pope's style, for in a letter to Keate, he stated that the verses in Shakespeare's tragedies 'ne sont certainement pas élégants et châtiez, comme ceux de Pope' (Best.D10322, 10 February 1762). Although he told the Nevilles ten years later that Pope lacked gaiety and imagination, he admitted that Pope had taste, for Pope 'savait faire de beaux vers, et choisir toujours le mot le plus propre, et . . . avait aussi – that best and wisest art, the art to blot' (*Voltaire's British visitors*, p.155).

It would therefore appear unwise to talk of Voltaire's mere acquaintance with Pope's satirical writings. It is likely that Voltaire used his knowledge of these in his works. There was nothing to be ashamed of in this, for Voltaire's predecessors and contemporaries cultivated the art of 'imitation'. Voltaire took the precaution of writing in 1756 in the

Lettres philosophiques that nearly everything was imitation (Lanson, ii. 136), while in *A Letter to a noble lord*, written against Hervey in 1733, Pope unashamedly declared: 'I am a mere imitator of Homer, Horace, Boileau, Garth, etc, which I have the less cause to be ashamed of since they were imitators of one another' (Elwin and Courthope, v. 438). The truth is that both Voltaire and Pope were no ordinary imitators: their satires bear the unmistakable mark of their strong individual personalities.

It was by no mere coincidence that Voltaire brought up the names of Pope, Dryden and Boileau in connection with Churchill in the *Gazette littéraire*. Some thirty years earlier he had found it most appropriate to refer to Boileau and his satires when talking of Rochester in the *Lettres philosophiques*, while in the *Conseils à un journaliste*, he placed Boileau, Rochester and Dryden on the same level. He was thus deliberately showing how familiar he was with both the English and French traditions in satirical writing. Yet it was no pedantic spirit in Voltaire that prompted his comparative method. Whatever may have been his pronouncements on satire and his attitude to English writers on the whole, Voltaire showed that he was determined to make the most of his extensive knowledge of English satirists. He had stated his position quite plainly in the *Lettres philosophiques*: 'Les Anglais ont beaucoup profité des ouvrages de notre langue, nous devrions à notre tour emprunter d'eux après leur avoir prêté' (Lanson ii. 139). This is what he in fact did, although he occasionally showed some contempt for English satirists.

It was natural that Voltaire should have looked to England even in matters of style. For the most famous of Augustan satirists had themselves found inspiration in Boileau, who also happened to be a constant source of reference for French satirists, including Voltaire. This, after all, was a period of interpenetration of English and French influences, despite French strictures against English taste arising from a failure to understand the aims and methods of English literature, especially the drama. As his experience in comedy had been enriched by English attempts to improve on Molière, Voltaire must have been fascinated by similar efforts to improve on Boileau's satires. At times he was impressed by Dryden's elegance. However, even in the most successful satire of the Augustan period, *Absalom and Achitophel*, Dryden paid lip service to the lofty principles of the *Discourse concerning satire* in the presentation of Zimri. His method in that particular instance was nearer to that of Pope who could be as blunt and as insulting as Voltaire. Voltaire and Pope were indeed kindred spirits in satirical methods, if not in thought.

Voltaire was deeply interested in Dryden's satires as well as in his critical writings and may have remembered to show some of Dryden's generosity when circumstances permitted, especially when he did not feel provoked. But Dryden was not all generosity and the example he set in his treatment of Shadwell in *Mac Flecknoe* could not easily be forgotten by any succeeding satirist. Besides, there was Pope to remind Voltaire of Dryden's technique against Shadwell. Voltaire's enthusiasm for the earlier satirist was thus extended to his brilliant successor through personal contacts with him.

Because of the insistence on decorum and propriety of words in English Augustan literature, H. Peyre was led to conclude that England was, par excellence, the 'country of understatement' (*Qu'est-ce que le classicisme?* p.155). If this remark about England were always true, Pope would have produced quite different works. There is little substance in the notion that English Augustan poets were unwilling to 'call a spade a spade'. A glance at any satire of Pope would suffice to prove the point. And Voltaire gave more than a glance at poems such as *The Dunciad* and the *Epistle to dr. Arbuthnot*. The denigration of Hervey in the latter poem is as vitriolic as Voltaire's onslaught on Desfontaines and Fréron. Can one have serious doubts about some of the sources of Voltaire's inspiration in his attacks against his two inveterate enemies?

Voltaire was perhaps disappointed to find that the greatest Augustan satirists, Dryden and Pope, sometimes lacked elegance. However, he had some compensation in that he found it where he might not have expected it, in the work of Prior. By using Prior as he did, Voltaire wanted to suggest that in his view the former diplomat was not such a 'minor' poet after all and that he came close to Dryden and Pope.

5

Voltaire's use of English prose

≈≈≋≈≈

i. *Voltaire's thoughts on prose fiction*

MOST traditional literary genres flourished in France in the seventeenth century, but tended to disintegrate in the eighteenth century as barriers between them fell away. In general, writers are in search of a form which can show to advantage their literary, social, philosophical and personal interests. How does Voltaire go about this search for an appropriate medium? In the first half of the eighteenth century, Voltaire, it is generally accepted, owed his fame mainly to the drama and to an epic poem and he had no hesitation in proclaiming his views on these well-established genres. Yet today his success as the author of the *contes philosophiques* is emphasized at the expense of his achievement in other fields and although this does little justice to a figure of such stature, it is important to know what he thought of prose fiction,[1] to which he devoted a good deal of his time once he was fully launched on his literary career.

Unlike Lenglet Du Fresnoy, author of *De l'usage des romans* (1734) or Aubert de La Chesnaye Des Bois, author of the *Lettres amusantes et critiques sur les romans en général anglois et françois* (1743), Voltaire has left no systematic essay on the novel. For a proper assessment of his position on the subject, therefore, Voltaire's views, which were expressed in a number of public and private utterances, require close examination. Moreover, Voltaire was no static critic who confided his thoughts to the world once and for all. He was forever changing his position and this flexibility is nowhere better illustrated than in his

---

[1] without subscribing to the view of P. Morillot as expressed in *Le Roman français* (*1610-1800*) (London 1920), p.161: 'Qu'est-ce qu'un conte? C'est un roman auquel personne ne croit, ni auteur, ni lecteur. Car il n'y a pas à dire: nous croyons aux personnages des vrais romans, à Virginie de La Tour, à Manon Lescaut', it is perhaps not necessary to distinguish between *conte* and *roman*. Voltaire himself did not make the distinction when commenting on *Zadig* (see below, p.238).

234

attitude to the novel.[2] He would contradict everyone and himself in the space of a single year or day so that it is by no means easy to ascertain what his views really were. Hence the need to proceed with care when we are dealing with Voltaire as a theorist of the novel.

It was some time before Voltaire turned to the resources of prose fiction. It was not that he was unaware in the early part of his career of the limitations of a serious treatise as an instrument of propaganda.[3] If that were the case, he would not have written in a letter to his friend Formont in connection with the *Lettres philosophiques* (Best. D617, *c.* 1 June 1733):

En vérité, ce qu'il y a de plus passable dans ce petit ouvrage, est ce qui regarde la philosophie; et c'est, je crois, ce qui sera le moins lu. On a beau dire, le siècle est philosophe. On n'a pourtant pas vendu deux cents exemplaires du petit livre de m. de Maupertuis, où il est question de l'attraction; et si on montre si peu d'empressement pour un ouvrage écrit de main de maître, qu'arrivera-t-il aux faibles essais d'un écolier comme moi?

Nevertheless he went on to write the argumentative *Traité de méta-physique* in 1734 and the *Eléments de la philosophie de Newton*, which was published in 1738. It was only some twenty years later that Voltaire came to prefer the *conte* to serious philosophical treatises. Four years after the publication of *Candide*, he began to extol the virtues of light, simple narrative.

If in the early 1730s Voltaire perhaps did not think of the *conte* as the right medium to express his ideas, how are we to account for the fact that soon afterwards he was to systematically use this genre by composing works like the *Songe de Platon* and *Micromégas*?[4] Can it be that Voltaire at first believed in the coexistence of a serious form such as a treatise and a light form such as the *contes philosophiques* or, to use

---

[2] in the earlier part of his career, Voltaire remained true to the teaching of the Jesuits and the rhetorical tradition which emphasized three literary genres and excluded prose fiction. He shared the prejudice of the early eighteenth century against fiction, which sought respectability by calling itself 'mémoire' or 'histoire'. Even Diderot's *Eloge de Richardson* (1762) betrayed the prejudice. See J. Van den Heuvel, *Voltaire dans ses contes* (Paris 1967), pp.15-19.

[3] see Richard A. Brooks, *Voltaire and Leibniz* (Geneva 1964), p.88.

[4] mme Du Châtelet may have played an important role here. She combined mathematical pursuits with light reading and under her influence, Voltaire too read novels, developed a more flexible taste, and, finally, tried his hand at the harmless game of mocking at Plato through a *conte*. See Van den Heuvel, pp.53-67.

his own words, the *rogatons?* This would not be too surprising from a writer who spent much of his life denigrating satire in theory while actually writing it. It is also worth noting that the genesis of Voltaire's early *contes* coincides with a period that witnessed the climax of official persecution of the novel.[5] This might to some extent explain Voltaire's reticence, at least in theory, towards prose fiction in these years.

Voltaire had become interested in the novel even before the 1730s. In 1727, for example, he showed that he was a discerning critic who was alive to the impact of madame de Lafayette's novel *Zaïde* on the reading public, especially women. In the *Essay on epick poetry*, he wrote: 'it is very strange, yet true, that among the most Learn'd and the greatest Admirers of Antiquity, there is scarce one to be found, who ever read the *Iliad*, with that Eagerness and Rapture, which a Woman feels when she reads the Novel of *Zaïda*' (White, p.90).

He makes certain concessions to the novel in the epistle *A un premier commis* which was composed in June 1733, but published for the first time in 1746. In it he states that he is aware that a poor novel is in the realm of books what a fool who wants to show off his imagination is in the world. One scoffs at the novel, but one puts up with it. Why? It is because (M.xxxiii. 353):

Ce roman fait vivre et l'auteur qui l'a composé, et le libraire qui le débite, et le fondeur, et l'imprimeur, et le papetier, et le relieur, et le colporteur, et le marchand de mauvais vin, à qui tous ceux-là portent leur argent. L'ouvrage amuse encore deux ou trois heures quelques femmes avec lesquelles il faut de la nouveauté en livres, comme en tout le reste. Ainsi, tout méprisable qu'il est, il a produit deux choses importantes: du profit et du plaisir.

About the same time, however, he also chose to lay more stress on the negative aspects of the novel in other writings. In the *Essai sur la poésie épique*, for example, with the seventeenth-century novel in mind, he concluded that it was fit only to entertain frivolous youth (M.viii.362). In Voltaire's view, the eighteenth-century novel too shares this frivolous character. For he subsequently harps on its frivolous nature and its tendency to sink into oblivion after being fashionable for a while. He tells Thieriot (Best.D2586, 19 January 1742):

[5] see Georges May, *Le Dilemme du roman au XVIIIe siècle* (New Haven 1963), pp.100-101.

je ne crois point parceque le frivole est bien reçu que la nation n'aime que le frivole. Les livres sensez et instructifs ont un succez plus durable, ils passent à la postérité et les petits romans sont bientôt oubliez . . . et on ne lira pas plu les confessions du comte de [by C. P. Duclos] que les honnêtes gens ne lisent celles de st Augustin.

On the same day, Voltaire contradicts himself with regard to Duclos's novel. He tells d'Argental that he has read it and that although it is better than st Augustine's work, it is simply 'un journal de bonnes fortunes, une histoire sans suitte, un roman sans intrigue, un ouvrage qui ne laisse rien dans l'esprit' (Best.D2584). Yet he admits to being impressed by its natural and lively style and he concludes that its subject-matter and its portraits must have pleased all readers.

Voltaire could appreciate a novel if it were written in a 'pure' and natural style. *Le Siège de Calais* (1739), a novel by mme de Tencin and Pont-de-Veyle, apparently satisfied this criterion. He told mlle Quinault that the work had such a style and that he had sought it for a long time (Best.D2052, 27 July 1739). If Le Sage's *Gil Blas* is still read, it is because it is natural (*Siècle de Louis XIV*, M.xiv.98).

In the *Siècle de Louis XIV*, Voltaire condemned the seventeenth-century novel on account of its superficiality and on aesthetic grounds as well, although he was careful enough to spare the reputation of madame de La Fayette. He complained that France had been submerged by all these novels (M.xiv.142):

ils ont presque tous été, excepté *Zaïde*, des productions d'esprits faibles qui écrivent avec facilité des choses indignes d'être lues par les esprits solides; ils sont même pour la plupart dénués d'imagination, et il y en a plus dans quatre pages de l'Arioste que dans tous ces insipides écrits qui gâtent le goût des jeunes gens.[6]

It was in 1748 in a parody of the 'approbation' which was then required for the publication of a book and which he prefaced to an edition of *Zadig* that Voltaire appears to have approved of the novel without any reservation for the first time.[7] He finds *Zadig* 'curieux,

---

[6] he hoped sir Everard and lady Fawkener did not care very much for romances. But he conceded to Fawkener: 'Yet there are some writ in a very lively manner. Nothing is more pleasing in that scurrilous way than the performances of our Hamilton' (Best. D4851, 27 March 1752).

[7] for tactical reasons perhaps, Voltaire told d'Argental in the same year that he wished to have nothing to do with novels. He resented the fact that *Zadig* was attributed to him (Best.D3759, 19 September 1748).

amusant, moral, philosophique, digne de plaire à ceux mêmes qui haïssent les romans'. Yet to please the keeper of the seal he says that he denigrated it, adding that he had assured 'M. le cadi-lesquier que c'est un ouvrage détestable' (M.xxi. 31).

Even if it is assumed that in his comment on *Zadig* Voltaire was to some extent making a special plea for himself, his sudden change must still be accounted for. One of the reasons surely is that he must have felt some of the impact the English novel was having in France. He did not, however, maintain a favourable attitude towards the novel as a genre for long. Before his struggles with *l'infâme*, he did not hesitate to attack the novel when and where he wanted. In the eighth book of *La Pucelle*, which had been composed by 1755, he ironically congratulates the abbé Tritême (that is, the theologian Johannes Heidenberg (1462-1516)) for having chosen to write on the theme of Agnès and Jeanne. Then he goes on to denigrate the novel for its dullness and indifference to verisimilitude, even parodying Boileau to make his point (Vercruysse, pp.391-92):

> Que je l'admire et que je me sais gré
> D'avoir toujours hautement préféré
> Cette lecture honnête et profitable
> A ce fatras d'insipides romans
> Que je vois naître et mourir tous les ans,
> De cerveaux creux avortons languissants!
> De Jeanne d'Arc l'histoire véritable
> Triomphera de l'envie et du temps.
> Le vrai me plaît, le vrai seul est durable.

If Voltaire felt a special dislike of the sentimental novel, it was partly because of *La Nouvelle Héloïse* (published in 1761), Rousseau's 'malheureux fatras intitulé roman', as he described it in a letter to mme Du Deffand (Best.D9670, 6 March 1761). In his letter to the duc de Nivernois, he thought it was high time for France to be concerned with its men of genius and not with those 'viles brochures et . . . ces malheureux romans qui nous déshonorent' (Best.D9794, 27 May 1761). He was more scathing in his *Lettres à m. de Voltaire sur la Nouvelle Héloïse ou Aloisia* published in February 1761 (M.xxiv.165-79) and his *Notes sur la Lettre . . . à m. Hume* published towards the end of 1766. Although Voltaire's attacks betray his hatred of Rousseau, they also took into account aesthetic and linguistic factors. They were made within a wider background in which there was nostalgic regret for standards of the *grand siècle* because of the barbarities of the new aesthetic in French tragedy.[8] It was concern for the French classical theatre which had been invaded by romance that made Voltaire appear so harsh towards the novel.

Even in his violent denigration of Rousseau, Voltaire could not help showing his appreciation of a good novel. Had he not wished that mme de La Fayette could come back to the world? (Best.D9670). In the *Notes sur la Lettre ... à m. Hume* he even expressed admiration for the tone in which *La Princesse de Clèves* and *Zaïde* were written. If in his *Commentaires sur Corneille* Voltaire did not hesitate to censure Corneille for having pandered to the medieval romance,[9] how could he spare the sentimental novel? It was *Pamela* and *Clarissa* which, in Voltaire's judgment, had encouraged the vogue of sentimentalism, the flouting of moral and aesthetic standards, of which *La Nouvelle Héloïse* was the worst example.

Voltaire even improved on his technique of denigrating the novel when he included in *Le Droit du seigneur*,[10] a comedy set in sixteenth-century Picardy, a delightful interlude which he himself called 'la tirade des romans' in a letter to Damilaville (Best.D9823, 15 June 1761). Apparently, he had been advised by friends to cross out this 'tirade' but 'cette madame Denis ... mangerait les yeux de quiconque voudrait supprimer la tirade des romans'.

In act II, scene iii of the *Droit du seigneur*, Acanthe who has been brought up by a former servant and is betrothed to Mathurin, a farmer, asks her friend Colette whether she has read any novels. Colette replies in the negative, but Acanthe says that the bailiff Métaprose has lent her some. Voltaire skilfully exploits the resources of Moliéresque comedy and its element of fantasy to ridicule the novel. At the beginning of the dialogue, the vocabulary of Acanthe is strongly reminiscent of M. Jourdain who stands amazed when listening to the explanations of the Maître de Philosophie on phonetics and is only capable of uttering: 'Ah! les belles choses! les belles choses!'. The irony at the expense of

---

[8] see David Williams, 'Voltaire on the sentimental novel', *Studies on Voltaire* (1975), cxxxv. 115-34.

[9] both Corneille and Racine had been accused of succumbing to the taste for the romanesque as far back as 1714 by Fénelon in his 'Projet d'un traité sur la tragédie' in *Lettre à m. Dacier sur les occupations de l'Académie, Œuvres*, (Paris 1824), xxi. 214-16.

[10] the comedy was performed under the title of *L'Ecueil du sage* on 18 January 1762 and published in 1763.

this world of fantasy which the novel allegedly produces reaches its
climax when Acanthe tells Colette how she came to like novels: she
had a vivid memory of a visit of a 'beau seigneur' to their part of the
country and of his exploits in boar-hunting:

ACANTHE

De son départ je fus encor témoin:
On l'entourait, je n'étais pas bien loin.
Il me parla ... Depuis ce jour, ma chère,
Tous les romans ont le don de me plaire:
Quand je les lis, je n'ai jamais d'ennui;
Il me paraît qu'ils me parlent de lui.

COLETTE

Ah! qu'un roman est beau!

ACANTHE

C'est la peinture
Du cœur humain, je crois, d'après nature.

While on the one hand Voltaire continued his attack on the novel,
particularly the sentimental novel, he began to speak more positively
of prose fiction in general in the same period. How can we account for
this dichotomy? The fact is that Voltaire was being subjected to the
pressing needs of his campaign against *l'infâme*. In the *Epître aux
fidèles* of July 1763, a kind of manifesto intended for the *philosophes*
and corrected at the suggestion of Helvétius,[11] Voltaire states: 'Il
paraît convenable de n'écrire que des choses simples, courtes, intelli-
gibles aux esprits les plus grossiers' (Best.D Appendix 233). He writes
to Damilaville that: 'Les ouvrages métaphisiques sont lus de peu de
personnes, et trouvent toujours des contradicteurs. Les faits évidents,
les choses simples et claires, sont à la portée de tout le monde et font
un effet immanquable' (Best.D11445, 4 October 1763). One's first
impression is that Voltaire has only light prose in mind and not prose
fiction. This impression is, however, dispelled when he writes to
Marmontel some months later. Here is his recommendation to his
friend: 'Vous devriez bien nous faire des contes philosophiques, où

---

[11] see also his letter to Helvétius where he says: 'C'est à peu près dans ce goust
simple que je voudrais qu'on écrivît' (Best.D11208, *c.* 15 May 1763).

vous rendriez ridicules certains sots, et certaines sottises, certaines méchancetés et certains méchants; le tout avec discrétion, en prenant vôtre temps et en rognant les ongles de la bête quand vous la trouverez un peu endormie' (Best.D11667, 28 January 1764). This letter is particularly significant because it has given us Voltaire's own definition of the *conte philosophique*.

After he had written on the *conte* in such favourable terms, Voltaire could tell Panckoucke in the same breath, in reply to the latter's proposal (Best.D11876, 16 May 1764) to publish a new edition of his tales: 'je vous réponds que si j'ai fait des romans j'en demande pardon à dieu; mais tout au moins je n'y ai jamais mis mon nom, pas plus qu'à mes autres sottises' (Best.D11889, 24 May 1764). This should not perhaps be taken too seriously: it may have been a tactical stand.[12] Voltaire was more serious when it was a matter of supporting the Enlightenment and defending light prose fiction, for he was quick to draw conclusions from the difficulties that beset the *Encyclopédie*. He told d'Alembert plainly: 'Jamais vingt volumes in-folio ne feront de révolution; ce sont les petits livres portatifs à trente sous qui sont à craindre. Si l'évangile avait coûté douze cents sesterces, jamais la religion chrétienne ne se serait établie' (Best.D13235, 5 April 1766).

Voltaire elaborated further on his concept of the *conte* in the *Taureau blanc* which he wrote in 1772 and published in 1773. In the tale Amaside wants this type of fiction to be based on verisimilitude and not to be always like a dream. It should contain nothing trivial or extravagant. What it needs above all is that under the cloak of the fable[13] it 'laissât entrevoir aux yeux exercés quelque vérité fine qui échappe au vulgaire'. With regard to style, Amaside is tired of the sun and the moon 'dont une vieille dispose à son gré, des montagnes qui dansent, des fleuves qui remontent à leur source, et des morts qui ressuscitent; mais surtout quand ces fadaises sont écrites d'un style ampoulé et inintelligible, cela me dégoûte horriblement' (Bénac, p.594).

---

[12] I owe this suggestion to professor Haydn Mason.

[13] in the *Dialogues des morts*, Fontenelle had stressed the necessity of dressing up truth through fables because of a permanent affinity between the human mind and what is false. But Voltaire took him to task for this in the article 'Fraude' of the *Dictionnaire philosophique*. The article was reproduced in 1771 in the *Questions sur l'encyclopédie*. To Bambabef's question: 'Quoi! vous croyez qu'on peut enseigner la vérité au peuple sans la soutenir par des fables?', Ouang replied: 'Je le crois fermement'. (M.xix.207). See Roland Mortier, *Clartés et ombres du siècle des Lumières* (Geneva 1969), pp.66-75. On the use of fables too Voltaire is changing his position.

History also could teach Voltaire a few lessons. His research for the *Essai sur les mœurs*, in particular, showed him how demoralising the history of mankind was. One of the central ideas of his work was that if one went through the history of the world, one would find petty crimes punished, but the major ones unpunished and the whole of the universe was nothing but a 'vaste scène de brigandage' abandoned to fortune. Voltaire takes up this point in the twelfth dialogue of the *A, B, C* which was composed towards 1767: he would like all civil and ecclesiastical history books to be burnt, for he finds in them only a record of crimes. He recalls having once read Maimbourg's *Histoire du grand schisme d'occident* where the treachery of popes was described. But since the papacy had survived despite all its excesses and since all these horrors reformed no one, he concludes that history is worthless. This leads him to think that the novel is full of potential, although in the hands of Homer and Fénelon its potential had been wasted. 'Oui, je conçois que le roman vaudrait mieux: on y est maître du moins de feindre des exemples de vertu; mais Homère n'a jamais imaginé une seule action vertueuse et honnête dans tout son roman monotone de l'*Iliade*. J'aimerais beaucoup mieux le roman de *Télémaque*, s'il n'était pas tout en digressions et en déclamations.' (*Dialogues philosophiques*, ed. R. Naves (Paris 1966), p.320) This represents a dramatic swing from his earlier position. Had he not first written in the *Essai sur la poésie épique* in 1733 of 'un roman frivole, qui n'est qu'un tissu de petites intrigues, lesquelles n'ont besoin ni de l'autorité de l'histoire, ni du poids d'aucun nom célèbre' (M.viii. 322), concluding that people prefer history to the novel (p.362)?

The triumph of the novel over history can be studied in a different way. One has only to look at the varying fortune of two representative seventeenth-century novels (*Clélie* and *L'Astrée*) in Voltaire's estimate. In the *Essai sur la poésie épique*, Voltaire says that they attract no contemporary readers (M.viii.362). He prefaced a letter to Frederick, whom he asked to read his play *Oreste*, with a poem where he has nothing but contempt for *L'Astrée* and its hero (Best.D4128, 17 March 1750):

> Et j'estime encor que son frère
> Ne doit point être un Celadon:
> Ce héros fort atrabilaire
> N'étoit point né sur le Lignon.

Yet writing to mme Du Deffand in 1769, Voltaire almost chides her for not having read *Clélie* and *L'Astrée*. He says (Best.D15605, 24 April 1769):

Je parie que vous n'avez jamais lu Clélie ni l'Astrée . . . Clélie est un ouvrage plus curieux qu'on ne pense. On y trouve les portraits de tous les gens qui fesaient du bruit dans le monde du tems de Mlle Scudéri. Tout Port roial y est. Le château de Villars qui apartient aujourd'hui à Mr Le Duc de Praslin y est décrit avec la plus grande éxactitude.

It is a glowing tribute to the novel's ability to reconstruct with historical accuracy the atmosphere of a period. Voltaire even suggests to mme Du Deffand that she should have learnt Italian in order to be able to read Ariosto who surpasses all other novelists.

However, the novel which had gradually been growing in status in Voltaire's eyes made its greatest impression on him in 1775 when he wrote a letter to the *Bibliothèque universelle des romans*.[14] This letter, crucial for a final analysis of Voltaire's attitude to prose fiction, was apparently published only in the *Mercure de France*. In it Voltaire said (Best.D19605, 15 August 1775):

Vous rendez un vrai service, messieurs, à la littérature en faisant connaître les romans, & on a une vraie obligation à m. le marquis de Paulmy de vouloir bien ouvrir sa bibliothèque à ceux qui veulent nous instruire dans un genre qui a précédé celui de l'histoire. Tout est roman dans nos premiers livres; Hérodote, Diodore de Sicile, commencent tous leurs récits par des romans. L'Iliade est elle autre chose qu'un beau roman en vers hexamètres? & les amours d'Enée & de Didon dans Virgile, ne sont-ils pas un roman admirable?

Si vous vous en tenez aux contes qui nous ont été donnés pour ce qu'ils sont, pour de simples ouvrages d'imagination, vous aurez une assez belle carrière à parcourir. On voit dans presque tous les anciens ouvrages de cette espèce, un tableau fidèle des mœurs du temps. Les faits sont faux, mais la peinture est vraie.

The novel appears to be endowed with more than potential: it includes among its achievements those of being consecrated by time and showing a faithful mirror of society. It may be inferred from this letter

[14] published from July 1775 to June 1789 in 224 volumes, it has been described as a sort of 'encyclopédie' of the world's prose fiction, aiming to offer contemporary readers the best novels not only of eighteenth-century France, but of classical antiquity, of the middle ages, of all modern European literature and of the Orient! See John M. Clapp, 'An eighteenth-century attempt at a critical view of the novel: the *Bibliothèque universelle des romans*', *PMLA* (Baltimore 1910), xxv. 60-96.

that Voltaire would not have raised any serious objection to his own epic, *La Henriade*, being described as a novel!

If *Candide* can be said to represent Pascal's revenge on Voltaire to a certain extent, the novel as a genre has a similar claim in this direction. Admittedly, Voltaire's *volte-face* may not be as complete as Boileau's in the quarrel between ancients and moderns. His change of position is at any rate more understandable than Boileau's, for the great seventeenth-century critic had begun by pontificating on and attacking the novel in book iii of the *Art poétique*, only to end by vaunting, in the *Lettre à Perrault* in 1700, the merit of 'ces poèmes en prose que nous appelons romans, dont nous avons chez nous des modèles qu'on ne saurait trop estimer' (*Œuvres de Boileau*, ed. M. de Saint-Marc (Amsterdam 1772), v. 193). Boileau says that the Latin writers never knew this type of writing which can be criticised only on moral grounds. Unlike him, Voltaire grew up in a century which witnessed major developments in the novel. However reluctant he may have been in the earlier part of his career to acknowledge the merits of this so-called *minor* genre, Voltaire showed that in this particular field he did not cling desperately to the models of the *grand siècle*, that in certain literary matters he was not the arch conservative that he has been made out to be for so long. He was even forward looking and gave some intimation of the great novels of the nineteenth century.[15] Despite the risks to which one is exposed in generalising about Voltaire, a fairly clear pattern has emerged with regard to his thoughts on prose fiction. From 1763 to the end of his career, excepting the period of his attacks on the *Nouvelle Héloïse*, in which wider issues were at stake, Voltaire appears to have made himself a champion of the novel, even if in 1777 he talked of the 'charlatanerie' of novelists. What part did the English novelists play in bringing about this change in Voltaire?

ii. *The influence of Swift and Sterne on Voltaire*

Whatever may have been his reservations on fiction at certain stages in his career and whatever may have been his ambition in the epic and

---

[15] from the pursuit of verisimilitude which Voltaire stresses as being characteristic of the novel, one goes to its logical development, the importance to be attached to the physical environment, which looms large in Balzac, for example. See Ian Watt, *The Rise of the novel* (Harmondsworth 1968), p.28.

the drama, Voltaire was not necessarily opposed to prose as such. For prose was the medium used by masters of polemics such as Pascal and Bayle in whom he was deeply interested. Even when he attacked an author in a particular context, this did not prevent Voltaire from using him in a different one. The same Pascal whom he satirised in the *Lettres philosophiques*, Voltaire did not hesitate to use against the Jesuits in the *Relation du jésuite Berthier*. He may have found Pascal useful, for like Corneille and Racine, Pascal was a writer in the rhetorical tradition, a tradition which can provide writers and orators of all ages with some of the finest techniques of persuasion.

Bayle is perhaps more significant for our purpose, for unlike Pascal he had some interest in English literature. When in *De l'Allemagne* mme de Staël stated that Bayle was the arsenal from which all witticisms and jokes dealing with sceptical thought were drawn and that Voltaire had made them more biting by his verve and polish, she was thinking of Bayle's influence on French writers primarily. English men of letters like Sterne also went to him for inspiration.[16] While he was a prebendary of York Minster Sterne used the Minster library which contained the second English edition of Bayle's *Dictionnaire historique et critique* (1734-38) and he borrowed the five volumes for ten months between 1752 and 1753. Sterne exploited the scurrilous jokes of the *Dictionnaire* in *Tristram Shandy*. He particularly enjoyed reading about theories of generation and sexual jokes such as those appearing in the articles 'Anaxagoras', 'Arodon', 'Vayer'. It would, however, be a mistake to assume that these were the only items of interest to him. Apart from the obscenities, Bayle's *Dictionnaire* must have delighted the writer who fulminated against Roman Catholics in *Tristram Shandy*. Bayle may justifiably be regarded as a common source that was tapped by both French and English writers and as a bridge between Voltaire, Swift and Sterne. Moreover, Voltaire was interested in any savage denunciation of religious sectarian feeling wherever it took place, in France or in England. It is therefore appropriate to say a word about Bayle as a religious polemicist before discussing Swift and Sterne.

There can be little doubt that Voltaire was influenced by Bayle, not only from the point of view of ideas, but also from that of style. It seems that literary history too repeats itself with few changes. For

[16] see F. Doherty, 'Bayle and *Tristram Shandy*: stage-loads of chymical nostrums and peripatetic lumber', *Neophilologus* (Amsterdam July 1974), lviii. 339-48.

all the bitterness which characterized religious controversy in the seventeenth century reappeared in a slightly different form in the eighteenth century. The violent hatred shown by Protestants against Catholics and vice-versa in the earlier period is now replaced by the virulent denunciations of the 'philosophes' against religion in general, or *l'infâme*. Voltaire was conspicuous in the battle of the *philosophes*, even if he managed to avoid committing himself to the extreme stand taken by some *encyclopédistes*. But as far as techniques were concerned, there is no doubt that the example of oustanding precursors proved useful to him both in his private and his public polemics. He must have found their practice very relevant to his own writings. In particular, he must have been impressed by the way Bayle polarized into black and white all conflicting opinions. He certainly remembered the crude denigration and invectives used against his opponents by the Protestant writer, especially in the pamphlet *Ce que c'est que la France toute catholique sous le règne de Louis le Grand* (1686). It was natural that Voltaire should have used his French background at the same time that he was exploiting the resources of English prose. It is even likely that Bayle stimulated his interest in English polemical writers. For Bayle's vituperative language against Roman Catholics can be paralleled by the tone of Swift's and Sterne's denigration of the papists in their writings. Bayle, Swift, Sterne and Voltaire have at least one common characteristic: their aggressive denunciation of what they dislike.

In spite of all the criticisms he could level at the English novel in his correspondence and elsewhere, Voltaire must have watched with interest the development of a type of writing which was establishing itself in France. It is true that Fougeret de Montbron, author of the *Préservatif contre l'anglomanie* (1757) denigrated the English novel even more vehemently, but he did not exert much influence. There were others like Lenglet Du Fresnoy, La Chesnaye Des Bois and Voltaire's disciple, Marmontel,[17] who militated in its favour. Arnaud and Suard, who edited the *Journal étranger* at first and then the *Gazette littéraire* were equally well-disposed towards English literature. The *Année littéraire* of Fréron mentioned all the major English novels, especially between 1766 and 1771.

As far back as 1713 the *Journal littéraire* mentioned several of Swift's works and later published parts of *Gulliver's travels* and the *Tale of a*

---

[17] J. F. Marmontel wrote an *Essai sur les romans* which was published in 1787.

tub. In 1721 Juste Van Effen (1684-1735) translated and published the *Tale of a tub* at the Hague, while in France Desfontaines translated *Gulliver* as best he could in 1727. Desfontaines's translation was well-received in France. The *Mercure de France* and the *Journal des savants*, on the whole, responded favourably to *Gulliver*. Desfontaines sub-sequently published an imitation of *Gulliver's travels* called *Le Nouveau Gulliver* (1730). This imitation, in the form of philosophic voyages, was very popular: it appeared in English and Italian translations in 1731 and it was reedited many times in France. Paradis de Moncrif, author of an essay read before the French Academy in 1741 and entitled 'Réflexions sur quelques ouvrages faussement appellez: Ouvrages d'imagination', appears to have been the only hostile critic of *Gulliver's travels* in France.

The name of Swift was frequently quoted on the continent. The *Bibliothèque angloise* published by M. de La Roche and A. de La Chapelle in Amsterdam between 1717 and 1728 with the aim of informing foreigners, especially those who did not know English, about books written in England, wrote that Swift had long acquired the reputation of thinking and writing differently from others. His works, it added, always had a distinctive trait that defied imitation (viii.108). Prévost wrote glowing accounts of him in the *Pour et contre*. He first described Swift as being 'connu par la finesse et l'agrément de son esprit, et père d'une infinité de petits ouvrages qui portent ces deux caractères' (iii.57). In a later volume, Prévost remarked that by his countless works – both in prose and in verse – Swift had come to be looked upon as the model of subtle irony and of the most ingenious and pleasant witticisms. He thought that Swift was known in France only for his *Gulliver* and the *Tale of a tub* and wished someone could translate his poetry (vi. 8-9).

Prévost's hope was fulfilled, for the abbé Yart translated many of Swift's poems, including the *Elegy on the death of Partridge*, in his *Idée de la poésie anglaise* which appeared in eight volumes between 1749 and 1756. Yart also made the following comment on Swift: 'Sa manière singulière d'appercevoir des choses que personne n'avoit apperçues, et de dire ce qu'on n'avoit point encore dit... doit faire passer par dessus le désordre grotesque de ses tableaux. Il faut avoir la même indulgence pour le Calot de la Poësie Anglaise que nous en avons pour les portraits ridicules de notre Calot, en faveur de la gaieté originale que l'un et l'autre ont répandue sur leurs Ouvrages'

(v. 265). This judgment is interesting because it is reminiscent of Voltaire's judgment on Sterne (see below). It is probable that Voltaire read Yart's work: it is listed in the Ferney Catalogue. Yart wrote to Voltaire shortly before the latter's death and hinted that the great man had perhaps heard of the *Idée de la poésie anglaise*. He claimed that some fifty years back their common friend Cideville had sent Voltaire a few epigrams from him and that he, Voltaire, had quoted one of them (Best.D21097, 9 March 1778).

Voltaire showed his great esteem for Swift, Pope's lifelong friend, in a letter to Thieriot in 1727 (Best.D308, 2 February 1727). Thieriot apparently allowed Desfontaines to read this letter. The abbé says in the preface to his translation of *Gulliver's travels* that a friend of Voltaire had shown him a recent letter written from London. He adds that Voltaire's highly favourable account and his view that *Gulliver* was worth translating were among the factors that led him to undertake the translation. In his letter Voltaire wrote:

Si vous voulez remplir les vues dont vous me parlez, par la traduction d'un livre anglois, Gulliver est peutêtre le seul qui vous convienne. C'est le Rabelais d'Angleterre comme je vous l'ay déjà mandé, mais c'est un Rabelais sans fatras et le livre seroit très amusant par luy même par les imaginations singulières dont il est plein, par la légèreté de son stile, etc. quand il ne seroit pas d'ailleurs la satire du genre humain.[18]

Yet about a month later, Voltaire has reservations about the second volume of *Gulliver* which he says interests only England. He writes to Thieriot (Best.D310, 11 March 1727):

You will find in the same pacquet the second volume of mr Gulliver which by the by j don't advise you to translate. Stick to the first, the other is over-strain'd. The reader's imagination is pleased and charmingly entertaind by the new prospects of the lands which Gulliver discovers to him, but that continued series of new fangled follies, of fairy tales, of wild inventions, palls at last upon our taste. Nothing unnatural may please long. T'is for this reason that commonly the second parts of romances are so insipid.

He seems to be lending support to critics who attacked the novel for its artificiality and for its excessive pandering to fancy.

[18] Voltaire sent Thieriot an earlier letter with two volumes of *Gulliver*. The text of this letter is lost, but Besterman has summarized its contents by means of a reconstruction from Desfontaines's preface to his translation. Voltaire presumably said that he had never read anything wittier and more entertaining (Best.D306, *c*. 15 November 1726).

It is perhaps for this reason that Voltaire does not specifically mention *Gulliver* in the *Lettres philosophiques* (cf. Dédéyan, p. 67). It may also be that Voltaire, who up to 1728 was on fairly good terms with Desfontaines, had read the latter's translation of *Gulliver*, although he did not have a high opinion of him as a translator in general (see Best.D336, 25 June 1728). He certainly knew of the existence of this translation, for he told Thieriot: 'J hear that mr Gulliver is now translated' (Best.D315, 27 May 1727). It was a free translation, but the preface was well-balanced. Desfontaines recognised the merit of the work but could not help pointing out it weaknesses, 'the impenetrable allegories, insipid allusions, puerile details, low thoughts, boring repetitions, coarse jokes'[19] – things which would have offended French taste. Publicising *Gulliver* in the *Lettres philosophiques* would be tantamount to promoting the cause of Desfontaines and Voltaire's generosity did not go as far as that.

These so-called weaknesses did not prevent Voltaire later on from exploiting the *Gulliver* theme and techniques in *Micromégas*, *Zadig*, the *Voyages de Scarmentado* and *Candide*. In *Micromégas*, the imitation of *Gulliver* is fairly obvious. Both tales have a strange setting, draw a contrast between giants and dwarfs, show contempt for man's cruelty, ignorance and stupidity and use similar jokes.

For the measurement of Micromégas, Voltaire's tale imitates *Gulliver* to some extent and at one point Swift's name is even quoted. In chapter 6 Micromégas lies fully stretched on the ground, for if he had stood up his head would have towered above the clouds. By placing together a number of triangles, the philosopher concluded that they were looking at a young man of 'cent vingt mille pieds de roi'. In book i, chapter 6 of *Gulliver*, the seamstress took Gulliver's measure as he lay on the ground, 'one standing at my neck, and another at my mid-leg . . . while the third measured the length of the cord with a rule of an inch long. Then they measured my right thumb, and desired no more; for by a mathematical computation, that twice round the thumb is once round the wrist . . . they fitted me exactly.'

Many of the sparks that shine in *Micromégas*, *Zadig* and *Candide* were inspired by the genius of Swift. Fréron had no hesitation in stating that since Voltaire possessed the art of imitation to the happiest degree, he had in many of his prose pieces made use of the substance and often the form of *Gulliver* (*Année littéraire* (1762), iv. 259-63).

[19] the quotation is from *Swift*, ed. Kathleen Williams (London 1970), p.79.

Even more uncharitable was the following judgment from a friend, Chesterfield: 'a most poor performance, called *Micromégas* ... it is so very unworthy of him; it consists only of thoughts, stolen from Swift, but miserably mangled and disfigured' (*The Letters of Chesterfield*, v. 1991).

In *Zadig*, we hear of a fifteen hundred year old dispute in Babylon between two sects: one claimed that the temple of Mithras should always be entered with the left foot first; the other, which hated that custom, always entered it by the right foot. This ridiculous situation is not unlike that obtaining in *Gulliver*, book i, where Reldresal, prime minister of Lilliput, explains the origin of the war between Lilliput and Blefuscu. This stemmed from the encouragement given by the latter to exiles from Lilliput. The exiles had been punished for refusing to obey an imperial decree ordering the inhabitants to break the smaller end of their eggs instead of the larger end before eating them.[20]

In the eighteenth chapter of *Candide*, Cacambo wonders how one should greet the king of Eldorado. He naturally asks: 'si on se jetait à genoux ou ventre à terre; si on mettait les mains sur la tête ou sur le derrière; si on léchait la pousière de la salle'. The last possibility was probably suggested to Voltaire by what happens to the hero in book iii of *Gulliver*. When Gulliver arrives at the court of Luggnagg and wishes to be received in audience, he has to lick the dust on the ground.

In June 1727, Voltaire recommends Swift to Du Noquet and continues his praise of him. 'La personne qui vous rendra cette lettre est l'illustre monsieur Swift ... Je vous prie mon cher Dunoquet de luy rendre tous les services qui dépendront de vous' (Best.D316, 14 June 1727). His recommendation to the comte de Morville is as warm, for he speaks of the famous Swift, one of the most extraordinary men England had produced, who does honour to a nation Morville holds in esteem and whom he takes the liberty of introducing to him (Best.D318, 16 June 1727). This letter was enclosed with a letter to Swift. In it Voltaire says that in case Swift travels to France via Rouen he will give him letters of introduction to a lady (mme de Bernières) who will receive him well. Swift would also find some of Voltaire's friends who are 'yr admirers and who have learn'd English since j am in England' (Best.D319).

[20] apart from Swift, Voltaire, it may be remembered, was also indebted in *Zadig* to Thomas Parnell whose poem, *The Hermit*, was one of the sources of the chapter entitled 'L'Hermite'.

Arising from his desire to enlist Swift's support for subscriptions to the *Henriade*, Voltaire becomes even more lyrical in his eulogy. He sends Swift his *Essay on epick poetry* with these words (Best.D323, 14 December 1727):

You will be surprised in receiving an English essay from a french traveller. Pray, forgive an admirer of you, who ows to yr writings, the love he bears to yr language, which has betray'd him into the rash attempt of writing in english . . . Do not forbid me to grace my relation with yr name. Let me indulge the satisfaction of talking of you as posterity will do.

Swift responded warmly with a 'short account of the author' in the 1728 Dublin edition of the *Essay*. And in the last letter written to Swift during the English visit, Voltaire again pays tribute to Swift's greatness. 'J have not seen mr Pope this winter, but j have seen the third volume of the miscelanea, et the more j read yr works, the more j am ashamed of mines' (Best.D328, March 1728).

The *Letters concerning the English nation* confirm the high opinion Voltaire has of Swift in the correspondence. In letter xxii, he has nothing but praise for 'the Works of the ingenious Dean *Swift*, who has been call'd the English Rabelais'. He adds: 'This Gentleman has the Honour (in common with Rabelais) of being a Priest, and like him laughs at every Thing. But in my humble Opinion, the Title of the *English Rabelais* which is given the Dean is highly derogatory to his Genius' (pp.213-14). In an attempt to elevate Swift's status, he does everything he can to lower Rabelais who, he claims, 'has been vastly lavish of Erudition, of Smut, and insipid Raillery' (p.214). But Swift is '*Rabelais* in his Senses, and frequenting the politest Company. The former indeed is not so gay as the latter, but then he possesses all the Delicacy, the Justness, the Choice, the good Taste, in all which Particulars our giggling rural Vicar *Rabelais* is wanting. The poetical Numbers of Dean *Swift* are of a singular and almost inimitable Taste; true Humour whether in Prose or Verse, seems to be his peculiar Talent' (p.215).

Swift appears like a towering figure in letter xxiv and the homage paid to him is both direct and indirect. There is a direct reference to his plan to found an 'Academy for the *English* Tongue upon the Model of that of the French' (p.235). Swift may even be the wit who asked Voltaire for the memoirs of the French Academy. It is also likely that his Academy of Laputa offered Voltaire the model with which to attack the disorder prevailing in the Royal Society.

In the 'Leningrad notebooks', Voltaire wrote a short piece entitled 'Sermon du docteur Suif sur l'orgueil devant le parlement d'Irlande'. He must have enjoyed the wit of the sermon which he reproduced thus (*Notebooks*, i. 418):

Messieurs

Il y a trois sortes d'orgueil, celuy de la naissance, celuy des places, celuy de l'esprit. A l'égard du troisième comme personne de cette auguste compagnie ne peut être accusé de ce vice, je n'auray pas l'honneur de vous en parler.

Generous tribute is paid to Swift in the *Siècle de Louis XIV* when Voltaire says: 'Il y a du doyen Swift plusieurs morceaux dont on ne trouve aucun exemple dans l'antiquité: c'est Rabelais perfectionné' (M.xiv.560).

In 1752, Voltaire shows interest in a different type of writing by Swift. This is the *Account of the death of mr Partrige the almanack-maker*, a copy of which Voltaire possessed, although it is not listed in either of the catalogues of his library (see Best.D4815, c. 24 February 1752, n.1). He refers to it in his letter to Darget: 'Le crieur d'enterrement du docteur Patridge aurait pu nous soutenir à tous deux que nous étions ses pratiques' (Best.D4815). Some months later, he makes an even more precise allusion to Swift's book when he writes to Frederick: 'La réponse grave de Maupertuis n'était pas ce qu'il fallait. C'était bien le cas d'imiter Suift, qui persuadait à l'astrologue Partrige qu'il était mort' (Best.D5008, 5 September 1752).

It seems that Voltaire drew some inspiration from Swift for the *Relation du jésuite Berthier*. In the *Predictions of the year 1708*, Bickerstaff (Swift) prophesied that Partrige the almanack-maker would 'infallibly die upon the 29th March next, about eleven at night, of a raging fever'.[21] He was advised to settle his affairs in time. In the *Account of the death of mr Partrige* Partrige, who was on his death bed, 'declared himself a Nonconformist, and had a fanatick Preacher to be his Spiritual Guide' (Davis, p.155). The *Relation* begins in this manner: 'Ce fut le 12 octobre 1759 que frère Berthier alla, pour son malheur, de Paris à Versailles avec frère Coutu, qui l'accompagne ordinairement.' Berthier has to go through a series of humiliating acts, such as the

[21] *Bickerstaff papers and pamphlets on the Church*, ed. H. Davis (Oxford 1941), p.145.

swallowing of a page of the *Encyclopédie* dipped in white wine[22] –
presumably as a punishment for his manœuvres against it – and
confessing to a Jansenist. What he claims Maupertuis failed to do, that
is to imitate Swift, Voltaire certainly did. In the *Relation* he tried to
kill Berthier in 1759, whereas the latter in fact died much later in 1782,
after having successfully become tutor to the king's children at
Versailles for a while, travelled abroad and returned to Paris in 1776
to write religious works like the *Réflexions spirituelles*.[23] Voltaire may
have also found the *Tale of a tub* useful for his attack on Berthier. Has
not Swift presented Jack as the prototype of religious enthusiasm who
had gone out of his wits and confirmed the report of his illness by
falling into the oddest whimsies that a sick brain ever conceived?

Because of the element of fantasy which recalls Swift's prose
writings and Voltaire's *contes*, the satire in the *Relation* lacks the
bitterness found in the attacks that are grounded in reality. It is kinder
than the *Akakia* pamphlets to which it offers some parallel. It is true
that both in the *Akakia* and in the *Relation* Voltaire's aim was to depict
a sick man. In the former Maupertuis, who had hallucinations, was given
'tisanes rafraichissantes'. But Voltaire resorted to personal denigration
in the *Akakia* and could not obtain the same effect as in the *Relation*.

In the preface to his translation of the *Tale of a tub*, Van Effen wrote
that pious people in England thought that work represented extreme
views held by a free thinker, whose sole intention was to lay the foundations of irreligion on the ruin of all Christian sects. He himself felt
that there was no trace of freethinking or irreligion in the *Tale* where
perfectly sustained allegory simply ridiculed the stupid credulity of the
Roman Church and the spirit of enthusiasm and fanaticism of the
Protestants. He wished only that Swift had not mingled with his irony
certain ribald turns of phrase which shock a delicate imagination.

It was perhaps this very work that made the most profound impression on Voltaire. In the 1756 addition to the *Lettres philosophiques*,

---

[22] this type of remedy was frequently used in the eighteenth century, though not
necessarily against an opponent. In chapter xlvi of *Les Bijoux indiscrets* (1748), Diderot
made a doctor prescribe to the sultan a drug which contained a mixture of various works,
including the novels of Marivaux and Crébillon. To cheer up his wife who was ill,
Diderot described in a letter to his daughter dated 28 July 1781 how he gave mme
Diderot a number of adventure novels together with his own *Jacques le fataliste* (Diderot, *Correspondance*, ed. G. Roth (Paris 1970), xv. 253-54).

[23] see J. Pappas, *Berthier's* Journal de Trévoux *and the* philosophes, Studies on
Voltaire (1957), iii. 58-60.

he observed: 'Dans ce pays, qui paraît si étrange à une partie de l'Europe, on n'a point trouvé trop étrange que le Révérend Swift Doyen d'une cathédrale, se soit moqué dans son *Conte du tonneau* du Catholicisme, du Luteranisme et du Calvinisme: il dit pour ses raisons qu'il n'a pas touché au Christianisme. Il prétend avoir respecté le Père en donnant cent coups de fouet aux trois enfants. Des gens difficiles ont cru que les verges étaient si longues qu'elles allaient jusqu'au Père' (Lanson, ii. 136). From there he goes on to speak of the sources of this 'fameux *Conte du tonneau*'.

Voltaire was reading or rereading the *Tale of a tub* in 1759. When he wrote to mme Du Deffand in that year, he commented (Best. D8533, 13 October 1759):

Plût à Dieu, Madame, pour le bien que je vous veux, qu'on eût pû aumoins copier fidèlement le conte du Tonneau, du doyen Suift! C'est un trésor de plaisanteries dont il n'y a point d'idée ailleurs. Pascal n'amuse qu'aux dépends des Jésuïtes, Suift divertit et instruit aux dépends du genre humain. Que j'aime la hardiesse anglaise! que j'aime les gens qui disent ce qu'ils pensent! C'est ne vivre qu'à demi que de n'oser penser qu'à demi.

It is not likely that Voltaire was thinking only of a general attack on mankind by Swift. The reference to English daring suggests that in Voltaire's eyes Swift was good at attacking all Christian denominations in contrast to Pascal who had singled out the Jesuits.

It must not be imagined that Voltaire was happy to maintain the light vein of the *Lettres philosophiques* and the *Relation* in his use of Swift after 1759. There is a marked change of tone from that year. This can be seen from a letter he wrote to d'Alembert in 1760 when he said: 'J'aime mieux les ridicules que les héros. Le Conte du tonneau a fait plus de mal à l'église romaine que Henri VIII' (Best.D9137, 13 August 1760). Having first imitated the *Account of the death of mr Partrige*, Voltaire repeated the performance with the *Tale of a tub* and thus practised what he preached to mme Du Deffand about faithfully imitating the *Tale*. His imitation, however, lacked the jokes he had admired in Swift.

In the *Tale*, Swift describes Peter's bulls with Rabelaisian gusto: 'they would roar, and spit, and belch, and Piss, and Fart, and Snivel out Fire, and keep a perpetual Coyl, till you flung them a bit of gold.' Shortly afterwards, Peter, who had dined at an alderman's in the city, proclaimed to his brothers: 'Bread, dear brothers, is the staff of life; in which bread is contained, inclusive, the quintessence of beef, mutton, veal, venison, partridge, plum-pudding, and custard' (Davis, p.72). The next day, he tried to pass off his brown bread as excellent mutton, but the trick did not work on anyone and Peter used abusive language to convince his brothers. 'Such a thundering proof as this left no further room for objection; the two unbelievers began to gather and pocket up their mistake as hastily as they could' (p.73).

The episode must have struck Voltaire,[24] for he appears to have used it against the Roman Catholic religion with the most devastating violence in the article 'Transsubstantiation' of the *Dictionnaire philosophique* in 1767. With not only Swift, but Bayle and Sterne as well, in mind he wrote: 'Les protestants, et surtout les philosophes protestants regardent la transsubstantiation comme le dernier terme de l'impudence des moines et de l'imbécillité des laïques ... du vin changé en sang, et qui a le goût du vin; du pain qui est changé en chair et en fibres, et qui a le goût du pain: tout cela inspire tant d'horreur et de mépris aux ennemis de la religion catholique, apostolique et romaine ... Leur horreur augmente, quand on leur dit qu'on voit tous les jours, dans les pays catholiques, des prêtres, des moines qui, sortant d'un lit incestueux, et n'ayant pas encore lavé leurs mains souillées d'impuretés, vont faire des dieux par centaines, mangent et boivent leur dieu, chient et pissent leur Dieu' (Benda and Naves, p.411). The vocabulary here is reminiscent of that used to describe Peter's bulls. Instead of drawing a general parallel regarding bread and wine, Voltaire could have made more of the witty invective found in Swift. But perhaps he was in no mood to be witty after Calas, Sirven and La Barre.

It is also possible that Voltaire used the *Tale of a tub* for his attack against *l'infâme* in the *Pot-pourri* which he composed towards the end of 1764. The way he skips from tale to tale, from anecdote to anecdote in the *Pot-pourri* is reminiscent of Swift's interpolated story. The resemblance is too striking to be mere coincidence (Goulding, p.51).[25] Be that as it may, Swift is, like Sterne, the kind of writer

[24] Fougeret de Montbron may have used the *Tale* – albeit at a more superficial level – in his burlesque tale, *Le Cosmopolite*, where he describes a once all-powerful magician now reduced to selling charms which cure everything, provided one has faith. This charlatan boasted having a stone 'qui enlève jusqu'aux moindres souillures de l'âme'. See Sybil Goulding, *Swift en France* (Paris 1924), p.50. In 1721, René Macé had adapted the *Tale* under the title of *Les Trois just-au-corps*.
[25] C. Thacker discusses this point in greater detail in 'Swift and Voltaire', *Hermathena* (Dublin 1967), civ. 58-61.

whom Voltaire would have found useful in the most militant period of his career.

Voltaire devotes the fifth of the *Lettres à s. a. mgr le prince de *** sur Rabelais et d'autres auteurs accusés d'avoir mal parlé de la religion chrétienne* (1767) to Swift. It is a corroboration of his former eulogy of the dean in the *Lettres philosophiques*, who apparently is 'le seul écrivain anglais de ce genre qui ait été plaisant' (M.xxvi. 489). But as is typical of Voltaire, the eulogy is qualified when he speaks of the *Tale of a tub*. With one eye on the recipient of the letter, he does not refrain from making remarks worthy of orthodox thinkers. He seems to continue the tradition of hostile French critics when he describes it as a 'raillerie impie'. Yet as a writer who had indulged in such practices himself, Voltaire must have liked the frontispiece of the work to which he refers: it was a print representing three methods of public speaking. The first was the theatre of harlequins and clowns, the second a preacher speaking from a pulpit made of a half-cask, and the third the ladder from the top of which a man about to be hanged makes his last speech to the people. Voltaire has no hesitation in saying that a preacher between a clown and a condemned criminal does not make an impressive figure. He claims that Swift's three heroes, that is, Peter, Martin and Jack, who represent the Pope, Luther and Calvin respectively, performed more extravagant acts than Cervantes's Don Quixote, or Ariosto's Roland. He finds that the work is badly translated and is convinced that it was impossible to find equivalents for the comic passages which give it its flavour. He identifies the source of the comedy: the quarrels between the Anglican and Presbyterian Churches, customs and events unknown to the French, and word play peculiar to the English language. For example, the word signifying a papal bull also means in English a *bœuf* (bull). This gives rise to puns and jokes entirely lost on a French reader. In the conclusion of his *Lettre*, Voltaire says that Swift was much less learned than Rabelais, but that his wit was sharper and subtler; he was the Rabalais of polite company (M.xxvi. 491).[26]

The last time Voltaire mentioned Swift was in his article on Sterne's *Tristram Shandy* in 1777 in the *Journal de politique et de littérature*. He claimed that Swift was the author of several works like *Tristram*, adding that the dean had written in his own language with much more

[26] cf. *Swift*, ed. K. Williams, p.76.

purity and delicacy than Rabelais did in his. Swift's verses were worthy of Horace in their elegance and simplicity.

It was not pure coincidence that made Voltaire link Swift with Sterne. He was struck by the fact that such extraordinary prose came from writers who were priests. Sterne was destined to make an impact as strong as Swift's on him. It is worth noting how different were the reactions Sterne provoked in John Ferriar, a medical doctor who was interested in Sterne's literary sources. In his paper entitled 'Comments on Sterne (1791-1793)' and his book *Illustrations of Sterne* (1798)[27] Ferriar attempted to show every borrowing Sterne made from Rabelais, Burton, Swift and others so that he could condemn him as a plagiarist 'in possession of every praise but that of curious erudition, to which he had no great pretence, and of unparalleled originality, which ignorance only can ascribe to any polished writer' (Howes, p.286). In Voltaire's eyes, Sterne was simply another Rabelais – perhaps superior to his model – produced by England. It did not matter whether Swift had written many books in the style of Sterne before. He felt that Rabelais, Swift and Sterne all wrote in the same jesting and bold tradition.

Sterne was first brought to the attention of the French by a review of *Tristram Shandy* published in the *Journal encyclopédique* on 15 April 1760. The reviewer described it as a book with moral, penetrating, delicate, salient, sound, strong, blasphemous, indiscreet and rash thoughts. In his opinion, its author had neither plan nor principles, nor system, yet one listened to him on account of his lively imagination, the dazzling quality of his portraits and the distinctive character of his reflections. The reviewer stressed how the English found mystery in it and admired it. The same periodical changed its tone subsequently. In an article published on 1 May 1761, another reviewer complained that *Tristram Shandy*'s only merit was to heap buffooneries, obscenities on obscenities and to diffuse over all an original and curious cast of thought. The *Journal encyclopédique* for 1 March 1762 referred to the novel's tedious digressions and the fact that Sterne was not so original as the English had thought, since Rabelais was his model.

French interest in Sterne was kept alive by his two journeys to France in 1762-64 and 1765-66. On his first visit, Sterne met Diderot at the home of d'Holbach to whom he sent six volumes of *Tristram Shandy* in 1762. Writing to Sophie Volland on 7 October 1762 and

[27] see *Sterne*, ed. Alan B. Howes (London 1974), pp.283-92.

substituting *Tristram* for its author, Diderot said that this book so mad, so wise and so gay was the Rabelais of the English, that it was impossible to give any idea of it other than that of a universal satire. He also pointed out that its author was another priest.[28] It does not seem that there was a direct exchange of letters between Diderot and Sterne, but Diderot's name together with those of d'Holbach, Crébillon fils and Voltaire appeared on the list of subscribers to the third and fourth volumes of Sterne's sermons which were published in 1766.[29]

As far as Voltaire is concerned, he first mentioned *Tristram Shandy* in a letter to Algarotti in 1760. He wrote: 'Have you read Tristram Shandi? T'is a very unaccountable book; an original one. They run mad about it in England'[30] (Best.D9227, September 1760). Voltaire was naturally flattered by Sterne's reference to *Candide* in chapter nine of the first volume of *Tristram Shandy*. This chapter ends with a dedication to the Moon

who, by the bye, of all the PATRONS or MATRONS I can think of, has most power to set my book a-going, and make the world run mad after it.
> *Bright Goddess*
If thou are not too busy with CANDID and Miss CUNEGUND's affairs, – take *Tristram Shandy's* under thy protection also.
(*Tristram Shandy*, ed. Douglas Grant (London 1950), p.39)

It seems that Voltaire's information to Algarotti about the book's popularity in England may have been derived from what Sterne himself writes in *Tristram Shandy*.

We next hear of *Tristram Shandy* and its author in Voltaire's review of Churchill's *Poems* which appeared in the *Gazette littéraire*

[28] Diderot had already referred to the maddest, the wisest and the gayest of books without naming *Tristram* in a letter to Sophie on 26 September 1762 (Roth, iv. 172).

[29] cf. Alice G. Fredman, *Diderot and Sterne* (New York 1955), p. 7. Diderot openly imitated *Tristram Shandy* in *Jacques le fataliste*, for two episodes in Diderot's novel, Jacques's wound and Denise's massage of Jacques, are taken from book viii of *Tristram Shandy*. Diderot himself admits: 'Voici le second paragraphe copié de *la vie de Tristram Shandy*' (*Œuvres complètes*, Assézat-Tourneux (Paris 1875-78), v. 284).

[30] Voltaire is referring to the original text in English. A copy of it in six volumes up to 1762 is listed in his library at Leningrad. The catalogue of his library at Ferney mentions six volumes of *Tristram* up to 1767. Voltaire definitely refers to the translation by Joseph Pierre Frénais in 1776 entitled *La Vie et les opinions de Tristram Shandy* in a letter to Panckoucke: 'Je n'ai point reçu le *Tristram Shandi* en français' (Best.D20565, 15 February 1777). Th. Besterman was mistaken when he spoke of a translation of *Tristram* in 1760 (Best.D9227, n.5 & D20565, n.1). No such translation exists.

in 1764. Up to a point Churchill resembled Sterne for his wit, digressions and incoherence. His remarks on Sterne must have been noticed by Voltaire and must have stimulated the latter's interest further. In book iii of *The Ghost*, Churchill wrote:

> Could I, whilst *Humour* held the Quill,
> Could I digress with half that skill,
> Could I with half that skill return,
> Which we so much admire in STERNE,
> Where each *Digression*, seeming vain,
> And only fit to entertain,
> Is found, on better recollection,
> To have a just and nice Connection,
> To help the whole with wond'rous art,
> Whence it seems idly to depart.
> (*The Poetical works of C. Churchill*,
> ed. D. Grant, p.131).

In the 1763 edition of *The Rosciad*, Churchill thought that Sterne was 'too gay' a judge to decide the contest among the actors, while Johnson was 'too grave' (Grant, p.5):

> For MURPHY some few *pilf'ring* wits declar'd,
> Whilst FOLLY clap'd her hands and WISDOM shar'd.

Voltaire pointed out the resemblance between Churchill and Sterne in his *Gazette littéraire* article. He noted how in *The Rosciad* Churchill satirises the different actors of two London theatres. He thought that this was a rather strange subject to start a theologian of the Church of England on his career. Sterne, a prebendary of York, had the same kind of beginning with his 'roman plus gai que décent de *Tristram Shandy*' (M.xxv. 167). To a certain extent Voltaire therefore shared the views of English critics of the eighteenth century who often censured both Churchill and Sterne for writing works which were not suitable to the character of a clergyman. The anonymous poem *The Anti-Times* (1764), which was addressed to Churchill, proved that Sterne was no fit ambassador from hell. Robert Lloyd, a friend of Churchill, emphasized Sterne's indecency in his poem *The New river-head* (1764).[31] After the success he had obtained with works such as *Candide* and *La*

---

[31] see *Sterne*, ed. Howes, pp.155, 235.

Pucelle, which in parts had something 'plus gai que décent' to offer,[32] Voltaire nevertheless secretly enjoyed reading the spicy sections of *Tristram Shandy*.

The *Gazette littéraire* of 1765 printed a review on the occasion of the publication of volumes vii and viii of *Tristram Shandy*. It is not certain who wrote the article which was published in volume v of the periodical and has usually been excluded from Voltaire's works. Beuchot's reasons for doing so do not seem convincing. He states (M.xxv. 167, n.1): 'D'après la manière dont Voltaire en parle dans le premier de ses *Articles extraits du Journal*..., il ne doit pas être l'auteur de l'article sur Sterne inséré au tome v de la *Gazette littéraire de l'Europe*.' Yet internal evidence does point to Voltaire.

There appears to be a close connection between the article published in the *Gazette littéraire* of 18 April 1764, that of 1765 and what Voltaire subsequently said about Sterne in the article on *Tristram Shandy* published in the *Journal de politique et de littérature* of 25 April 1777. The phrase 'roman plus gai que décent de *Tristram Shandy*' of the first article can be matched by a remark found in the second article in which Sterne and Rabelais are compared, that Sterne 'est aussi gai, & souvent aussi peu décent'. In the latter article, *Tristram Shandy* is referred to as 'un des ouvrages les plus bizarres qui aient jamais paru dans aucune langue ... une espèce de Roman bouffon écrit à pe u près dans le goût de *Pantagruel* & de *la Satyre Ménippée*'. The writer adds: 'Ceux qui cherchent finesse à tout découvroient un sens profond dans des bouffonneries qui n'en avoient aucun ... il est très difficile de donner une légère idée de ce livre extraordinaire ... Tout se passe en digressions.' As for the author of *Tristram*, the writer's conclusion is that 'M. Sterne s'étoit diverti aux *dépens du Public*'. Now if we turn to the last article for Voltaire's views on *Tristram Shandy*, we note that 'tout l'ouvrage est en préliminaires et en digressions.[33] C'est une bouffonnerie continuelle dans le goût de Scarron.' Though *Tristram Shandy* will not lead to any revolution, we must be grateful, says Voltaire, to the translator for having suppressed 'des bouffonneries un peu grossières qu'on a quelque fois reprochées à l'Angleterre'.

[32] for example, in *Candide* at the beginning of chapter xvi where two naked girls 'couraient légèrement au bord de la prairie, tandis que deux singes les suivaient en leur mordant les fesses' and in *La Pucelle* where Voltaire took delight in writing on the genesis of Hermaphrodix and explaining how in order to satisfy the 'fausse délicatesse' of virtuous ladies, he had transformed him from Conculix (Vercruysse, p.329).

[33] cf. Churchill's comments above, p.259.

Sterne himself, concludes Voltaire, was born 'pauvre et gai, il voulait rire aux dépens de l'Angleterre, et gagner de l'argent'. The last remark suggests that Voltaire had read Sterne's *Letters*. Had not Sterne declared there that he wanted to make his labour financially and socially advantageous to himself?[34]

Whoever may have been the author[35] of the article in the *Gazette littéraire* of 1765, it is certain that Voltaire had more than a fleeting interest in Sterne: the evidence suggests that he was fascinated by him from 1760 almost until the time of his death. His interest was not limited to *Tristram*. A 1769 edition of the *Sermons of mr Yorick* and the *Letters from Yorick to Eliza* (1775), which contain ten of Sterne's letters to mrs Draper, are listed in the catalogue of Voltaire's library at Ferney. With regard to the *Sermons*, Sterne did his best to attract attention to them with advanced publicity in *Tristram Shandy*. He decided to interpolate in the novel his own sermon on 'The abuses of Conscience' and to stress that 'in case the character of parson Yorick, and this sample of his sermons is liked, – there are now in the possession of the *Shandy* family, as many as will make a handsome volume' (*Tristram Shandy*, p.135).

Sterne's technique produced the desired effect on Voltaire, who was obviously thrilled by the *Sermons*. He wrote an uncollected[36] review of them for the *Gazette littéraire* in 1764. This review was included in the material published by Boiteux in his paper on 'Voltaire et le ménage Suard' (*Studies on Voltaire* (1955), i. 25). Despite Sterne's indebtedness to Swift, Voltaire thought that his sermons were very original as they struck him as being a very novel course of moral instruction. Sterne appeared to differ from other preachers. In his article, Voltaire laid stress on the seventh sermon entitled 'The vindication of human nature'. What he liked was that instead of depicting man as being essentially inclined towards evil, Sterne gave the assurance that he was born good. Sterne proved his point by stressing the innocence of childhood, the trusting nature and simplicity of youth. Even old age was praised: although self-centred, an old man still loves his children. Sterne also referred to the pity man has for the unhappy, a sentiment which is inborn and which dies out only in

---

[34] see *Letters of Laurence Sterne*, ed. L. P. Curtis (Oxford 1935), p.89.
[35] see Appendix.
[36] I am indebted to the late Theodore Besterman for helping me trace the source of this review.

monsters. His method of reminding man of his dignity and of rousing his sense of honour is as good as the usual method of making him feel horror for his being. That is why, concluded Voltaire, these sermons which have the merit of being very short and dispensing with division or exordium went into five editions in six months.

It is perhaps not profitable to restrict oneself to what Voltaire openly acknowledged in a work or in an author when it is a question of establishing influences on him. More often than not it is worth considering what Voltaire specifically avoids mentioning. In the most militant phase of his career, Voltaire, one may argue, would no doubt have been interested in almost any source that could give him material with which to conduct his campaign against *l'infâme*. Had he not revealed in a letter to Clavel de Brenles that he was keen on English books on account of their anticlerical tendency? He wrote: 'je reçois la cargaison des livres anglais sur les quels je n'avais plus compté. J'avais fait venir, il y a six mois, les mêmes volumes de Londres . . . On n'en saurait trop avoir, tous ces livres sont contre les prêtres' (Best.D7929, 2 November 1758).

There were at least five titles in Sterne's *Sermons of mr Yorick* which could not fail to evoke a response in Voltaire. These were 'The Levite and his concubine', 'Felix's behaviour towards Paul examin'd', 'Penances', 'On enthusiasm' and 'On conscience'. The first contained a jibe at the Old Testament prophet Solomon 'whose excesses became an insult upon the privileges of mankind; for by the same plan of luxury, which made it necessary to have forty thousand stalls of horses, – he had unfortunately miscalculated his other wants; and so had seven hundred wives, and three hundred concubines' (*The Sermons of mr Yorick* (Oxford 1927), i. 63-64). The interest in the second title is to be found in the definition of popery which it contains, namely that 'it is a pecuniary system, well contrived to operate upon men's passions and weakness whilst their pockets are o'picking' (i. 224). This definition is repeated in the sermon on 'Penances' with a slight variation: popery is a 'system put together and contrived to operate upon men's weaknesses and passions, – and thereby to pick their pockets, – and leave them in a fit condition for its arbitrary designs' (*Sermons*, ii. 180). In this sermon, Sterne castigates the practice of penance in the Church of Rome where 'almost the whole of religion is made to consist in the pious fooleries of penances and sufferings' (p.179). His conclusion is that by the doctrine of penances which are raised to the number of sacraments and other tenets 'no less politic and inquisitional, popery has found out the art of making men miserable in spite of their senses' (p.180). The Methodists too do not escape censure: for their keenness to alienate themselves from the world and sell all their possessions is to be ascribed to 'the same mistaken enthusiastic principle, which would cast so black a shade upon religion, as if the kind Author of it had created us on purpose to go mourning, all our lives long, in sack-cloth and ashes, – and sent us into the world, as so many saint-errants, in quest of adventures full of sorrow and affliction' (p.176). This was just the type of writing to appeal to Voltaire, as he had censured the austerity of the Jansenists in works such as the *Lettres philosophiques* and *Le Mondain*.

However, nothing could be as stimulating for Voltaire as the sermon 'On enthusiasm' which like most of the others had been written before 1751, but was only published in 1769. In it Sterne describes the mistaken enthusiast ostentatiously clothed in the outward garb of sanctity to attract the eyes of the vulgar and arrogantly thanking his God for being different from other men (ii. 195). With more than papal uncharitableness, the enthusiast very liberally allots the portion of the damned, to every Christian whom he, partial judge, deems less perfect than himself. Then Sterne refers to the religious conflict of the seventeenth century in England when the Church of Christ was torn asunder into various sects and factions, 'when some men pretended to have Scripture precepts, parables, or prophecies to plead, in favour of the most impious absurdities that falsehood could advance' (p.196). The behaviour of these modern enthusiasts is undoubtedly that of fanatics. To ascribe to the holy spirit of God the hallucinations of a frantic brain is blasphemous. Yet Sterne thinks that many of these deluded people demand our tenderest compassion because their disorder is in the head rather than in the heart. They ask for the help of a physician to cure their bodies rather than for someone to alleviate their mental anguish. They are, however, beyond the skill of either physician or spiritual guide. Unless God checks the progress of enthusiasm, it may cause havoc in Britain.

It seems that Voltaire drew some inspiration from Sterne's sermon for his article 'Enthousiasme' in the *Questions sur l'encyclopédie* two years later. At the beginning of the article, he tries to define enthusiasm and its various states. He then illustrates these. The sectarian spirit is well disposed towards enthusiasm and there is no sect that does not have its fanatics. A passionate man has in his eyes, in his voice and gestures a subtle poison which is thrust like a jet among the men of his faction. That is why queen Elizabeth of England imposed a six-month ban on preaching, (unless a written authorization were obtained from her) in order to maintain peace in the country. The ground has been well-prepared for a description of the excesses caused by enthusiasm. St Ignace whose head is full of wild notions reads the life of the desert fathers after he has read novels. This leads to a double enthusiasm: first he wants to enrol as a knight of the Virgin Mary and he has visions of her. In one of these visions, she tells him that his society must only be called after Jesus. A more serious consequence is that Ignace communicates his enthusiasm to Xavier who spreads it to his disciples. Enthusiasm becomes such an epidemic that Xavier's disciples form after his death what they call a Christian society in Japan. What is the result of all this? 'Cette chrétienté finit par une guerre civile et par cent mille hommes égorgés: l'enthousiasme alors est parvenu à son dernier degré, qui est le fanatisme; et ce fanatisme est devenu rage' (M.xviii.553). The idea of hallucinations caused by a brain teeming with weird notions may be basically Sterne's, but the manner of writing about them is undoubtedly Voltaire's.

How charming is Voltaire's portrait of the young fakir who sees the end of his nose while saying his prayers, becomes increasingly so excited as to believe that if he carries chains weighing fifty pounds, the supreme being will owe him a great obligation! The fakir goes to sleep, his thoughts completely taken up with Brama whom he does not fail to see in his dream. Sometimes in the state when one is neither asleep nor awake, sparks come out of his eyes; he sees Brama in full splendour, he has ecstasies and the disease often becomes incurable. The rest of the article is devoted to reasonable enthusiasm in literature.

Granted that Voltaire was interested in Sterne in a variety of ways and that there was between them something more than a mere affinity in Rabelaisian humour, in what type of work then are we to look for a possible influence of *Tristram Shandy* on Voltaire? It has been maintained with justification that his deeper affinities with Molière as a comic writer must be sought not in Voltaire's theatre but in his *contes philosophiques*.[37] If this is a true picture of the situation, is there no legitimate ground for asserting that Voltaire may have used *Tristram Shandy* outside his fictional writing for his attack against *l'infâme*?

[37] William H. Barber, 'Voltaire and Molière', p.213.

It was not without cause that Voltaire first became interested in Sterne's novel in 1760, the year in which the first two volumes were published, with the sermon on conscience appearing in the second volume. He was to use it subsequently, after having made such alterations to it as suited his polemical purpose. In section iii of the article 'Conscience', entitled 'De la conscience trompeuse', published in the *Questions* in 1771, Voltaire introduces his subject thus: 'Ce qu'on a peut-être jamais dit de mieux sur cette question importante se trouve dans le livre comique de *Tristram Shandy*, écrit par un curé nommé Sterne, le second Rabelais d'Angleterre; il ressemble à ces petits satyres de l'antiquité qui renfermaient des essences précieuses' (M.xviii. 237). The first Rabelais was, of course, Swift. There was logic in Voltaire's pinpointing the similarity between Swift and Sterne: one may, *inter alia*, note the fact that Sterne's sermon on conscience was based on Swift's discourse entitled 'On the testimony of conscience'.[38] The question of conscience as such appears to be a *trompe l'œil*, for what really matters to Voltaire is the attack on French theologians: (M.xviii.237):

Deux vieux capitaines à demi-paye, assistés du docteur Slop, font les questions les plus ridicules. Dans ces questions, les théologiens de France ne sont pas épargnés. On insiste particulièrement sur un Mémoire présenté à la Sorbonne par un chirurgien, qui demande la permission de baptiser les enfants dans le ventre de leurs mères, au moyen d'une canule qu'il introduira proprement dans l'utérus, sans blesser la mère ni l'enfant.[39]

Although Frénais stated in the 'Avertissement' to his translation in 1776 that *Tristram Shandy* was one of the most difficult works ever written in English and that he had had to prune the original considerably and to make good what he had removed, he gave a fairly close rendering of the section dealing with Roman Catholic baptism of a child in cases of danger before it is born. In both the original text

---

[38] see L. Hammond, *Laurence Sterne's Sermons of mr Yorick* (New Haven 1948), p.83.

[39] a similar story appears in Diderot's letter of 12 October 1760 to Sophie Volland (Roth, iii. 132). Diderot says that he was told this 'anecdote polissonne' by père Hoop who in his younger days had followed a course on midwifery given by a doctor Grégoire. Either Diderot or père Hoop could have got the story from *Tristram*. Intra-uterine baptism seems to have been topical, for a work on this subject entitled *Abrégé de l'embryologie sacrée* appeared in the same period and was reviewed in a letter dated 24 July 1762 in the *Année littéraire*. I am grateful to Peter France for pointing out Diderot's letter to me.

and in Frénais's translation which Voltaire read before publishing his
article in the *Journal de politique* in 1777, there is no question of
introducing 'une canule . . . proprement dans l'utérus', although there
is mention in the translation of children who are 'renfermés dans le
sein de leurs Mères . . . infantes in maternis uteris existentes' and
of a surgeon who 'prétend, par le moyen d'une petite canule, de
pouvoir baptiser immédiatement l'enfant, sans faire aucun tort à la
mère'.

Voltaire bestows lavish praise on Sterne whose sketches are described as being superior to those of Rembrandt and Callot, because
he draws the picture of a man who leads a life of pleasure and debauchery and dies without the slightest remorse. Thereupon 'le
docteur Slop interrompt le lecteur pour dire que cela est impossible
dans l'Eglise anglicane, et ne peut arriver que chez des papistes'
(M.xviii. 237).

Voltaire's interpretation of this incident does not seem accurate. To
begin with, Slop – in actual life dr John Burton, author of books on
midwifery – is described as a papist in the original. Trim, who had
suggested that conscience was engaged on such things as talking loud
against petty larceny and executing vengeance upon puny crimes while
the man was enjoying himself, was interrupted. '[If he was of our
church tho', quoth Dr. *Slop*, he could not] . . . [All this is impossible
with us, quoth Dr. *Slop*, turning to my father, – the case could not
happen in our Church. – It happens in ours, however, replied my
father, but too often' (*Tristram Shandy*, pp.123-24). Voltaire may
have become confused as to who the papist was, but his interest lay
elsewhere.

The writer who had enjoyed with such witty relish the tussle between
Jesuits and Jansenists in the *Relation du jésuite Berthier* some years
earlier was probably delighted with the description of the petty dispute
he read in *Tristram Shandy* between Anglicans and Roman Catholics.
The equally futile dispute between Anglicans and Puritans during the
English civil war had made a strong impression on him and had been
used to advantage in his satirical writings. Setting one sect or one
religion against another is a constant in Voltaire's polemical technique.
In *Zaïre* Christians and Moslems hurl abuse at one another, in the
Lettres philosophiques, Quakers are set against other Christian de-
nominations and in the *Lettres d'Amabed*, Hinduism is contrasted with
Christianity.

Voltaire concludes the article 'Conscience' of the *Questions* with the remark 'enfin le curé Sterne cite l'exemple de David, qui a, dit-il, tantôt une conscience délicate et éclairée, tantôt une conscience très ténébreuse'.[40] As he had already enjoyed Sterne's jibe at Solomon in the *Sermons of mr Yorick*, Voltaire was delighted to have Sterne's support for one of his various attacks on another Old Testament prophet.[41] In the article 'David' published in 1767 in the *Dictionnaire philosophique*, Voltaire wrote (Benda and Naves, pp.160-62):

Je suis un peu scandalisé que David, l'oint du Seigneur, l'homme selon le cœur de Dieu, . . . s'en aille avec quatre cents bandits mettre le pays à contribution, aille voler le bonhomme Nabal, qu'immédiatement après Nabal se trouve mort et que David épouse la veuve sans tarder . . . Je ne parlerai pas ici de l'assassinat abominable d'Urie, et de l'adultère de Bethsabée . . . Je ne demande pas maintenant comment Jerieu a eu l'insolence de persécuter le sage Bayle pour n'avoir pas approuvé toutes les actions du bon roi David.

In a 1771 addition to the article, Voltaire asked (p.504):

Qu'importe le nom de celui qui égorgeait les femmes et les enfants de ses alliés, qui faisait pendre les petits-fils de son roi, qui faisait scier en deux, brûler dans des fours, déchirer sous des herses, des citoyens malheureux? . . . le nom n'augmente ni ne diminue le crime. Plus on révèle David comme réconcilié avec Dieu par son repentir, et plus on condamne les cruautés dont il s'est rendu coupable.

The sermon on conscience found in *Tristram Shandy* made such an impression on Voltaire that he came back to it in his article on the book, which appeared on 25 April 1777 in the *Journal de politique et de littérature*. He thought the publication of the sermon there was a 'plaisanterie' (M.xxx. 380). Why did he make the assessment that this sermon was 'un des meilleurs dont l'éloquence anglaise puisse se faire

---

[40] Sterne did not actually say this, either in the original or in Frénais's translation, but this is what he clearly meant and Voltaire is therefore more accurate here. Sterne wrote: 'When *David* surprized *Saul* sleeping in the Cave, and cut off the skirt of his robe . . . his heart smote him for what he had done:– But in the matter of *Uriah* . . . where conscience had so much greater reason to take the alarm, his heart smote him not. A whole year had almost passed from the first commission of that crime, to the time *Nathan* was sent to reprove him; and we read not once of the least sorrow or compunction of heart . . . for what he had done' (*Tristram Shandy*, p.126).

[41] Voltaire also used Peter Annet's *The Life of David* and Bayle's *Dictionnaire* article on David. The original material for the attack on David came from Bayle, though Voltaire found Annet more outspoken. See H. T. Mason, *Pierre Bayle and Voltaire*, pp.21, 29-30.

honneur' (M.xxx.380)? It is really because Sterne had made Trim
conclude his sermon with a devastating attack on the Roman Catholic
religion, despite the numerous interruptions from Slop (*Tristram
Shandy*, pp.130-31):

Examine the history of the Roman Church . . . see what scenes of cruelty,
murders, rapines, blood-shed, have all been sanctified by a religion not
strictly governed by morality . . . In how many kingdoms of the world has
the crusading sword of this misguided saint-errant spared neither age, or
merit or sex, or condition? – and, as he fought under the banners of a religion
which set him loose from justice and humanity, he shewed none; mercilessly
trampled upon both, – heard neither the cries of the unfortunate, nor pitied
their distresses . . . If the testimony of past centuries in this matter is not
sufficient, – consider at this instant, how the votaries of that religion are every
day thinking to do service and honour to God, by actions which are a dis-
honour and scandal to themselves. To be convinced of this, go with me for a
moment into the prisons of the inquisition . . . Behold Religion, with Mercy
and Justice chained down under her feet, – there sitting ghastly upon a black
tribunal, propp'd up with racks and instruments of torment. – Hark! hark!
what a piteous groan . . . See the melancholy wretch who uttered it just
brought forth to undergo the anguish of a mock trial, and endure the utmost
pains that a studied system of cruelty has been able to invent . . . Behold this
helpless victim delivered up to his tormentors, – his body so wasted with
sorrow and confinement, you will see every nerve and muscle as it suffers.

Using his discretion as a translator, Frénais had shifted the blame from
the Roman Catholic Church on to religion in general and had written:
'Que de crimes ce zèle mal entendu de religion sans morale a causé dans
le monde! . . . que de scènes de cruauté, de meurtre, de rapine, d'ef-
fusion de sang il a produits.'[42]

By this time it was open to Voltaire to read *Tristram Shandy* in the
original and in translation. He certainly found in that novel evidence
to justify what he had been saying so often against *l'infâme*. The champion of Calas, Sirven and La Barre could not be indifferent. Sterne's
sermons, as they appear in the *Sermons of mr Yorick* and in *Tristram
Shandy*, reflect the violent hatred against Rome prevalent in 1745.[43]
Then every church was full of denunciations of Rome. Addressing a

[42] *La Vie et les opinions de Tristram Shandy*, trans. Frénais (York and Paris 1776),
p.239.
[43] W. L. Cross, *The Life and times of Laurence Sterne* (New Haven 1925), i. 78-80.

large congregation from the pulpit of St Peter's, York on 29 July 1750, Sterne drew a portrait of the victim of the Inquisition. This militant phase had passed by the time *Tristram Shandy* was written, but the material incorporated in the novel and in the sermons was still relevant to Voltaire's purpose. Moreover, Sterne must have roused in him the same kind of feelings he had had on reading Bayle. In *Ce que c'est que la France toute catholique*, Bayle had concluded his violent denunciation of the Roman Catholic religion in these terms (*Œuvres diverses*, ii. 350):

Ne doit-on pas croire que c'est une Religion qui aime le sang, et le carnage; qui veut violenter le corps et l'âme; qui pour établir sa tirannie sur les consciences et faire des fourbes et des hipocrites, en cas qu'elle n'ait pas l'adresse de persuader ce qu'elle veut, met tout en usage, mensonges, faux-sermons, Dragons, Juges iniques, Chicaneurs et Solliciteurs de méchans procès, faux-témoins, Bourreaux, Inquisitions et tout cela.

Voltaire acknowledged in the article on *Tristram Shandy* in the *Journal de politique et de littérature* that there were in Sterne's work 'des éclairs d'une raison supérieure, comme on en voit dans Shakespeare' (M.xxx.380). On the other hand, the linking of Sterne with Shakespeare suggests qualified approval on the part of Voltaire, as he had never been whole-heartedly in favour of Shakespeare. One of his reservations with regard to Sterne was that the latter had violated decorum. Voltaire agrees with Frénais for having suppressed some coarse jokes: 'il y a même des morceaux considérables que le traducteur de Sterne n'a pas osé rendre en français, comme la formule d'excommunication usitée dans l'église de Rochester: nos bienséances ne l'ont pas permis' (M.xxx.382).[44] What he says about the excommunication formula is not exact, for it does appear in Frénais's translation, although in a modified form. The Latin of the formula 'Maledictus sit . . . quiescendo, mingendo, cacando, flebotomando' is rendered by Sterne as 'may he be cursed in resting, in pissing, in shitting and in blood-letting' (*Tristram Shandy*, p.159). Frénais simply writes 'etc' for the last part of the sentence.

Voltaire's final appraisal of Sterne is tempered by criticism, but it is not difficult to understand his stand. For despite the sparks, despite the wit and the wisdom he found in Sterne, Voltaire felt that Sterne, like other Englishmen, was making an improper use of a genre which

[44] this shows how familiar Voltaire was with the English text.

did not constantly win his support. Like many French writers of the seventeenth and eighteenth centuries, Voltaire enjoyed opposing English *thought* to English *literature*. Whenever he could he would opt for the former. That is perhaps why he wrote: 'Il eût été à désirer que le prédicateur n'eût fait son comique roman que pour apprendre aux Anglais à ne plus se laisser duper par la charlatanerie des romanciers, et qu'il eût pu corriger la nation, qui tombe depuis longtemps, abandonne l'étude des Locke et des Newton pour les ouvrages les plus extravagants et les plus frivoles' (M.xxx.380).

It is worth remembering that his review of Sterne's novel in the *Journal de politique et de littérature* came soon after the conclusion of his anti-Shakespeare campaign, which reached its height in the *Lettre à l'Académie française* in 1776. His denigration of Shakespeare may have slightly influenced his judgement on Sterne, although it does not appear to have modified his attitude to Swift. He reluctantly acknowledged his debt to English literature and one could understand his reluctance in this particular instance, as the inspiration was not of the most delicate. One cannot, however, take Voltaire too seriously: his *pudeur* may be false. He had himself paid little attention to standards of decorum when in the article 'Transsubstantiation' of the *Dictionnaire philosophique* he described what happened in Catholic countries.

If there can be no question of his imitating Sterne in his works of the late 1750s, one can surely talk of certain affinities drawing Voltaire to him in the 1760s. These affinities were initially at a superficial level: that of grotesque humour. But as had happened in the case of Butler (see above), Voltaire found that he could use Sterne for more serious matters, particularly for his attack against *l'infâme*. This may explain why he became so interested in Sterne's sermons in the 1760s and 1770s. After he had made the most of them, Voltaire could afford to look down on Sterne and talk of French decorum.

iii. *Voltaire, Richardson and Fielding*

Considering that Voltaire had enjoyed good relations with Swift and had liked his works and those of Sterne, one might have expected him to spare the English novel from a general condemnation of the genre. Despite his attitude to Rousseau's *Nouvelle Héloïse*, one might also have expected him to feel some of the impact the sentimental and the 'realist' novels were having in France. La Chesnaye Des Bois, who had translated Richardson's *Pamela* in 1741, noted that to be fashionable in Paris one had to have a copy of *Pamela* in one's possession. Louis de Boissy and Nivelle de La Chaussée produced their own adaptations of *Pamela* in the form of comedies in 1743, while Baculard d'Arnaud published a story with the title *Nancy ou la nouvelle Paméla* in the periodical, *Le Discoureur*, in 1762. Baculard's story then appeared in book form in 1764 as *Fanni ou l'heureux repentir* and then in 1767 as *Fanni ou la nouvelle Paméla*.

At a time when the English sentimental novel was being widely acclaimed in France, would Voltaire choose to strike an entirely different note? Here one must take into consideration the personal element that is involved. For in the latter part of his literary career, one must remember that Voltaire was interested in fighting against certain aspects of English literature which he had been among the first to introduce in France, especially in the 1730s. One of the reasons underlining his attitude is that he could not remain indifferent when he saw his reputation as a translator of Shakespeare being eclipsed by Le Tourneur's.[45] The same Le Tourneur was winning success as a translator of English novels. La Place too had translated *Tom Jones* in 1750.

This may explain why Voltaire revealed such hostile feelings towards English sentimental and 'realist' novels in his correspondence. He, however, did them justice in his review of Frances Brooke's *History of Lady Julia Mandeville* published in the *Gazette littéraire* of 30 May 1764. He wrote: 'L'*Histoire de Julie Mandeville* est peut-être le meilleur roman de ce genre qui ait paru en Angleterre depuis *Clarisse* et *Grandisson*. On y trouve de la vérité et de l'intérêt; et c'est l'art d'intéresser qui fait le succès des ouvrages dans tous les genres, même dans l'histoire; à plus forte raison dans les romans, qui sont des histoires supposées' (M.xxv.181). He also tried to account for the success of the novel in England in this article. He ascribed it to the frivolity of English readers and to social and educational factors prevailing in England. 'Ce qui est remarquable, c'est que ces livres de pur agrément ont plus de lecteurs en Angleterre qu'en France ... c'est que l'état mitoyen est plus riche et plus instruit en Angleterre qu'en France, et qu'un très-grand nombre de familles anglaises passent neuf mois de l'année dans

---

[45] see D. Williams, *Voltaire: literary critic*, p.329.

leurs terres; la lecture leur est plus nécessaire qu'aux Français rassemblés dans les villes' (M.xxv.182-83).

Voltaire was critical of mme Du Deffand in a letter he wrote to her in 1759, for she had apparently suggested that he should read English novels: 'mais je ne vous passe point de vouloir me faire lire les romans anglais quand vous ne voulez pas lire l'ancien Testament' (Best.D8533, 13 October 1759). Mme Du Deffand did not wish that Voltaire's attack should remain unchallenged. She wrote back stressing the merit of English novels. After she had made a minor concession that they might appear too long, she argued that they were 'traités de morale en actions qui sont très intéressants et peuvent être fort utiles; c'est Pamela, Clarisse et Grandissonn; l'auteur est Richerson, il me parois avoir bien de l'esprit' (Best.D8559, 28 October 1759).[46]

Mme Du Deffand's enthusiasm for Richardson apparently made some impression on Voltaire. He read *Clarissa* in the original or perhaps in Prévost's translation, the *Lettres angloises ou histoire de Miss Clarisse Harlowe* (1751), of which he had a copy in his library. Voltaire gave his friend his impressions of the novel on 12 April 1760. He claimed that he read it as a distraction from his work: 'pendant ma fièvre; cette Lecture m'allumait le sang'. It was cruel for a man as lively as himself to read nine whole volumes in which one finds nothing and which serve only to show that Clarissa is in love with a rake named Lovelace. Even if these people were related to him or his friends, he could not be interested in them. He sees in Richardson nothing more than a skilful author who knows how men are curious and who always promises something from volume to volume in order to sell his work. He has seen Clarissa in a place of ill repute in the tenth volume and he has been deeply moved. Pierre Corneille's Theodore cannot match Clarissa in her situation and her feelings. Yet, apart from the terrible predicament of the beautiful English girl, Voltaire finds that the rest of the novel has not given him any pleasure and that he would not like to be condemned to reread it (Best.D8846).

The publication of Diderot's *Eloge de Richardson* in 1762 was perhaps destined to rouse hostile feelings in Voltaire. It coincided with

---

[46] Diderot told Sophie Volland in his letter dated 20 October 1760 of the conflicting reactions *Clarissa* provoked in readers. He had a copy of it and was annoyed that she did not have one and he added: 'Je ne serai content ni de vous ni de moi que je ne vous aie amenée à goûter la vérité de *Paméla*, de *Tom Jones*, de *Clarice* et de *Grandison*' (Roth, iii. 173-74).

the beginning of his attack on *La Nouvelle Héloïse*. If Diderot helped to elevate the status of the sentimental novel in France, would he also not spread the influence of Rousseau's novel? Diderot waxed lyrical about Richardson, describing his novels as 'ouvrages . . . qui élèvent l'esprit, qui touchent l'âme, qui respirent partout l'amour du bien (A.T., v. 212-14). Voltaire must have particularly objected to the description of Richardson as a unique genius whom Diderot would always read. Diderot even stated that if he were forced by pressing needs to sell his books, he would keep Richardson and place him on the same shelf as Moses, Homer, Euripides and Sophocles.

Voltaire was no doubt aware of the success of Richardson's novels. In his article published in the *Gazette littéraire* of 30 May 1764, he stated that English novels were hardly read in Europe before *Pamela*. This type of novel appeared very exciting. *Clarissa* had less success than *Pamela* though it deserved more. In a letter he wrote to d'Argental in 1767, he said he did not like the long and unbearable novels of *Pamela* and *Clarissa*. He claimed that they owed their success to the fact that they had stimulated the curiosity of the reader 'à travers un fatras d'inutilités' (Best.D14179, 16 May 1767). All these disparaging remarks did not prevent Voltaire from rereading *Clarissa* in 1776. He seems to have been obsessed by Richardson's novel even when he complained that *Clarissa* made him lose the train of his thoughts. In the twelfth of the *Lettres chinoises, indiennes, et tartares*, published in 1776, he says he is absorbed in a mathematical problem. Then some anglomaniacs vaunt to him the excellence of *Clarissa*: to listen to them one would think that this was the only novel which a wise man could read. Voltaire admits that he is mad enough to read it; by so doing, he loses his time and his concentration (M.xxix.498).

In these circumstances, is there any chance of Richardson having made a real impact on Voltaire? At first sight this seems unlikely. Yet the possibility seems less remote when we remember that for all his adverse comments, Voltaire did not hesitate to use *Clarissa* in a chapter of *L'Ingénu*. The similarity between the agony of mademoiselle de St Yves in chapter xx of Voltaire's tale and Clarissa's has been noted.[47] This point is worth recording because it is not a regular technique of Voltaire to use material from another author in basically the same type of writing. With regard to the influence of the English 'realist' novel

[47] see Joseph Texte, *Jean-Jacques Rousseau et les origines du cosmopolitisme littéraire* (Paris 1895), p.275.

on Voltaire, it has been argued that it is not so much in the latter's *contes philosophiques* as in his theatre that that influence may be traced. For example, the play *Nanine* (1749), where the heroine reads an English book whose author 'prétend que tous les hommes sont frères' might recall certain features of *Pamela* (Dédéyan, p.77). According to the same view, Nanine's denouement is that of the 'préjugé vaincu', another title of Voltaire's play. On the other hand, Voltaire may also have been thinking of Marivaux, one of whose comedies is called *Le Préjugé vaincu* (1746).

Even when he was critical of Richardson, Voltaire must have been strongly impressed by the English novelist to think of writing an epistolary novel 'dans le goust de Pamela', as he himself stated in a letter to mme Denis (Best.D5535, 1 October 1753), and based on his correspondence with her. If his niece could write an unpublished play, *Pamela,* and provide him with one of his sources for l'*Ecossaise*,[48] Voltaire could oblige with a novel. From an earlier letter it appears that Voltaire intended to chastise Frederick for his despicable conduct towards mme Denis in a pseudo documentary and historical novel (Best.D5500, 3 September 1753). The novel was to be published after Voltaire's death and the heroine of his *Pamela* was to be mme Denis, as she was a victim of the wrath of Frederick, who had had her arrested a few months before. Theodore Besterman believed that Voltaire simply invented this story in order to humour his niece's vanity and persuade her to return his papers (Best.D5535, n.2).

It should be mentioned, however, that Voltaire confided in a third person about his *Pamela*. For on 10 October 1753, he wrote to d'Argental: 'je ne peux parvenir à peindre les infortunes de ceux qu'on appelle les héros des siècles passez à moins que je ne trouve quelque princesse mise en prison pour avoir été secourir un oncle malade. Cette avanture me tient plus au cœur que touttes celles de Denis et d'Hieron' (Best. D5543). If Voltaire had simply intended a hoax, perhaps it was not strictly necessary for him to write the last sentence to d'Argental. What is certain is that this mysterious *Pamela* has never been found. J. Nivat[49] maintained that *Pamela* was nothing more than the correspondence of the years 1750-53, although Voltaire's intention to use

---

[48] see Colin Duckworth, 'Madame Denis's unpublished *Pamela*', *Studies on Voltaire* (1970), lxxvi. 37-53.
[49] 'Quelques énigmes de la correspondance de Voltaire', *Revue d'histoire littéraire* (Paris 1953), liii. 439-63.

these letters for a novel was *bona fide*. A. Jovicevich, on the other hand, has a more plausible explanation. He believes that Voltaire did complete the novel and publish it in a modified form as the *Lettres d'Amabed*.[50]

While it is not certain that he intended mme Denis to be the heroine of *Pamela*, it is clear that Voltaire himself thought of the *Lettres d'Amabed* as being written in the manner of *Pamela*. For in 1769 he told Thieriot: 'Il [the *Lettres d'Amabed*] est écrit en forme de Lettres dans le goût de Paméla' (Best.D15668, 29 May 1769). Did Voltaire really achieve the objective he had set himself some sixteen years before of writing a novel in the manner of *Pamela*? He was convinced that his *Lettres d'Amabed* were superior to Richardson's novel. He was confident enough to add: 'Mais dans les six tomes de Paméla il n'y a rien. Ce n'est qu'une petite fille qui ne veut pas coucher avec son maître à moins qu'il ne l'épouse, et les lettres d'Amabed sont le tableau du monde entier depuis les rives du Gange jusqu'au Vatican.'

It requires some stretch of the imagination to find a parallel between Voltaire and Richardson in these two prose works. There are, however, certain superficial resemblances between them. Both use the epistolary form, but from the point of view of technique and to a certain extent that of substance, the *Lettres d'Amabed* are more reminiscent of the *Lettres persanes*.[51] The impressions Amabed and Adaté have of Europeans are not unlike those of Usbek and Rica. At first these are very unfavourable. The Persians eventually come to appreciate Europeans, as the Indians do in Voltaire's tale. As in the *Lettres persanes* and in his own *Le Monde comme il va*, the worst and the best co-exist in the *Lettres d'Amabed*. Like the Persian of Montesquieu, like Babouc, Amabed allows himself to be swayed by the pleasures of life. Often the same flowery language is used in these oriental tales.

It is clear that in the *Lettres d'Amabed* Voltaire never expected any tears of sympathy from the reader as Richardson did in *Pamela*, although the priest Shastasid claims to have shed 'des ruisseaux de larmes' over the three letters Adaté sent him to describe her rape. Fundamental questions such as chastity which the servant girl Pamela

[50] 'A propos d'une Paméla de Voltaire', *The French review* (Worcester, Mass. 1962-63), xxxvi. 276-83.

[51] see Diderot on the *Lettres d'Amabed* in *Miscellanea littéraires*: 'c'est la meilleure réparation qu'il pût faire à l'auteur des *Lettres persanes*' (A. T., vi. 367).

considered to be of great importance and which was rewarded by a considerable income later in Richardson's novel, the persistent scheming of Pamela and her parents for a decent social status, the opposed conceptions of sex and marriage held by two different social classes and the distinction of classes do not interest Voltaire. On the other hand, the model of feminine virtue exemplified by the heroine and her rape by Lovelace in *Clarissa* may have made a greater impression on him. It is perhaps this aspect of the novel which Voltaire seizes upon and uses in the *Lettres d'Amabed*, albeit in the most distorted form. Like Clarissa, Adaté is virtuous and innocent. But the wife of Amabed is raped by the dominican priest Fa tutto who pretended to be her friend.

If the similarities between Voltaire and Richardson appear slight, why then did the former insist that he was writing a novel in the manner of *Pamela*? It is possible that he thought of the *Lettres d'Amabed* as a convenient way of ridiculing Richardson and his admirers[52] in France. By mentioning the length of *Pamela* which had become a standard joke, he tried to show that where Richardson required volumes, Rousseau hundreds of pages, he could manage with a few pages. In fact he may have intended his *Lettres* to be an anti-*Pamela*. He had a good precedent in Fielding, a writer who interested him in various ways. Had not Fielding written his anti-*Pamela* in the form of *Joseph Andrews*? *Shamela* too ridiculed *Pamela*: it was most probably by Fielding. Or perhaps Voltaire was thinking of an anti-*Nouvelle Héloïse*. In the *Notes sur la lettre à m. Hume*, he had pointed out that Rousseau's novel was a bad imitation of *Pamela* and *Clarissa* because it contained 'ni exposition, ni nœud, ni dénouement, ni aventures intéressantes, ni raison, ni esprit' (M.xxvi.43). His *Lettres d'Amabed* would therefore show all the qualities which *Pamela* and its imitation lacked.

However, it is also likely that Voltaire was using Richardson's *Pamela* as a camouflage for one of his attacks against *l'infâme*. In the

---

[52] in his appreciation of *Clarissa*, Marmontel wrote in the *Essai sur les romans*: 'Tout est simple dans ce roman, hormis le caractère atroce et monstrueux, mais malheureusement encore trop naturel, de Lovelace: nulle affectation d'éloquence, nul épisode tiré de loin et artistement enchâssé, nul détail curieusement travaillé, nulle ostentation d'esprit ni de philosophie. L'auteur ne s'y montre jamais; on ne soupçonne pas même qu'il y ait un ... tout y est naturel et comme spontané' (*Œuvres complètes* (Paris 1819), x. 338). Marmontel explained that the substance of his *Essai* which appeared in 1787 was the same as what he had said in the *Mercure* of August 1758 and that time had barely changed his impressions.

latter part of his career, Voltaire showed an increasing tendency to look on English literature as a scapegoat for his vendetta. The *Lettres d'Amabed* enabled him to flog his hobby-horse once more: monks, Roman Catholicism, the Inquisition, the Bible – all came under attack.[53]

What has not been sufficiently noted in the eighteenth century, for example, is that taking Richardson's description of a rape as a starting-point, Voltaire used it to explore a current trend in the French novel: eroticism. In the fifth letter, père Fa tutto bursts into Adaté's bedroom: 'le détestable Fa tutto a fait pleuvoir dans mon sein la brûlante rosée de son crime.' Adaté wishes her ravisher to be turned into a young Indian girl after death while she herself changes into a dominican so that she may inflict the same pain on the wrong-doer and be even more merciless. Such a thought has nothing to do with Richardson or with *l'infâme*. If in the *Lettres d'Amabed* we see a travesty of Richardson, it is because Voltaire deliberately wanted it to be like this. He had not mis-read *Pamela* and *Clarissa*, since in his article in the *Gazette littéraire* on May 1764, he had suggested that the latter was superior to the former and deserved more success. He thus proved how sound his judgement was with regard to the two novels – a judgement confirmed by posterity.[54]

Voltaire was at first interested in Fielding as a dramatist. In his *Vie de Molière*, he thought that Fielding was a better and more modest poet than Shadwell. Fielding translated Molière's *L'Avare* as *The Miser* and Voltaire felt that in his translation Fielding had added some fine traits in the dialogue. These traits were typical of the English nation and Fielding's version had been performed thirty times. In Voltaire's opinion, Fielding obtained a very rare success in London because for the most popular plays one could expect only a maximum of fifteen performances there (M.xxiii.115). It was Fielding's novels, however, that attracted more attention in France.

Before translating *Joseph Andrews* in 1744, Desfontaines wrote a favourable review of the novel in the *Observations sur les écrits modernes*

---

[53] in Diderot's unkind words, this tale was 'sans goût, sans finesse, sans invention, un rabâchage de toutes les vieilles polissonneries que l'auteur a débitées contre Moïse et Jésus-Christ, les prophètes et les apôtres, l'Eglise, les papes, les cardinaux, les prêtres et les moines; nul intérêt, nulle chaleur, nulle vraisemblance, force ordures, une grosse gaîté... Si l'on reconnaît par ci par là l'ongle du lion, c'est l'ongle du lion caduc' (A. T., vi. 367).

[54] see, for example, A. Kettle, *An Introduction to the English novel* (London 1962), i. 69-76.

in 1743. He placed it on the same footing as Cervantes's *Don Quixote* and Scarron's *Roman comique*. He thought it was a judicious and moral work which exalted virtue. As for its style, it was comic throughout, excepting the passages where a tender and lawful love created the interest. Desfontaines went so far as to say that England had not hitherto produced such a perfect example of this genre. Moreover, *Joseph Andrews* could instruct the reader in the customs of the English, which were completely unknown in France, and it contained a hundred particulars worth the attention of the most serious person (xxxii. 189-91).[55]

Grimm gave an account of La Place's translation of *Tom Jones* (1750) in the *Correspondance littéraire*. He started off with the plot of the novel and then observed that despite the fact that it had been condensed it was too long. The characters were sufficiently well-drawn and varied, but the multitude of dramatis personae produced some confusion. The interest the reader must take in the two heroes was weakened by the attention he must devote to all the subordinate characters. Grimm criticised the vulgar episodes of *Tom Jones* and found the translation rather 'gothic' (i. 410).[56]

When Fréron wrote his lengthy review of *Tom Jones* in the *Lettres sur quelques écrits de ce temps* in July 1751, he commended La Place for having suppressed the prefaces, digressions and treatises found in the novel. But another, he added, would have suppressed all the 'low' comic scenes scattered in profusion throughout the work; he would, for instance, have spared the reader the barber Partridge, a detestable joker and dull pedagogue, who reels off scraps of latin at the least excuse. Some readers might also have wished that La Place had corrected the lack of verisimilitude in the story. Despite these defects, however, Fréron was forced to admit that he had read it twice with great pleasure. It had moving passages, sentiments expressed with such force and truth, characters so real and well-sustained that one could not deny the author's great genius and his ability to portray men. Moreover, the aim Fielding set himself was so noble and in general so happily fulfilled that one had to pardon his errors which were due more to the traditions of his country than to his own genius (v. 3-22).[57] In the *Essai sur les romans*, Marmontel emphasized the subtle

---

[55] cf. *Henry Fielding*, eds R. Paulson and T. Lockwood (London 1969), pp.126-27.
[56] cf. *Fielding*, pp.228-29.   [57] cf. *Fielding*, pp.275-81.

distinction made by Fielding between error and vice and contrasted the characters Blifil and Jones (*Œuvres*, x. 337).

Although Fielding's novels did not make as great an impact on Voltaire as other English novels, he was not indifferent to them. He certainly read *Tom Jones*, possibly in La Place's translation, a copy of which he had in his library. He spoke of *Tom Jones* disparagingly in a letter to mme Du Deffand, but unlike Fréron, he showed that he appreciated the barber Partridge in the novel: 'Quoi que Tobie ne soit pas si bon, cependant cela me parait meilleur que *Tom Jones*, dans lequel il n'y a rien de passable que le caractère d'un barbier' (Best. D8533, 13 October 1759). Voltaire must also have read other novels by Fielding. In his review in the *Gazette littéraire* of 30 May 1764 he first talked of Richardson's novels, then added: 'Les romans de Fielding présentèrent ensuite d'autres scènes, d'autres mœurs, un autre ton: ils plurent, parce qu'ils avaient de la vérité et de la gaieté' (M.xxv.182). Whilst he appreciated verisimilitude and gaiety in Fielding's novels, Voltaire also took the opportunity to show his disapproval of the imitators of Fielding: 'le succès des uns et des autres en a fait éclore ensuite une foule de mauvaises copies qui n'ont pas fait oublier les premiers, mais en ont sensiblement diminué le goût'. The objection then is not so much to Fielding as to his imitators, who pander to the whims and vanity of idle people, and, in particular, to a middle-class female reading public.

It has been suggested that Voltaire used the realism of the English novel in his drama. 'S'il n'écrit pas en effet de romans à la Richardson, ou à la Fielding, il songe à utiliser l'enseignement qu'ils donnent d'une vie vécue, d'une psychologie vraie' (Dédéyan, p.77). To support his point the author quotes the preface of Voltaire's play *L'Ecossaise* (1760). Is Voltaire to be taken literally? In this preface he claims that the ending of the play, the character of Lindane and that of Freeport have no parallel in the French theatre. Even if that were the case, it is doubtful whether *L'Ecossaise* really shows any realism or true psychology in so far as the character Frélon, that is Voltaire's bitter enemy Fréron, is concerned. Frélon is not plausibly integrated into the central plot of *L'Ecossaise*, whereas Zoïlin, that is Desfontaines, another enemy, is better integrated into the play *L'Envieux* (1739). Frélon appears to be an incidental element in the play, and as Voltaire is not really interested in the development of character, but in damning his opponent, Frélon puts in relatively few appearances. Once Voltaire has illustrated his thesis, which is to represent Frélon as a thoroughly worthless person, he makes him disappear from the scene after the fourth act.

Frélon's disappearance fits in with Voltaire's conception of his role. Since Frélon is regarded as a despicable scoundrel, so he might well illustrate the moral truth that 'l'homme le plus méprisable peut servir de contraste au plus galant homme'. This, however, is not to be taken literally. For Voltaire is not really interested in teaching any lesson. He is interested in Frélon in so far as his enemy can be shown to debase himself. This is part of the technique of distortion: Frélon is repulsive above everything else.

What happens in *L'Ecossaise* is that Voltaire used English novels such as Fielding's merely as a pretext for his devastating attack against Fréron. By attacking Fréron as he did he could argue that he was following precedents set up abroad. As the *Lettres d'Amabed* were destined to be written in the so-called 'goût de Paméla', so *L'Ecossaise*, Voltaire would have us believe, 'paraît un peu dans le goût de ces romans anglais qui ont fait tant de fortune' (M.v. 409). He claimed in his preface that the play had the same touches, and portrayed manners in the same way as these novels. Like the English novels, *L'Ecossaise* contained nothing far-fetched: it did not aim to appear witty and to let the author intervene directly when it should be showing only the characters. It was free from digressions, tirades worthy of schoolboys and those trivial maxims which masquerade as action. As English daring in the field of thought was generally accepted, Voltaire imagined that he could make capital out of English daring in the field of literature. All this was of course not done by way of homage to the English genius, but simply as a protection from critics who would challenge his methods. Every blemish in his writings could be attributed to the influence of the 'goût anglais'. Voltaire gladly admitted that Frélon might not be worthy of a play in France, but claimed that he was basing himself on the English artist who does not scorn anything. The latter sometimes takes delight in drawing objects which can shock other nations. To the English, the subject does not matter, provided it is true. Voltaire then added: 'Ils disent que la comédie étend ses droits sur tous les caractères et sur toutes les conditions; que tout ce qui est dans la nature doit être peint; que nous avons une fausse délicatesse' (M.v.410). By this Voltaire meant that his comedy of

L'Ecossaise was performing the same function as English novels. One must therefore note how Voltaire used both Richardson and Fielding in the cause of general and personal polemics.

Of the four English prose writers whose works Voltaire knew, Swift and Sterne seem to have made the greatest impact on him. This is not surprising since Voltaire had always been interested in the thought and style of religious polemicists, French or English. The extraordinary prose written in English by two priests is enough to explain Voltaire's fascination. The fact that he had also enjoyed good personal relations with Swift accounts for his favourable reactions towards him. In fact Voltaire was unflinching in his admiration for Swift and it lasted many years after the latter's death. It was some time before Swift's influence made itself felt in Voltaire's writings. The Voltaire of the *contes philosophiques* found Swift useful for the denunciation of man's vanity, his stupid wars and his countless abuses. English prose thus proved complementary to the inspiration found in English verse satire such as that written by Butler and Rochester. As important as the matter was the manner of Swift's prose writings. Voltaire succeeded in capturing the light-hearted spirit of Swift's fantasy as well as his vehemence in his own *contes*, the *Relation du jésuite Berthier* and the *Dictionnaire philosophique*. With Sterne, it was the virulence of the attack that made the most profound impression on Voltaire. The reference to *Candide* in *Tristram* no doubt paved the way for Voltaire's reciprocal treatment of Sterne. However, since he chose to exploit Sterne's techniques outside his prose fiction, Voltaire' article on Sterne in the *Questions sur l'Encyclopédie* has the deadly seriousness that is sometimes found in his imitation of Swift. Not having had the pleasure of Sterne's acquaintance, Voltaire could occasionally be unfair towards him.

If Voltaire appeared harsh towards Richardson, it was for different reasons. Richardson was gaining too much popularity in France for Voltaire's liking and Diderot's *Eloge* must have appeared to Voltaire like the consecration of a foreign intruder. Hence the constant hostility shown towards Richardson in the correspondence. Yet Voltaire did not want to appear unfashionable: he too could produce his epistolary novel in the manner of *Pamela*, the *Lettres d'Amabed*. This *tale* could be regarded as proof that Voltaire recognized the status of Richardson, since his intention was to outdo him. Even if the intention was also to reduce the importance of Richardson, the result may well be what

Diderot thought, that is, Voltaire had only succeeded in making it up to Montesquieu.

Why do Voltaire's objections to Fielding appear so mild? One of the reasons must be that Fielding did not have the same impact as Richardson in France. There was therefore little competition to fear from him. It was only fair that Voltaire should have spared the Englishman who showed a detailed knowledge of his *Histoire de Charles XII* when he translated Gustav Adlerfeld's *Military history of Charles XII* which was published in 1740.[58] Moreover, Fielding's imitators could never have had the same status as Richardson's principal imitator, Rousseau. Fielding's realism may have proved useful to Voltaire in his personal polemics in *L'Ecossaise*. Voltaire was also well-disposed towards him because of his achievement in the drama. In fact, whoever imitated Molière without attacking him was sure to earn Voltaire's respect. Although Voltaire's reactions to these English prose writers varied to some extent, one of the most significant influences they collectively exerted on him was that they helped alter his view of prose fiction. Gradually, but inexorably, the novel stopped being a despised genre to Voltaire.

[58] see J. E. Wells, 'Henry Fielding and the *History of Charles XII*', *Journal of English and Germanic philology* (1912), xi. 603-13.

Conclusion

IN a study of Voltaire's reactions to English literature, it is worth recalling that Voltaire's interest was not restricted to those writers who distinguished themselves in the drama, the epic, satire and prose fiction. In the *Essay on epick poetry*, for example, he showed that he was acquainted with the lyric poetry of Waller and Denham (White, p.111). In letter xxi of the *Lettres philosophiques*, he discussed Waller at the same time as Rochester. There he compared Waller with Voiture and translated his poem *Upon the death of the Lord Protector*, which he enjoyed. Voltaire had known Young in England and had had stimulating discussions on Milton with him; he could not have been indifferent to Young's *The Complaint, or night-thoughts on life, death, and immortality* (1742-45) since the poem gained European fame. He nevertheless did not appreciate Young's melancholy, as can be seen from his letter to Le Tourneur, the translator of *Night-thoughts*. In it he claimed that Le Tourneur had done great honour to his old friend Young and that the translator had more taste than the author. He criticised Young's work for its clichés, written in a bombastic and obscure style, and he added that sermons were not meant to be written in verse. He thought that Louis Racine's poem, *La Religion*, was much better than all of Young's poems (Best.D15680, 7 June 1769).

Voltaire made hostile comments on the nature poetry of Thomson in his letter to Dupont de Nemours where he drew a parallel between Saint Lambert's *Saisons* and Thomson's *Seasons*. He found no difficulty in preferring the Frenchman's poetry because his descriptions were more moving and cheerful, while Thomson's verses lacked harmony and suffered from the prosaic languor of blank verse. Worse still, a man from the north was incapable of celebrating the seasons as well as a man from the south, where the climate is more favourable (Best. D15679, 7 June 1769). In the article 'Flatterie' of the *Questions sur l'Encyclopédie* (1771), Voltaire even attacked Thomson on the ground that each book of the *Seasons* is dedicated to a wealthy man (M.xix.147). Yet many years before, in 1736, he had not hesitated to imitate Thomson's poem *To the memory of Newton* in his own *Epître à mme Du Châtelet*.[1]

It is likely that Voltaire appreciated Gay's play, *The Beggar's opera* (1728); according to major W. Broom, Gay showed Voltaire the manuscript before the performance (*Voltaire's British visitors*, p.94). Had he not expressed to Thieriot his admiration for the works and person of 'sr Ovid Gay' (Best.D492, 26 May 1732)? However, the works of Waller, Young and Gay do not appear to have made a profound impact on Voltaire, since he took only a passing interest in them. It would be difficult to find traces of their influence in his writings.

However 'minor' an English author might be, it sufficed that he was writing in a *grand* genre like tragedy for Voltaire's curiosity to be roused. Despite his criticisms of Thomson, Voltaire showed that he had read his tragedies. If he read Thomson's drama he had more reason to read Addison who was close to the French in taste. Voltaire read Addison with such enthusiasm that he elevated the latter's status at Shakespeare's expense. How ironical that he should spend so much of his time denigrating Shakespeare, the greatest of English dramatists, while at the same time looking for his 'fire' in the works of lesser writers! However, no amount of denigration could conceal the fact that it was Shakespeare who made the greatest impact on him. Voltaire was unlike many other critics because the more he attacked an English author, the greater the impact that author is likely to have made on him. The vehemence of his attack of course depended on whether he considered the author to be a serious rival in his own field and what the latter's reputation was in France. That is why Voltaire at times appears so hostile to Shakespeare. On the other hand, he had no legitimate ground to censure a writer like Congreve. It was also natural that he should have spoken favourably of Englishmen who had profited from French literature.

If we are to believe Goldsmith who visited Voltaire at Lausanne at his house called Montriond in 1756, Voltaire felt provoked by Fontenelle's attack on English taste and learning. Goldsmith was not impressed by Diderot's vindication of English literature, but then there was Voltaire who 'began his defense with the utmost elegance mixed with spirit'. Goldsmith was so much charmed that he never remembered

[1] see Ruth T. Murdoch, 'Voltaire, James Thomson and a poem for the marquise Du Châtelet', *Studies on Voltaire* (1958), vi. 147-53.

'so absolute a victory as he [Voltaire] gained in this dispute' (*Works*, ed. Friedman, iii. 247-48). Was Voltaire on his best behaviour in order to please Goldsmith? It seems that in general he passed favourable judgements on English writers in the presence of his visitors. To Charles Burney, Voltaire expressed regret in 1770 that the English had 'no one who lords it over the rest like Dryden, Pope and Swift' (*Voltaire's British visitors*, p.141). Likewise he told Martin Sherlock in 1776 that though he could not perfectly pronounce English, his ear was sensible of the language and of the versification; that Pope and Dryden had the most harmony in poetry, Addison in prose (p.184). Voltaire himself suggested that his praise of English writers stemmed from a firm conviction and not from a mere desire to please. He told the Nevilles in 1772 that he had 'censured fully the foolish love scenes and far-fetched conspiracies so introduced in Cato' and that he could speak 'as freely of crowned heads as of authors' (p.156).

Fairmindedness was hardly a constant with Voltaire. One can, however, understand the bitterness of his attacks against Milton. Voltaire had perhaps not realised at first the threat that Milton presented to his reputation as an epic poet. When he realised his 'mistake', it was too late. He had helped to focus attention on Milton and, ironically, to undermine his own status in this field. Was he not justified in making the best of a bad situation? Having failed as an epic poet, Voltaire could still hope to succeed as a polemicist. As this study has shown, Milton's *Paradise lost* was useful to Voltaire in many of his writings, the polemical works in particular.

It was Dryden and Pope who taught their French admirer how to use Milton's epic for polemical purposes. Their lessons helped Voltaire to become their counterpart in France.[2] Although Voltaire was dramatist, philosopher, historian and diplomat, the importance and overall significance of satire for this key figure of the Enlightenment cannot be underestimated: satire formed the very basis of his art. Voltaire no doubt found some inspiration in Boileau, but the latter often wrote on behalf of a clique and his satire dealt mainly with flatterers and bad taste in writing. Voltaire's satire, on the other hand, has something of the depth and breadth of his life and career. It is often personal, but it is also general in that it is linked with the central issues of the times.

[2] for a different view, see W. G. Moore, *French achievement in literature* (London 1969), p.100. Dr. Moore believed that La Bruyère was the counterpart to Dryden, Pope and Swift.

Can there be any doubt about the contribution of English satirical works towards Voltaire's achievement in satire? The verse satire of Garth, Churchill, Rochester, Butler, Prior, Dryden and Pope appealed to Voltaire in increasing order of importance. It is by no means easy to determine which of the last two satirists had a greater impact on the Frenchman. The *Temple du goût*, for instance, may have been directly inspired by Dryden's dedication to the *Aeneis*. In the dedication, Dryden argues that after the *Iliad*, the *Aeneid* and *Gerusalemme liberata* have been accepted as epic poems, some critic of authority should be set before the door, to keep out a crowd of little poets who press for admission and are not of quality. Le Moyne, Scudéry, Chapelain and even Milton are refused a place (Watson, ii. 232-33). Is the situation described in the *Temple du goût* not identical? There 'une foule d'écrivains de tout rang . . . qui gratoient à la porte, et qui prioient la Critique de les laisser entrer' were turned away (Carcassonne, p.72). Voltaire used English satire for better and for worse. In the *Temple du goût*, he achieved the same kind of effect as Dryden in the dedication to the *Aeneis*. He perhaps did not obtain equally good results in all his satirical writings. No other satirist, however, has succeeded in doing this. Dryden at his best found it hard to maintain the same standard in one satirical poem: one can note different levels of writing in his masterpiece, *Absalom and Achitophel*.

Voltaire's knowledge and use of English satire cannot be held against him. As if to rebut in advance the charge of some future hostile critic that he was devoid of any originality, he included in the 1756 edition of the *Lettres philosophiques* the remark that 'les esprits les plus originaux empruntent les uns des autres' (Lanson, ii. 136) and that many English writers had copied the French without any acknowledgement. His attitude towards English writers then appeared harsher than in 1734 when his advice to the French was simply to borrow from the English, as they had borrowed from the French. Despite the change in tone Voltaire's remark in 1756 can be taken as an indirect acknowledgement of his sources; sometimes he directly acknowledged them, but often he made no acknowledgement at all. Voltaire behaved like Dryden who was capable of paying the most generous tribute to Boileau, in his view a 'living Horace and a Juvenal . . . whose numbers are excellent, whose expressions are noble, whose thoughts are just; whose language is pure, whose satire is pointed' (*Discourse concerning satire*, Watson, ii. 81). Yet the same Dryden was capable of expressing the most chauvinistic feelings against the French. It is clear that in spite of a certain reluctance to reveal their indebtedness to the writers on the opposite side of the Channel, both English and French authors derived considerable benefit from their mutual intercourse. Voltaire's talents were enriched by his contacts with writers such as Pope and Swift, though the francophile Chesterfield must have also encouraged him in his tendency to belittle English literary achievements.

It was inevitable that there should be gaps in Voltaire's knowledge of English literature. Even today, few people apart from specialists of English literature would know the works of every major English author between the sixteenth and eighteenth centuries. It would have been virtually impossible for an eighteenth-century Frenchman to show the same familiarity with all the major works produced between the time of Shakespeare and Sterne. Nevertheless, it is rather surprising to note that Voltaire did not know anything about Defoe in as much as he was interested in the development of prose fiction in France and in England. One might have thought that Voltaire would know at least *Robinson Crusoe* since it had been translated by Saint-Hyacinthe in 1720, a year after its publication in the original. A plausible explanation is that Voltaire wanted to make a conscious selection in his reading of English prose. So he remained indifferent to Smollett who had translated *Micromégas* in 1752 and been influenced by *Candide* in his novel *Humphry Clinker*.[3] His preference for Swift and Sterne was instinctive: there was a common bond between all three and it was not just Diderot who was influenced by Sterne.[4] The intellectual climate in France and, up to a point, pressures from friends such as mme Du Deffand induced Voltaire to read Richardson and Fielding. As there was less commitment in their works, their impact had certain limits. Even so, his own achievement as 'conteur', combined with that of other French prose writers and English novelists led him to conlcude towards the end of his career that the novel preceded history and was superior to what had hitherto been regarded as the greatest genre – the epic. Coming from a writer who had tried his hand at every genre, this judgement was of great significance for the future status of the novel.

[3] see E. T. Helmick, 'Voltaire and *Humphry Clinker*', *Studies on Voltaire* (1969), lxvii. 59-64.

[4] there is hardly a mention of Voltaire in F. B. Barton, *Etude sur l'influence de Laurence Sterne en France au dix-huitième siècle* (Paris 1911).

Despite Voltaire's shortcomings, few eighteenth-century French writers could have read as deeply as he into English literature. He had studied the English and been influenced by them in every genre in which they wrote. At one time it was even thought that he was the pioneer in introducing almost every major English author to the French. In one sense, he was largely responsible for the creation of this legend as he repeatedly made the claim in his private and public utterances. His claim no longer appears justified in many cases, although he cannot be refused the distinction of having introduced Milton to his countrymen. Yet, such was Voltaire's personality and influence that even when others had beaten him at the post, it was his comments on English writers that made the most profound impression. Often his reactions seemed full of prejudice, prejudice encouraged by his French literary background and by his entourage. Prejudice sometimes made him attack the greatest names in English literature. There was, however, some poetic justice here. In his constant denunciation of English taste, he tried to overthrow what he thought were the idols. He replaced these by a few of his own making, endowing them with qualities which they did not possess. At the same time, he apparently failed to notice that he was destroying the myth he had inherited from his French background – that the English could sometimes have genius, but taste never.

Appendix

‹‹‹❦›››

NOTE on the authorship of the review of *Tristram Shandy* in the *Gazette littéraire* of 1765.

It is difficult to establish who was the author of this unsigned article. There is nothing in the French article to suggest that the editors wrote it. It could very well have been Jean Baptiste Suard who was the translator of many English works and considered by some as an authority on English literature. He had met Sterne during his Paris visits. François Arnaud was a good classicist, but his knowledge of English is not established. The evidence for attributing authorship to Suard rests mostly on Voltaire's word and the *London chronicle* which translated the article in its number for 16-18 April 1765 in vol. xvii. The periodical wrote that it was 'An account of the two last Volumes of the Life of *TRISTRAM SHANDY*, by the ingenious Author of the Gazette Litteraire de l'Europe'.

Now we know that Voltaire wanted to remain an anonymous contributor to the *Gazette littéraire*. He wrote to the d'Argentals: 'Je supplie instamment les sages qui travaillent à la gazette littéraire de me garder toujours le plus profond secret' (Best.D11933, 18 June 1764). A few days later, he asked the same correspondents to pass on the message to the editors of the *Gazette* (Best.D11943, 22 June 1764). He may then have had a particular book in mind about which they should keep quiet. But in 1763, even before the publication of the *Gazette*, the first number of which appeared on 7 March 1764, he had expressed to the d'Argentals his wish for secrecy (Best.D11214, 19 May, 1763). In 1764 he wrote to the *Gazette littéraire* disavowing publications circulated under his name by 'forgers' (Best.D12255, 24 December 1764). Two days later he mentioned the books in a letter to Arnaud, requesting his help for the disavowal (Best.D12264). Could he not therefore have written the article himself and kept quiet about it?

The present case is different from that of the *Connaissance des beautés*, which was long attributed to Voltaire, but which was in fact written by Durand. See Theodore Besterman, 'Note on the authorship of the *Connaissance des beautés'*, *Studies on Voltaire* (1957), iv. 291-94. Whereas with regard to the *Connaissance des beautés*, Voltaire emphatically denied authorship, here he simply says that the article was by a French journalist. We cannot take him too literally. Too much praise is heaped on the journalist for him not to be Voltaire himself. In the *Conseils à un journaliste*, Voltaire had stated that a good journalist must know at least English and Italian, the two European languages that were most necessary for a Frenchman (M.xxii.261). Voltaire certainly knew English and Italian well, and he had some knowledge of Spanish too. Remarks such as 'alors on rendit une exacte justice à ce livre. Aussi l'auteur de la *Gazette littéraire* était-il aussi instruit dans les principales langues de l'Europe que capable de bien juger tous les écrits' are too reminiscent of Voltaire's conceited assertions about himself in the *Temple du goût*.

Bibliography

Voltaire Texts

COLLECTED EDITIONS

Œuvres complètes de Voltaire, ed. Louis Moland. Paris 1877-83, 52 vols
Les Œuvres complètes de Voltaire | The Complete works of Voltaire, eds W. H. Barber *et al.* Geneva 1968-70, Banbury 1971-75, Oxford 1976-
Dialogues et anecdotes philosophiques, ed. Raymond Naves. Paris 1955
Romans et contes, ed. Henri Bénac. Paris 1960

CORRESPONDENCE

Correspondence and related documents, ed. Theodore Besterman (1968-77), in the *Complete works of Voltaire*, vols 85-135
Correspondance de Voltaire (1726-1729), ed. Lucien Foulet. Paris 1913

INDIVIDUAL WORKS

Candide ou l'optimisme, ed. André Morize. Paris 1913
Commentaires sur Corneille, ed. David Williams (1974-75), in the *Complete works of Voltaire*, vols 53-55
Dictionnaire philosophique, eds Julien Benda and Raymond Naves. Paris 1961
Essay on epic poetry, ed. Florence D. White. Albany 1915
La Henriade, ed. Owen R. Taylor (1970), in the *Complete works of Voltaire*, vol. 2
Histoire du Docteur Akakia et du natif de St Malo. ed. Jacques Tuffet. Paris 1967
Letters concerning the English nation. London 1733
Lettres philosophiques, ed. Gustave Lanson, revised by André-M. Rousseau. Paris 1964. 2 vols
Notebooks, ed. Theodore Besterman (1968), in the *Complete works of Voltaire*, vols 81-82
La Pucelle d'Orléans, ed. Jeroom Vercruysse (1970), in the *Complete works of Voltaire*, vol. 7
Le Temple du goût, ed. Elie Carcassonne. Paris 1938
Traité de métaphysique, ed. H. Temple Patterson. Manchester 1937

Eighteenth-century French periodicals

Année littéraire, ed. Elie Fréron, etc. (1754-90), 292 vols
Bibliothèque angloise, eds. M. de La Roche and A. de La Chapelle (1717-28), 17 vols
Bibliothèque française, eds Camusat, Du Sauzet, etc. (1723-46), 50 vols
Bibliothèque universelle des romans (1775-89), 224 vols
Gazette littéraire de l'Europe, eds François Arnaud and Jean Baptiste Suard (1764-66), 8 vols
Journal encyclopédique, eds P. Rousseau, etc. (1756-59, 1760-73), 288 vols
Journal littéraire, eds Albert Henri Sallengre, etc. (1713-22, 1729-36), 24 vols
Journal de Trévoux, eds Tournemine, Brumoy, Berthier (1701-67), 265 vols
Lettres sur quelques écrits de ce temps, ed. Elie Fréron (1749-54), 13 vols

Bibliography

Mercure de France, eds Dufresny, de La Roque, etc. (1724-91), 977 vols
Observations sur les écrits modernes, eds F. G. Desfontaines, etc. (1735-43),

34 vols
Pour et contre, ed. Antoine François Prévost (1733-40), 20 vols

Other texts before 1800

Addison, Joseph, Works, ed. R. Hurd. London 1811, 6 vols
— The Spectator, ed. D. F. Bond. Oxford 1965, 5 vols
Adlerfeld, Gustav, The Military history of Charles XII, trans. H. Fielding. London 1740, 3 vols
Andreini, Giovanni Battista, Adamo. Milan 1613
Arbuthnot, John, Memoirs of Martinus Scriblerus. London 1714

Baculard d'Arnaud, François Thomas, Fanni ou la nouvelle Paméla. Paris 1767
Baretti, Giuseppe, Discours sur Shakespeare et sur monsieur de Voltaire. London 1777
Bayle, Pierre, Dictionnaire historique et critique. Rotterdam 1697
— Œuvres diverses, ed. Desmaizeaux. The Hague 1725-31, 4 vols
Boileau, Nicolas, Œuvres, ed. M. de Saint Marc. Amsterdam 1772, vol. v
— Œuvres, ed. G. Mongrédien. Paris 1961
Boyer, Abel, Dialogues familiers [1712?]
— Cato. London 1714
Breval, John, Epistle to Addison. London 1717
Brooke, Frances, The History of lady Julia Mandeville. London 1763
Butler, Samuel, Characters and passages from Notebooks, ed. A. R. Waller. Cambridge 1908
— Hudibras, ed. John Wilders. Oxford 1967
Bysshe, Edward, The Art of poetry. London 1702

Chappuzeau, Samuel, Le Théâtre françois. Paris 1674
Chesterfield, Philip Dormer Stanhope, 4th earl of, Miscellaneous works. London 1779, 2 vols

— The Letters of lord Chesterfield, ed. Bonamy Dobrée. London 1932, 5 vols
Chevreau, Urbain, L'Ecole du sage. Paris 1646
Churchill, Charles, The Poetical works of C. Churchill, ed. Douglas Grant. Oxford 1956
Cibber, Colley, Dramatic works. London 1777, 5 vols
Cocchi, Antonio, 'Lettre sur la Henriade', trans. Elderchen. Paris 1733
Congreve, William, Complete plays, ed. H. Davis. London 1967
Constantin de Magny, Claude François, Dissertation critique sur le Paradis perdu. Paris 1729
Corneille, Pierre, Théâtre, ed. R. Bray. Paris 1949, 2 vols

Dacier, André, Préface sur les satires d'Horace in Remarques critiques sur les œuvres d'Horace. Paris 1687
Dennis, John, Miscellanies in verse and prose (1693)
— The Critical works of John Dennis, ed. E. N. Hooker. Baltimore 1939-43, 2 vols
Deschamps, François, Caton d'Utique. Paris 1715
Desfontaines, François Guyot, Le Nouveau Gulliver. Paris 1730
Destouches, Philippe Néricault, Le Glorieux. Paris 1732
Diderot, Denis, Œuvres complètes, eds J. Assézat and M. Tourneux. Paris 1875-77, 20 vols
— Correspondance, eds G. Roth and J. Varloot. Paris 1955-70, 16 vols
Dryden, John, The Works of John Dryden, ed. W. Scott. London 1892, vol. xvii
— The Dramatic works of J. Dryden, ed. Montague Summers. London 1931

— *The Poetical works*, ed. G. Noyes. Cambridge, Mass. 1950

— *Of Dramatic poesy and other critical essays*, ed. George Watson. London 1962, 2 vols

— *The Poems and fables of John Dryden*, ed. J. Kinsley. Oxford 1970

Du Bocage, Anne-Marie, *Le Paradis terrestre*. Londres 1748

Du Bas, Jean-Baptiste, *Réflexions critiques sur la poésie et sur la peinture*. Paris 1719, 3 vols

Dupré de St Maur, Nicolas-François, *Le Paradis perdu de Milton*. Paris 1729, 3 vols

Durand, David, *La Chute de l'homme*. Londres 1729

— *Connaissance des beautés*. Paris 1749

Du Resnel, Jean-François, *Essai sur la critique*. Paris 1730.

Fénelon, François de Salignac, *Télémaque*. Paris 1699

— *Lettre à l'Académie*. Paris 1714

Fenton, Elijah, *Mariamne*. London 1723

— *Paradise lost*. London 1725

Fielding, Henry, *Joseph Andrews*, trans. Desfontaines. Paris 1744

— *Tom Jones*, trans. La Place. Paris 1750

— *Works*, ed. L. Stephen. London 1882, 10 vols

Fontenelle, Bernard Le Bovier de, *Œuvres*. Paris 1758, 10 vols

Fougeret de Montbron, Louis-Charles, *Le Cosmopolite*. Paris 1753

— *Préservatif contre l'anglomanie*. Paris 1757

Garth, Samuel, *The Dispensary*. London 1699

Gay, John, *The Beggar's opera*. London 1728

Goldsmith, Oliver, *Collected works*, ed. Arthur Friedman. Oxford 1966, 5 vols

Grimm, Friedrich Melchior, *Correspondance littéraire*, ed. M. Tourneux. Paris 1877-82, 16 vols

Grotius, Hugo, *Adamus exul*, trans. F. Barham. London 1839

Hall, Joseph, *Characters of virtues and vices*. London 1608

Hill, Aaron, *The Dramatic works*. London 1760, 2 vols

Holwell, John, *Interesting historical events relative to the provinces of Bengal*. London 1766

Jeffreys, George, *Miscellanies in verse and prose*. London 1754

Jonson, Ben, *Works*, eds C. H. Herford and P. Simpson. London 1925-51, 11 vols

Kahle, Martin, *Examen du livre intitulé 'La Métaphysique de Newton', ou parallèle des sentiments de Newton et de Leibnitz, par m. de Voltaire*, trans. Gautier de Saint-Blancard. The Hague 1744

Keate, George, *The Alps*. London 1763

La Baume, Jacques-François, *La Christiade ou le Paradis reconquis pour servir de suite au Paradis perdu de Milton*. Brussels 1753, 6 vols

La Bruyère, Jean de, *Les Caractères*, ed. R. Garapon. Paris 1962

La Chesnaye Des Bois, François Alexandre Aubert de, *Lettres amusantes et critiques sur les romans en général*. Paris 1743

La Fayette, Marie Madeleine de, *Zaïde*. Paris 1670

— *La Princesse de Clèves*. Paris 1678

La Fosse, Antoine de, *Manlius Capitolinus*. Paris 1698

La Place, Antoine, *Théâtre anglais*. Paris 1746-49, 8 vols

Le Blanc, J. B., *Lettres d'un François*. The Hague 1745

Le Bossu, René, *Traité du poème épique*. Paris 1675

Lebrun, Antoine Louis, *J'ay vu*. Paris 1714

Legrand, Antoine, *L'Impromptu de la folie*. 1726

Lenglet Du Fresnoy, Nicolas, *De l'usage des romans*. Paris 1734

Le Tourneur, P., *Shakespeare traduit de l'anglois*. Paris 1776-82, 20 vols

Lloyd, Robert, *The New river-head*. London 1764

Lucan, Marcus Annaeus, *Pharsalia*, trans. Nicholas Rowe. London 1722

Maimbourg, Louis, *Histoire du grand schisme d'occident*. Paris 1678
— *Histoire du calvinisme*. Paris 1682
Marmontel, Jean-François, *Essai sur les romans* in *Œuvres complètes*. Paris 1819, x. 287-361
Maupertuis, Pierre Louis Moreau de, *Discours sur la différente figure des astres*. Paris 1732
Milton, John, *Paradise lost* in *The Poetical works of J. Milton*, ed. Helen Darbishire. Oxford 1952
— *Complete prose works of J. Milton*, eds Don M. Wolfe *et al.* New Haven 1953-
Molière, Jean-Baptiste Poquelin, *Œuvres complètes*, ed. R. Jouanny. Paris 1962, 2 vols
Montagu, Elizabeth, *An Essay on the writings and genius of Shakespeare with some remarks upon the misrepresentation of m. de Voltaire*. London 1769
Montagu, Mary Wortley, *The Complete letters of lady Wortley Montagu*, ed. Robert Halsband. Oxford 1965-67
Muralt, Louis Béat de, *Lettres sur les Anglois et les François*. Paris 1725
Murphy, Arthur, *The Orphan of China*. London 1759
— *Letter from the author of 'The Orphan of China'*. London 1759

Otway, Thomas, *Works*, ed. J. C. Ghosh. Oxford 1932, 2 vols

Palissot de Montenoy, Charles, *La Dunciade*. Paris 1764, 1771
Panckoucke, Henri, *La Mort de Caton d'Utique*. Paris 1768
Parnell, Thomas, *The Hermit* [1718?]
Pascal, Blaise, *Lettres provinciales*, ed. H. F. Stewart. Manchester 1920
Perrault, Charles, *Parallèle des anciens et des modernes*. Paris 1688-97
Philips, John, *Blenheim*. London 1705
— *The Splendid shilling*. London 1705
Pope, Alexander, *The Works of Alexander Pope*, eds W. Elwin and W. J. Courthope. London 1871-89, 10 vols
— *Correspondence of Alexander Pope*, ed. George Sherburn. Oxford 1956, 5 vols

— *The Poems of Alexander Pope*, ed. John Butt. London 1963
Prévost, Antoine François, *Mémoires et aventures d'un homme de qualité*, ed. Mysie E. Robertson. Paris 1927
Prior, Matthew, *The Literary works of Matthew Prior*, eds H. Bunker Wright and Monroe K. Spears. Oxford 1971

Racine, Jean, *Théâtre complet*, ed. M. Rat. Paris 1960
Ramsay, Andrew Michael, *Les Aventures de Télémaque*. Paris 1717
Rapin, René, *Réflexions sur la poétique d'Aristote*. Paris 1674
Richardson, Samuel, *Pamela*, trans. La Chesnaye Des Bois. Paris 1741
— *Lettres angloises ou histoire de miss Clarisse Harlowe*, trans. Prévost. Paris 1751
— *Works*, ed. L. Stephen. London 1883-84, 12 vols
Rivarol, Antoine, *De l'universalité de la langue française*. Paris 1784
Rochester, John Wilmot, *The Poetical works of John Wilmot, earl of Rochester*, ed. Q. Johns. Halifax 1933
Rolli, Paolo, *Remarks upon m. Voltaire's Essay on the epick poetry of the european nations*. London 1728
Rollin, Charles, *Traité des études*. Paris 1730-31, 4 vols
Rousseau, Jean-Jacques, *La Nouvelle Héloïse*, ed. R. Pomeau. Paris 1963
Routh, Bernard, *Lettres critiques sur le Paradis perdu et reconquis de Milton*. Paris 1731
Rutlidge, James, *Essay on the characters and manners of the French* (1770)
— *Le Bureau d'esprit*. Paris 1776
— *Observations à messieurs de l'Académie française*. Paris 1776
— *La Quinzaine anglaise*. Paris 1776
Rymer, Thomas, *A Short view of tragedy*. London 1693

Saint-Evremond, Charles de, *Œuvres*, ed. Desmaizeaux. Paris 1753, 10 vols
— *Œuvres en prose*, ed. R. Ternois. Paris 1962-69, 4 vols

Saint Réal, César de, *Conjuration des Espagnols contre la république de Venise*. Paris 1674

Scudéry, Madeleine de, *Clélie* (1654-60)

Sewell, George, *Observations upon Cato*. London 1713

Shadwell, Thomas, *Complete works*, ed. M. Summers. London 1927, 5 vols

Shakespeare, William, *The Complete works*, ed. Peter Alexander. London 1951

— *King Henry VIII*, ed. R. A. Foakes. London 1957

Sheffield, John, *The Tragedy of Julius Caesar*. London 1722

— *The Tragedy of Marcus Brutus*. London 1722

Sherlock, Martin, *Letters from an English traveller*. London 1780

Smollett, Tobias George, *Works*, ed. G. Saintsbury. London 1895, 12 vols

Sorbière, Samuel, *Relation d'un voyage en Angleterre*. Paris 1664

Spence, Joseph, *Observations, anecdotes, and characters of books and men*, ed. J. M. Osborn. Oxford 1966, 2 vols

Sprat, Thomas, *Observations on m. de Sorbière's voyage into England*. London 1665

Steele, Richard, *The Conscious lovers*. London 1722

Sterne, Laurence, *La Vie et les opinions de Tristram Shandy, traduites par M. Frénais*. York 1776-85, 6 vols

— *The Sermons of Mr. Yorick*. Oxford 1927

— *Letters of Laurence Sterne*, ed. Lewis Perry Curtis. Oxford 1935

— *Sterne (Memoirs, Tristram Shandy, etc.)*, ed. Douglas Grant. London 1950

Swift, Jonathan, *The Prose works of Jonathan Swift*, ed. Davis. Oxford 1939-68, 14 vols

— *Correspondence of Jonathan Swift*, ed. H. Williams. Oxford 1963-65, 5 vols.

Tasso, Torquato, *Gerusalemme liberata* (1581)

Thomson, James, *Works*, ed. George Lyttelton. London 1750, 4 vols

Titon Du Tillet, Everard, *Le Parnasse français*. Paris 1755

Urfé, Honoré d', *L'Astrée*. 1607-27

Vanbrugh, sir John, *Sir John Vanbrugh*, ed. W. C. Ward. London 1893, 2 vols

Veiras, Denis, *Histoire des Sévarambes*. Paris 1677, 2 vols

Waller, Edmund, *Poems*, ed. G. Thorn Drury. London 1905, 2 vols

Wycherley, William, *Plays*, ed. W. C. Ward. London 1888

Yart, Antoine, *Idée de la poésie anglaise*. Paris 1749-56, 5 vols

Young, Edward, *Complete works*, ed. J. Doran. London 1854, 2 vols

Criticism and other works

Alekseev, M. P. and Kopreeva, J. K., eds *Bibliothèque de Voltaire: catalogue des livres*. Leningrad 1961

Audra, Emile, *L'Influence française dans l'œuvre de Pope*. Paris 1931

Baldensperger, Fernand, 'Voltaire anglophile avant son séjour d'Angleterre', *RLC* (1929), ix. 25-61

Ballantyne, Archibald, *Voltaire's visit to England 1726-29*. London 1893

Balcou, Jean, *Fréron contre les philosophes*. Genève 1975

Barber, William Henry, *Leibniz in France from Arnauld to Voltaire*. Oxford 1955

— 'L'Angleterre dans *Candide*', *RLC* (1963), xxxviii. 202-15

— 'Voltaire and Molière' in *Molière: stage and study*, eds W. D. Howarth and M. Thomas. Oxford 1973, pp.201-17

— 'Voltaire at Cirey: art and thought' in *Studies in eighteenth-century French literature*, eds J. M. Fox *et al.* Exeter 1975, pp.1-13

Barling, T. J., 'Voltaire's correspondence with lord Hervey: three new letters', *Studies on Voltaire* (1968), lxii. 13-27

Barnard, T., ed. *Pope.* London 1973

Barton, F. B., *Etude sur l'influence de Laurence Sterne en France au dix-huitième siècle.* Paris 1911

Beljame, Alexandre, *Le Public et les hommes de lettres en Angleterre au dix-huitième siècle*, trans. E. O. Lorimer. London 1948

Bellessort, André, *Essai sur Voltaire.* Paris 1925

Bengesco, Georges, *Voltaire: bibliographie de ses œuvres.* Paris 1882-1890, 4 vols

Besterman, Theodore, *Voltaire on Shakespeare*, Studies on Voltaire (1967), vol. liv

Boiteux, L. A., 'Voltaire et le ménage Suard', *Studies on Voltaire* (1955), i. 19-109

Bonno, Gabriel, *La Culture et la civilisation britanniques devant l'opinion française de la paix d'Utrecht aux 'Lettres philosophiques'.* Philadelphia 1948

Bredvold, Louis I., *The Intellectual milieu of J. Dryden.* Michigan 1934

Brooks, Richard A., *Voltaire and Leibniz.* Geneva 1964

Bullitt, John Marshall, *Jonathan Swift and the anatomy of satire.* Cambridge, Mass. 1953

Chateaubriand, François René de, *Essai sur la littérature anglaise.* Paris 1836

Clark, Alexander Frederick Bruce, *Boileau and the French classical critics in England (1660-1830).* Paris 1925

Cobban, Alfred, *A History of modern France.* Harmondsworth 1966, vol. i

Cornou, François, *Trente années de luttes contre Voltaire et les philosophes du dix-huitième siècle: E. Fréron.* Paris 1922

Cross, Wilbur L., *The Life and times of Laurence Sterne.* New Haven 1925

De Beer, Gavin R. and André-M. Rousseau, ed. *Voltaire's British visitors,* Studies on Voltaire (1967), vol. xlix

Dédéyan, Charles, *Voltaire et la pensée anglaise.* Paris 1956

Desvignes, Lucette, *Marivaux et l'Angleterre.* Paris 1970

Dixon, Peter, *The World of Pope's satires.* London 1973

Dobrée, Bonamy, *Restoration comedy.* Oxford 1924

— *Restoration tragedy.* Oxford 1929

Doherty, F., 'Bayle and *Tristram Shandy*: stage-loads of chymical nostrums and peripatetic lumber', *Neophil* (1974), lviii. 339-48

Duckworth, Colin, 'Madame Denis's unpublished *Pamela*', *Studies on Voltaire* (1970), lxxvi. 37-53

Dunbar, Howard Hunter, *The Dramatic career of Arthur Murphy.* New York 1946

Eliot, Thomas Sterne, *Homage to John Dryden.* London 1924

Fellows, Otis, 'Metaphysics and the *Bijoux indiscrets*: Diderot's debt to Prior', *Studies on Voltaire* (1967), lvi. 509-40

Faguet, Emile, 'Jugements particuliers de Voltaire sur plusieurs grands écrivains', *RCC* (1900), vol. ix

Fenger, Henning, 'Voltaire et le théâtre anglais', *Orbis litterarum* (1949), vii. 161-287

Fletcher, Dennis, J., 'The Fortunes of Bolinbroke in France in the eighteenth century', *Studies on Voltaire* (1966) xlvii. 207-32

Ford, Boris, ed. *The Pelican guide to English literature.* Harmondsworth 1968, vols. iv and v

Fredman, Alice G., *Diderot and Sterne.* New York 1955

Genuist, André, *Le Théâtre de Shakespeare dans l'œuvre de Pierre Le Tourneur 1776-1783.* Paris 1971

Gillet, Jean, *Le Paradis perdu dans la littérature française, de Voltaire à Chateaubriand.* Paris 1975

Goulding, Sybil, *Swift en France*. Paris 1924

Green, Frederick Charles, *Minuet, a critical survey of French and English literary ideas in the eighteenth-century*. London 1935

Guerinot, Joseph V., *Pamphlet attacks on Alexander Pope 1711-1744*. London 1969

Hall, Gaston, 'Molière, Chevreau's *Ecole du sage* and Joseph Hall's *Characters*', *FS* (1975), xxix. 398-410

Halsband, Robert, *The Life of lady Mary Wortley Montagu*. Oxford 1956

Hammond, Lansing van der Heyden, *Laurence Sterne's Sermons of Mr. Yorick*. New Haven 1948

Hartley, K. H., 'The Sources of Voltaire's *Mariamne*', *AUMLA* (1964), xxi.5-14

Havens, George R., *The Abbé Prévost and English literature*. Princeton 1921

Havens, G. R. and Torrey, Norman L., eds *Voltaire's catalogue of his library at Ferney*, Studies on Voltaire (1959), vol. ix

Helmick, E. T., 'Voltaire and *Humphry Clinker*', *Studies on Voltaire* (1969), lxvii. 59-64

Henderson, J. S., *Voltaire's Tancrède*, Studies on Voltaire (1968), vol. lxi

Hodges, John Cunyns, *William Congreve, the man*. London 1941

Hoffman, Arthur Wolf, *J. Dryden's imagery*. Gainesville 1962

Howes, Alan B., ed. *Sterne*. London 1974

Hunter, Alfred C., 'Le *Conte de la femme de Bath* en français au xviiie siècle', *RLC* (1929), ix. 117-40

Ilchester, Giles Stephen Holland, earl of, *Lord Hervey and his friends, 1726-1738*. London 1950

Jack, Ian, *Augustan satire: intention and idiom in English poetry 1660-1750*. Oxford 1952, 1966

Jeune, Simon, '*Hamlet* d'Otway, *Macbeth* de Dryden, ou Shakespeare en France en 1714', *RLC* (1962), xxxvi. 500-504

Jovicevich, Alexandre, 'A propos d'une Paméla de Voltaire', *FR* (1962-63), xxxvi. 276-83

Jusserand, Jean Adrien Antoine Jules, *Shakespeare en France sous l'ancien régime*. Paris 1898

Kettle, Arnold, *An Introduction to the English novel*. London 1962, 2 vols

Knapp, Richard Gilbert, *The Fortune of Pope's Essay on man in eighteenth-century France*, Studies on Voltaire (1971), vol. lxxxii

Lancaster, H. Carrington, *A History of French dramatic literature in the seventeenth century*. Baltimore 1929-42, 9 vols

Lanson, Gustave, *Histoire de la littérature française*. Paris 1894

— *L'Art de la prose*. Paris 1908

Macdonald, W. L., *Pope and his critics*. London 1951

Maillet, Albert, 'Dryden et Voltaire', *RLC* (1938), xviii. 272-86

Marmier, Jean, *Horace en France au dix-septième siècle*. Paris 1962

Mason, Haydn T., *Pierre Bayle and Voltaire*. Oxford 1963

May, Georges, *Le Dilemme du roman au XVIIIe siècle*. New Haven 1963

Moore, Will G., *French achievement in literature*. London 1969

Morillot, P., *Le Roman français 1610-1800*. London 1920

Mortier, Roland, *Clartés et ombres du siècle des lumières*. Geneva 1969

— 'Les formes de la satire chez Voltaire', *Documentatieblad werkgroep 18' eeuw* (April 1972), pp.43-64

— 'La satire, "ce poison de la littérature"': Voltaire et la nouvelle déontologie de l'homme de lettres', *Essays in the age of Enlightenment in honor of I. O. Wade*, ed. J. Macary. Geneva 1977, pp. 233-46

Murdoch, Ruth T., 'Voltaire, James Thomson and a poem for the marquise Du Châtelet', *Studies on Voltaire* (1958), vi. 147-53

Muir, Kenneth, *The Comedy of manners*. London 1970

Myers, William, *Dryden*. London 1973

Naves, Raymond, *Le Goût de Voltaire*. Paris 1938

Nicoll, Allardyce, *A History of English drama 1660-1900*. Cambridge 1955, vol. ii

Nivat, Jean, 'Quelques énigmes de la correspondance de Voltaire', *RHL* (1953), liii. 439-63

Pappas, John, *Berthier's Journal de Trévoux and the philosophes*, Studies on Voltaire (1957), vol. iii

Paulson, R. and Lockwood, T., eds *Henry Fielding*. London 1969

Perry, Norma, *Sir Everard Fawkener, friend and correspondent of Voltaire*, Studies on Voltaire (1975), vol. cxxxiii

Peyre, Henri, *Qu'est-ce que le classicisme?* Paris 1965

Pike, Robert E., 'Voltaire: le *Patriot insulaire*', *MLN* (1942), lvii. 354-55

Pomeau, René, *La Religion de Voltaire*. Paris 1956, 1969

Quintana, Ricardo, *The Mind and art of Jonathan Swift*. London 1953

Ridgway, Ronald S., *La Propagande philosophique dans les tragédies de Voltaire*, Studies on Voltaire (1961), vol. xv

Robertson, J. G., 'The knowledge of Shakespeare on the continent at the beginning of the eighteenth century', *MLR* (1906), i. 312-21

— 'Milton's fame on the continent', *Proceedings of the British Academy* (1908), iii. 319-28

Roper, Alan, *Dryden's poetic kingdoms*. London 1965

Rousseau, André-Michel, *L'Angleterre et Voltaire*, Studies on Voltaire (1976), vols. cxlv-cxlvii

Russell, Trusten Wheeler, *Voltaire, Dryden and heroic tragedy*. New York 1946

— 'Dryden, inspirateur de Voltaire', *RLC* (1948), xxii. 321-28

Sareil, Jean, 'La mission diplomatique de Voltaire en 1743', *Dhs* (1972), pp. 271-99

Smith, D. N., ed. *Eighteenth-century essays on Shakespeare*. Oxford 1963

Sonet, Edouard, *Voltaire et l'influence anglaise*. Rennes 1926

Spingarn, Joel Elias, ed. *Critical essays of the seventeenth century*. London 1908, 3 vols

Staël, mme de, *De l'Allemagne*. Paris 1810

Streeter, Harold Wade, *The Eighteenth-century English novel in French*. New York 1936

Telleen, John Martin, *Milton dans la littérature française*. Paris 1904

Texte, Joseph, *Jean-Jacques Rousseau et les origines du cosmopolitisme littéraire*. Paris 1895

Thacker, Christopher, 'Swift and Voltaire', *Hermathena* (1967), no. 104, pp. 51-66

Tillotson, Geoffrey, *On the poetry of Pope*. Oxford 1950

Torrey, Norman L., 'Voltaire's English notebook', *MP* (1929), xxvi. 307-25

Van den Heuvel, Jacques, *Voltaire dans ses contes*. Paris 1967

Van Doren, Mark, *The Poetry of John Dryden*. Cambridge 1931

Van Tieghem, Paul, *La Découverte de Shakespeare sur le continent*, in *Le Préromantisme*. Paris 1947, vol. iii

Wade, Ira Owen, *The Intellectual development of Voltaire*. New Jersey 1969

Watt, Ian, *The Rise of the novel*. Harmondsworth 1968

Wells, J. E., 'Henry Fielding and the *History of Charles XII*', *JEGP* (1912), xi. 603-13

Williams, David, *Voltaire: literary critic* Studies on Voltaire (1966), vol. xlviii

— 'Voltaire on the sentimental novel', *Studies on Voltaire* (1975), cxxxv. 115-34

Williams, Kathleen, ed. *Swift*. London 1970

Index